TABLE OF CONTENTS

DC COMICS INC.

Jenette Kahn
President & Publisher

Dick Giordano
Co-Editor

Denny O'Neil
Co-Editor

Richard Bruning
Art Director

Bob Rozakis
Production Manager

Julia Sabbagh
Asst. Art Director

Pat Bastienne
Mgr. Editorial Coord

Terri Cunningham
Mgr. Editorial Admin.

Paul Levitz
Executive V.P.

Joe Orlando
V.P.-Creative Director

Ed Shukin
V.P.-Circulation

Bruce Bristow
Marketing Director

Patrick Caldon
Controller

DC Comics Inc.
666 Fifth Ave., New York, NY 10103

(W) A Warner Communications Company

Printed in Canada
Seventh Printing
10 9 8 7

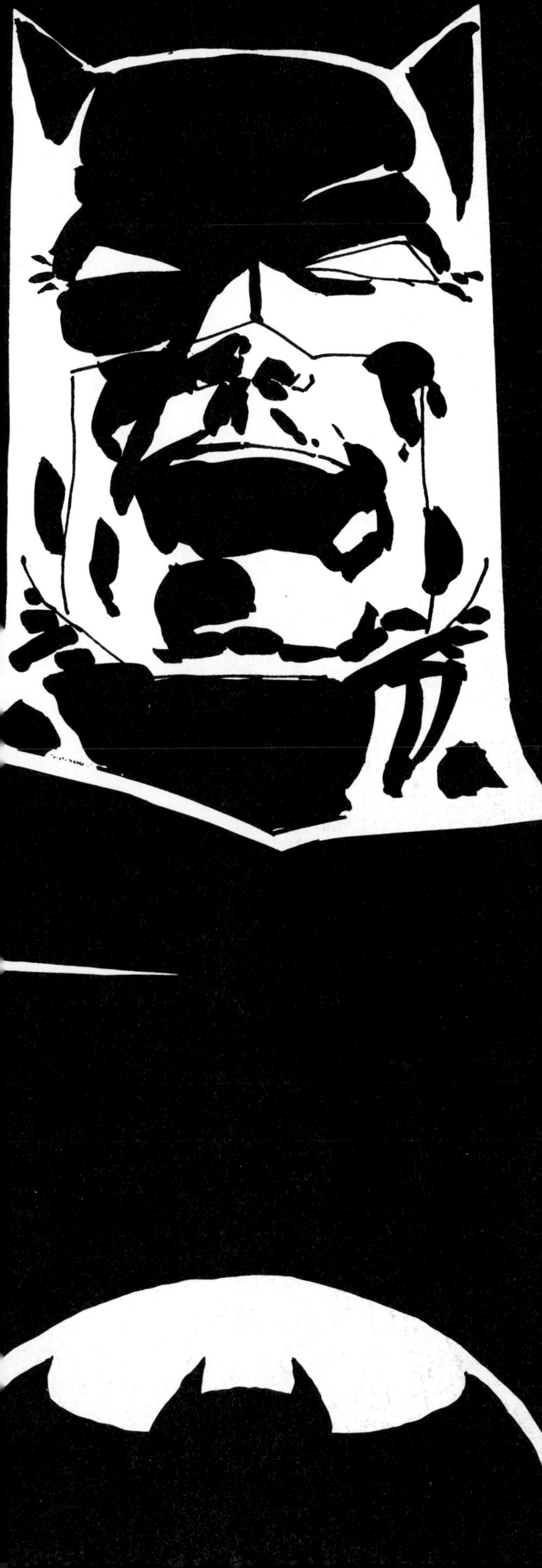

BATMAN™

THE DARK KNIGHT™ RETURNS

FRANK MILLER
Story and Pencils

KLAUS JANSON
FRANK MILLER
Inks

LYNN VARLEY
Colors and Visual Effects

JOHN COSTANZA
Letters

Based on characters
created by BOB KANE

THE MARK OF BATMAN

OF

BATMAN

AN INTRODUCTION

As anyone involved in fiction and its crafting over the past fifteen or so years would be delighted to tell you, heroes are starting to become rather problem. They aren't what they used to be...or rather they *are*, and therein lies the heart of the difficulty.

The world about us has changed and is continually changing at an ever-accellerating pace. So have we. With the increase in media coverage and information technology, we see more of the world, comprehend its workings a little more clearly, and as a result our perception of ourselves and the society surrounding us has been modified. Consequently, we begin to make different demands upon the art and culture that is meant to reflect the constantly shifting landscape we find ourselves in. We demand new themes, new insights, new dramatic situations.

BY ALAN MOORE

We demand new heroes.

The fictional heroes of the past, while still retaining all of their charm and power and magic, have had some of their credibility stripped away forever as a result of the new sophistication in their audience. With the benefit of hindsight and a greater understanding of anthropoid behavior patterns, science fiction author Philip Jose Farmer was able to demonstrate quite credibly that the young Tarzan would almost certainly have indulged in sexual experimentation with chimpanzees and that he would just surely have had none of the aversion to eating human flesh that Edgar Rice Burroughs attributed to him. As our political and social consciousness continues to evolve, Alan Quartermain stands revealed as just another white imperialist out to exploit the natives and we begin to see that the overriding factor in James Bond's psychological makeup is his utter hatred and contempt for women. Whether most of us would prefer to enjoy the above-mentioned gentlemen's adventures without spoiling things by considering the social implications is beside the point. The fact remains that we have changed, along with our society, and that were such characters created today they would be subject to the most extreme suspicion and criticism.

So, unless we are to somehow do without heroes altogether, how are the creators of fiction to go about redefining their legends to suit the contemporary climate?

The fields of cinema and literature have to some extent been able to tackle the problem in a mature and intelligent fashion, perhaps by virtue of having a mature and intelligent audience capable of appreciating and supporting such a response. The field of comic books, seen since its inception as a juvenile medium in which any interjection of adult themes and subject matter are likely to be met with howls of outrage and the threat or actuality of censorship, has not been so fortunate. Whereas in novels and movies we have been presented with such concepts as the anti-hero or the classical hero reinterpreted in a contemporary manner, comic books have largely had to plod along with the same old muscle-bound oafs spouting the same old muscle-bound platitudes while attempting to dismember each other. As the naivety of the characters and the absurdity of their situations become increasingly embarrassing and anachronistic to modern eyes, so does the problem become more compounded and intractable. Left floundering in the wake of other media, how are comic books to reinterpret their traditional icons so as to interest an audience growing progressively further away from them? Obviously, the problem becomes one that can only be solved by people who understand the dilemma and, further to that, have an equal understanding of heroes and what makes them tick.

Which brings me to Frank Miller, and to Dark Knight.

In deciding to apply his style and sensibilities to The Batman, Frank Miller has come up with a solution to the difficulties outlined above that is as impressive and elegant as any that I've seen. More strikingly still, he has managed to do it while handling a character who, in the view of the wider public that exists beyond the relatively tiny confines of the comic audience, sums up more than any other the essential silliness of the comic book hero. Whatever changes may have been wrought in the comics themselves, the image of Batman most permanently fixed in the mind of the general populace is that of Adam West delivering outrageously straight-faced camp dialogue while walking up a wall thanks to the benefit of stupendous special effects and a camera turned on its side. To lend such a subject credibility in the eyes of an audience not necessarily enamored of super-heroes and their

trappings is no inconsiderable feat, and it would perhaps be appropriate to look a little more closely here at what exactly it is that Miller has done. (I hope Frank will forgive me for calling him 'Miller'. It seems a little brusque and rude and I would certainly never do it to his face, but somehow it's just the sort of thing you call people you know quite well when writing introductions for their books.)

He has taken a character whose every trivial and incidental detail is graven in stone on the hearts and minds of the comic fans that make up his audience and managed to dramatically redefine that character without contradicting one jot of the character's mythology. Yes, Batman is still Bruce Wayne, Alfred is still his butler and Commissioner Gordon is still chief of police, albeit just barely. There is still a young sidekick named Robin, along with a batmobile, a batcave and a utility belt. The Joker, Two-Face, and the Catwoman are still in evidence amongst the roster of villains. Everything is exactly the same, except for the fact that it's all totally different.

Gotham City, a place which during the comic stories of the forties and fifties seemed to be an extended urban playground stuffed with giant typewriters and other gargantuan props, becomes something much grimmer in Miller's hands. A dark and unfriendly city in decay, populated by rabid and sociopathic streetgangs, it comes to resemble more closely the urban masses which may very well exist in our own uncomfortably near future. The Batman himself, taking account of our current perception of vigilantes as a social force in the wake of Bernie Goetz, is seen as a near-fascist and a dangerous fanatic by the media while concerned psychiatrists plead for the release of a homicidal Joker upon strictly humanitarian grounds. The values of the world we see are no longer defined in the clear, bright, primary colors of the conventional comic book but in the more subtle and ambiguous tones supplied by Lynn Varley's gorgeous palette and sublime sensibilities.

The most immediate and overpowering difference is obviously in the portrayal both of The Batman and of Bruce Wayne, the man beneath the mask. Depicted over the years as, alternately, a concerned do-gooder and a revenge-driven psychopath, the character as presented here manages to bridge both of those interpretations quite easily while integrating them in a much larger and more persuasively realized personality. Every subtlety of expression, every nuance of body language, serves to demonstrate that *this* Batman has finally become what he should always have been: He is a legend.

The importance of myth and legend as a subtext to Dark Knight can't really be overstated, shining as it does from every page. The familiar Batman origin sequence with the tiny bat fluttering in through an open window to inspire a musing Bruce Wayne becomes something far more religious and apocalyptic under Miller's handling; the bat itself transformed into a gigantic and ominous chimera straight out of the darkest european fables. The later scenes of The Batman on horseback, evoking everything from the chivalry of the Round Table to the arrival in town of Clint Eastwood, serve to further demonstrate this mythical quality, as does Miller's startling portrayal of Batman's old acquaintance Superman: The Superman we see here is an earthbound god whose presence is announced only by the wind of his passing or the destruction left in his wake. At the same time, his doubtful position as an agent of the United States Government manages to treat an incredible situation realistically and to seamlessly wed the stuff of legend to the stuff of twentieth century reality.

Beyond the imagery, themes, and essential romance of Dark Knight, Miller has also man-

aged to shape The Batman into a true legend by introducing that element without which all true legends are incomplete and yet which for some reason hardly seems to exist in the world depicted in the average comic book, and that element is time.

All of our best and oldest legends recognize that time passes and that people grow old and die. The legend of Robin Hood would not be complete without the final blind arrow shot to determine the site of his grave. The Norse Legends would lose much of their power were it not for the knowledge of an eventual Ragnarok, as would the story of Davy Crockett without the existence of an Alamo. In comic books, however, given the commercial fact that a given character will still have to sell to a given audience in ten years' time, these elements are missing. The characters remain in the perpetual limbo of their mid-to-late twenties, and the presence of death in their world is at best a temporary and reversible phenomenon.

With Dark Knight, time has come to the Batman and the capstone that makes legends what they are has finally been fitted. In his engrossing story of a great man's final and greatest battle, Miller has managed to create something radiant which should hopefully illuminate things for the rest of the comic book field, casting a new light upon the problems which face all of us working within the industry and perhaps even guiding us towards some fresh solutions. For those of you who've already eagerly consumed Dark Knight in its softcover version, rest assured that in your hands you hold one of the few genuine comic book landmarks worthy of a lavish and more durable presentation. For the rest of you, who are about to enter entirely new territory, I can only express my extreme envy. You are about to encounter a new level of comic book storytelling. A new world with new pleasures and new pains.

A new hero.

Alan Moore
Northampton, 1986

Vowing upon
his parent's death
to rid the city
of the criminal element,
the Batman has,
over the years,
fought crime in its
many macabre forms...

For the last ten years
no one has seen
or heard from him...

that is, until now...

Dedicated to
WILL JUNGKUNTZ
1955-1985

BOOK ONE

THE DARK KNIGHT RETURNS

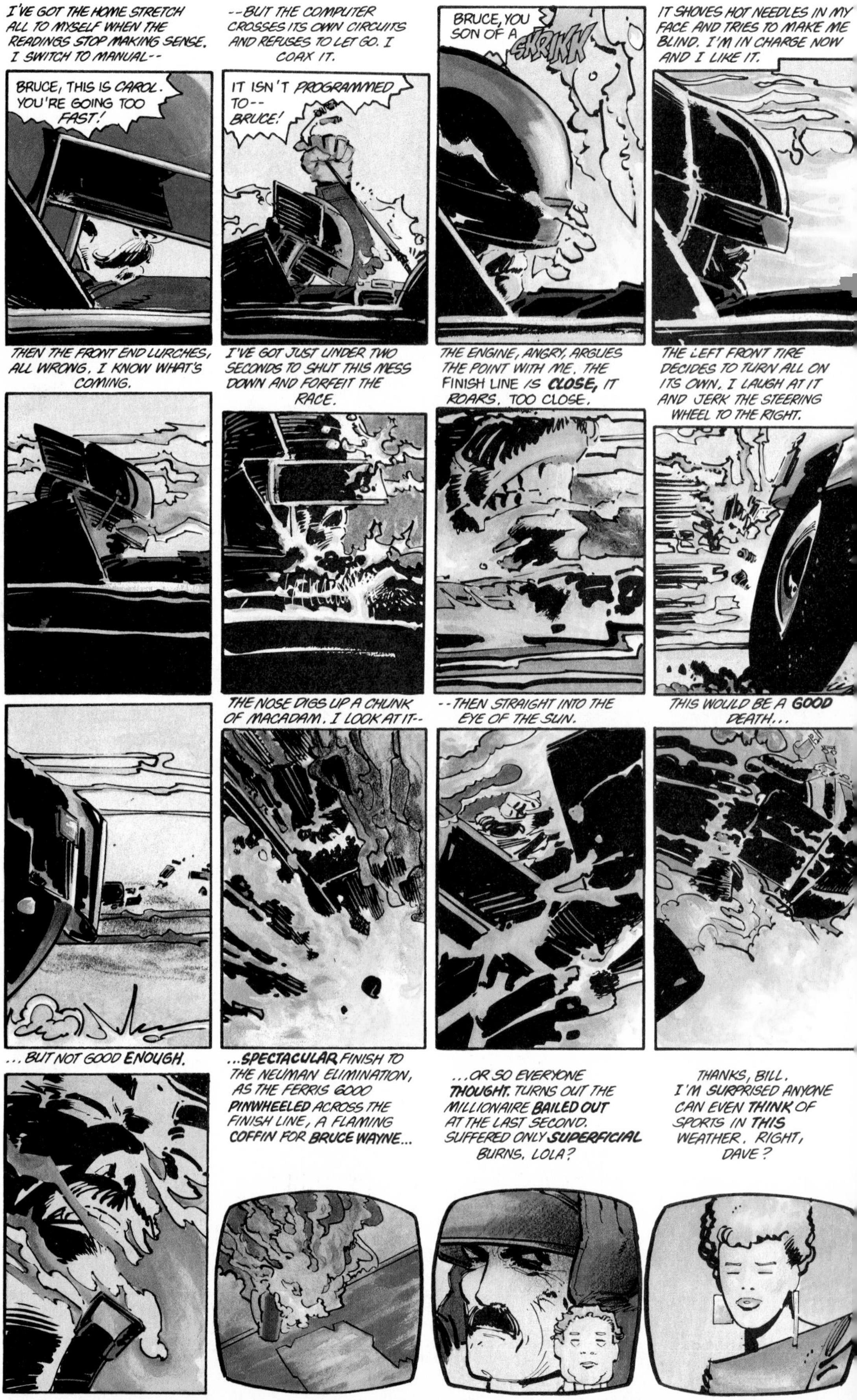
I'VE GOT THE HOME STRETCH ALL TO MYSELF WHEN THE READINGS STOP MAKING SENSE. I SWITCH TO MANUAL--
BRUCE, THIS IS CAROL. YOU'RE GOING TOO FAST!
--BUT THE COMPUTER CROSSES ITS OWN CIRCUITS AND REFUSES TO LET GO. I COAX IT.
IT ISN'T PROGRAMMED TO--
BRUCE!
BRUCE, YOU SON OF A
SKRIKK
IT SHOVES HOT NEEDLES IN MY FACE AND TRIES TO MAKE ME BLIND. I'M IN CHARGE NOW AND I LIKE IT.
THEN THE FRONT END LURCHES, ALL WRONG. I KNOW WHAT'S COMING.
I'VE GOT JUST UNDER TWO SECONDS TO SHUT THIS MESS DOWN AND FORFEIT THE RACE.
THE ENGINE, ANGRY, ARGUES THE POINT WITH ME. THE FINISH LINE IS CLOSE, IT ROARS. TOO CLOSE.
THE LEFT FRONT TIRE DECIDES TO TURN ALL ON ITS OWN. I LAUGH AT IT AND JERK THE STEERING WHEEL TO THE RIGHT.
THE NOSE DIGS UP A CHUNK OF MACADAM. I LOOK AT IT--
--THEN STRAIGHT INTO THE EYE OF THE SUN.
THIS WOULD BE A GOOD DEATH...
...BUT NOT GOOD ENOUGH.
...SPECTACULAR FINISH TO THE NEUMAN ELIMINATION, AS THE FERRIS 6000 PINWHEELED ACROSS THE FINISH LINE, A FLAMING COFFIN FOR BRUCE WAYNE...
...OR SO EVERYONE THOUGHT. TURNS OUT THE MILLIONAIRE BAILED OUT AT THE LAST SECOND. SUFFERED ONLY SUPERFICIAL BURNS, LOLA?
THANKS, BILL. I'M SURPRISED ANYONE CAN EVEN THINK OF SPORTS IN THIS WEATHER. RIGHT, DAVE?

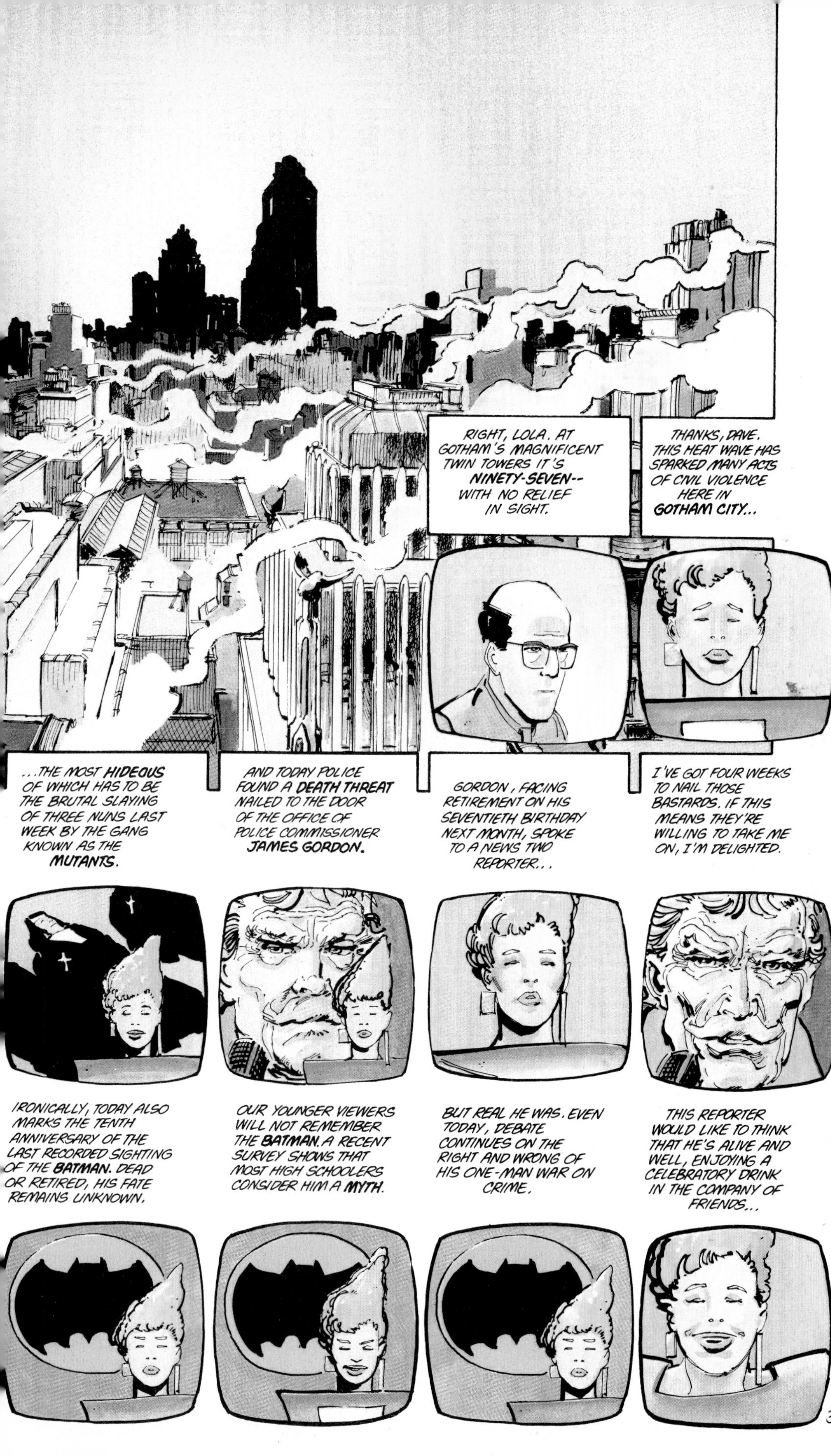

RIGHT, LOLA. AT GOTHAM'S MAGNIFICENT TWIN TOWERS IT'S NINETY-SEVEN-- WITH NO RELIEF IN SIGHT.
THANKS, DAVE. THIS HEAT WAVE HAS SPARKED MANY ACTS OF CIVIL VIOLENCE HERE IN GOTHAM CITY...
...THE MOST HIDEOUS OF WHICH HAS TO BE THE BRUTAL SLAYING OF THREE NUNS LAST WEEK BY THE GANG KNOWN AS THE MUTANTS.
AND TODAY POLICE FOUND A DEATH THREAT NAILED TO THE DOOR OF THE OFFICE OF POLICE COMMISSIONER JAMES GORDON.
GORDON, FACING RETIREMENT ON HIS SEVENTIETH BIRTHDAY NEXT MONTH, SPOKE TO A NEWS TWO REPORTER...
I'VE GOT FOUR WEEKS TO NAIL THOSE BASTARDS. IF THIS MEANS THEY'RE WILLING TO TAKE ME ON, I'M DELIGHTED.
IRONICALLY, TODAY ALSO MARKS THE TENTH ANNIVERSARY OF THE LAST RECORDED SIGHTING OF THE BATMAN. DEAD OR RETIRED, HIS FATE REMAINS UNKNOWN.
OUR YOUNGER VIEWERS WILL NOT REMEMBER THE BATMAN. A RECENT SURVEY SHOWS THAT MOST HIGH SCHOOLERS CONSIDER HIM A MYTH.
BUT REAL HE WAS. EVEN TODAY, DEBATE CONTINUES ON THE RIGHT AND WRONG OF HIS ONE-MAN WAR ON CRIME.
THIS REPORTER WOULD LIKE TO THINK THAT HE'S ALIVE AND WELL, ENJOYING A CELEBRATORY DRINK IN THE COMPANY OF FRIENDS...

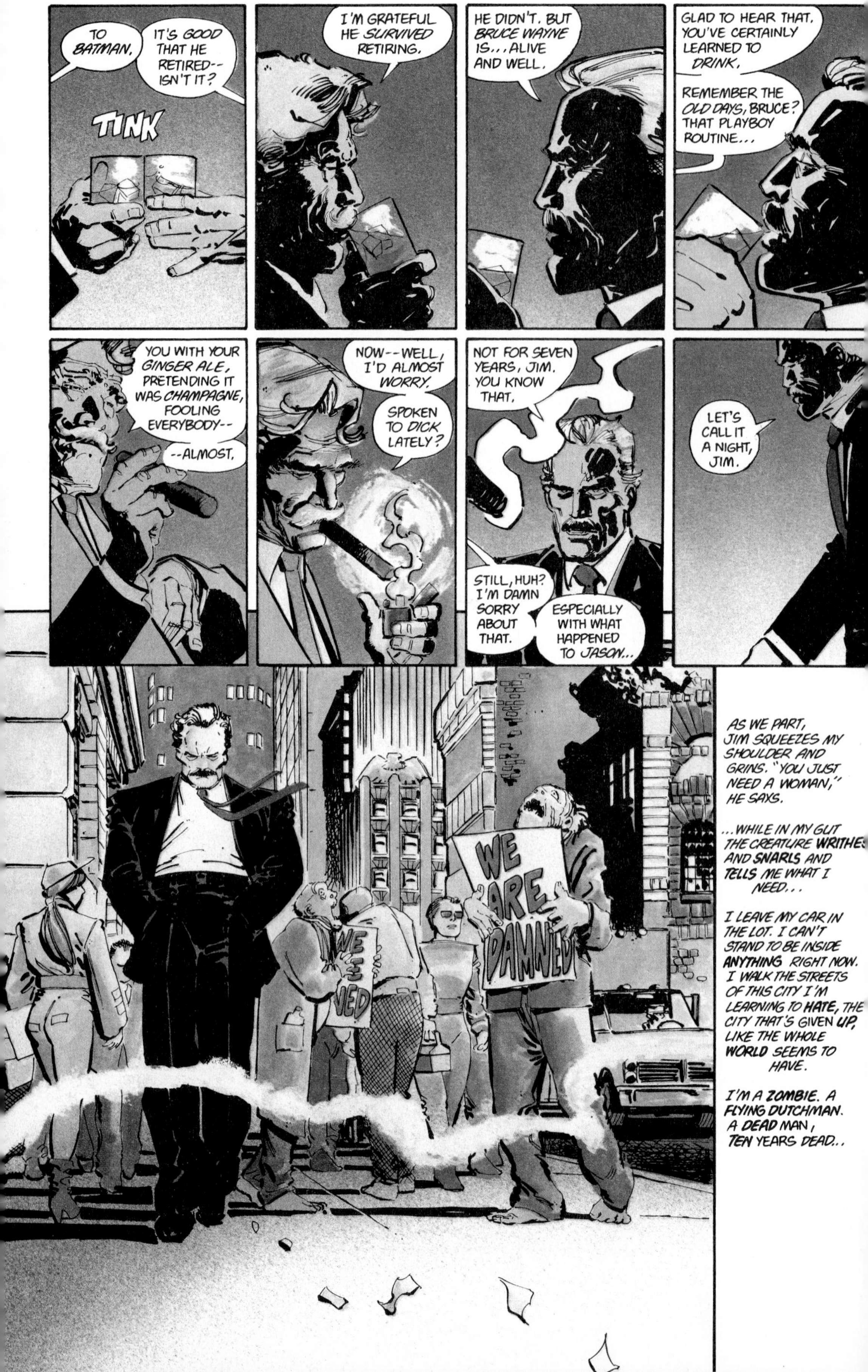
TO BATMAN.
IT'S GOOD THAT HE RETIRED-- ISN'T IT?
TINK
I'M GRATEFUL HE SURVIVED RETIRING.
HE DIDN'T. BUT BRUCE WAYNE IS... ALIVE AND WELL.
GLAD TO HEAR THAT. YOU'VE CERTAINLY LEARNED TO DRINK.
REMEMBER THE OLD DAYS, BRUCE? THAT PLAYBOY ROUTINE...
YOU WITH YOUR GINGER ALE, PRETENDING IT WAS CHAMPAGNE, FOOLING EVERYBODY--
--ALMOST.
NOW--WELL, I'D ALMOST WORRY.
SPOKEN TO DICK LATELY?
NOT FOR SEVEN YEARS, JIM. YOU KNOW THAT.
STILL, HUH? I'M DAMN SORRY ABOUT THAT.
ESPECIALLY WITH WHAT HAPPENED TO JASON...
LET'S CALL IT A NIGHT, JIM.
WE ARE DAMNED
WE ... NED
AS WE PART, JIM SQUEEZES MY SHOULDER AND GRINS. "YOU JUST NEED A WOMAN," HE SAYS.
...WHILE IN MY GUT THE CREATURE WRITHES AND SNARLS AND TELLS ME WHAT I NEED...
I LEAVE MY CAR IN THE LOT. I CAN'T STAND TO BE INSIDE ANYTHING RIGHT NOW. I WALK THE STREETS OF THIS CITY I'M LEARNING TO HATE, THE CITY THAT'S GIVEN UP, LIKE THE WHOLE WORLD SEEMS TO HAVE.
I'M A ZOMBIE. A FLYING DUTCHMAN. A DEAD MAN, TEN YEARS DEAD...

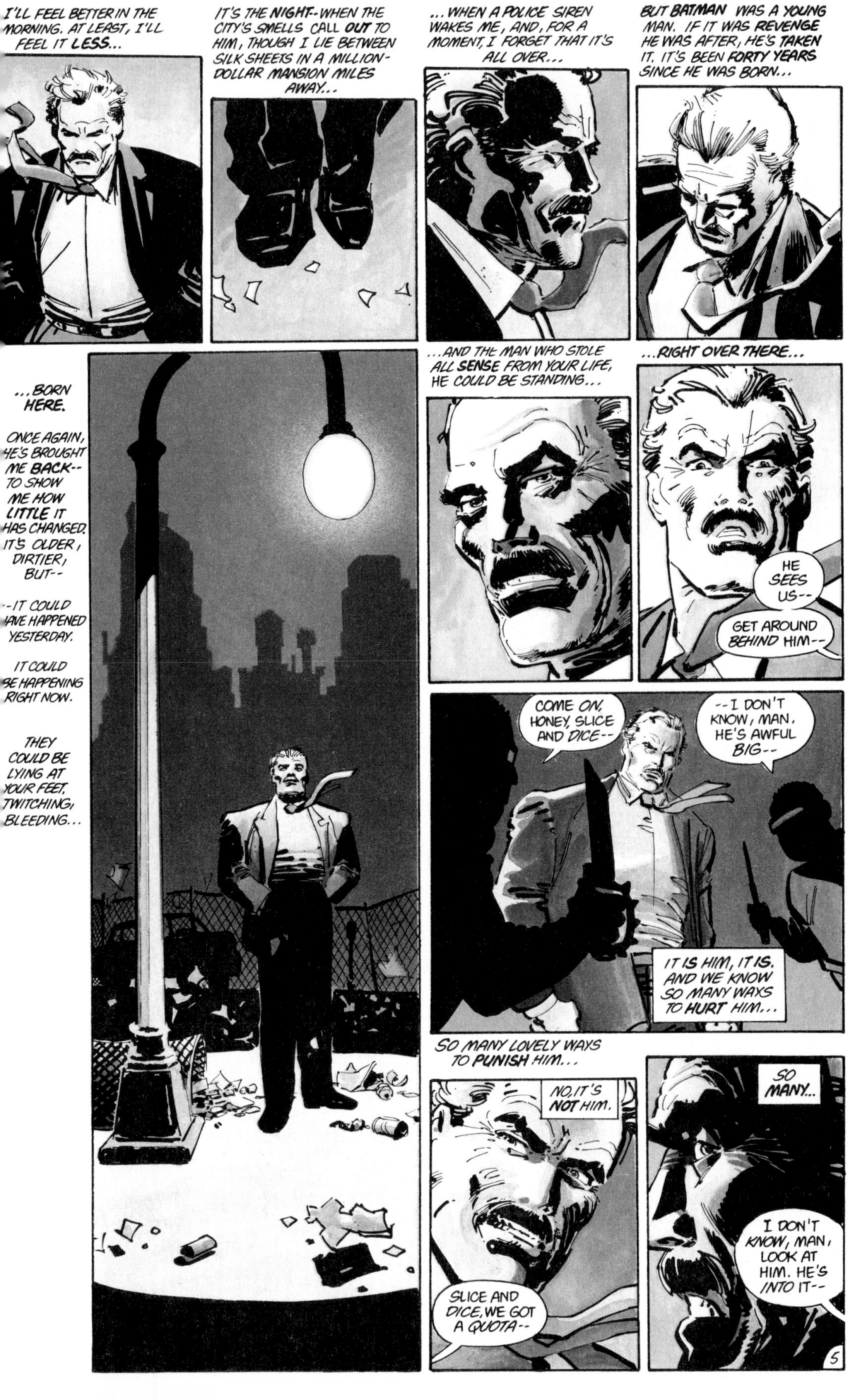

I'LL FEEL BETTER IN THE MORNING. AT LEAST, I'LL FEEL IT LESS...
IT'S THE NIGHT--WHEN THE CITY'S SMELLS CALL OUT TO HIM, THOUGH I LIE BETWEEN SILK SHEETS IN A MILLION-DOLLAR MANSION MILES AWAY...
...WHEN A POLICE SIREN WAKES ME, AND, FOR A MOMENT, I FORGET THAT IT'S ALL OVER...
BUT BATMAN WAS A YOUNG MAN. IF IT WAS REVENGE HE WAS AFTER, HE'S TAKEN IT. IT'S BEEN FORTY YEARS SINCE HE WAS BORN...
...BORN HERE.
ONCE AGAIN, HE'S BROUGHT ME BACK--TO SHOW ME HOW LITTLE IT HAS CHANGED. IT'S OLDER, DIRTIER, BUT--
--IT COULD HAVE HAPPENED YESTERDAY.
IT COULD BE HAPPENING RIGHT NOW.
THEY COULD BE LYING AT YOUR FEET, TWITCHING, BLEEDING...
...AND THE MAN WHO STOLE ALL SENSE FROM YOUR LIFE, HE COULD BE STANDING...
...RIGHT OVER THERE...
HE SEES US--
GET AROUND BEHIND HIM--
COME ON, HONEY, SLICE AND DICE--
--I DON'T KNOW, MAN, HE'S AWFUL BIG--
IT IS HIM, IT IS. AND WE KNOW SO MANY WAYS TO HURT HIM...
SO MANY LOVELY WAYS TO PUNISH HIM...
NO, IT'S NOT HIM.
SLICE AND DICE, WE GOT A QUOTA--
SO MANY...
I DON'T KNOW, MAN, LOOK AT HIM. HE'S INTO IT--

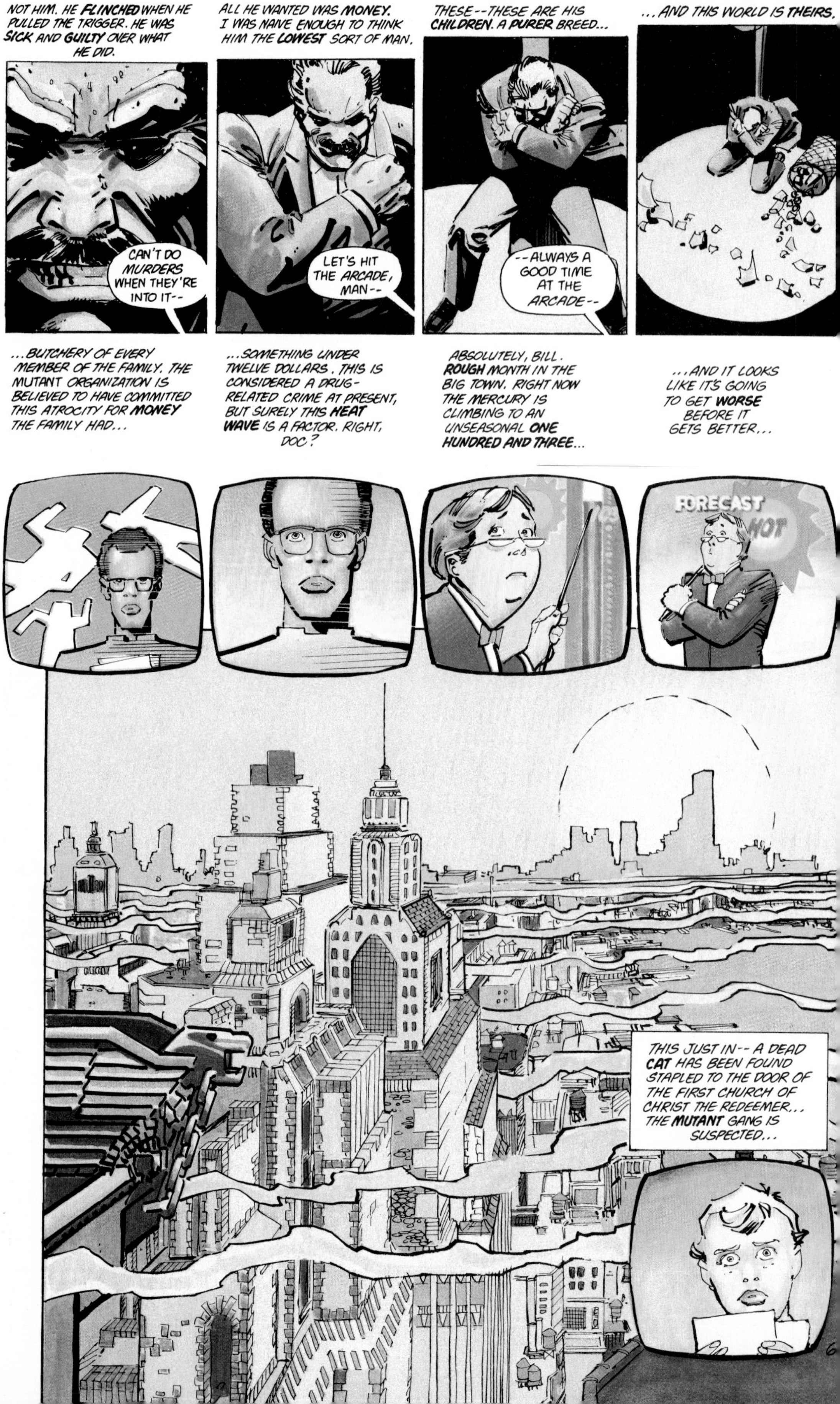

NOT HIM. HE FLINCHED WHEN HE PULLED THE TRIGGER. HE WAS SICK AND GUILTY OVER WHAT HE DID.
CAN'T DO MURDERS WHEN THEY'RE INTO IT--
ALL HE WANTED WAS MONEY. I WAS NAIVE ENOUGH TO THINK HIM THE LOWEST SORT OF MAN.
LET'S HIT THE ARCADE, MAN--
THESE--THESE ARE HIS CHILDREN. A PURER BREED...
--ALWAYS A GOOD TIME AT THE ARCADE--
...AND THIS WORLD IS THEIRS.
...BUTCHERY OF EVERY MEMBER OF THE FAMILY. THE MUTANT ORGANIZATION IS BELIEVED TO HAVE COMMITTED THIS ATROCITY FOR MONEY THE FAMILY HAD...
...SOMETHING UNDER TWELVE DOLLARS. THIS IS CONSIDERED A DRUG-RELATED CRIME AT PRESENT, BUT SURELY THIS HEAT WAVE IS A FACTOR. RIGHT, DOC?
ABSOLUTELY, BILL. ROUGH MONTH IN THE BIG TOWN. RIGHT NOW THE MERCURY IS CLIMBING TO AN UNSEASONAL ONE HUNDRED AND THREE...
...AND IT LOOKS LIKE IT'S GOING TO GET WORSE BEFORE IT GETS BETTER...
FORECAST
HOT
THIS JUST IN-- A DEAD CAT HAS BEEN FOUND STAPLED TO THE DOOR OF THE FIRST CHURCH OF CHRIST THE REDEEMER... THE MUTANT GANG IS SUSPECTED...

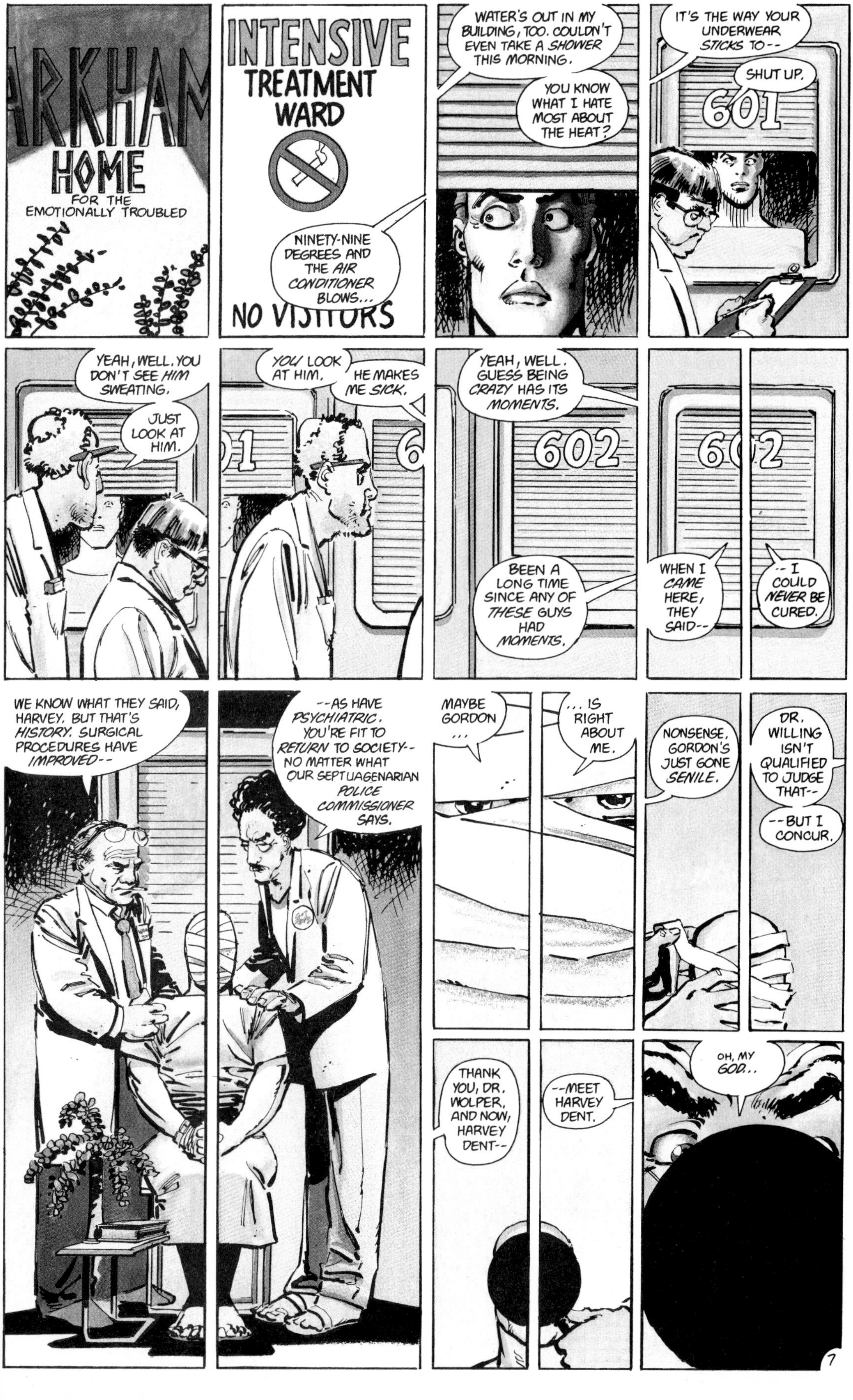
ARKHAM HOME FOR THE EMOTIONALLY TROUBLED
INTENSIVE TREATMENT WARD
NO VISITORS
NINETY-NINE DEGREES AND THE AIR CONDITIONER BLOWS...
WATER'S OUT IN MY BUILDING, TOO. COULDN'T EVEN TAKE A SHOWER THIS MORNING.
YOU KNOW WHAT I HATE MOST ABOUT THE HEAT?
IT'S THE WAY YOUR UNDERWEAR STICKS TO--
SHUT UP.
601
YEAH, WELL. YOU DON'T SEE HIM SWEATING.
JUST LOOK AT HIM.
YOU LOOK AT HIM.
HE MAKES ME SICK.
YEAH, WELL. GUESS BEING CRAZY HAS ITS MOMENTS.
602
BEEN A LONG TIME SINCE ANY OF THESE GUYS HAD MOMENTS.
WHEN I CAME HERE, THEY SAID--
--I COULD NEVER BE CURED.
WE KNOW WHAT THEY SAID, HARVEY. BUT THAT'S HISTORY. SURGICAL PROCEDURES HAVE IMPROVED--
--AS HAVE PSYCHIATRIC. YOU'RE FIT TO RETURN TO SOCIETY--NO MATTER WHAT OUR SEPTUAGENARIAN POLICE COMMISSIONER SAYS.
MAYBE GORDON ...
... IS RIGHT ABOUT ME.
NONSENSE. GORDON'S JUST GONE SENILE.
DR. WILLING ISN'T QUALIFIED TO JUDGE THAT--
--BUT I CONCUR.
THANK YOU, DR. WOLPER. AND NOW, HARVEY DENT--
--MEET HARVEY DENT.
OH, MY GOD...

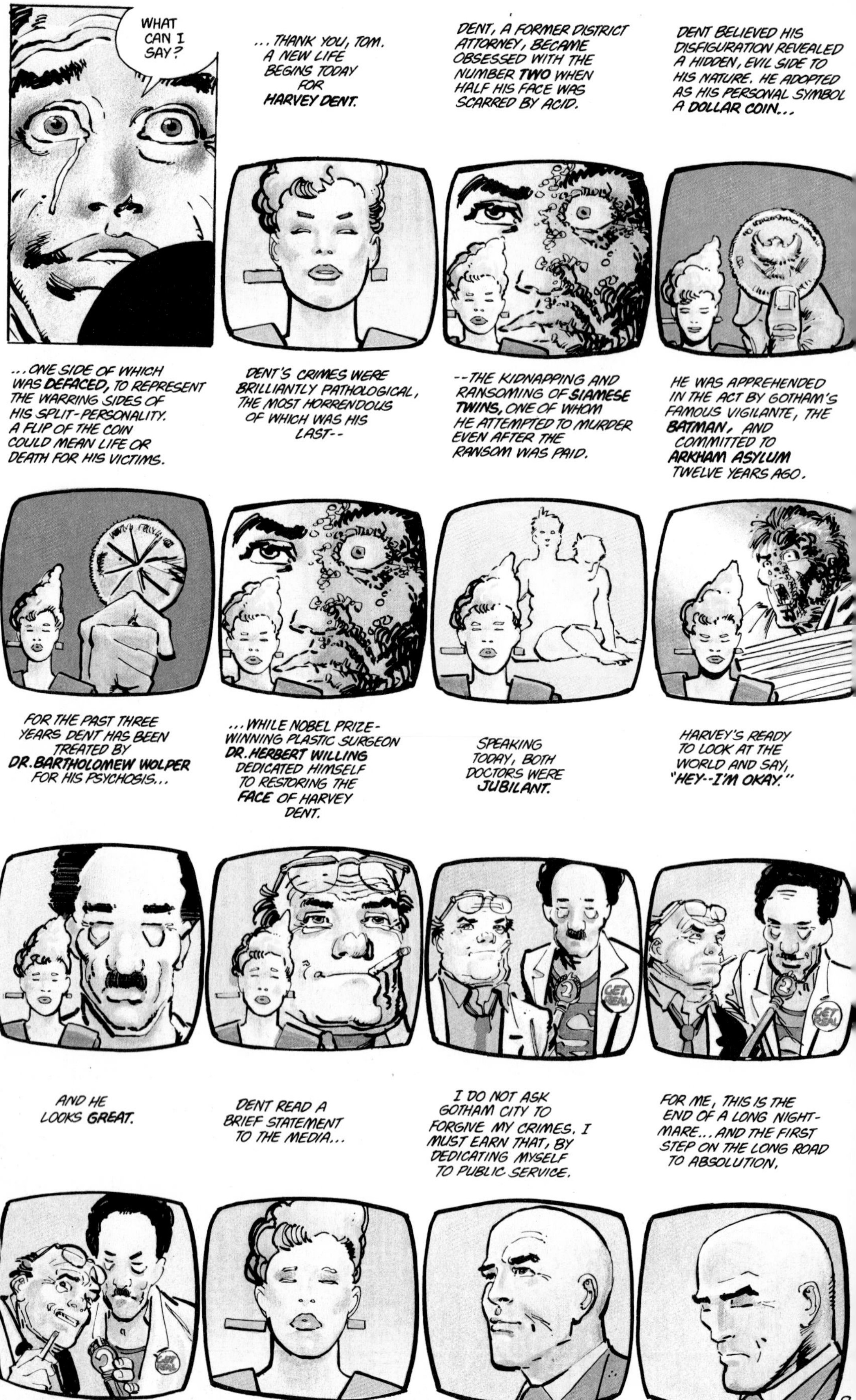

WHAT CAN I SAY?
...THANK YOU, TOM. A NEW LIFE BEGINS TODAY FOR HARVEY DENT.
DENT, A FORMER DISTRICT ATTORNEY, BECAME OBSESSED WITH THE NUMBER TWO WHEN HALF HIS FACE WAS SCARRED BY ACID.
DENT BELIEVED HIS DISFIGURATION REVEALED A HIDDEN, EVIL SIDE TO HIS NATURE. HE ADOPTED AS HIS PERSONAL SYMBOL A DOLLAR COIN...
...ONE SIDE OF WHICH WAS DEFACED, TO REPRESENT THE WARRING SIDES OF HIS SPLIT-PERSONALITY. A FLIP OF THE COIN COULD MEAN LIFE OR DEATH FOR HIS VICTIMS.
DENT'S CRIMES WERE BRILLIANTLY PATHOLOGICAL, THE MOST HORRENDOUS OF WHICH WAS HIS LAST--
--THE KIDNAPPING AND RANSOMING OF SIAMESE TWINS, ONE OF WHOM HE ATTEMPTED TO MURDER EVEN AFTER THE RANSOM WAS PAID.
HE WAS APPREHENDED IN THE ACT BY GOTHAM'S FAMOUS VIGILANTE, THE BATMAN, AND COMMITTED TO ARKHAM ASYLUM TWELVE YEARS AGO.
FOR THE PAST THREE YEARS DENT HAS BEEN TREATED BY DR. BARTHOLOMEW WOLPER FOR HIS PSYCHOSIS...
...WHILE NOBEL PRIZE-WINNING PLASTIC SURGEON DR. HERBERT WILLING DEDICATED HIMSELF TO RESTORING THE FACE OF HARVEY DENT.
SPEAKING TODAY, BOTH DOCTORS WERE JUBILANT.
HARVEY'S READY TO LOOK AT THE WORLD AND SAY, "HEY--I'M OKAY."
GET REAL
GET REAL
AND HE LOOKS GREAT.
GET REAL
DENT READ A BRIEF STATEMENT TO THE MEDIA...
I DO NOT ASK GOTHAM CITY TO FORGIVE MY CRIMES. I MUST EARN THAT, BY DEDICATING MYSELF TO PUBLIC SERVICE.
FOR ME, THIS IS THE END OF A LONG NIGHT-MARE... AND THE FIRST STEP ON THE LONG ROAD TO ABSOLUTION.

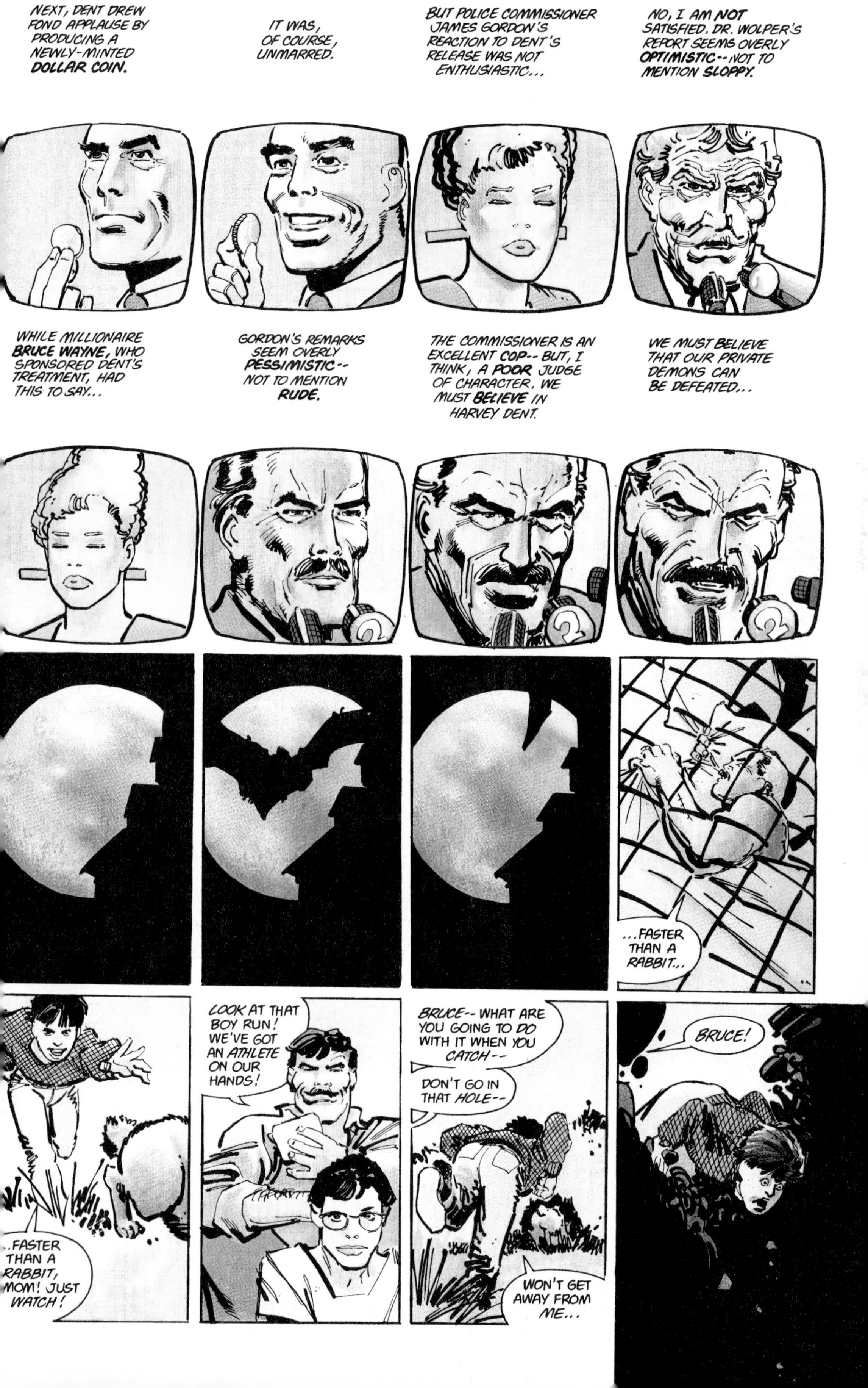
NEXT, DENT DREW FOND APPLAUSE BY PRODUCING A NEWLY-MINTED DOLLAR COIN.
IT WAS, OF COURSE, UNMARRED.
BUT POLICE COMMISSIONER JAMES GORDON'S REACTION TO DENT'S RELEASE WAS NOT ENTHUSIASTIC...
NO, I AM NOT SATISFIED. DR. WOLPER'S REPORT SEEMS OVERLY OPTIMISTIC-- NOT TO MENTION SLOPPY.
WHILE MILLIONAIRE BRUCE WAYNE, WHO SPONSORED DENT'S TREATMENT, HAD THIS TO SAY...
GORDON'S REMARKS SEEM OVERLY PESSIMISTIC-- NOT TO MENTION RUDE.
THE COMMISSIONER IS AN EXCELLENT COP-- BUT, I THINK, A POOR JUDGE OF CHARACTER. WE MUST BELIEVE IN HARVEY DENT.
WE MUST BELIEVE THAT OUR PRIVATE DEMONS CAN BE DEFEATED...
...FASTER THAN A RABBIT...
..FASTER THAN A RABBIT, MOM! JUST WATCH!
LOOK AT THAT BOY RUN! WE'VE GOT AN ATHLETE ON OUR HANDS!
BRUCE-- WHAT ARE YOU GOING TO DO WITH IT WHEN YOU CATCH--
DON'T GO IN THAT HOLE--
WON'T GET AWAY FROM ME...
BRUCE!

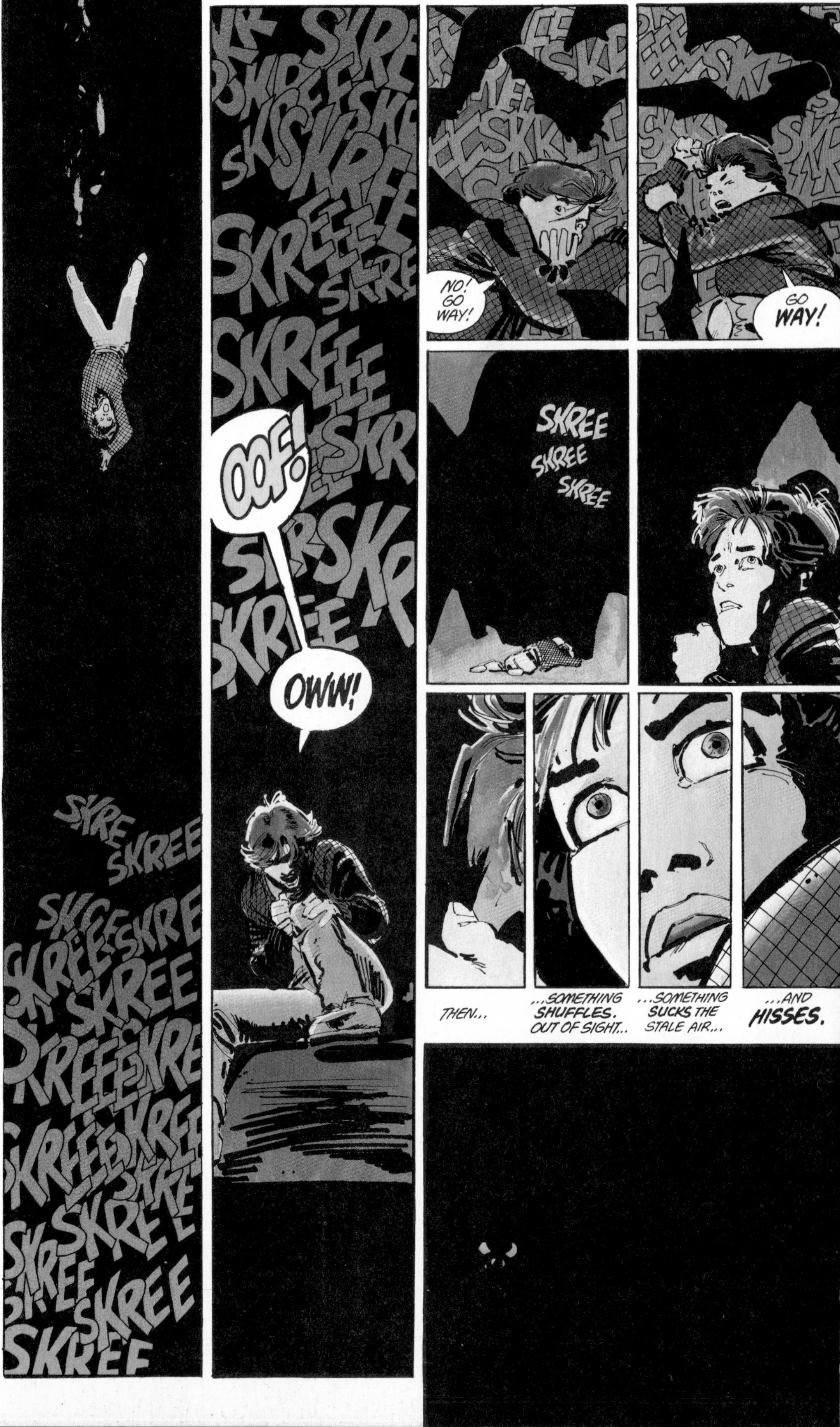

SKREE
OOF!
OWW!
NO! GO WAY!
GO WAY!
SKREE
SKREE
SKREE
THEN...
...SOMETHING SHUFFLES. OUT OF SIGHT...
...SOMETHING SUCKS THE STALE AIR...
...AND HISSES.

GLIDING WITH **ANCIENT** GRACE...

UNWILLING TO **RETREAT** AS HIS BROTHERS DID...

EYES **GLEAMING,** UNTOUCHED BY LOVE OR JOY OR SORROW...

BREATH **HOT** WITH THE TASTE OF FALLEN FOES...THE STENCH OF **DEAD** THINGS, **DAMNED** THINGS...

SURELY THE **FIERCEST** SURVIVOR-- THE **PUREST** WARRIOR...

GLARING, **HATING...**

...CLAIMING ME AS HIS **OWN.**

DREAMING...

I WAS ONLY SIX YEARS OLD WHEN THAT HAPPENED. WHEN I FIRST SAW THE **CAVE...**

...HUGE, EMPTY, SILENT AS A **CHURCH, WAITING,** AS THE **BAT** WAS WAITING.

AND NOW THE **COBWEBS** GROW AND THE DUST **THICKENS** IN HERE AS IT DOES IN **ME--**

--AND HE **LAUGHS** AT ME, CURSES ME. CALLS ME A **FOOL.** HE FILLS MY **SLEEP,** HE **TRICKS** ME. BRINGS ME HERE WHEN THE NIGHT IS **LONG** AND MY WILL IS **WEAK.** HE **STRUGGLES** RELENTLESSLY, HATEFULLY, TO BE **FREE--**

I WILL NOT **LET** HIM. I GAVE MY **WORD.**

FOR **JASON.**

NEVER.

NEVER AGAIN.

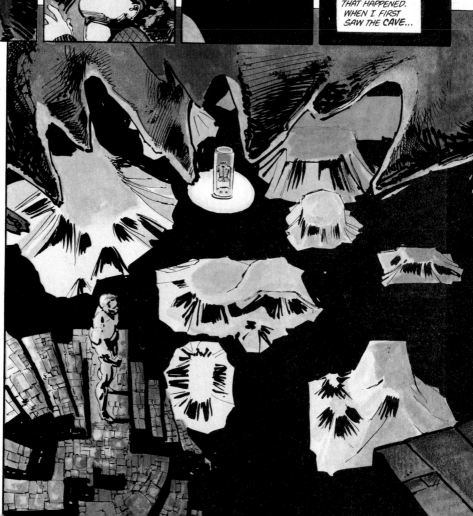

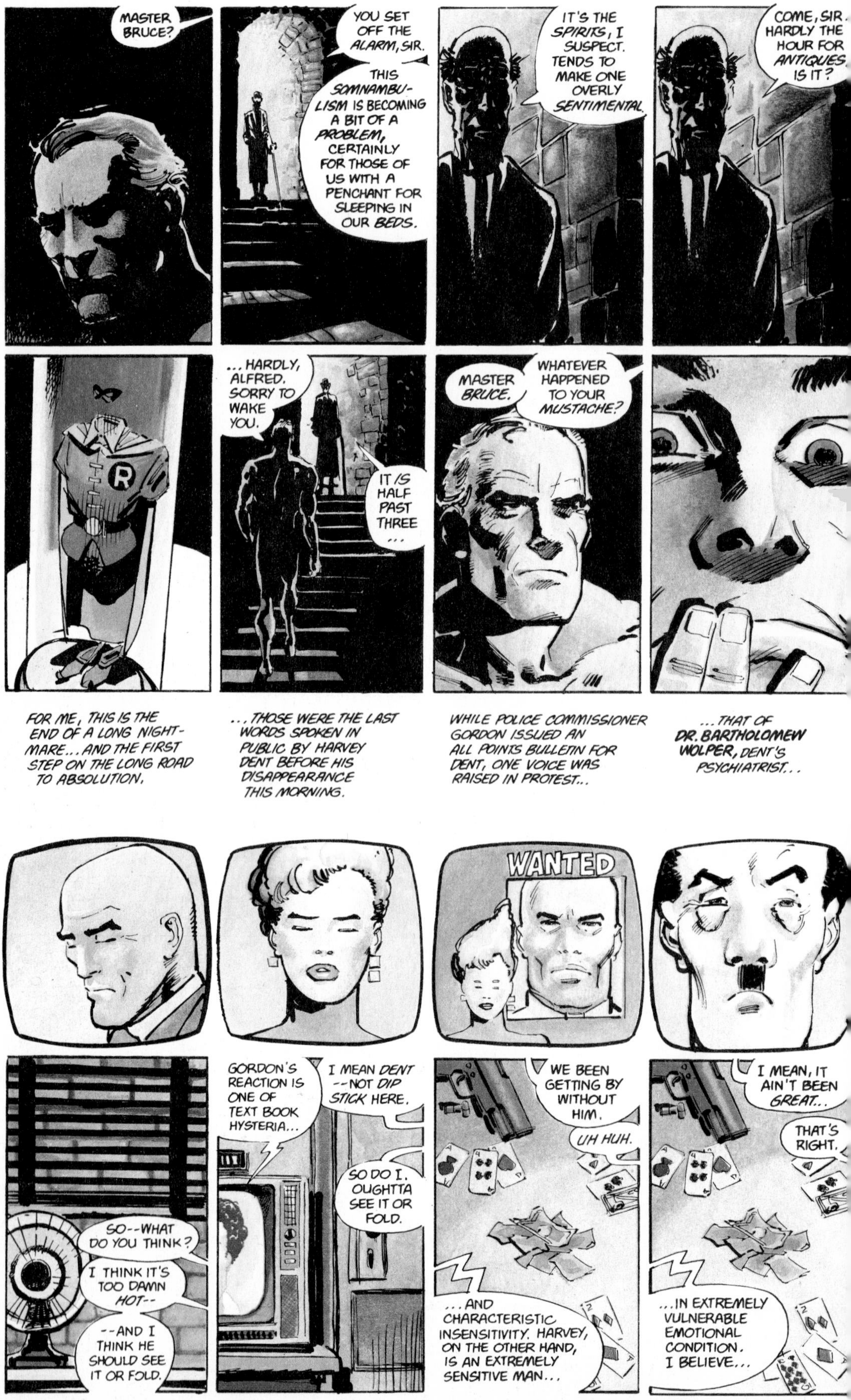
MASTER BRUCE?
YOU SET OFF THE ALARM, SIR.
THIS SOMNAMBULISM IS BECOMING A BIT OF A PROBLEM, CERTAINLY FOR THOSE OF US WITH A PENCHANT FOR SLEEPING IN OUR BEDS.
IT'S THE SPIRITS, I SUSPECT. TENDS TO MAKE ONE OVERLY SENTIMENTAL.
COME, SIR. HARDLY THE HOUR FOR ANTIQUES, IS IT?
...HARDLY, ALFRED. SORRY TO WAKE YOU.
IT IS HALF PAST THREE ...
MASTER BRUCE.
WHATEVER HAPPENED TO YOUR MUSTACHE?
FOR ME, THIS IS THE END OF A LONG NIGHTMARE... AND THE FIRST STEP ON THE LONG ROAD TO ABSOLUTION.
...THOSE WERE THE LAST WORDS SPOKEN IN PUBLIC BY HARVEY DENT BEFORE HIS DISAPPEARANCE THIS MORNING.
WHILE POLICE COMMISSIONER GORDON ISSUED AN ALL POINTS BULLETIN FOR DENT, ONE VOICE WAS RAISED IN PROTEST...
...THAT OF DR. BARTHOLOMEW WOLPER, DENT'S PSYCHIATRIST...
WANTED
SO--WHAT DO YOU THINK?
I THINK IT'S TOO DAMN HOT--
--AND I THINK HE SHOULD SEE IT OR FOLD.
GORDON'S REACTION IS ONE OF TEXT BOOK HYSTERIA...
I MEAN DENT --NOT DIP STICK HERE.
SO DO I. OUGHTTA SEE IT OR FOLD.
WE BEEN GETTING BY WITHOUT HIM.
UH HUH.
...AND CHARACTERISTIC INSENSITIVITY. HARVEY, ON THE OTHER HAND, IS AN EXTREMELY SENSITIVE MAN...
I MEAN, IT AIN'T BEEN GREAT...
THAT'S RIGHT.
...IN EXTREMELY VULNERABLE EMOTIONAL CONDITION. I BELIEVE...

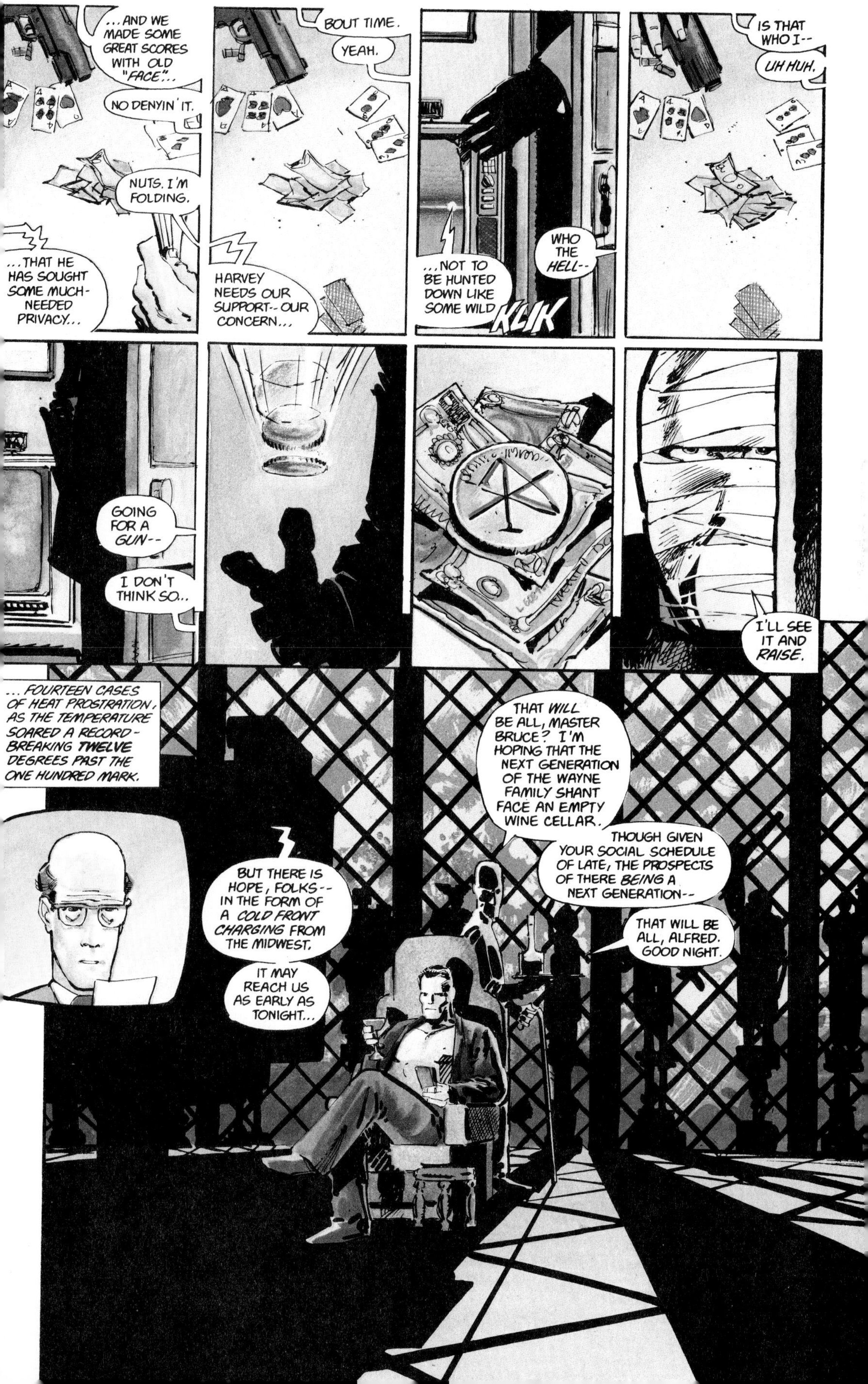
...AND WE MADE SOME GREAT SCORES WITH OLD "FACE"...
NO DENYIN' IT.
NUTS. I'M FOLDING.
...THAT HE HAS SOUGHT SOME MUCH-NEEDED PRIVACY...
BOUT TIME.
YEAH.
HARVEY NEEDS OUR SUPPORT-- OUR CONCERN...
...NOT TO BE HUNTED DOWN LIKE SOME WILD
KLIK
WHO THE HELL--
IS THAT WHO I--
UH HUH.
GOING FOR A GUN--
I DON'T THINK SO...
I'LL SEE IT AND RAISE.
... FOURTEEN CASES OF HEAT PROSTRATION, AS THE TEMPERATURE SOARED A RECORD-BREAKING TWELVE DEGREES PAST THE ONE HUNDRED MARK.
BUT THERE IS HOPE, FOLKS-- IN THE FORM OF A COLD FRONT CHARGING FROM THE MIDWEST.
IT MAY REACH US AS EARLY AS TONIGHT...
THAT WILL BE ALL, MASTER BRUCE? I'M HOPING THAT THE NEXT GENERATION OF THE WAYNE FAMILY SHANT FACE AN EMPTY WINE CELLAR.
THOUGH GIVEN YOUR SOCIAL SCHEDULE OF LATE, THE PROSPECTS OF THERE BEING A NEXT GENERATION--
THAT WILL BE ALL, ALFRED. GOOD NIGHT.

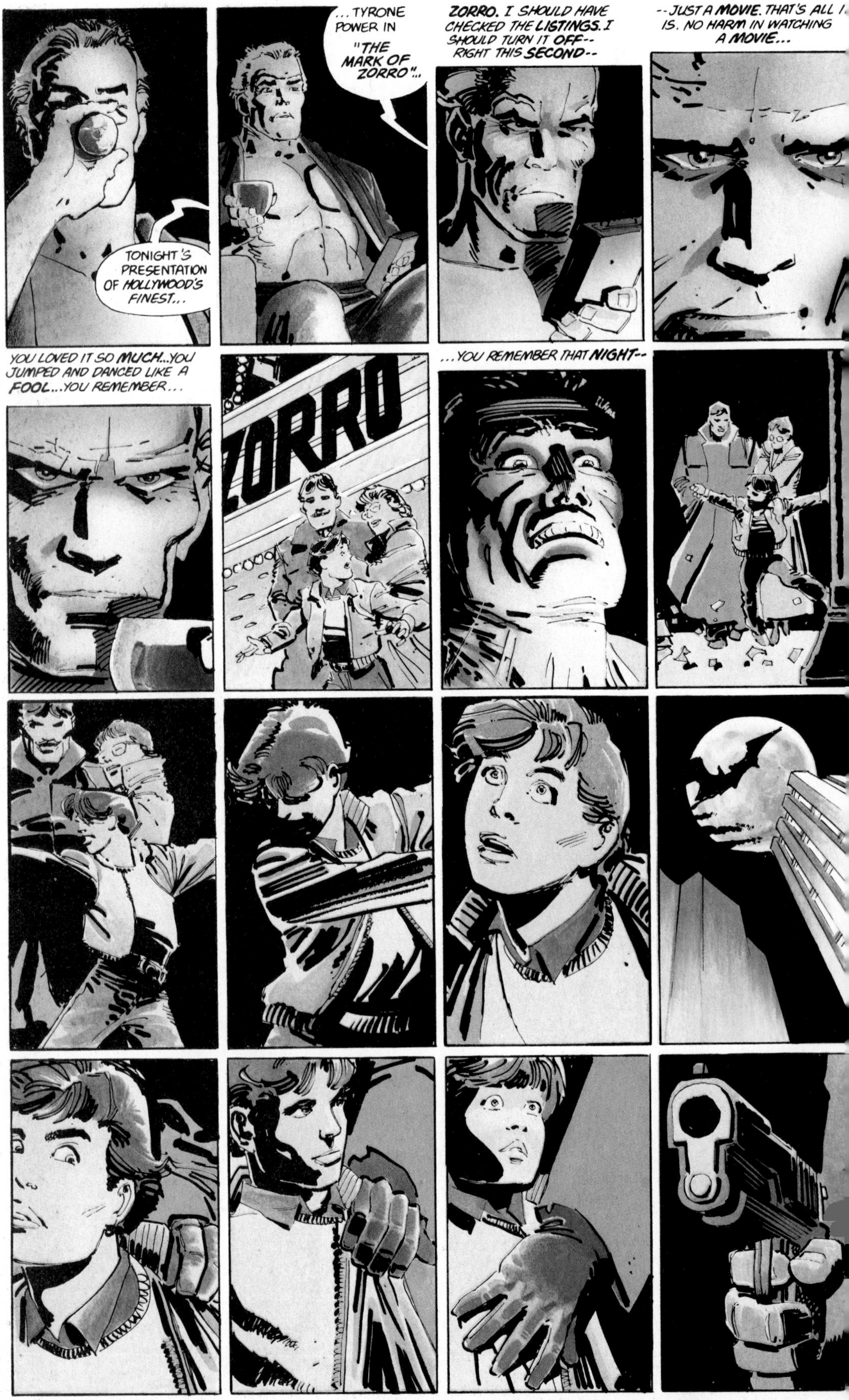
TONIGHT'S PRESENTATION OF HOLLYWOOD'S FINEST...
...TYRONE POWER IN "THE MARK OF ZORRO"...
ZORRO. I SHOULD HAVE CHECKED THE LISTINGS. I SHOULD TURN IT OFF-- RIGHT THIS SECOND--
--JUST A MOVIE. THAT'S ALL IT IS. NO HARM IN WATCHING A MOVIE...
YOU LOVED IT SO MUCH...YOU JUMPED AND DANCED LIKE A FOOL...YOU REMEMBER...
ZORRO
...YOU REMEMBER THAT NIGHT--

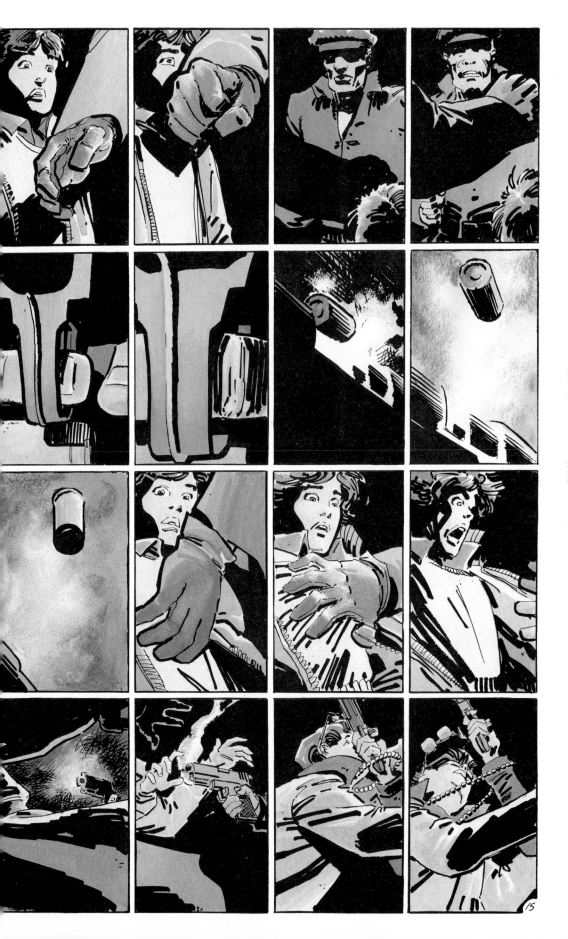

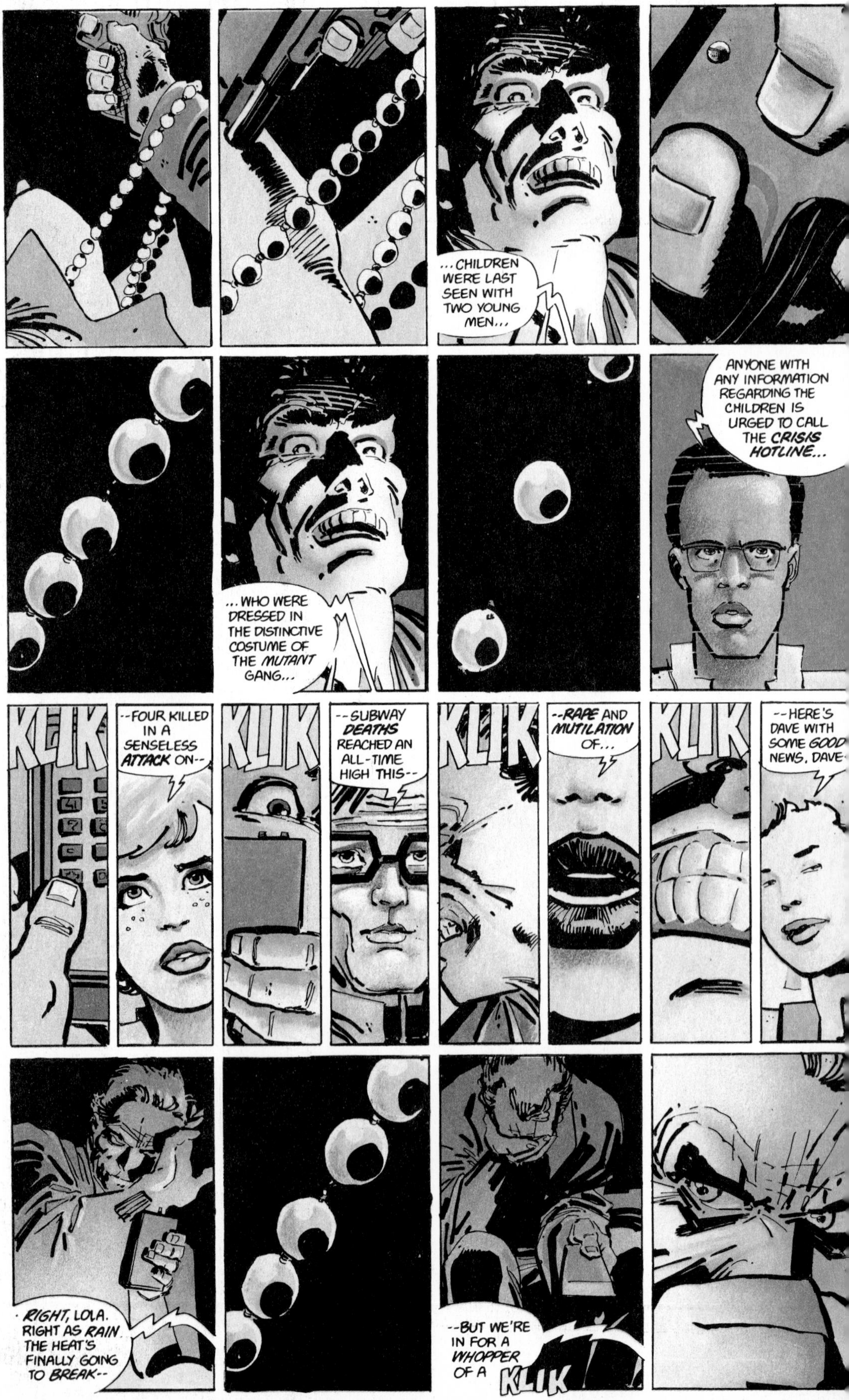
...CHILDREN WERE LAST SEEN WITH TWO YOUNG MEN...
...WHO WERE DRESSED IN THE DISTINCTIVE COSTUME OF THE MUTANT GANG...
ANYONE WITH ANY INFORMATION REGARDING THE CHILDREN IS URGED TO CALL THE CRISIS HOTLINE...
KLIK
--FOUR KILLED IN A SENSELESS ATTACK ON--
KLIK
--SUBWAY DEATHS REACHED AN ALL-TIME HIGH THIS--
KLIK
--RAPE AND MUTILATION OF...
KLIK
--HERE'S DAVE WITH SOME GOOD NEWS, DAVE--
RIGHT, LOLA. RIGHT AS RAIN. THE HEAT'S FINALLY GOING TO BREAK--
--BUT WE'RE IN FOR A WHOPPER OF A
KLIK

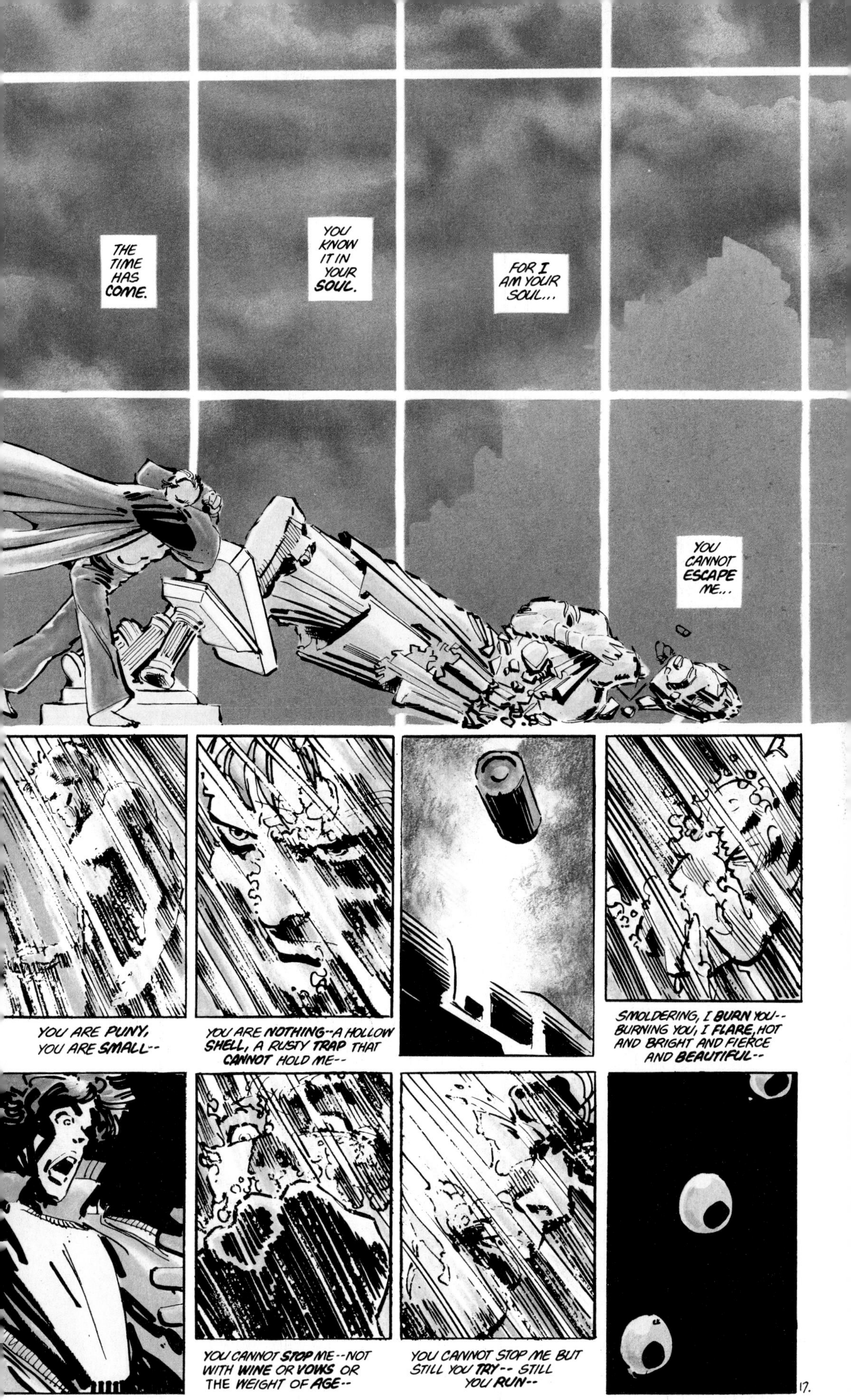
THE TIME HAS COME.
YOU KNOW IT IN YOUR SOUL.
FOR I AM YOUR SOUL...
YOU CANNOT ESCAPE ME...
YOU ARE PUNY, YOU ARE SMALL--
YOU ARE NOTHING--A HOLLOW SHELL, A RUSTY TRAP THAT CANNOT HOLD ME--
SMOLDERING, I BURN YOU--BURNING YOU, I FLARE, HOT AND BRIGHT AND FIERCE AND BEAUTIFUL--
YOU CANNOT STOP ME--NOT WITH WINE OR VOWS OR THE WEIGHT OF AGE--
YOU CANNOT STOP ME BUT STILL YOU TRY-- STILL YOU RUN--

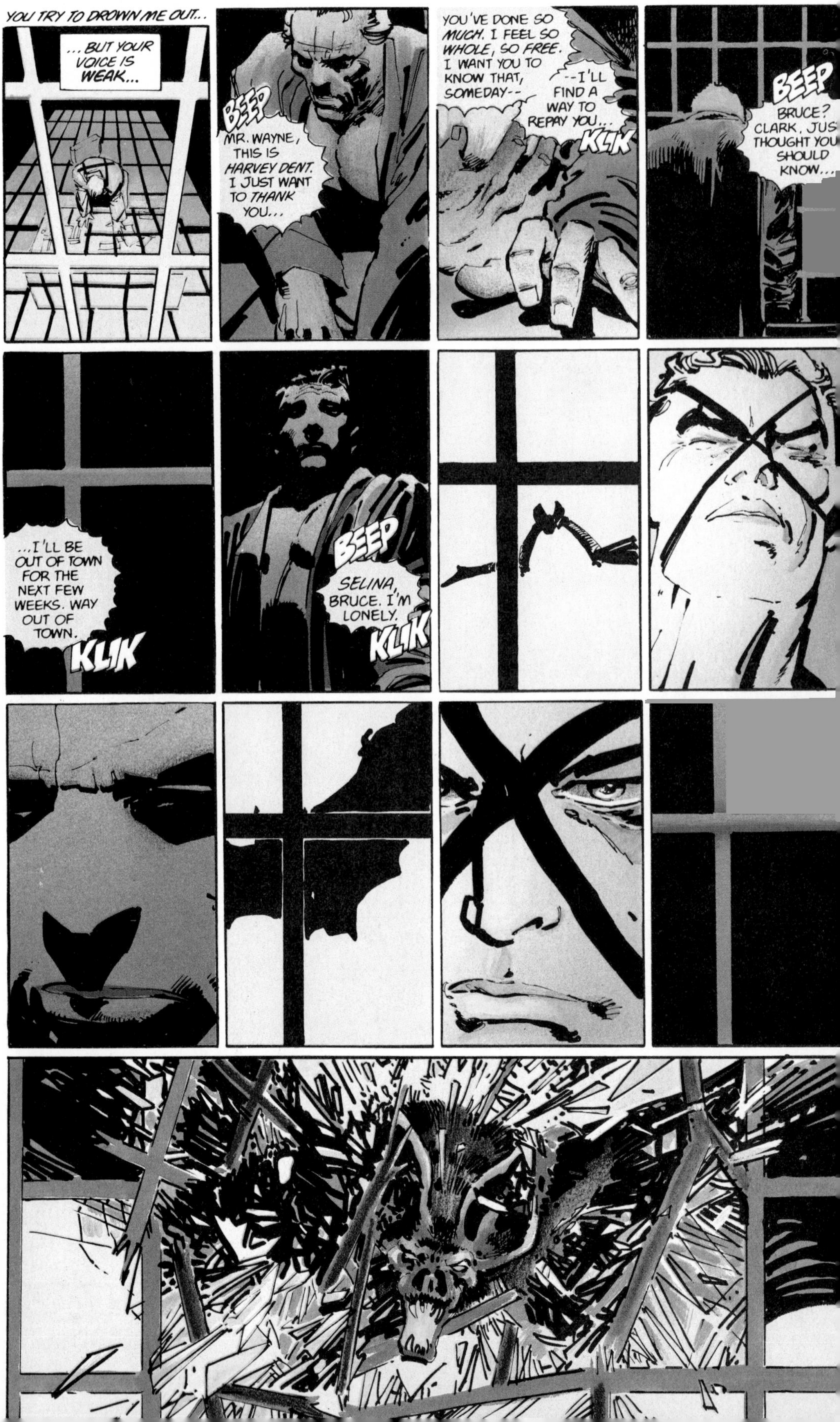

YOU TRY TO DROWN ME OUT...
...BUT YOUR VOICE IS WEAK...
BEEP
MR. WAYNE, THIS IS HARVEY DENT. I JUST WANT TO THANK YOU...
YOU'VE DONE SO MUCH. I FEEL SO WHOLE, SO FREE. I WANT YOU TO KNOW THAT, SOMEDAY--
--I'LL FIND A WAY TO REPAY YOU...
KLIK
BEEP
BRUCE? CLARK, JUS THOUGHT YOU SHOULD KNOW...
...I'LL BE OUT OF TOWN FOR THE NEXT FEW WEEKS. WAY OUT OF TOWN.
KLIK
BEEP
SELINA, BRUCE. I'M LONELY.
KLIK

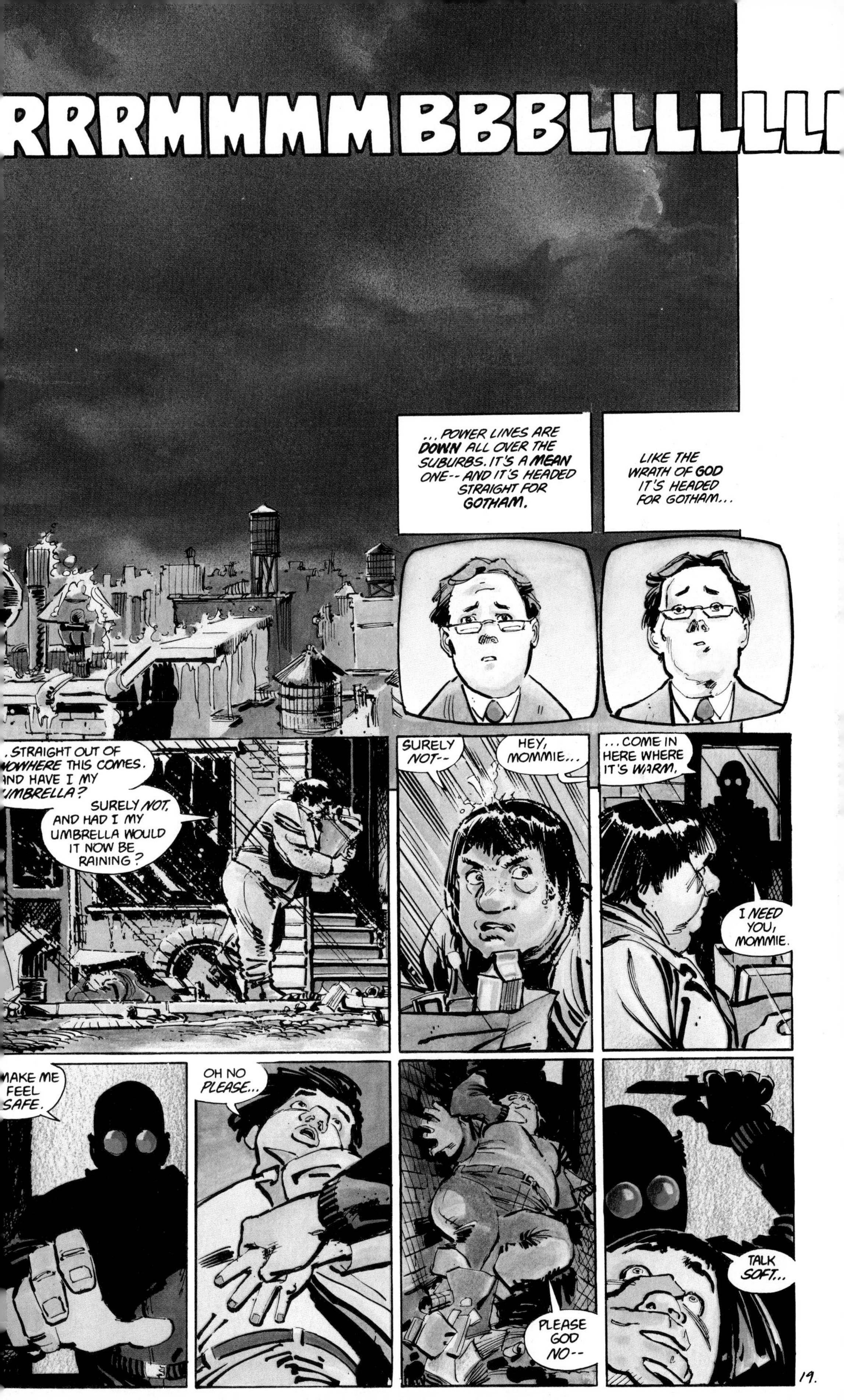

RRRMMMMBBBLLLLLL
...POWER LINES ARE DOWN ALL OVER THE SUBURBS. IT'S A MEAN ONE-- AND IT'S HEADED STRAIGHT FOR GOTHAM.
LIKE THE WRATH OF GOD IT'S HEADED FOR GOTHAM...
...STRAIGHT OUT OF NOWHERE THIS COMES. AND HAVE I MY UMBRELLA?
SURELY NOT. AND HAD I MY UMBRELLA WOULD IT NOW BE RAINING?
SURELY NOT--
HEY, MOMMIE...
...COME IN HERE WHERE IT'S WARM.
I NEED YOU, MOMMIE.
MAKE ME FEEL SAFE.
OH NO PLEASE...
PLEASE GOD NO--
TALK SOFT...

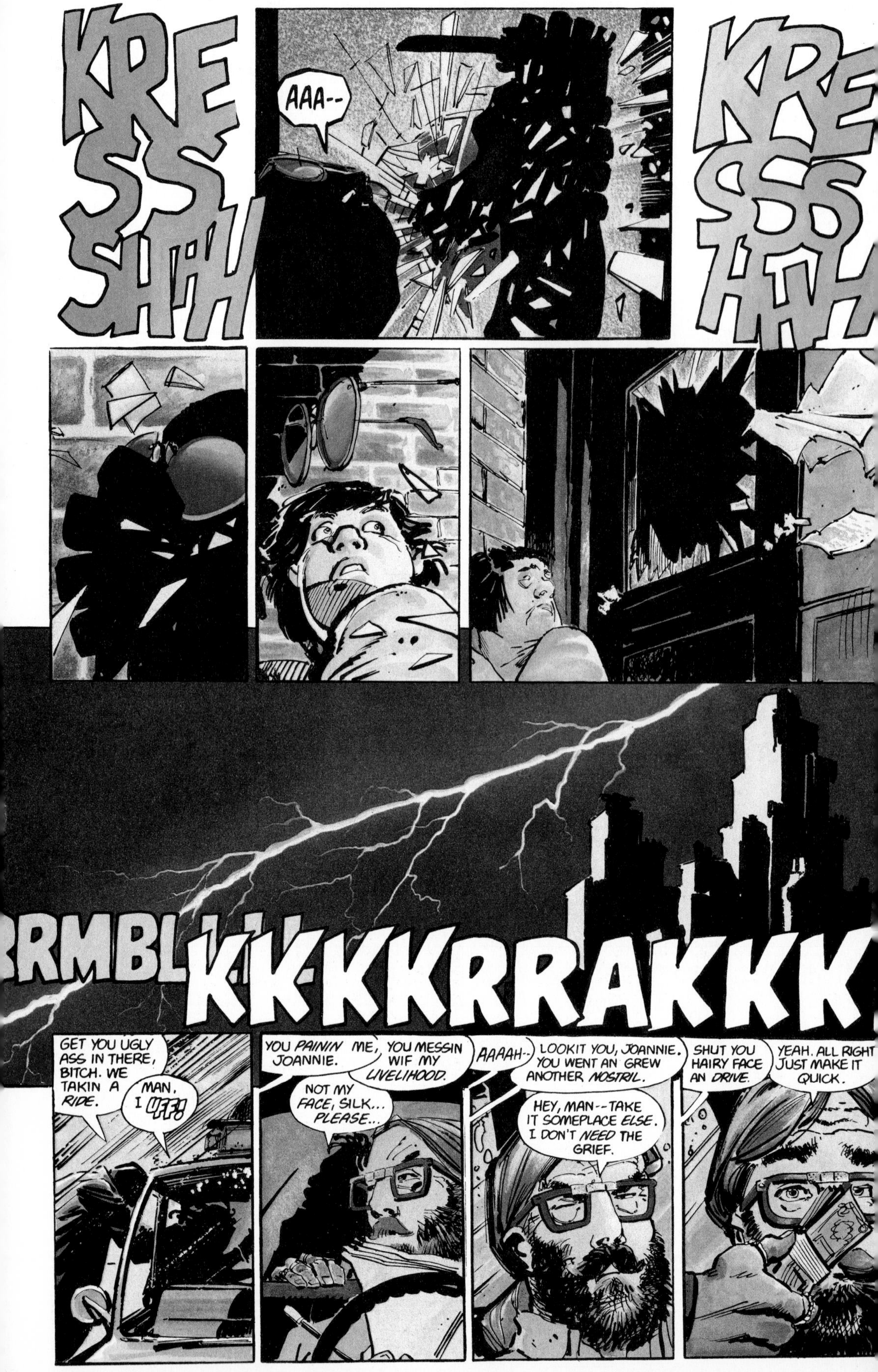
KRESSSHHH
AAA--
KRESSSHHH
RMBL
KKKKRRAKKK
GET YOU UGLY ASS IN THERE, BITCH. WE TAKIN A *RIDE*.
MAN, I *UFF!*
YOU *PAININ* ME, JOANNIE.
YOU MESSIN WIF MY *LIVELIHOOD*.
NOT MY *FACE*, SILK... PLEASE...
AAAAH--
LOOKIT YOU, JOANNIE. YOU WENT AN GREW ANOTHER *NOSTRIL*.
HEY, MAN--TAKE IT SOMEPLACE *ELSE*. I DON'T *NEED* THE GRIEF.
SHUT YOU HAIRY FACE AN *DRIVE*.
YEAH. ALL RIGHT JUST MAKE IT QUICK.

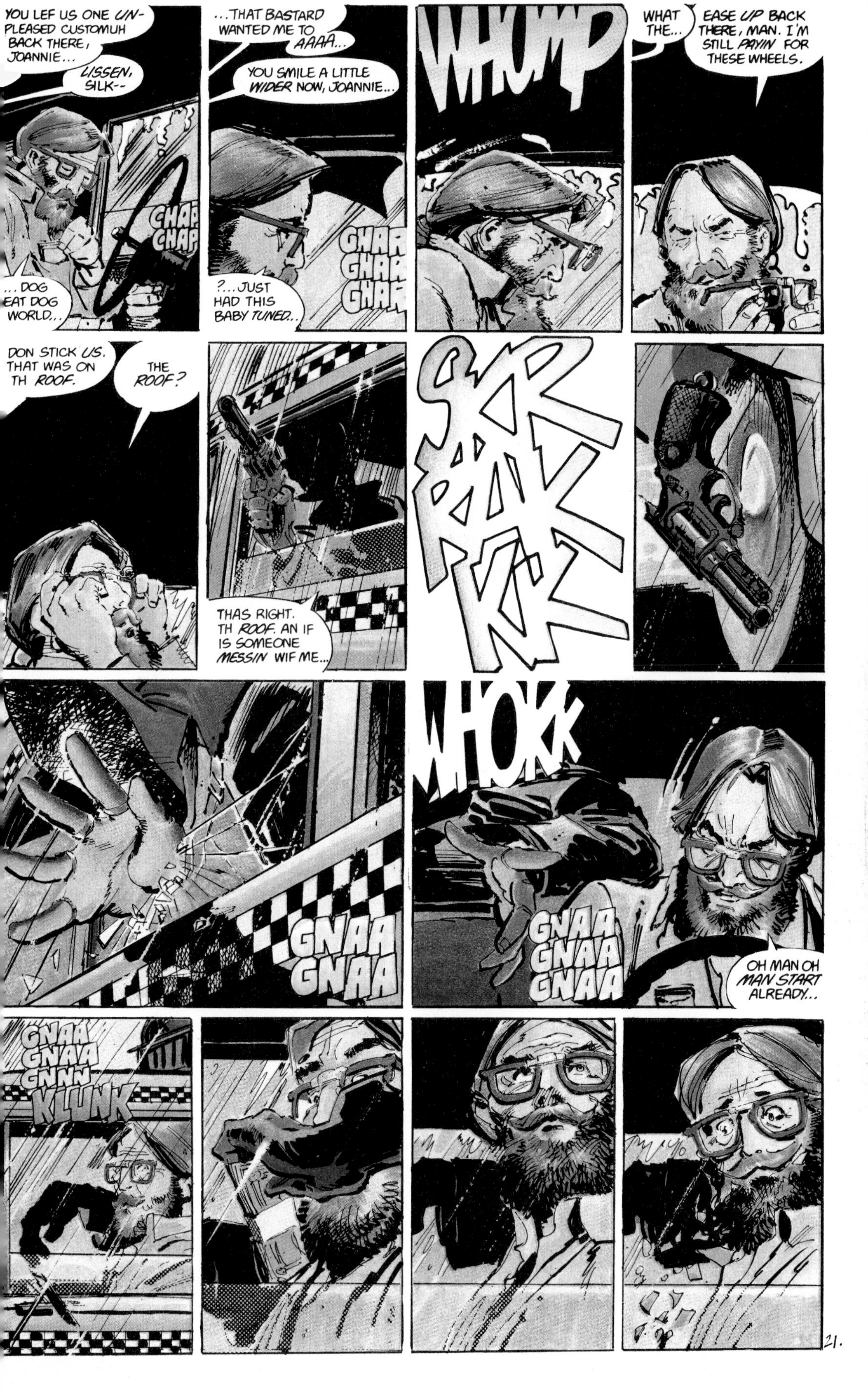
YOU LEF US ONE UN-PLEASED CUSTOMUH BACK THERE, JOANNIE...
LISSEN, SILK--
CHAP CHAP
...DOG EAT DOG WORLD...
...THAT BASTARD WANTED ME TO AAAA...
YOU SMILE A LITTLE WIDER NOW, JOANNIE...
GHAR GHAR GHAR
?...JUST HAD THIS BABY TUNED...
WHUMP
WHAT THE...
EASE UP BACK THERE, MAN. I'M STILL PAYIN FOR THESE WHEELS.
DON STICK US. THAT WAS ON TH ROOF.
THE ROOF?
THAS RIGHT. TH ROOF. AN IF IS SOMEONE MESSIN WIF ME...
SKRAKK
GNAA GNAA
WHOKK
GNAA GNAA GNAA
OH MAN OH MAN START ALREADY...
GNAA GNAA GNNN KLUNK

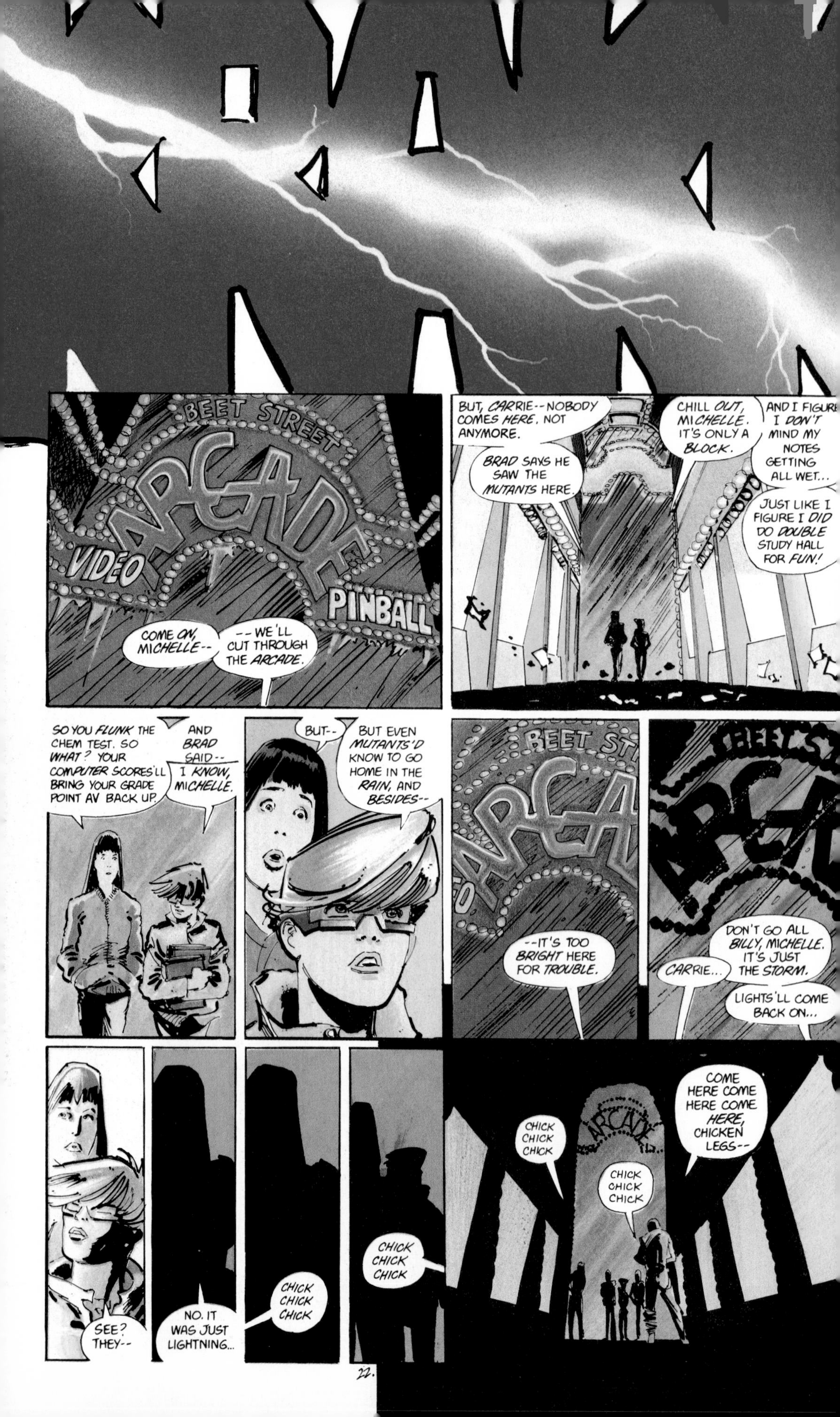

BEET STREET
VIDEO ARCADE
PINBALL
COME ON, MICHELLE--
--WE'LL CUT THROUGH THE ARCADE.
BUT, CARRIE--NOBODY COMES HERE. NOT ANYMORE.
BRAD SAYS HE SAW THE MUTANTS HERE.
CHILL OUT, MICHELLE. IT'S ONLY A BLOCK.
AND I FIGURE I DON'T MIND MY NOTES GETTING ALL WET...
JUST LIKE I FIGURE I DID DO DOUBLE STUDY HALL FOR FUN!
SO YOU FLUNK THE CHEM TEST. SO WHAT? YOUR COMPUTER SCORES'LL BRING YOUR GRADE POINT AV BACK UP.
AND BRAD SAID--
I KNOW, MICHELLE.
BUT--
BUT EVEN MUTANTS'D KNOW TO GO HOME IN THE RAIN, AND BESIDES--
--IT'S TOO BRIGHT HERE FOR TROUBLE.
CARRIE...
DON'T GO ALL BILLY, MICHELLE. IT'S JUST THE STORM.
LIGHTS'LL COME BACK ON...
SEE? THEY--
NO. IT WAS JUST LIGHTNING...
CHICK CHICK CHICK
CHICK CHICK CHICK
CHICK CHICK CHICK
ARCADE
CHICK CHICK CHICK
COME HERE COME HERE COME HERE, CHICKEN LEGS--

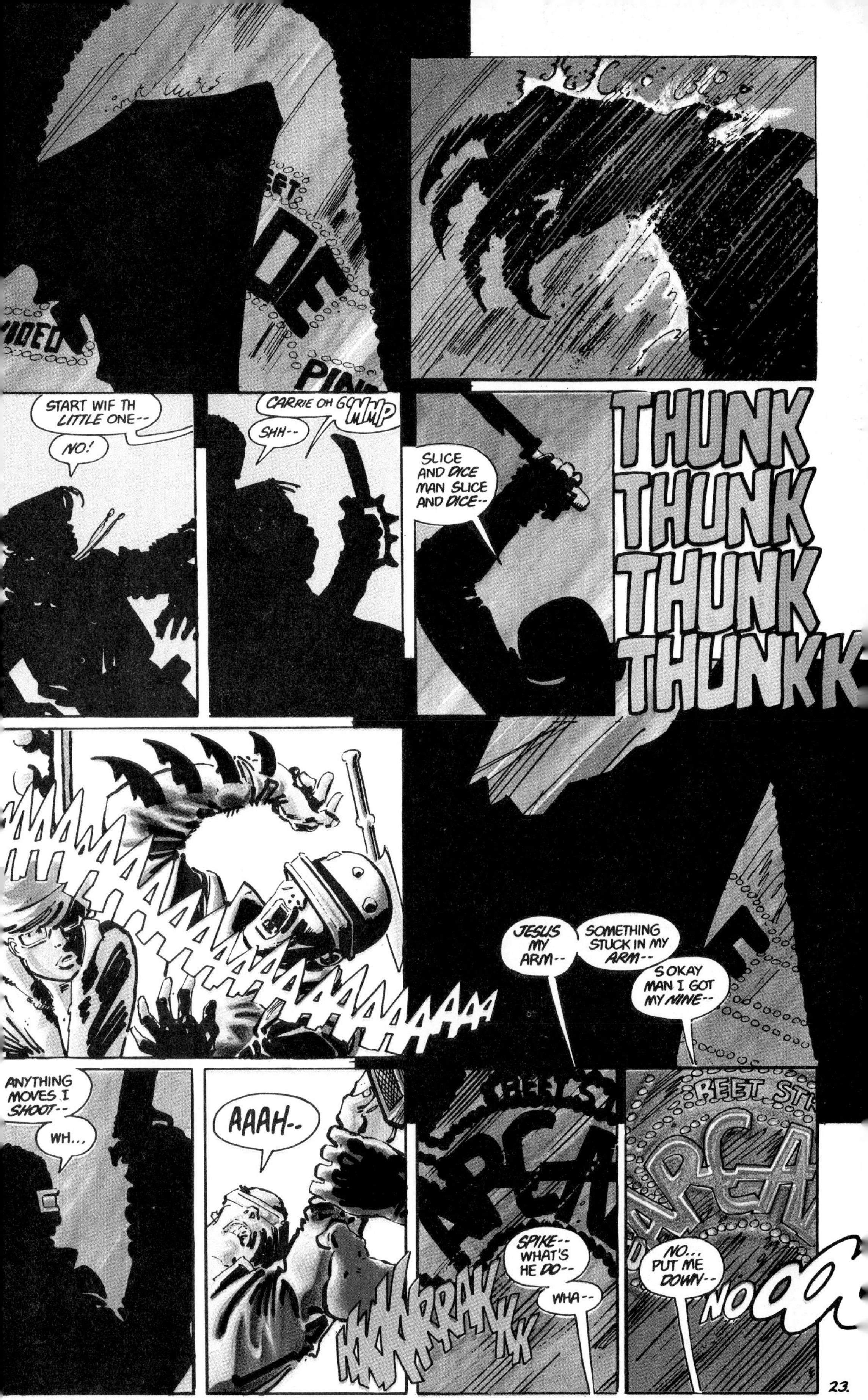
START WIF TH LITTLE ONE--
NO!
CARRIE OH GOMMP
SHH--
SLICE AND DICE MAN SLICE AND DICE--
THUNK
THUNK
THUNK
THUNKK
JESUS MY ARM--
SOMETHING STUCK IN MY ARM--
S OKAY MAN I GOT MY NINE--
ANYTHING MOVES I SHOOT--
WH...
AAAH--
SPIKE-- WHAT'S HE DO--
WHA--
NO... PUT ME DOWN--
NOOO

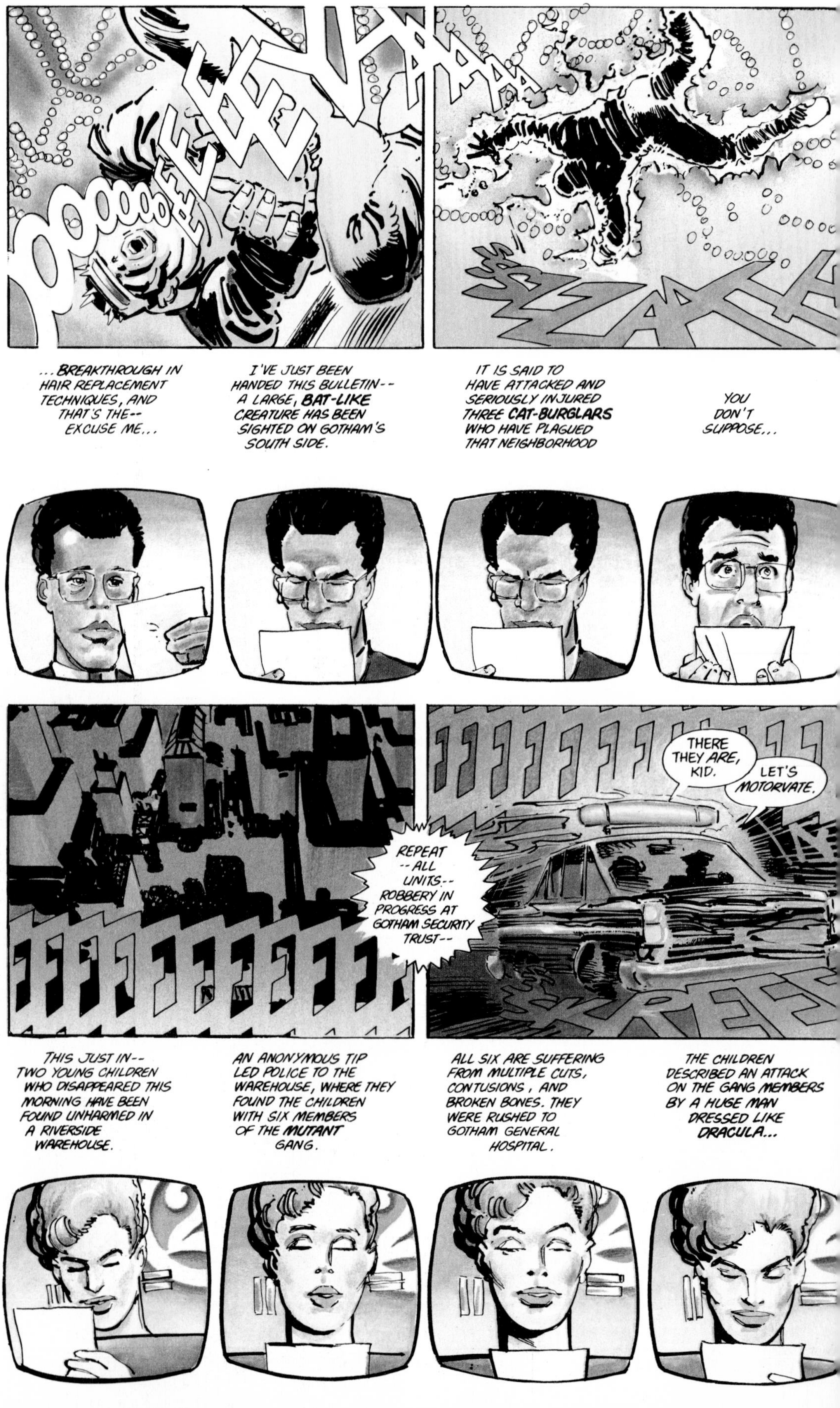
...BREAKTHROUGH IN HAIR REPLACEMENT TECHNIQUES, AND THAT'S THE-- EXCUSE ME...
I'VE JUST BEEN HANDED THIS BULLETIN-- A LARGE, BAT-LIKE CREATURE HAS BEEN SIGHTED ON GOTHAM'S SOUTH SIDE.
IT IS SAID TO HAVE ATTACKED AND SERIOUSLY INJURED THREE CAT-BURGLARS WHO HAVE PLAGUED THAT NEIGHBORHOOD
YOU DON'T SUPPOSE...
REPEAT --ALL UNITS-- ROBBERY IN PROGRESS AT GOTHAM SECURITY TRUST--
THERE THEY ARE, KID.
LET'S MOTORVATE.
THIS JUST IN-- TWO YOUNG CHILDREN WHO DISAPPEARED THIS MORNING HAVE BEEN FOUND UNHARMED IN A RIVERSIDE WAREHOUSE.
AN ANONYMOUS TIP LED POLICE TO THE WAREHOUSE, WHERE THEY FOUND THE CHILDREN WITH SIX MEMBERS OF THE MUTANT GANG.
ALL SIX ARE SUFFERING FROM MULTIPLE CUTS, CONTUSIONS, AND BROKEN BONES. THEY WERE RUSHED TO GOTHAM GENERAL HOSPITAL.
THE CHILDREN DESCRIBED AN ATTACK ON THE GANG MEMBERS BY A HUGE MAN DRESSED LIKE DRACULA...

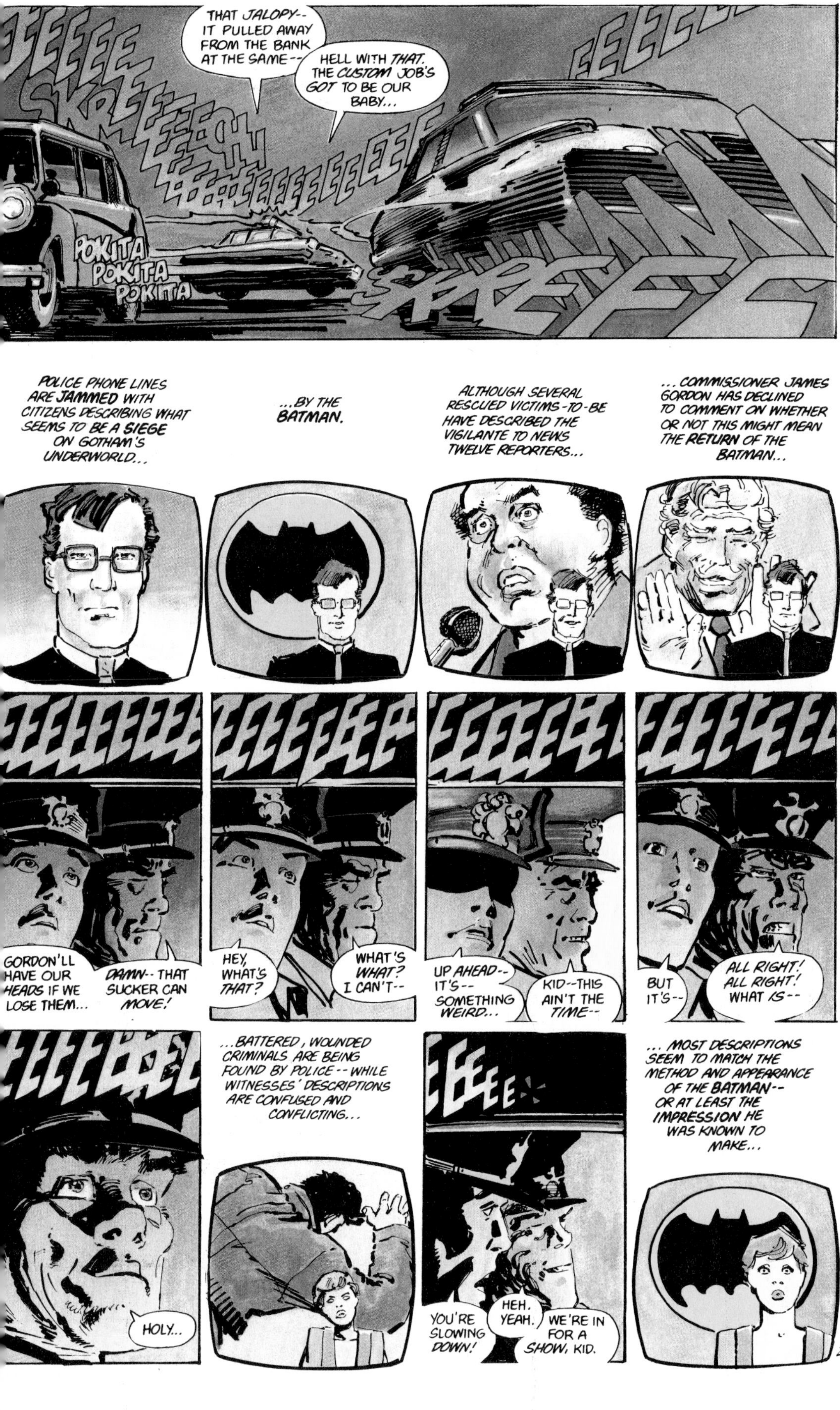
SKREEEEECH
THAT JALOPY-- IT PULLED AWAY FROM THE BANK AT THE SAME--
HELL WITH THAT. THE CUSTOM JOB'S GOT TO BE OUR BABY...
POKITA POKITA POKITA
...POLICE PHONE LINES ARE JAMMED WITH CITIZENS DESCRIBING WHAT SEEMS TO BE A SIEGE ON GOTHAM'S UNDERWORLD...
...BY THE BATMAN.
ALTHOUGH SEVERAL RESCUED VICTIMS-TO-BE HAVE DESCRIBED THE VIGILANTE TO NEWS TWELVE REPORTERS...
...COMMISSIONER JAMES GORDON HAS DECLINED TO COMMENT ON WHETHER OR NOT THIS MIGHT MEAN THE RETURN OF THE BATMAN...
GORDON'LL HAVE OUR HEADS IF WE LOSE THEM...
DAMN-- THAT SUCKER CAN MOVE!
HEY, WHAT'S THAT?
WHAT'S WHAT? I CAN'T--
UP AHEAD-- IT'S-- SOMETHING WEIRD...
KID--THIS AIN'T THE TIME--
BUT IT'S--
ALL RIGHT! ALL RIGHT! WHAT IS--
HOLY...
...BATTERED, WOUNDED CRIMINALS ARE BEING FOUND BY POLICE-- WHILE WITNESSES' DESCRIPTIONS ARE CONFUSED AND CONFLICTING...
YOU'RE SLOWING DOWN!
HEH. YEAH.
WE'RE IN FOR A SHOW, KID.
...MOST DESCRIPTIONS SEEM TO MATCH THE METHOD AND APPEARANCE OF THE BATMAN-- OR AT LEAST THE IMPRESSION HE WAS KNOWN TO MAKE...

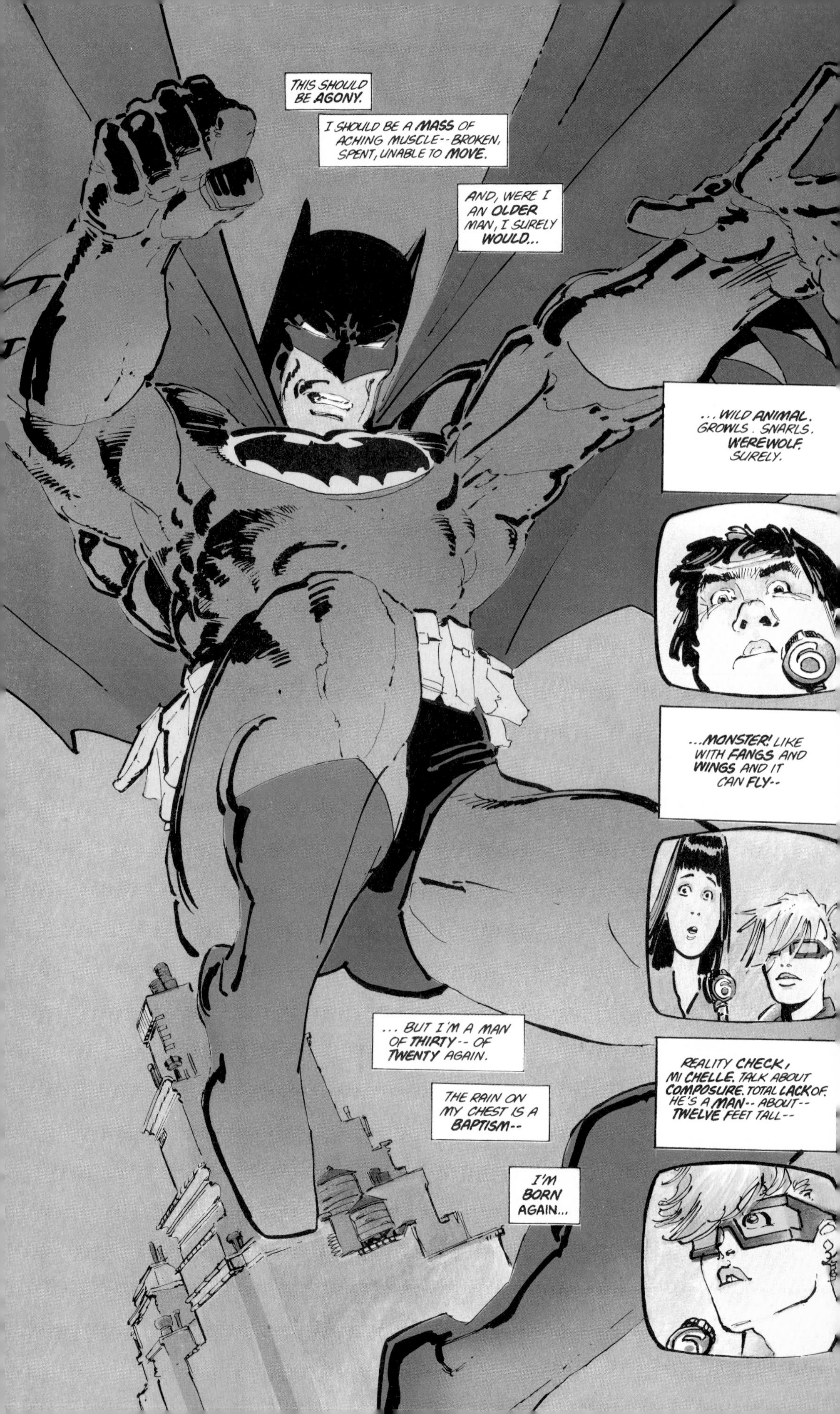
THIS SHOULD BE AGONY.
I SHOULD BE A MASS OF ACHING MUSCLE--BROKEN, SPENT, UNABLE TO MOVE.
AND, WERE I AN OLDER MAN, I SURELY WOULD...
...WILD ANIMAL. GROWLS. SNARLS. WEREWOLF. SURELY.
...MONSTER! LIKE WITH FANGS AND WINGS AND IT CAN FLY--
... BUT I'M A MAN OF THIRTY-- OF TWENTY AGAIN.
REALITY CHECK, MI CHELLE. TALK ABOUT COMPOSURE. TOTAL LACK OF. HE'S A MAN-- ABOUT-- TWELVE FEET TALL--
THE RAIN ON MY CHEST IS A BAPTISM--
I'M BORN AGAIN...

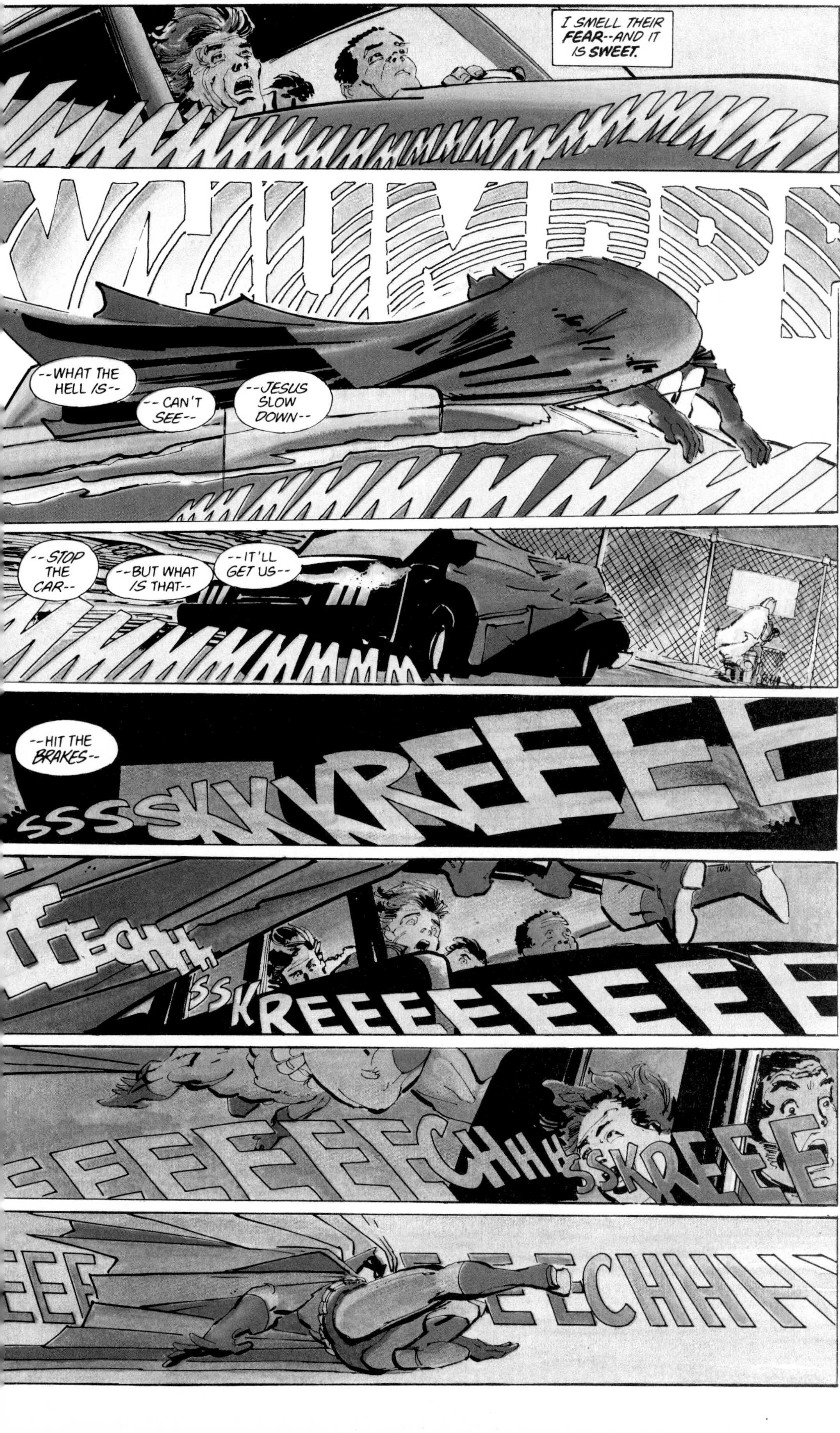
I SMELL THEIR FEAR--AND IT IS SWEET.
MMMMMMMMMMMMMMMMMM
WHUMPP
--WHAT THE HELL IS--
--CAN'T SEE--
--JESUS SLOW DOWN--
MMMMMMMMMMM
--STOP THE CAR--
--BUT WHAT IS THAT--
--IT'LL GET US--
MMMMMMMMMM
--HIT THE BRAKES--
SSSSKKREEEE
EECHHH
SSKREEEEEEEEEE
EEEEEEECHHH
SSKREEE
EEEEEECHHH

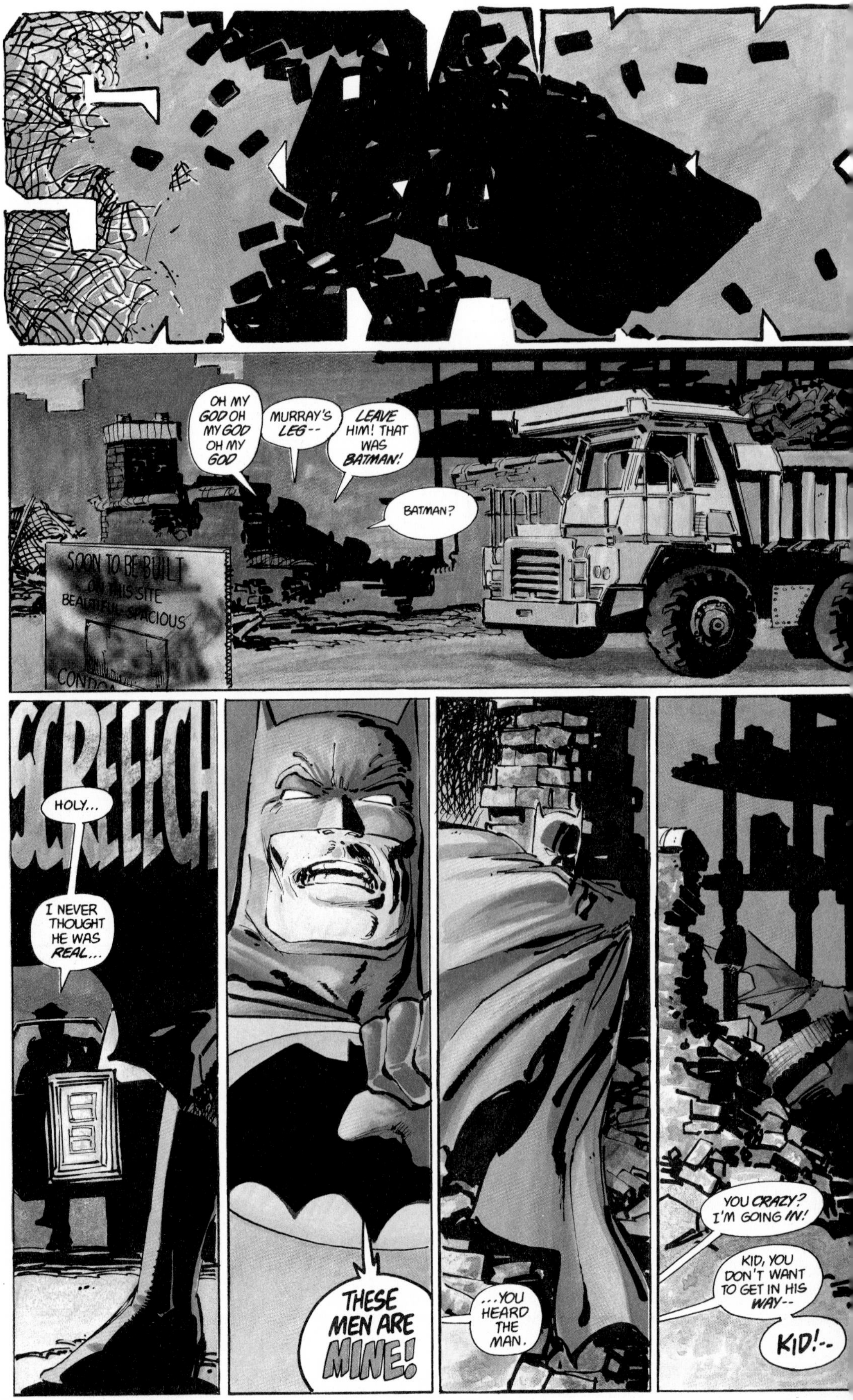
OH MY GOD OH MY GOD OH MY GOD
MURRAY'S LEG--
LEAVE HIM! THAT WAS BATMAN!
BATMAN?
SOON TO BE BUILT ON THIS SITE
SCREEECH
HOLY...
I NEVER THOUGHT HE WAS REAL...
THESE MEN ARE MINE!
...YOU HEARD THE MAN.
YOU CRAZY? I'M GOING IN!
KID, YOU DON'T WANT TO GET IN HIS WAY--
KID!--

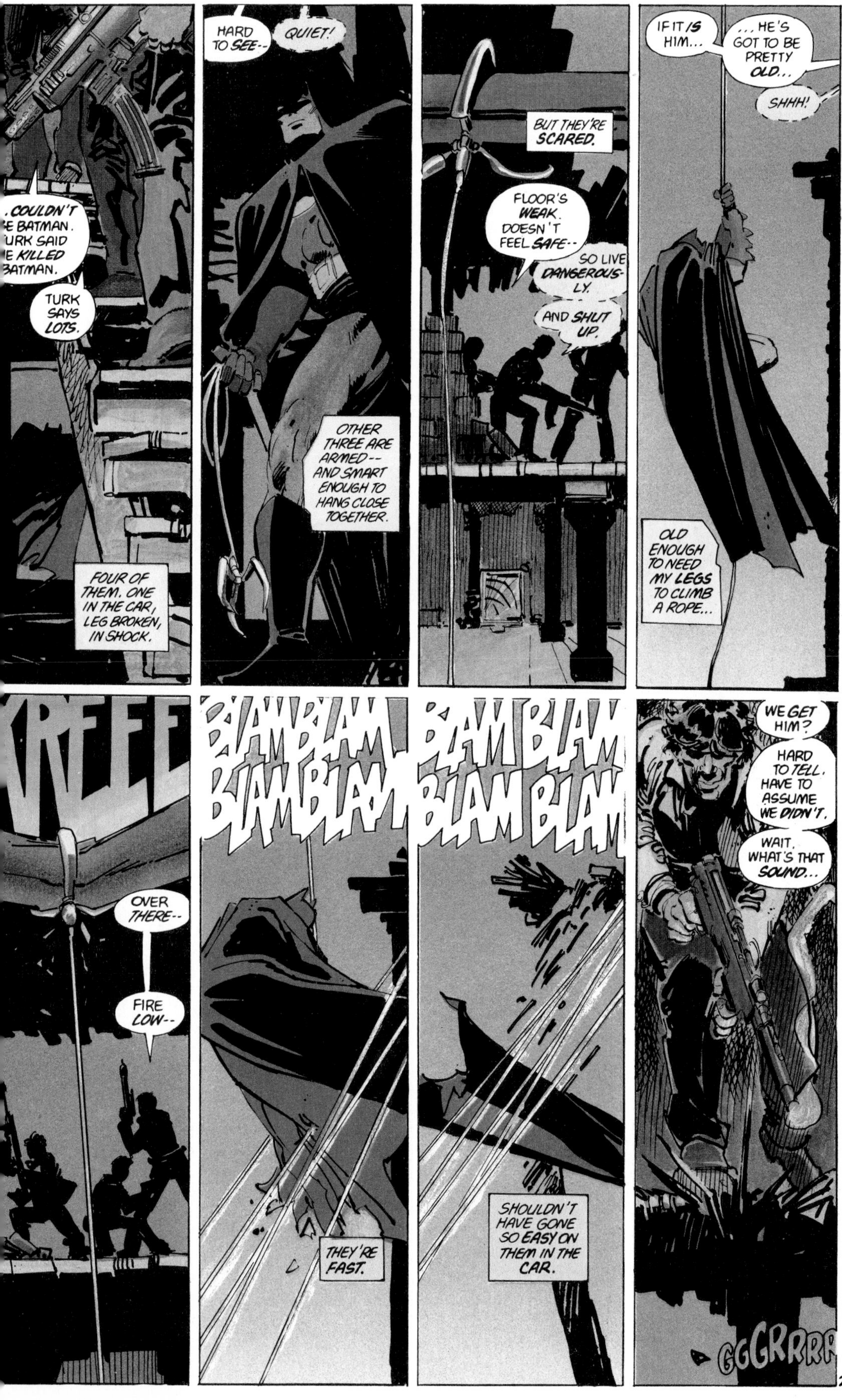

..COULDN'T
BE BATMAN. TURK SAID HE KILLED BATMAN.
TURK SAYS LOTS.
FOUR OF THEM. ONE IN THE CAR, LEG BROKEN, IN SHOCK.
HARD TO SEE--
QUIET!
OTHER THREE ARE ARMED-- AND SMART ENOUGH TO HANG CLOSE TOGETHER.
BUT THEY'RE SCARED.
FLOOR'S WEAK. DOESN'T FEEL SAFE--
SO LIVE DANGEROUSLY.
AND SHUT UP.
IF IT IS HIM...
...HE'S GOT TO BE PRETTY OLD...
SHHH!
OLD ENOUGH TO NEED MY LEGS TO CLIMB A ROPE...
REEE
OVER THERE--
FIRE LOW--
BLAM BLAM BLAM BLAM
THEY'RE FAST.
BLAM BLAM BLAM BLAM
SHOULDN'T HAVE GONE SO EASY ON THEM IN THE CAR.
WE GET HIM?
HARD TO TELL. HAVE TO ASSUME WE DIDN'T.
WAIT. WHAT'S THAT SOUND...
GGGRRRR

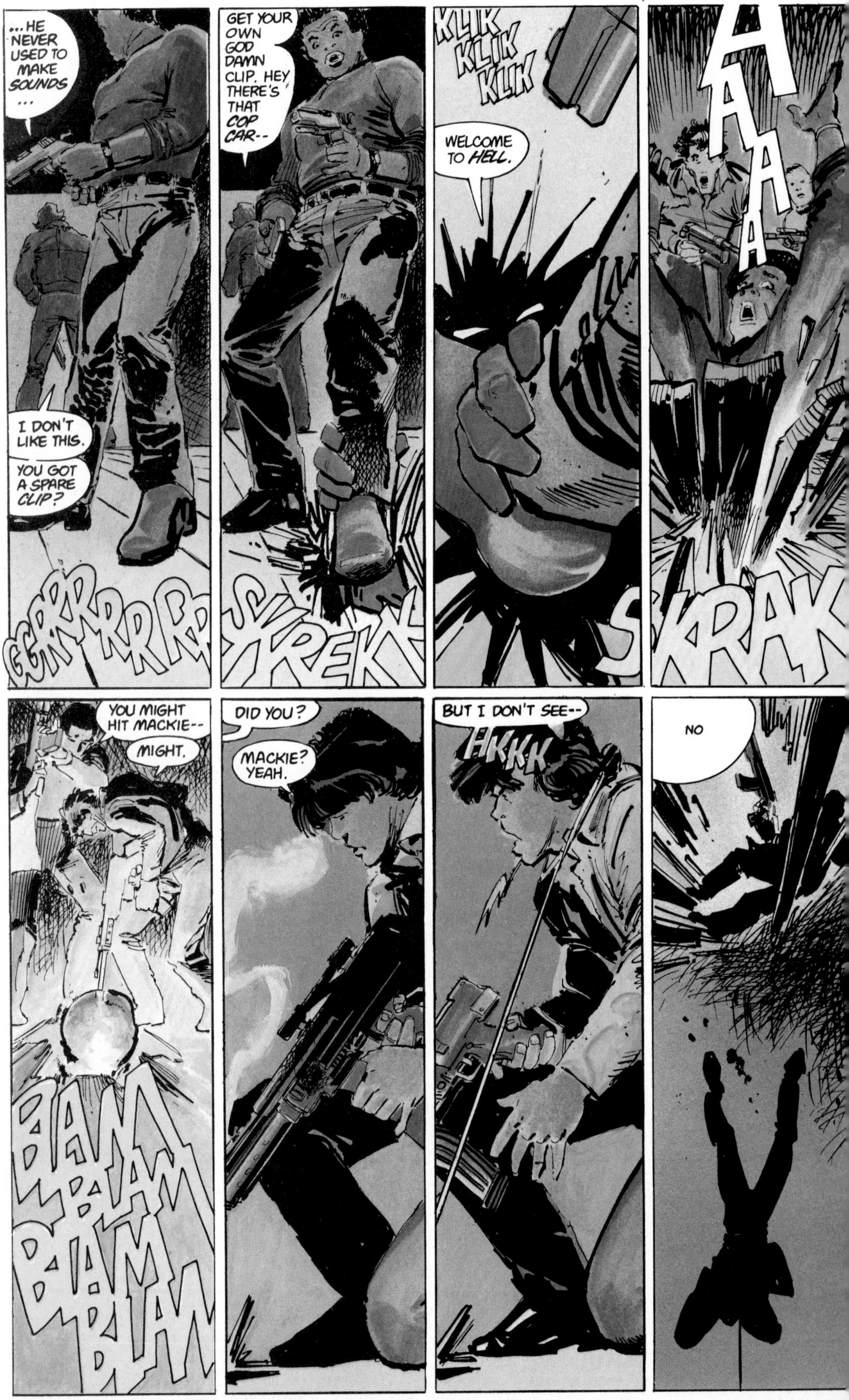
...HE NEVER USED TO MAKE SOUNDS ...
I DON'T LIKE THIS.
YOU GOT A SPARE CLIP?
GRRRRRRRR
GET YOUR OWN GOD DAMN CLIP. HEY THERE'S THAT COP CAR--
SKREKK
KLIK KLIK KLIK
WELCOME TO HELL.
AAAAA
SKRAK
YOU MIGHT HIT MACKIE--
MIGHT.
BLAM BLAM BLAM BLAM
DID YOU?
MACKIE? YEAH.
BUT I DON'T SEE--
HKKK
NO

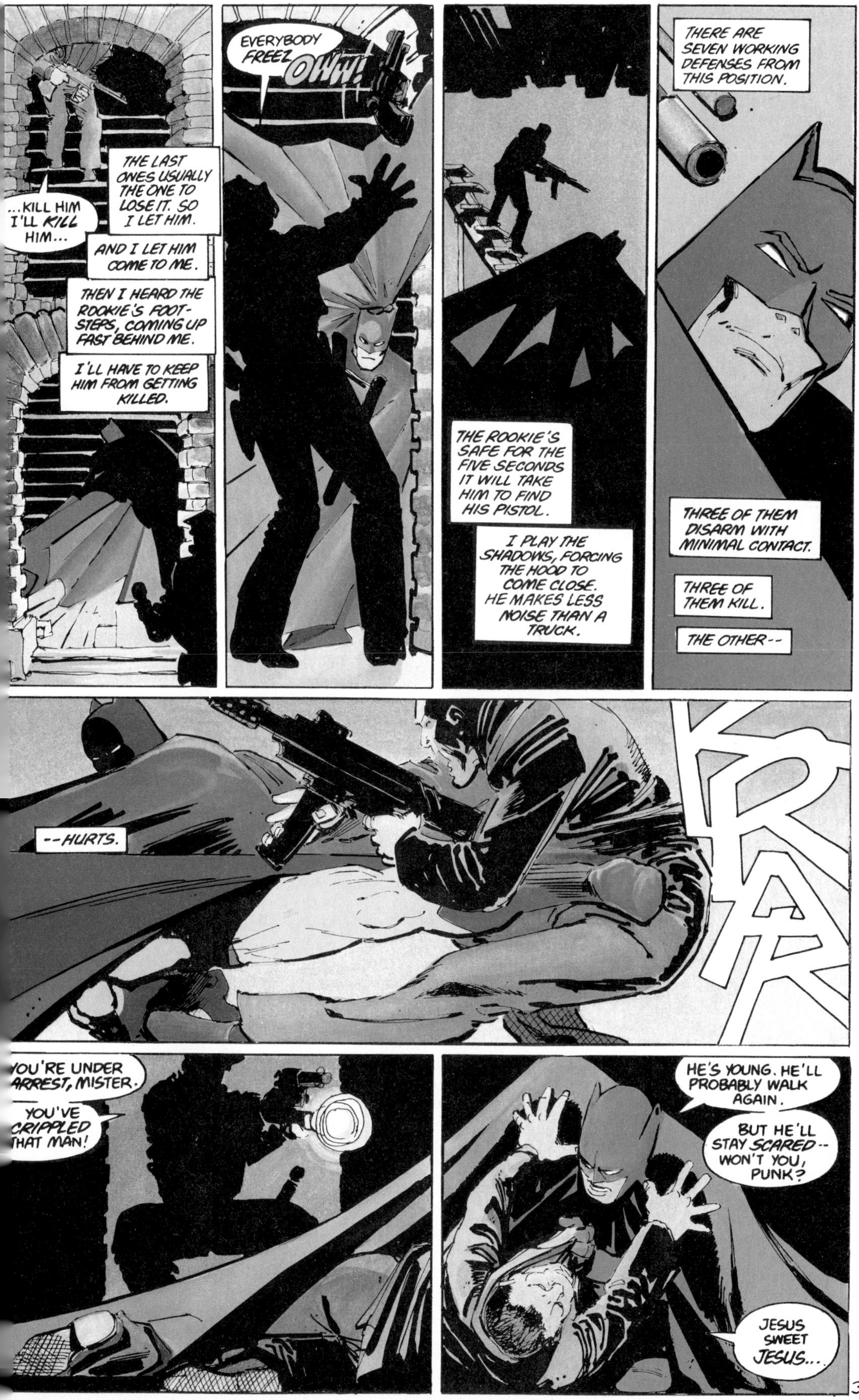
...KILL HIM
I'LL KILL
HIM...
THE LAST
ONES USUALLY
THE ONE TO
LOSE IT. SO
I LET HIM.
AND I LET HIM
COME TO ME.
THEN I HEARD THE
ROOKIE'S FOOT-
STEPS, COMING UP
FAST BEHIND ME.
I'LL HAVE TO KEEP
HIM FROM GETTING
KILLED.
EVERYBODY
FREEZ
OWW!
THE ROOKIE'S
SAFE FOR THE
FIVE SECONDS
IT WILL TAKE
HIM TO FIND
HIS PISTOL.
I PLAY THE
SHADOWS, FORCING
THE HOOD TO
COME CLOSE.
HE MAKES LESS
NOISE THAN A
TRUCK.
THERE ARE
SEVEN WORKING
DEFENSES FROM
THIS POSITION.
THREE OF THEM
DISARM WITH
MINIMAL CONTACT.
THREE OF
THEM KILL.
THE OTHER--
--HURTS.
KRAK
YOU'RE UNDER
ARREST, MISTER.
YOU'VE
CRIPPLED
THAT MAN!
HE'S YOUNG. HE'LL
PROBABLY WALK
AGAIN.
BUT HE'LL
STAY SCARED--
WON'T YOU,
PUNK?
JESUS
SWEET
JESUS...

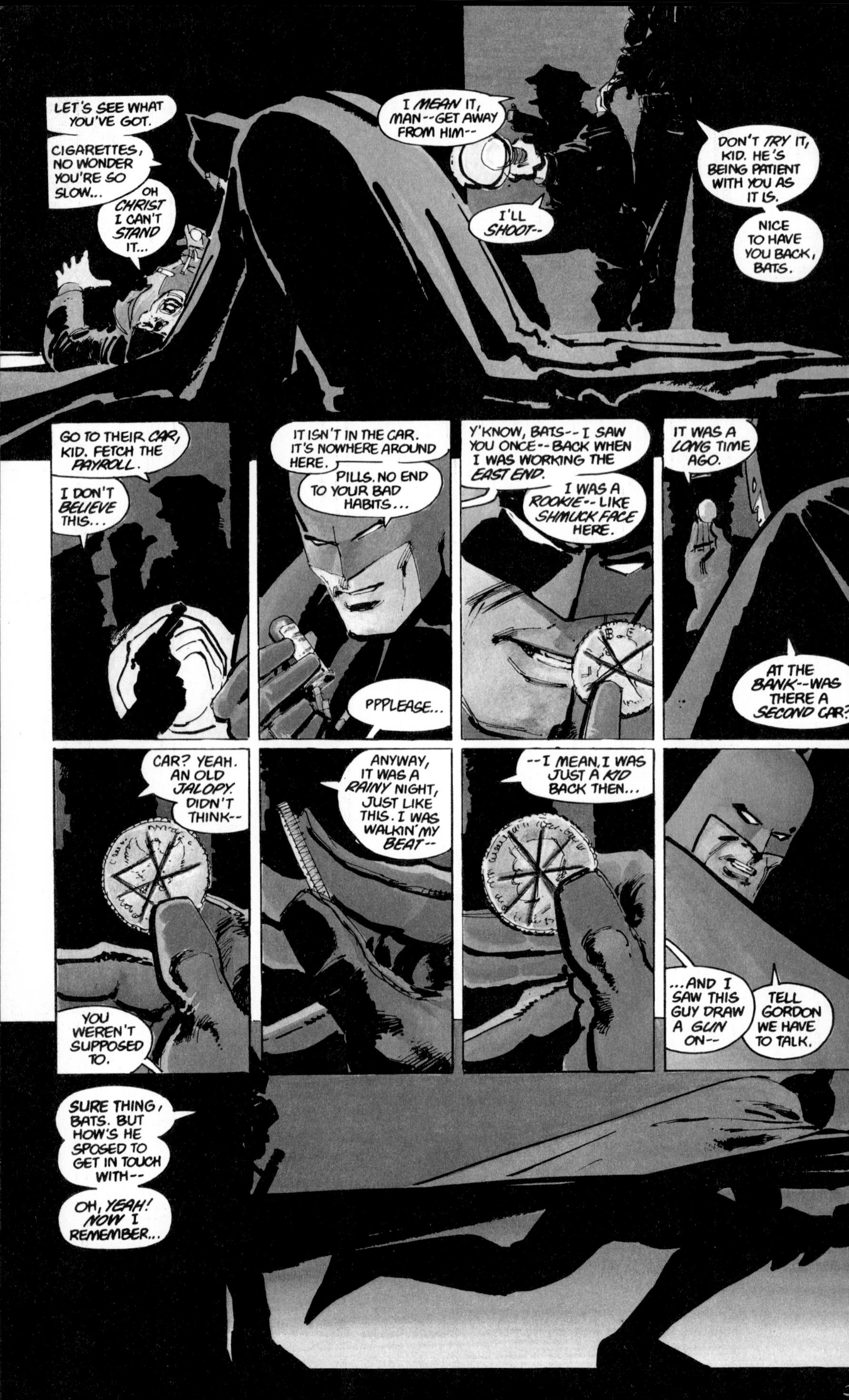
LET'S SEE WHAT YOU'VE GOT.
CIGARETTES, NO WONDER YOU'RE SO SLOW...
OH CHRIST I CAN'T STAND IT...
I MEAN IT, MAN--GET AWAY FROM HIM--
I'LL SHOOT--
DON'T TRY IT, KID. HE'S BEING PATIENT WITH YOU AS IT IS.
NICE TO HAVE YOU BACK, BATS.
GO TO THEIR CAR, KID. FETCH THE PAYROLL.
I DON'T BELIEVE THIS...
IT ISN'T IN THE CAR. IT'S NOWHERE AROUND HERE.
PILLS. NO END TO YOUR BAD HABITS...
PPPLEASE...
Y'KNOW, BATS--I SAW YOU ONCE--BACK WHEN I WAS WORKING THE EAST END.
I WAS A ROOKIE--LIKE SHMUCK FACE HERE.
IT WAS A LONG TIME AGO.
AT THE BANK--WAS THERE A SECOND CAR?
CAR? YEAH. AN OLD JALOPY. DIDN'T THINK--
YOU WEREN'T SUPPOSED TO.
ANYWAY, IT WAS A RAINY NIGHT, JUST LIKE THIS. I WAS WALKIN' MY BEAT--
--I MEAN, I WAS JUST A KID BACK THEN...
...AND I SAW THIS GUY DRAW A GUN ON--
TELL GORDON WE HAVE TO TALK.
SURE THING, BATS. BUT HOW'S HE SPOSED TO GET IN TOUCH WITH--
OH, YEAH! NOW I REMEMBER...

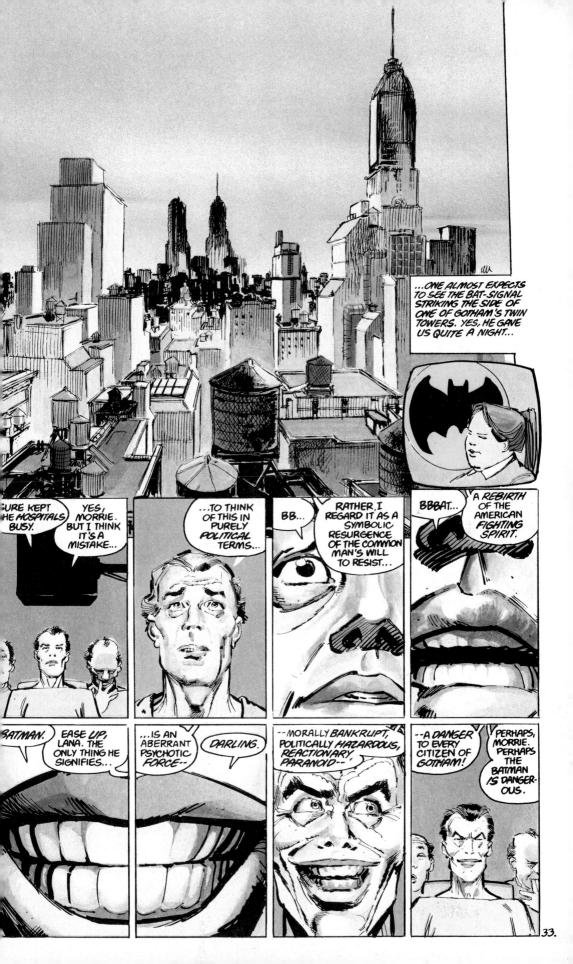

...ONE ALMOST EXPECTS TO SEE THE BAT-SIGNAL STRIKING THE SIDE OF ONE OF GOTHAM'S TWIN TOWERS. YES, HE GAVE US QUITE A NIGHT...

[URE KEPT] [HE] *HOSPITALS* BUSY.

YES, MORRIE. BUT I THINK IT'S A MISTAKE...

...TO THINK OF THIS IN PURELY *POLITICAL* TERMS...

BB...

RATHER, I REGARD IT AS A SYMBOLIC RESURGENCE OF THE COMMON MAN'S WILL TO RESIST...

BBBAT...

A *REBIRTH* OF THE AMERICAN *FIGHTING* SPIRIT.

[B]ATMAN. EASE *UP*, LANA. THE ONLY THING HE SIGNIFIES...

...IS AN ABERRANT PSYCHOTIC *FORCE*--

DARLING.

--MORALLY *BANKRUPT,* POLITICALLY *HAZARDOUS,* *REACTIONARY* PARANOID--

--A *DANGER* TO EVERY CITIZEN OF *GOTHAM!*

PERHAPS, MORRIE. PERHAPS THE *BATMAN IS* DANGEROUS.

33.

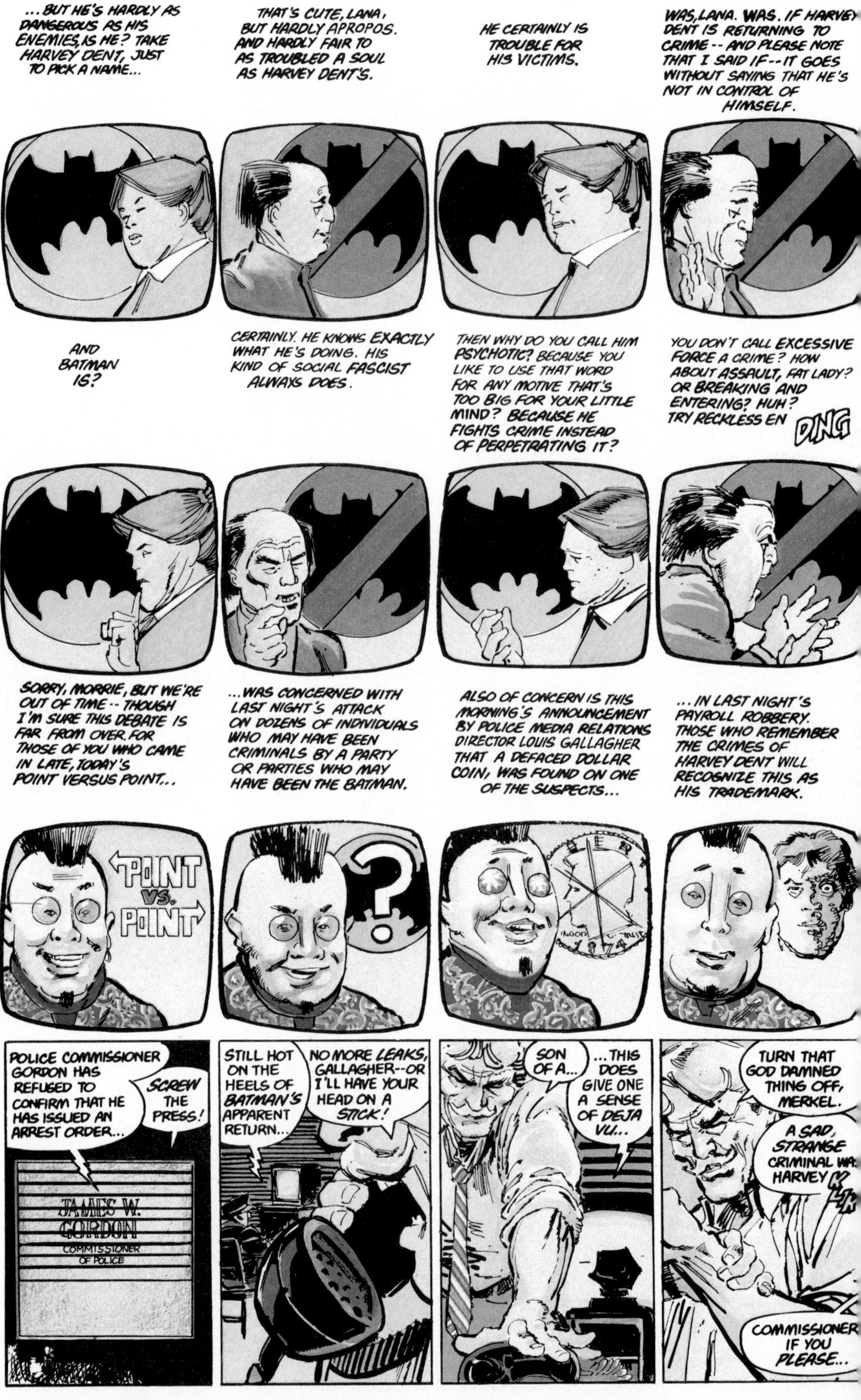

...BUT HE'S HARDLY AS DANGEROUS AS HIS ENEMIES, IS HE? TAKE HARVEY DENT, JUST TO PICK A NAME...
THAT'S CUTE, LANA, BUT HARDLY APROPOS. AND HARDLY FAIR TO AS TROUBLED A SOUL AS HARVEY DENT'S.
HE CERTAINLY IS TROUBLE FOR HIS VICTIMS.
WAS, LANA. WAS. IF HARVEY DENT IS RETURNING TO CRIME -- AND PLEASE NOTE THAT I SAID IF -- IT GOES WITHOUT SAYING THAT HE'S NOT IN CONTROL OF HIMSELF.
AND BATMAN IS?
CERTAINLY. HE KNOWS EXACTLY WHAT HE'S DOING. HIS KIND OF SOCIAL FASCIST ALWAYS DOES.
THEN WHY DO YOU CALL HIM PSYCHOTIC? BECAUSE YOU LIKE TO USE THAT WORD FOR ANY MOTIVE THAT'S TOO BIG FOR YOUR LITTLE MIND? BECAUSE HE FIGHTS CRIME INSTEAD OF PERPETRATING IT?
YOU DON'T CALL EXCESSIVE FORCE A CRIME? HOW ABOUT ASSAULT, FAT LADY? OR BREAKING AND ENTERING? HUH? TRY RECKLESS EN
DING
SORRY, MORRIE, BUT WE'RE OUT OF TIME -- THOUGH I'M SURE THIS DEBATE IS FAR FROM OVER. FOR THOSE OF YOU WHO CAME IN LATE, TODAY'S POINT VERSUS POINT...
POINT vs. POINT
...WAS CONCERNED WITH LAST NIGHT'S ATTACK ON DOZENS OF INDIVIDUALS WHO MAY HAVE BEEN CRIMINALS BY A PARTY OR PARTIES WHO MAY HAVE BEEN THE BATMAN.
ALSO OF CONCERN IS THIS MORNING'S ANNOUNCEMENT BY POLICE MEDIA RELATIONS DIRECTOR LOUIS GALLAGHER THAT A DEFACED DOLLAR COIN, WAS FOUND ON ONE OF THE SUSPECTS...
...IN LAST NIGHT'S PAYROLL ROBBERY. THOSE WHO REMEMBER THE CRIMES OF HARVEY DENT WILL RECOGNIZE THIS AS HIS TRADEMARK.
POLICE COMMISSIONER GORDON HAS REFUSED TO CONFIRM THAT HE HAS ISSUED AN ARREST ORDER...
SCREW THE PRESS!
JAMES W. GORDON
COMMISSIONER OF POLICE
STILL HOT ON THE HEELS OF BATMAN'S APPARENT RETURN...
NO MORE LEAKS, GALLAGHER--OR I'LL HAVE YOUR HEAD ON A STICK!
SON OF A...
...THIS DOES GIVE ONE A SENSE OF DEJA VU...
TURN THAT GOD DAMNED THING OFF, MERKEL.
A SAD, STRANGE CRIMINAL WA HARVEY
COMMISSIONER IF YOU PLEASE...

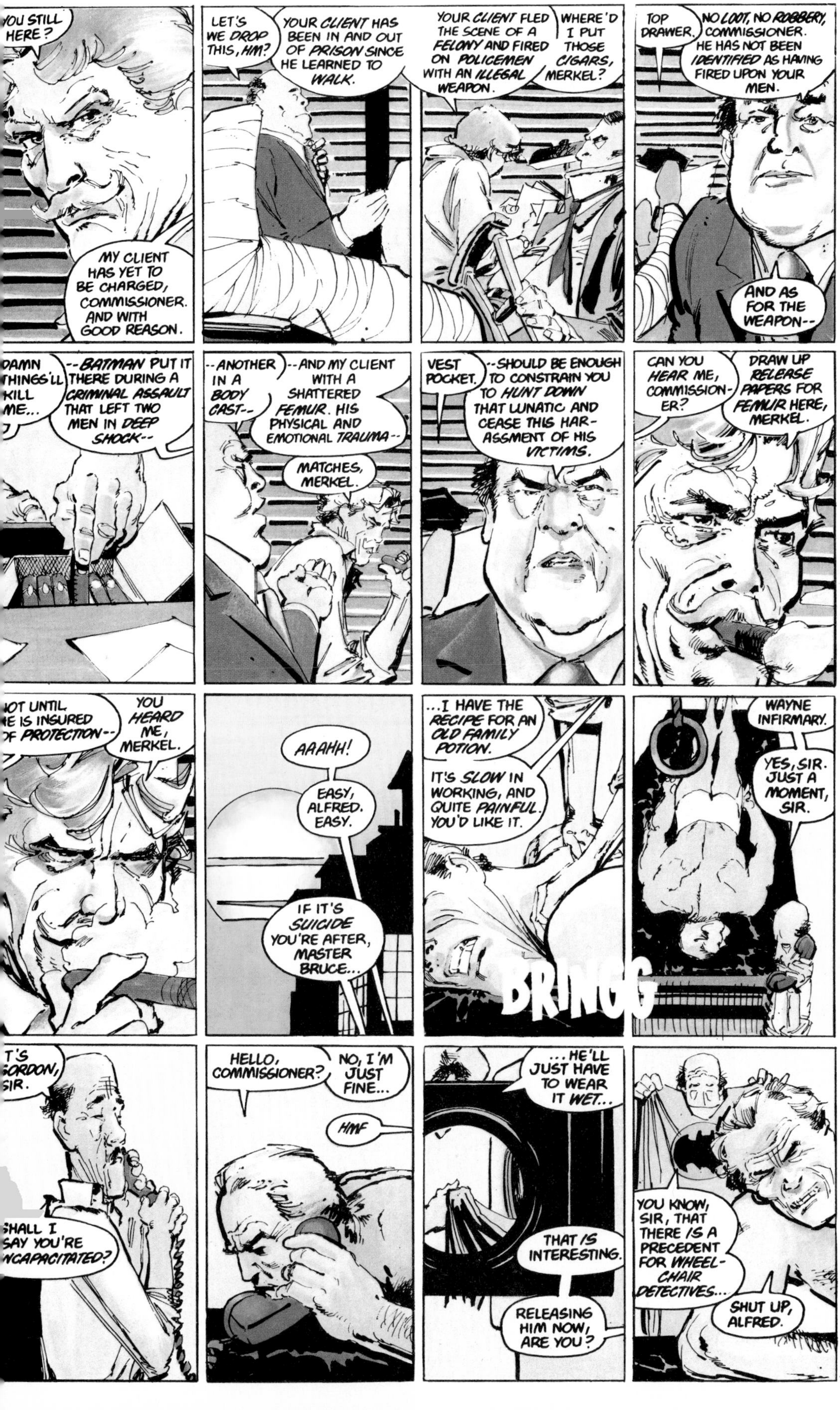
YOU STILL HERE?
MY CLIENT HAS YET TO BE CHARGED, COMMISSIONER. AND WITH GOOD REASON.
LET'S WE DROP THIS, HM?
YOUR CLIENT HAS BEEN IN AND OUT OF PRISON SINCE HE LEARNED TO WALK.
YOUR CLIENT FLED THE SCENE OF A FELONY AND FIRED ON POLICEMEN WITH AN ILLEGAL WEAPON.
WHERE'D I PUT THOSE CIGARS, MERKEL?
TOP DRAWER.
NO LOOT, NO ROBBERY, COMMISSIONER. HE HAS NOT BEEN IDENTIFIED AS HAVING FIRED UPON YOUR MEN.
AND AS FOR THE WEAPON--
DAMN THINGS'LL KILL ME...
--BATMAN PUT IT THERE DURING A CRIMINAL ASSAULT THAT LEFT TWO MEN IN DEEP SHOCK--
--ANOTHER IN A BODY CAST--
--AND MY CLIENT WITH A SHATTERED FEMUR. HIS PHYSICAL AND EMOTIONAL TRAUMA--
MATCHES, MERKEL.
VEST POCKET.
--SHOULD BE ENOUGH TO CONSTRAIN YOU TO HUNT DOWN THAT LUNATIC AND CEASE THIS HARASSMENT OF HIS VICTIMS.
CAN YOU HEAR ME, COMMISSIONER?
DRAW UP RELEASE PAPERS FOR FEMUR HERE, MERKEL.
NOT UNTIL HE IS INSURED OF PROTECTION--
YOU HEARD ME, MERKEL.
AAAHH!
EASY, ALFRED. EASY.
IF IT'S SUICIDE YOU'RE AFTER, MASTER BRUCE...
...I HAVE THE RECIPE FOR AN OLD FAMILY POTION.
IT'S SLOW IN WORKING, AND QUITE PAINFUL. YOU'D LIKE IT.
BRINGG
WAYNE INFIRMARY.
YES, SIR. JUST A MOMENT, SIR.
IT'S GORDON, SIR.
SHALL I SAY YOU'RE INCAPACITATED?
HELLO, COMMISSIONER?
NO, I'M JUST FINE...
HMF
...HE'LL JUST HAVE TO WEAR IT WET...
THAT IS INTERESTING.
RELEASING HIM NOW, ARE YOU?
YOU KNOW, SIR, THAT THERE IS A PRECEDENT FOR WHEELCHAIR DETECTIVES...
SHUT UP, ALFRED.

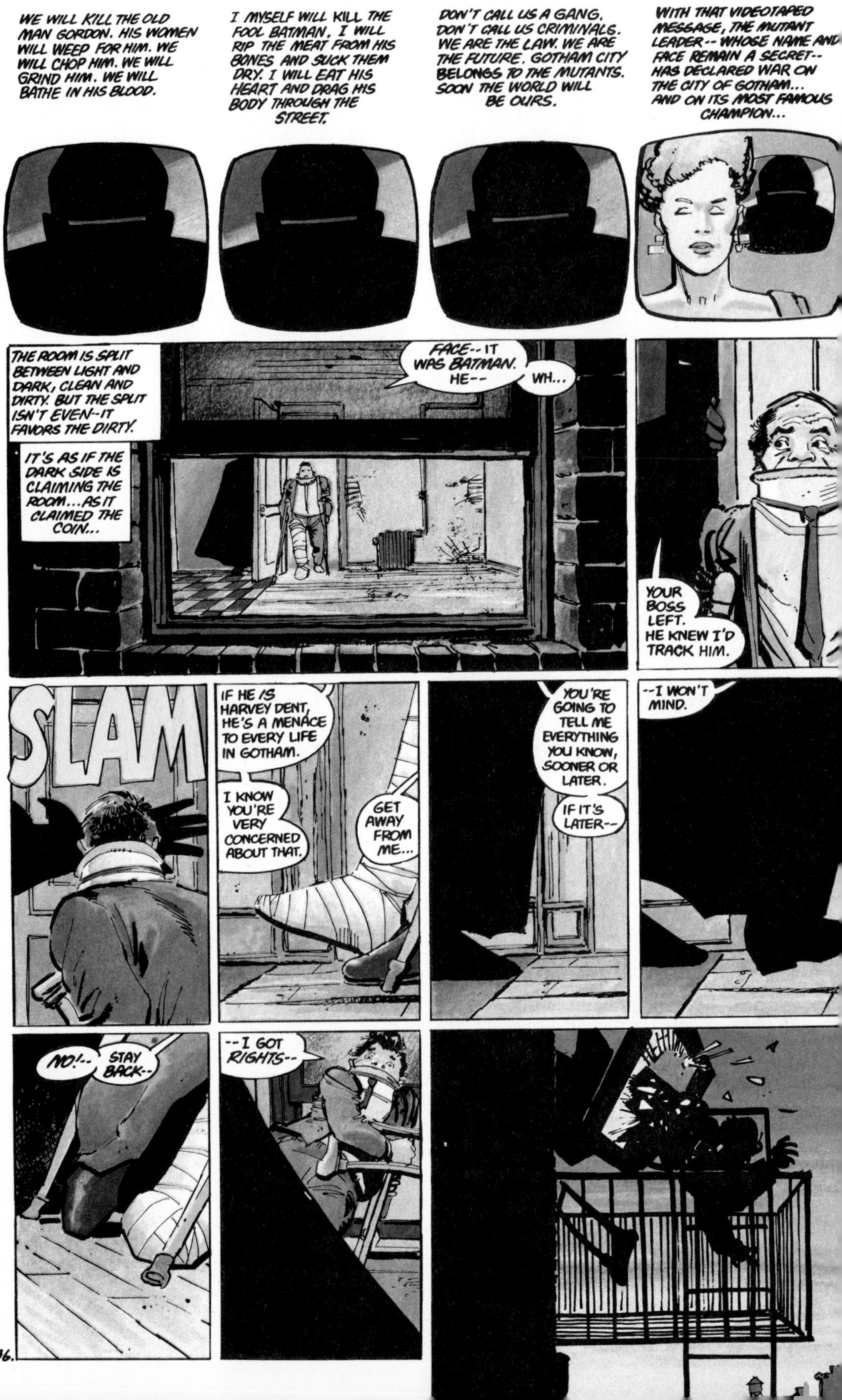
WE WILL KILL THE OLD MAN GORDON. HIS WOMEN WILL WEEP FOR HIM. WE WILL CHOP HIM. WE WILL GRIND HIM. WE WILL BATHE IN HIS BLOOD.
I MYSELF WILL KILL THE FOOL BATMAN. I WILL RIP THE MEAT FROM HIS BONES AND SUCK THEM DRY. I WILL EAT HIS HEART AND DRAG HIS BODY THROUGH THE STREET.
DON'T CALL US A GANG. DON'T CALL US CRIMINALS. WE ARE THE LAW. WE ARE THE FUTURE. GOTHAM CITY BELONGS TO THE MUTANTS. SOON THE WORLD WILL BE OURS.
WITH THAT VIDEOTAPED MESSAGE, THE MUTANT LEADER-- WHOSE NAME AND FACE REMAIN A SECRET-- HAS DECLARED WAR ON THE CITY OF GOTHAM... AND ON ITS MOST FAMOUS CHAMPION...
THE ROOM IS SPLIT BETWEEN LIGHT AND DARK, CLEAN AND DIRTY. BUT THE SPLIT ISN'T EVEN--IT FAVORS THE DIRTY.
IT'S AS IF THE DARK SIDE IS CLAIMING THE ROOM...AS IT CLAIMED THE COIN...
FACE-- IT WAS BATMAN. HE--
WH...
YOUR BOSS LEFT. HE KNEW I'D TRACK HIM.
SLAM
IF HE IS HARVEY DENT, HE'S A MENACE TO EVERY LIFE IN GOTHAM.
I KNOW YOU'RE VERY CONCERNED ABOUT THAT.
GET AWAY FROM ME...
YOU'RE GOING TO TELL ME EVERYTHING YOU KNOW, SOONER OR LATER.
IF IT'S LATER--
--I WON'T MIND.
NO!--
STAY BACK--
--I GOT RIGHTS--

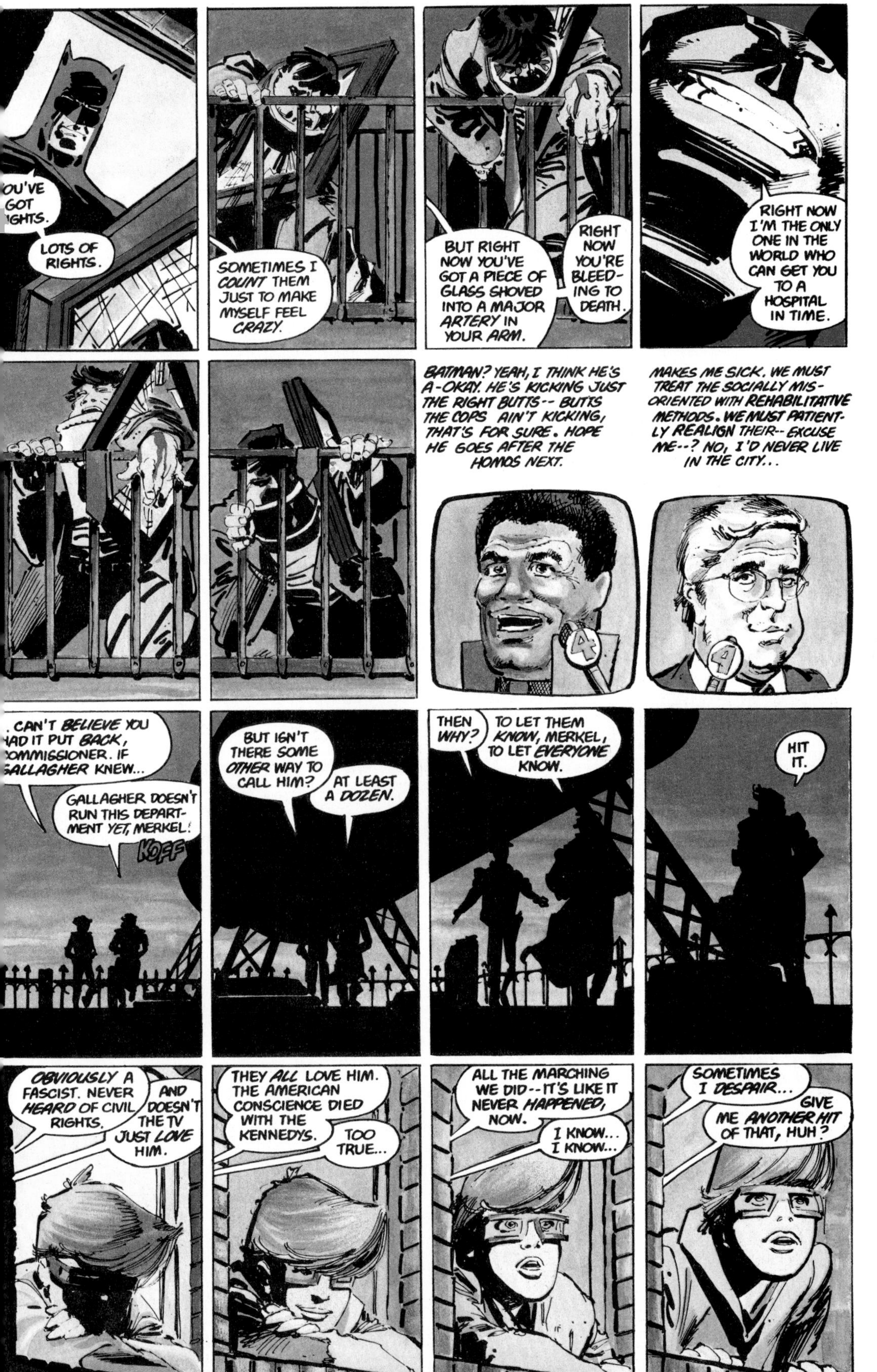
OU'VE GOT IGHTS.
LOTS OF RIGHTS.
SOMETIMES I COUNT THEM JUST TO MAKE MYSELF FEEL CRAZY.
BUT RIGHT NOW YOU'VE GOT A PIECE OF GLASS SHOVED INTO A MAJOR ARTERY IN YOUR ARM.
RIGHT NOW YOU'RE BLEEDING TO DEATH.
RIGHT NOW I'M THE ONLY ONE IN THE WORLD WHO CAN GET YOU TO A HOSPITAL IN TIME.
BATMAN? YEAH, I THINK HE'S A-OKAY. HE'S KICKING JUST THE RIGHT BUTTS -- BUTTS THE COPS AIN'T KICKING, THAT'S FOR SURE. HOPE HE GOES AFTER THE HOMOS NEXT.
MAKES ME SICK. WE MUST TREAT THE SOCIALLY MIS-ORIENTED WITH REHABILITATIVE METHODS. WE MUST PATIENTLY REALIGN THEIR-- EXCUSE ME--? NO, I'D NEVER LIVE IN THE CITY...
4
4
. CAN'T BELIEVE YOU HAD IT PUT BACK, COMMISSIONER.. IF GALLAGHER KNEW...
GALLAGHER DOESN'T RUN THIS DEPARTMENT YET, MERKEL!
KOFF
BUT ISN'T THERE SOME OTHER WAY TO CALL HIM?
AT LEAST A DOZEN.
THEN WHY?
TO LET THEM KNOW, MERKEL, TO LET EVERYONE KNOW.
HIT IT.
OBVIOUSLY A FASCIST. NEVER HEARD OF CIVIL RIGHTS.
AND DOESN'T THE TV JUST LOVE HIM.
THEY ALL LOVE HIM. THE AMERICAN CONSCIENCE DIED WITH THE KENNEDYS.
TOO TRUE...
ALL THE MARCHING WE DID--IT'S LIKE IT NEVER HAPPENED, NOW.
I KNOW... I KNOW...
SOMETIMES I DESPAIR...
GIVE ME ANOTHER HIT OF THAT, HUH?

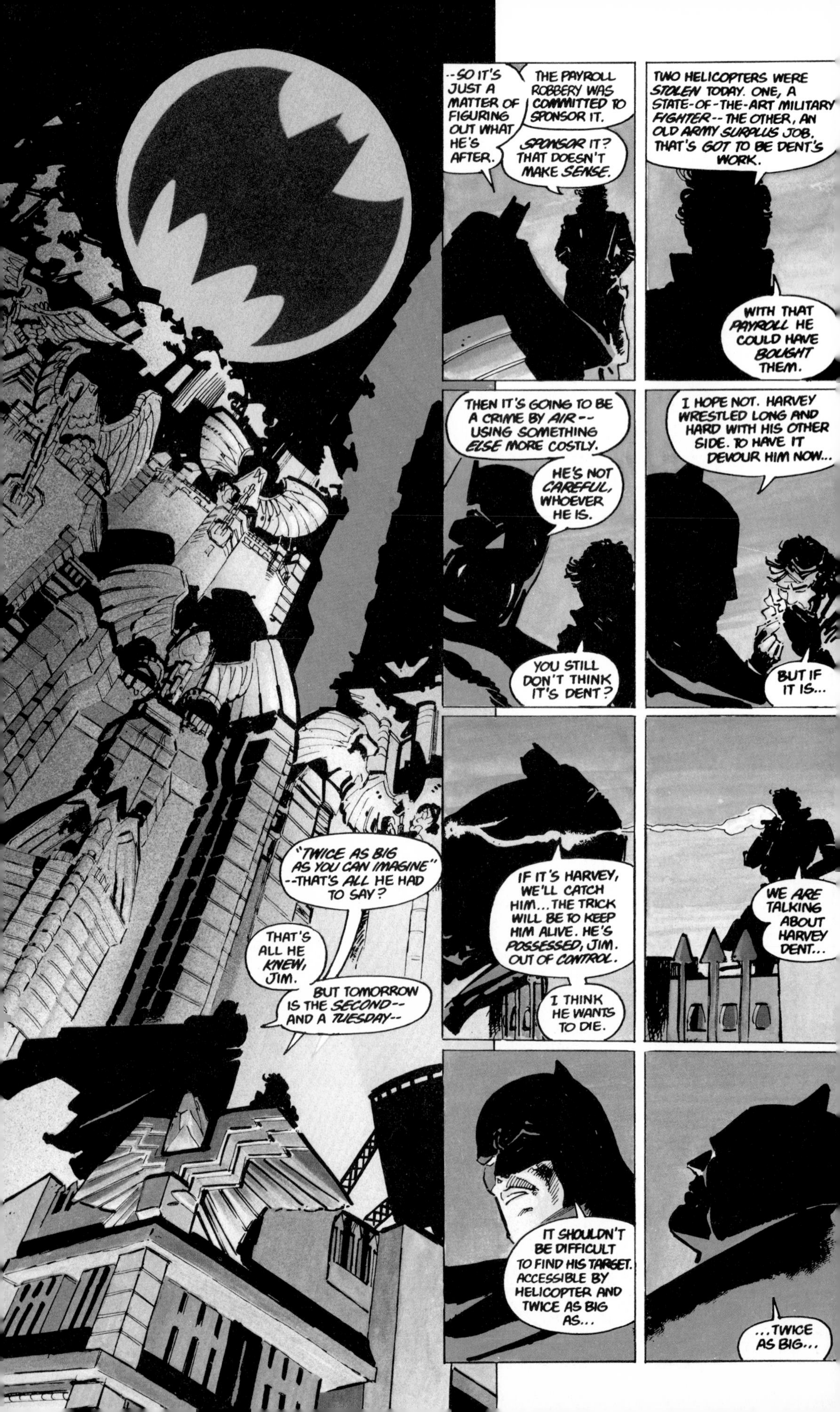
"TWICE AS BIG AS YOU CAN IMAGINE" --THAT'S ALL HE HAD TO SAY?
THAT'S ALL HE KNEW, JIM.
BUT TOMORROW IS THE SECOND-- AND A TUESDAY--
--SO IT'S JUST A MATTER OF FIGURING OUT WHAT HE'S AFTER.
THE PAYROLL ROBBERY WAS COMMITTED TO SPONSOR IT.
SPONSOR IT? THAT DOESN'T MAKE SENSE.
TWO HELICOPTERS WERE STOLEN TODAY. ONE, A STATE-OF-THE-ART MILITARY FIGHTER-- THE OTHER, AN OLD ARMY SURPLUS JOB. THAT'S GOT TO BE DENT'S WORK.
WITH THAT PAYROLL HE COULD HAVE BOUGHT THEM.
THEN IT'S GOING TO BE A CRIME BY AIR-- USING SOMETHING ELSE MORE COSTLY.
HE'S NOT CAREFUL, WHOEVER HE IS.
YOU STILL DON'T THINK IT'S DENT?
I HOPE NOT. HARVEY WRESTLED LONG AND HARD WITH HIS OTHER SIDE. TO HAVE IT DEVOUR HIM NOW...
BUT IF IT IS...
IF IT'S HARVEY, WE'LL CATCH HIM... THE TRICK WILL BE TO KEEP HIM ALIVE. HE'S POSSESSED, JIM. OUT OF CONTROL.
I THINK HE WANTS TO DIE.
WE ARE TALKING ABOUT HARVEY DENT...
IT SHOULDN'T BE DIFFICULT TO FIND HIS TARGET. ACCESSIBLE BY HELICOPTER AND TWICE AS BIG AS...
...TWICE AS BIG...

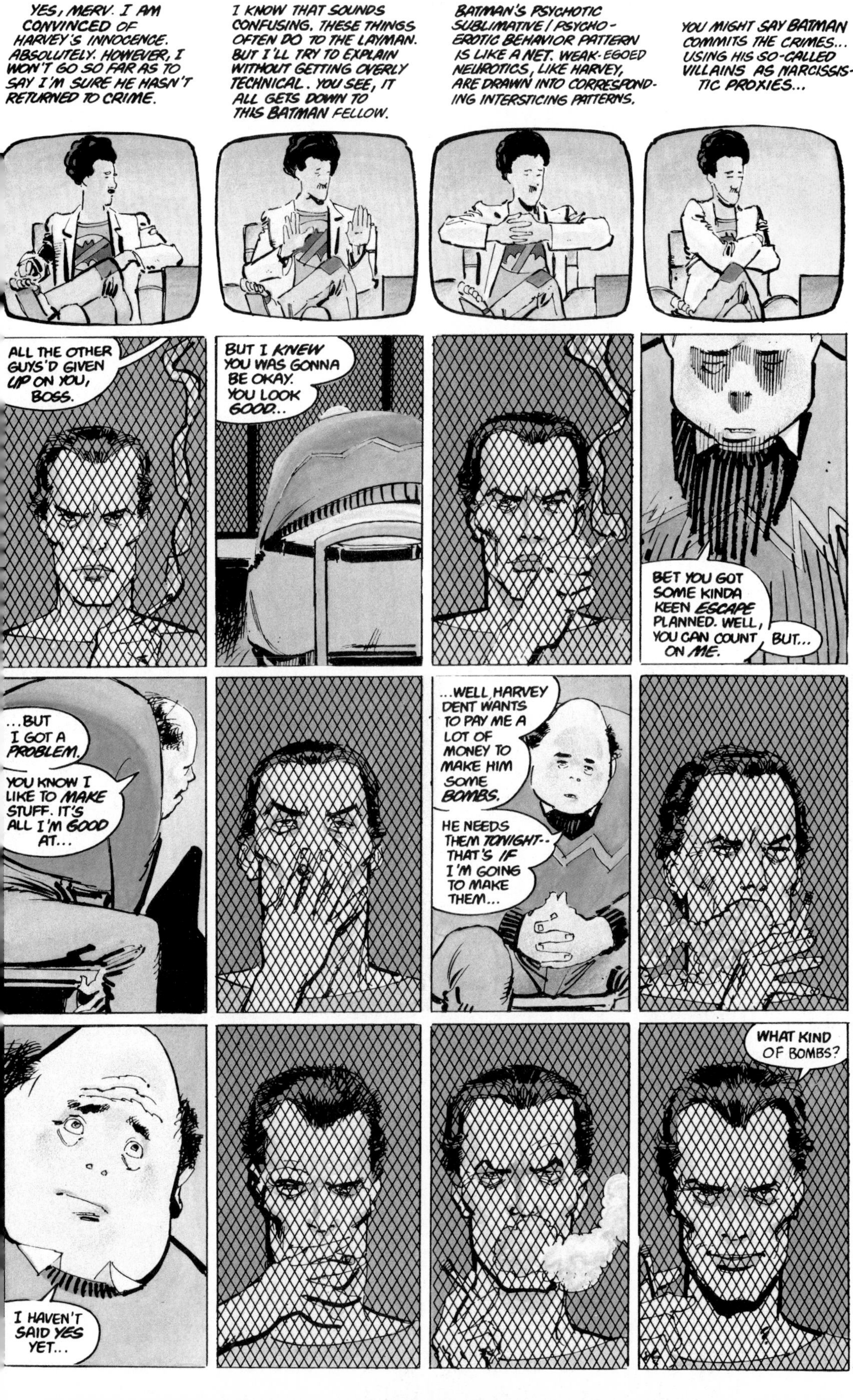
YES, MERV. I AM CONVINCED OF HARVEY'S INNOCENCE. ABSOLUTELY. HOWEVER, I WON'T GO SO FAR AS TO SAY I'M SURE HE HASN'T RETURNED TO CRIME.
I KNOW THAT SOUNDS CONFUSING. THESE THINGS OFTEN DO TO THE LAYMAN. BUT I'LL TRY TO EXPLAIN WITHOUT GETTING OVERLY TECHNICAL. YOU SEE, IT ALL GETS DOWN TO THIS BATMAN FELLOW.
BATMAN'S PSYCHOTIC SUBLIMATIVE / PSYCHO-EROTIC BEHAVIOR PATTERN IS LIKE A NET. WEAK-EGOED NEUROTICS, LIKE HARVEY, ARE DRAWN INTO CORRESPONDING INTERSTICING PATTERNS.
YOU MIGHT SAY BATMAN COMMITS THE CRIMES... USING HIS SO-CALLED VILLAINS AS NARCISSISTIC PROXIES...
ALL THE OTHER GUYS'D GIVEN UP ON YOU, BOSS.
BUT I KNEW YOU WAS GONNA BE OKAY. YOU LOOK GOOD...
BET YOU GOT SOME KINDA KEEN ESCAPE PLANNED. WELL, YOU CAN COUNT ON ME.
BUT...
...BUT I GOT A PROBLEM.
YOU KNOW I LIKE TO MAKE STUFF. IT'S ALL I'M GOOD AT...
...WELL, HARVEY DENT WANTS TO PAY ME A LOT OF MONEY TO MAKE HIM SOME BOMBS.
HE NEEDS THEM TONIGHT-- THAT'S IF I'M GOING TO MAKE THEM...
I HAVEN'T SAID YES YET...
WHAT KIND OF BOMBS?

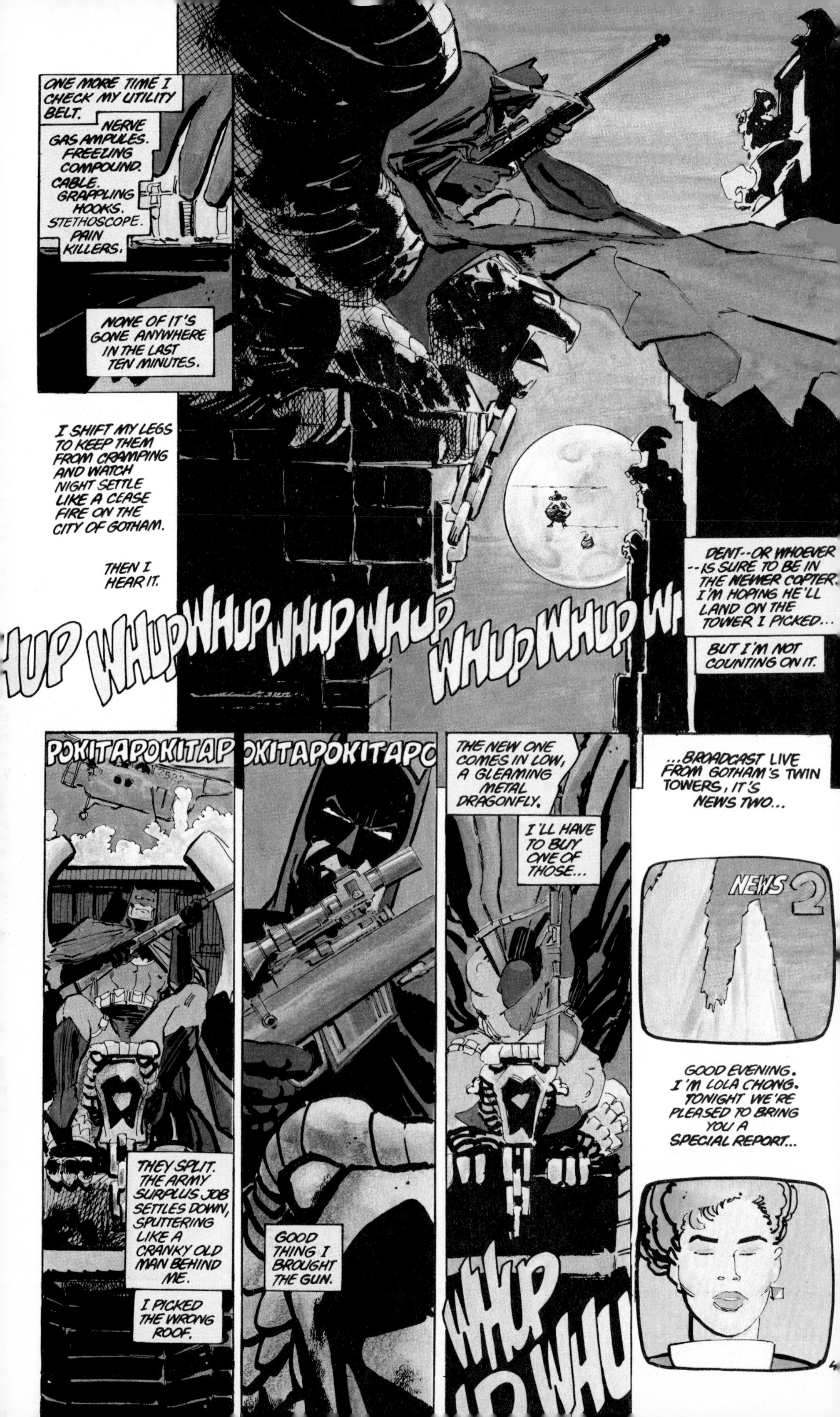

ONE MORE TIME I CHECK MY UTILITY BELT.
NERVE GAS AMPULES. FREEZING COMPOUND. CABLE. GRAPPLING HOOKS. STETHOSCOPE. PAIN KILLERS.
NONE OF IT'S GONE ANYWHERE IN THE LAST TEN MINUTES.
I SHIFT MY LEGS TO KEEP THEM FROM CRAMPING AND WATCH NIGHT SETTLE LIKE A CEASE FIRE ON THE CITY OF GOTHAM.
THEN I HEAR IT.
HUP WHUP WHUP WHUP WHUP WHUP WHUP WH
DENT--OR WHOEVER --IS SURE TO BE IN THE NEWER COPTER. I'M HOPING HE'LL LAND ON THE TOWER I PICKED...
BUT I'M NOT COUNTING ON IT.
POKITAPOKITAP
THEY SPLIT. THE ARMY SURPLUS JOB SETTLES DOWN, SPUTTERING LIKE A CRANKY OLD MAN BEHIND ME.
I PICKED THE WRONG ROOF.
OKITAPOKITAPO
GOOD THING I BROUGHT THE GUN.
THE NEW ONE COMES IN LOW, A GLEAMING METAL DRAGONFLY.
I'LL HAVE TO BUY ONE OF THOSE...
WHUP WHU
...BROADCAST LIVE FROM GOTHAM'S TWIN TOWERS, IT'S NEWS TWO...
NEWS 2
GOOD EVENING. I'M LOLA CHONG. TONIGHT WE'RE PLEASED TO BRING YOU A SPECIAL REPORT...

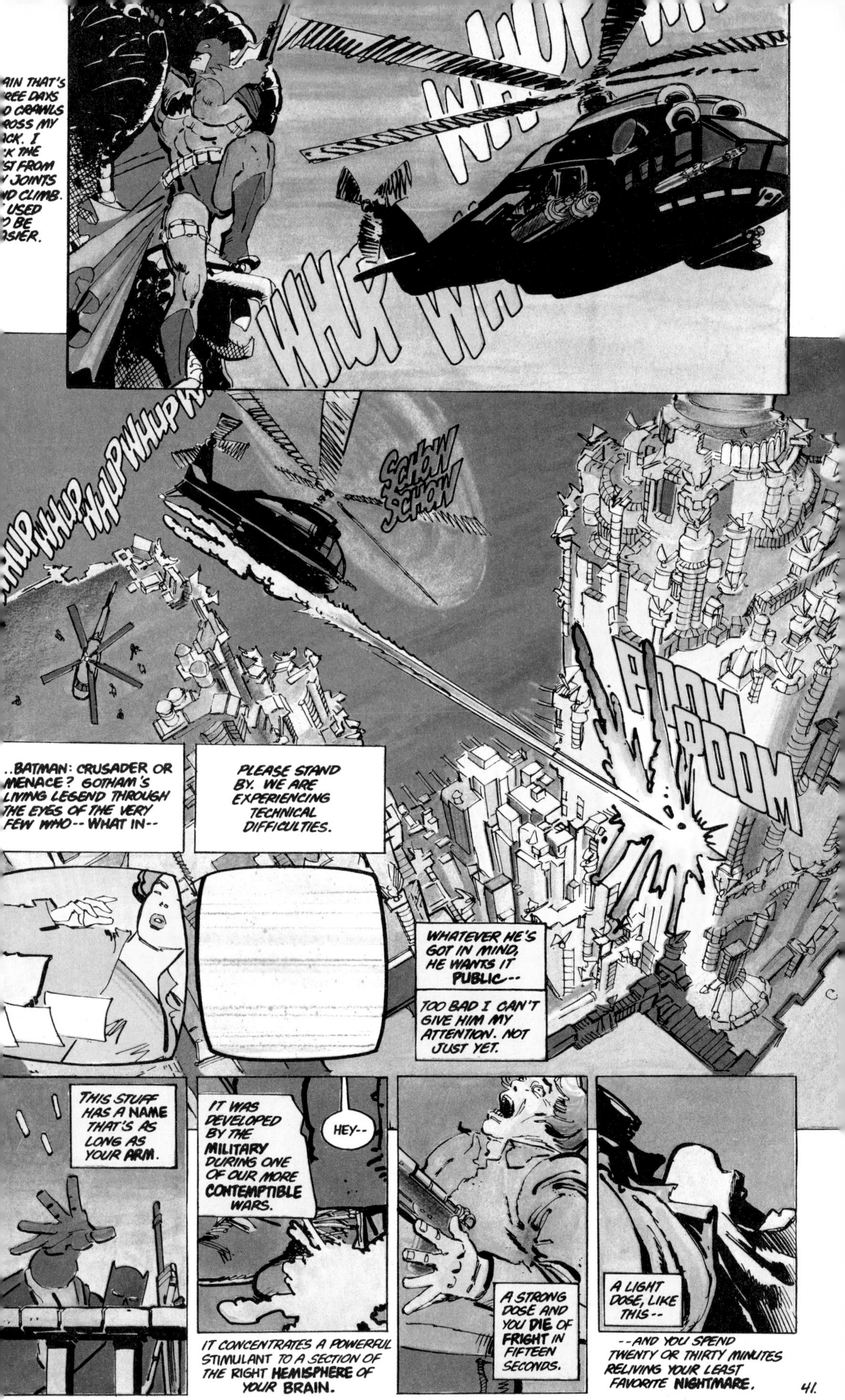
AIN THAT'S
REE DAYS
D CRAWLS
ROSS MY
ACK. I
K THE
ST FROM
JOINTS
D CLIMB.
USED
O BE
ASIER.
WHUP WHUP
SCHOW SCHOW
WHUP WHUP WHUP WHUP
BOOM BOOM
..BATMAN: CRUSADER OR MENACE? GOTHAM'S LIVING LEGEND THROUGH THE EYES OF THE VERY FEW WHO-- WHAT IN--
PLEASE STAND BY. WE ARE EXPERIENCING TECHNICAL DIFFICULTIES.
WHATEVER HE'S GOT IN MIND, HE WANTS IT PUBLIC--
TOO BAD I CAN'T GIVE HIM MY ATTENTION. NOT JUST YET.
THIS STUFF HAS A NAME THAT'S AS LONG AS YOUR ARM.
IT WAS DEVELOPED BY THE MILITARY DURING ONE OF OUR MORE CONTEMPTIBLE WARS.
HEY--
IT CONCENTRATES A POWERFUL STIMULANT TO A SECTION OF THE RIGHT HEMISPHERE OF YOUR BRAIN.
A STRONG DOSE AND YOU DIE OF FRIGHT IN FIFTEEN SECONDS.
A LIGHT DOSE, LIKE THIS--
--AND YOU SPEND TWENTY OR THIRTY MINUTES RELIVING YOUR LEAST FAVORITE NIGHTMARE.

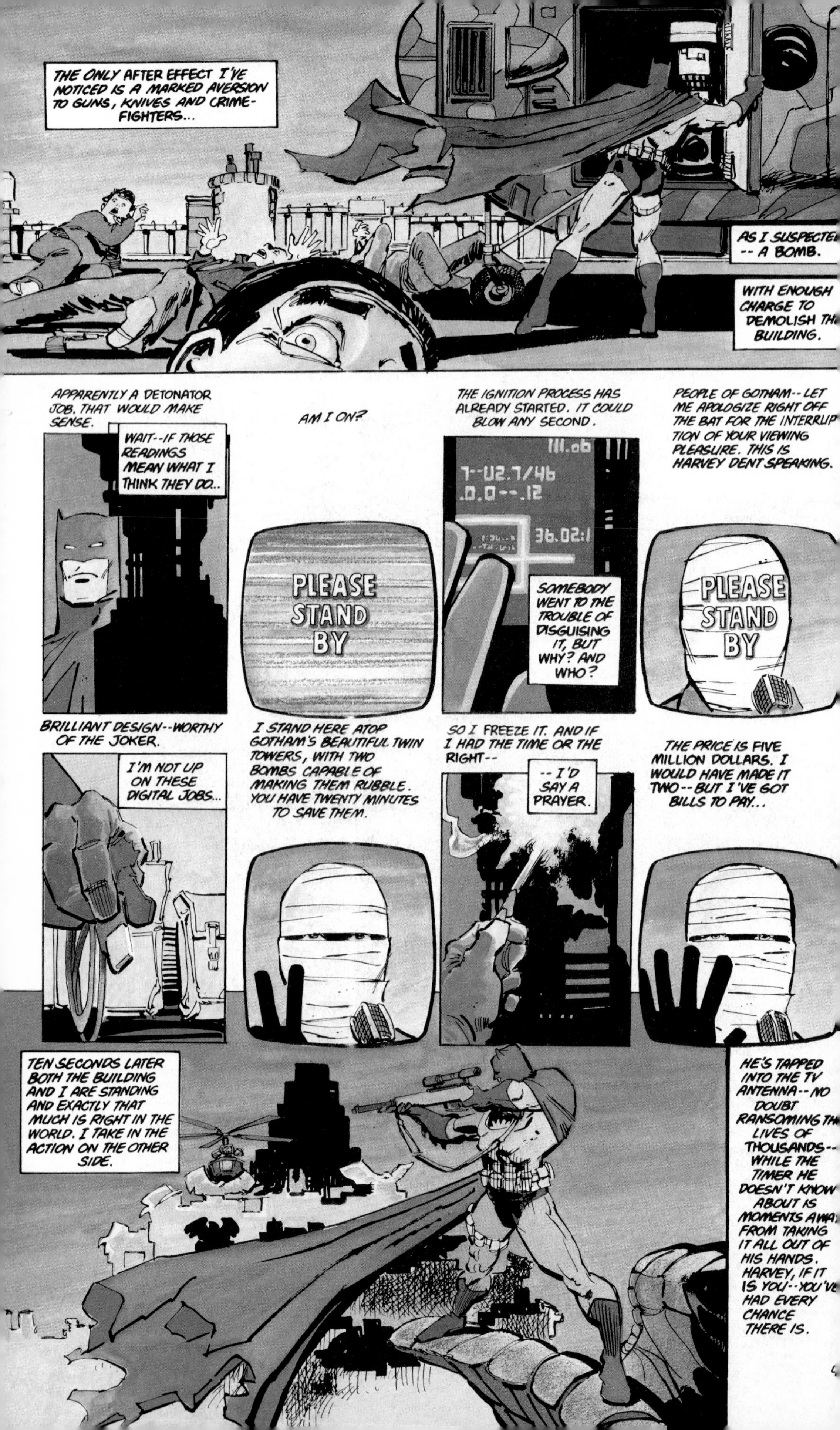
THE ONLY AFTER EFFECT I'VE NOTICED IS A MARKED AVERSION TO GUNS, KNIVES AND CRIME-FIGHTERS...
AS I SUSPECTE -- A BOMB.
WITH ENOUGH CHARGE TO DEMOLISH TH BUILDING.
APPARENTLY A DETONATOR JOB. THAT WOULD MAKE SENSE.
WAIT--IF THOSE READINGS MEAN WHAT I THINK THEY DO..
AM I ON?
PLEASE STAND BY
THE IGNITION PROCESS HAS ALREADY STARTED. IT COULD BLOW ANY SECOND.
SOMEBODY WENT TO THE TROUBLE OF DISGUISING IT, BUT WHY? AND WHO?
PEOPLE OF GOTHAM--LET ME APOLOGIZE RIGHT OFF THE BAT FOR THE INTERRUP TION OF YOUR VIEWING PLEASURE. THIS IS HARVEY DENT SPEAKING.
PLEASE STAND BY
BRILLIANT DESIGN--WORTHY OF THE JOKER.
I'M NOT UP ON THESE DIGITAL JOBS...
I STAND HERE ATOP GOTHAM'S BEAUTIFUL TWIN TOWERS, WITH TWO BOMBS CAPABLE OF MAKING THEM RUBBLE. YOU HAVE TWENTY MINUTES TO SAVE THEM.
SO I FREEZE IT. AND IF I HAD THE TIME OR THE RIGHT--
-- I'D SAY A PRAYER.
THE PRICE IS FIVE MILLION DOLLARS. I WOULD HAVE MADE IT TWO--BUT I'VE GOT BILLS TO PAY...
TEN SECONDS LATER BOTH THE BUILDING AND I ARE STANDING AND EXACTLY THAT MUCH IS RIGHT IN THE WORLD. I TAKE IN THE ACTION ON THE OTHER SIDE.
HE'S TAPPED INTO THE TV ANTENNA--NO DOUBT RANSOMING TH LIVES OF THOUSANDS-- WHILE THE TIMER HE DOESN'T KNOW ABOUT IS MOMENTS AWA FROM TAKING IT ALL OUT OF HIS HANDS. HARVEY, IF IT IS YOU--YOU'VE HAD EVERY CHANCE THERE IS.

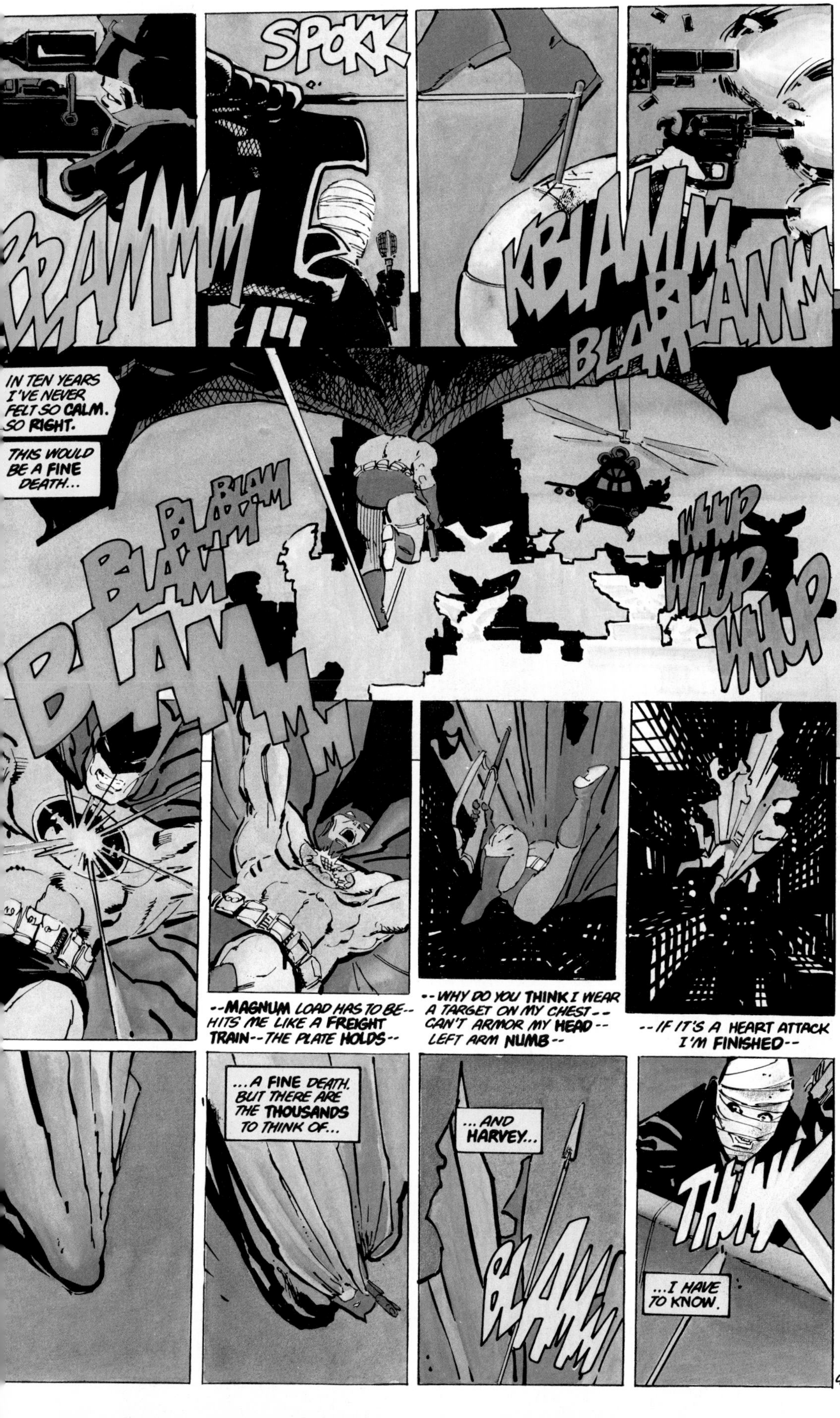
BRAMMM
SPOKK
KBLAMM
BLAMM
BLAMM
IN TEN YEARS I'VE NEVER FELT SO CALM. SO RIGHT.
THIS WOULD BE A FINE DEATH...
BLAM
BLAM
BLAM
BLAMM
WHUP
WHUP
WHUP
--MAGNUM LOAD HAS TO BE-- HITS ME LIKE A FREIGHT TRAIN--THE PLATE HOLDS--
--WHY DO YOU THINK I WEAR A TARGET ON MY CHEST-- CAN'T ARMOR MY HEAD-- LEFT ARM NUMB--
--IF IT'S A HEART ATTACK I'M FINISHED--
...A FINE DEATH. BUT THERE ARE THE THOUSANDS TO THINK OF...
...AND HARVEY...
BLAMM
THUNK
...I HAVE TO KNOW.

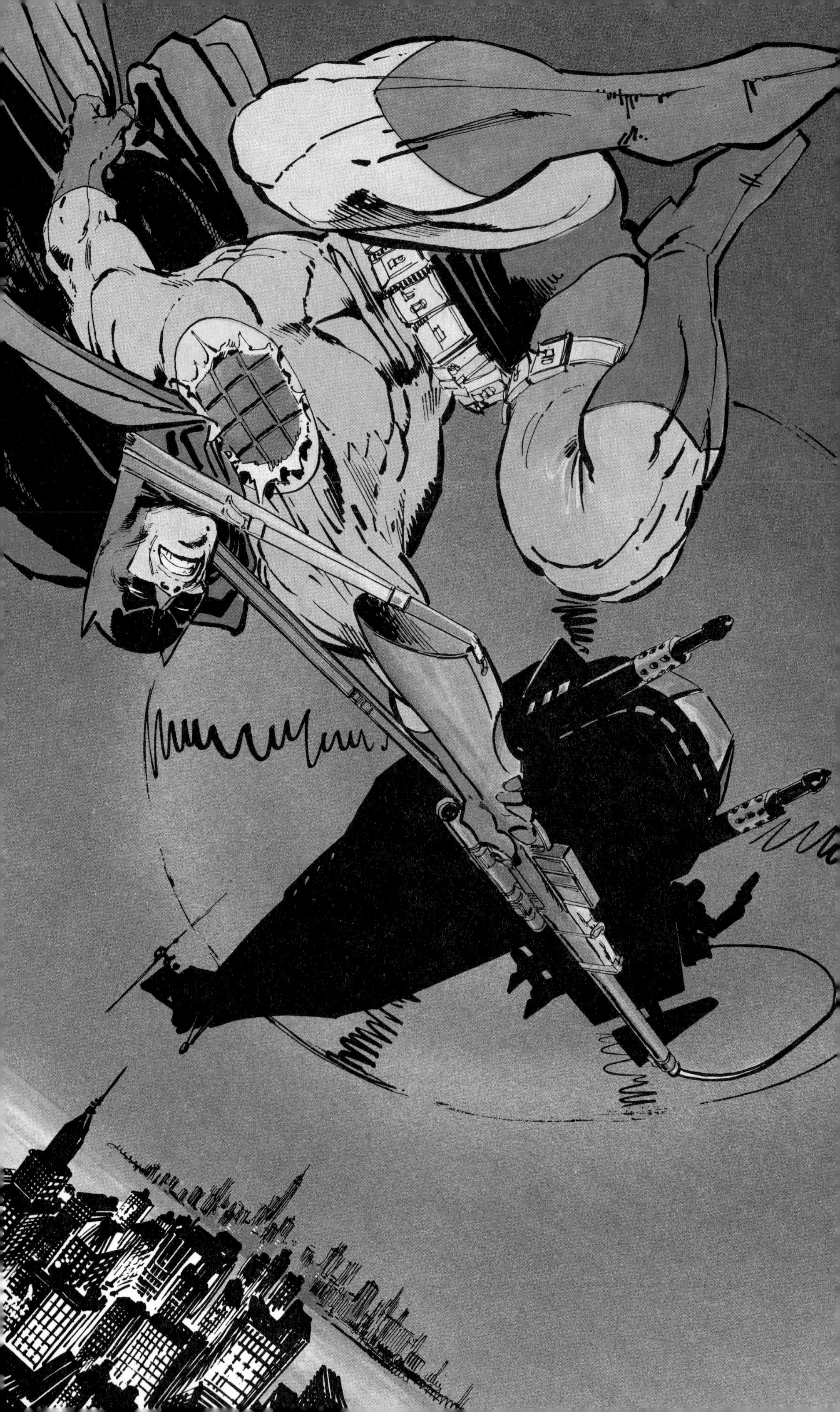

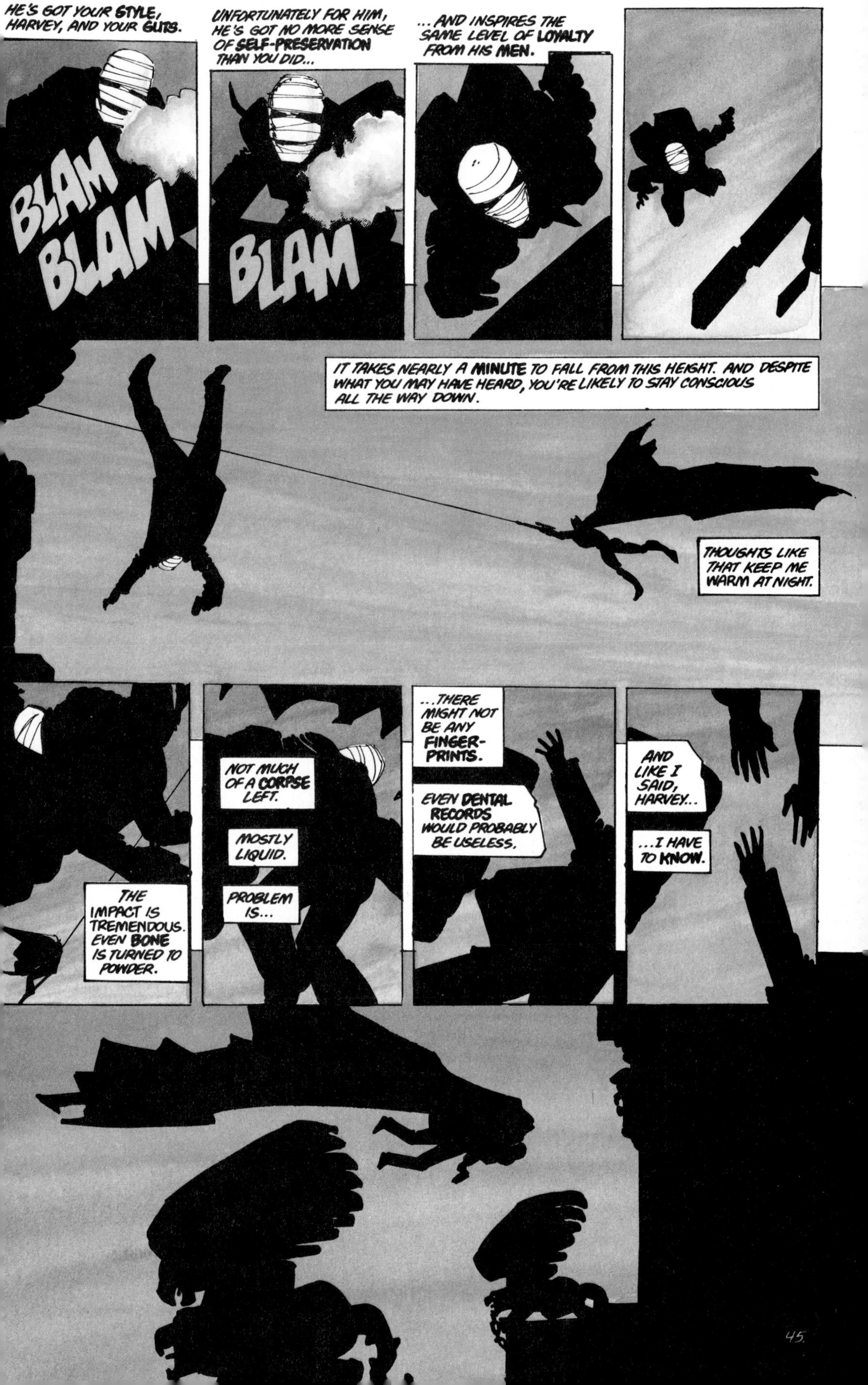
HE'S GOT YOUR STYLE, HARVEY, AND YOUR GUTS.
BLAM BLAM
UNFORTUNATELY FOR HIM, HE'S GOT NO MORE SENSE OF SELF-PRESERVATION THAN YOU DID...
BLAM
...AND INSPIRES THE SAME LEVEL OF LOYALTY FROM HIS MEN.
IT TAKES NEARLY A MINUTE TO FALL FROM THIS HEIGHT. AND DESPITE WHAT YOU MAY HAVE HEARD, YOU'RE LIKELY TO STAY CONSCIOUS ALL THE WAY DOWN.
THOUGHTS LIKE THAT KEEP ME WARM AT NIGHT.
THE IMPACT IS TREMENDOUS. EVEN BONE IS TURNED TO POWDER.
NOT MUCH OF A CORPSE LEFT.
MOSTLY LIQUID.
PROBLEM IS...
...THERE MIGHT NOT BE ANY FINGER-PRINTS.
EVEN DENTAL RECORDS WOULD PROBABLY BE USELESS.
AND LIKE I SAID, HARVEY...
...I HAVE TO KNOW.

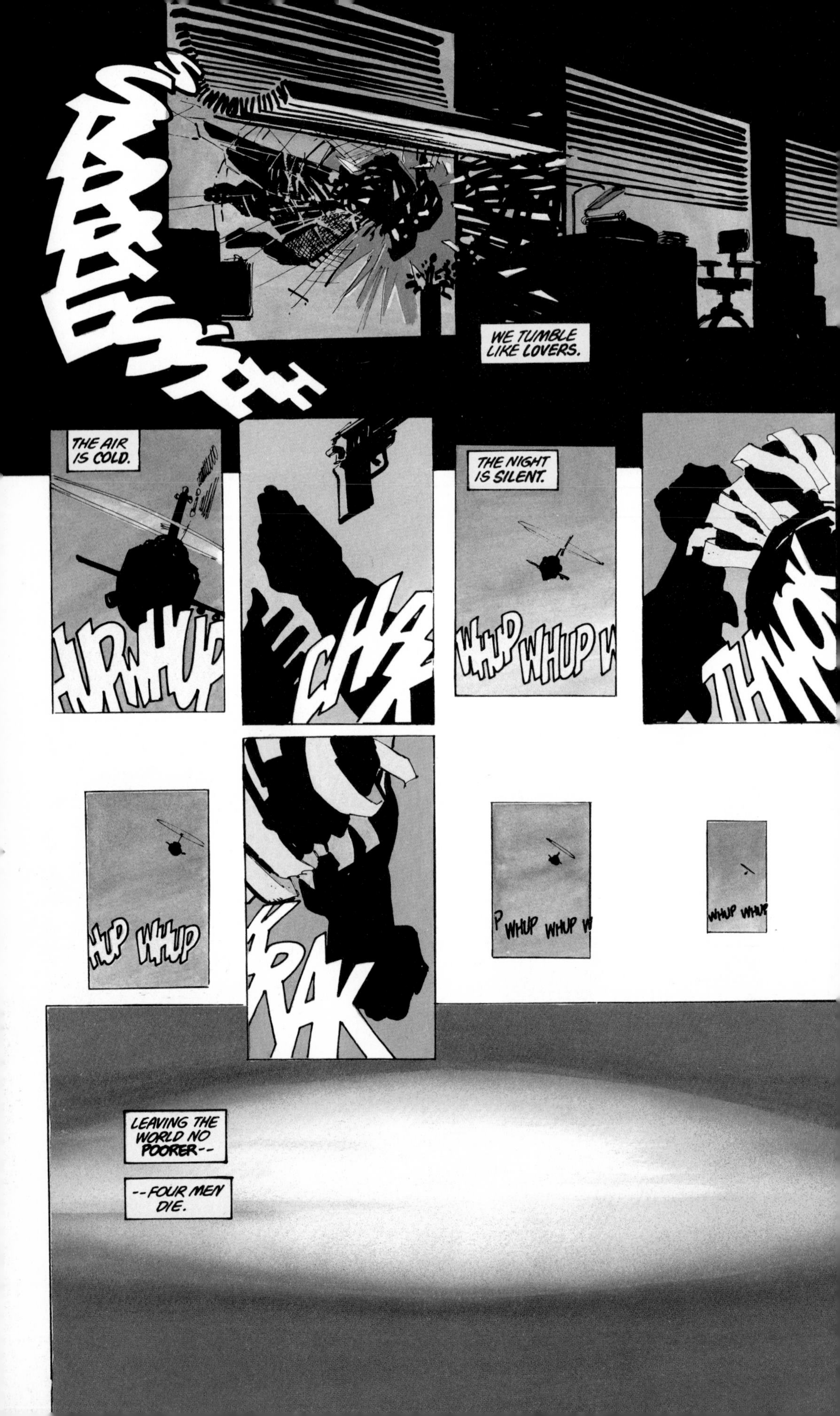
WE TUMBLE LIKE LOVERS.
THE AIR IS COLD.
THE NIGHT IS SILENT.
WHUP WHUP
WHUP WHUP
WHUP WHUP
WHUP WHUP
LEAVING THE WORLD NO POORER--
--FOUR MEN DIE.

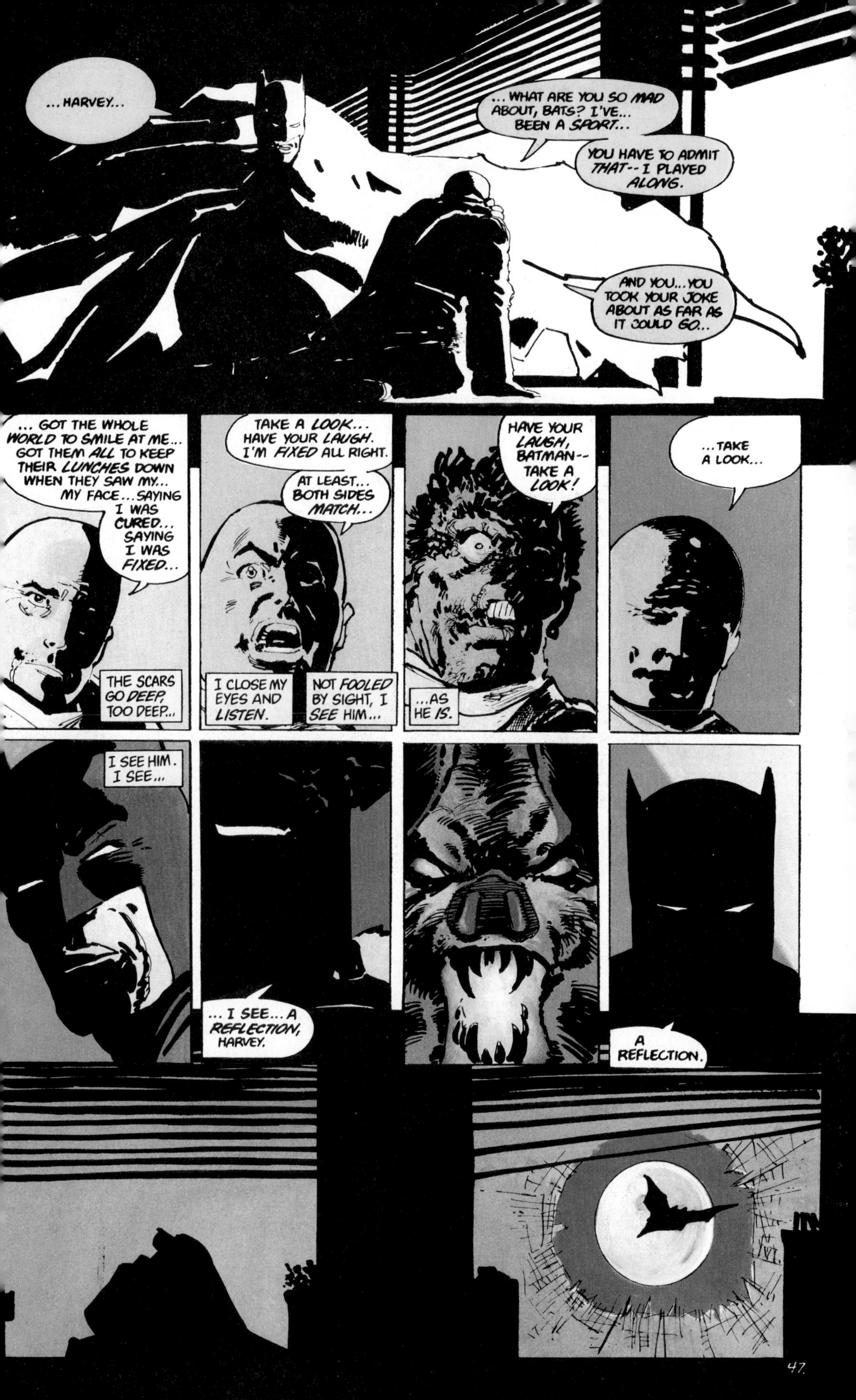

... HARVEY...
... WHAT ARE YOU SO MAD ABOUT, BATS? I'VE... BEEN A SPORT...
YOU HAVE TO ADMIT THAT-- I PLAYED ALONG.
AND YOU... YOU TOOK YOUR JOKE ABOUT AS FAR AS IT COULD GO...
... GOT THE WHOLE WORLD TO SMILE AT ME... GOT THEM ALL TO KEEP THEIR LUNCHES DOWN WHEN THEY SAW MY... MY FACE... SAYING I WAS CURED... SAYING I WAS FIXED...
THE SCARS GO DEEP, TOO DEEP...
TAKE A LOOK... HAVE YOUR LAUGH. I'M FIXED ALL RIGHT.
AT LEAST... BOTH SIDES MATCH...
I CLOSE MY EYES AND LISTEN.
NOT FOOLED BY SIGHT, I SEE HIM...
HAVE YOUR LAUGH, BATMAN-- TAKE A LOOK!
...AS HE IS.
...TAKE A LOOK...
I SEE HIM. I SEE...
... I SEE... A REFLECTION, HARVEY.
A REFLECTION.

BOOK TWO

THE
DARK
KNIGHT
TRIUMPHANT

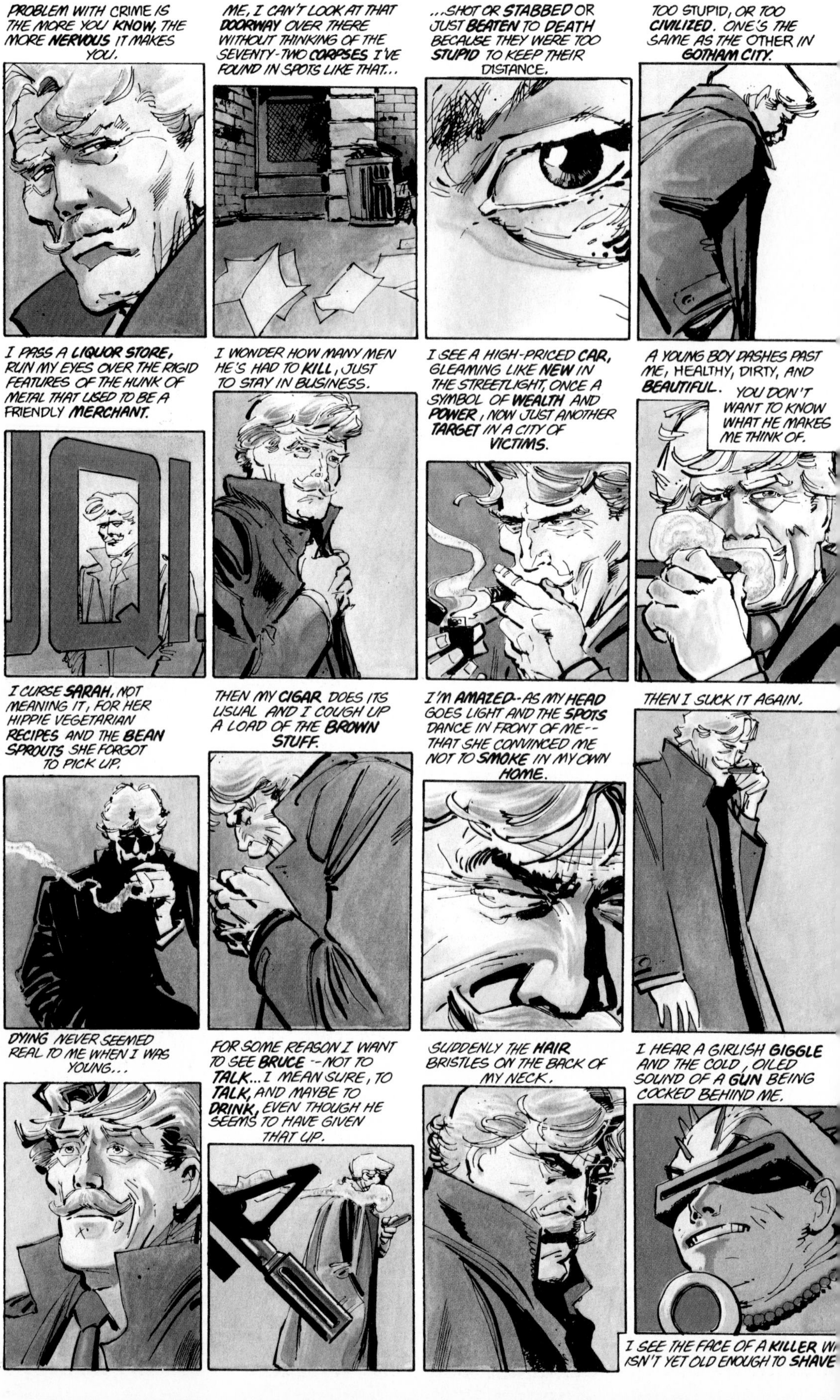
PROBLEM WITH CRIME IS THE MORE YOU KNOW, THE MORE NERVOUS IT MAKES YOU.
ME, I CAN'T LOOK AT THAT DOORWAY OVER THERE WITHOUT THINKING OF THE SEVENTY-TWO CORPSES I'VE FOUND IN SPOTS LIKE THAT...
...SHOT OR STABBED OR JUST BEATEN TO DEATH BECAUSE THEY WERE TOO STUPID TO KEEP THEIR DISTANCE.
TOO STUPID, OR TOO CIVILIZED. ONE'S THE SAME AS THE OTHER IN GOTHAM CITY.
I PASS A LIQUOR STORE, RUN MY EYES OVER THE RIGID FEATURES OF THE HUNK OF METAL THAT USED TO BE A FRIENDLY MERCHANT.
I WONDER HOW MANY MEN HE'S HAD TO KILL, JUST TO STAY IN BUSINESS.
I SEE A HIGH-PRICED CAR, GLEAMING LIKE NEW IN THE STREETLIGHT, ONCE A SYMBOL OF WEALTH AND POWER, NOW JUST ANOTHER TARGET IN A CITY OF VICTIMS.
A YOUNG BOY DASHES PAST ME, HEALTHY, DIRTY, AND BEAUTIFUL.
YOU DON'T WANT TO KNOW WHAT HE MAKES ME THINK OF.
I CURSE SARAH, NOT MEANING IT, FOR HER HIPPIE VEGETARIAN RECIPES AND THE BEAN SPROUTS SHE FORGOT TO PICK UP.
THEN MY CIGAR DOES ITS USUAL AND I COUGH UP A LOAD OF THE BROWN STUFF.
I'M AMAZED--AS MY HEAD GOES LIGHT AND THE SPOTS DANCE IN FRONT OF ME--THAT SHE CONVINCED ME NOT TO SMOKE IN MY OWN HOME.
THEN I SUCK IT AGAIN.
DYING NEVER SEEMED REAL TO ME WHEN I WAS YOUNG...
FOR SOME REASON I WANT TO SEE BRUCE --NOT TO TALK...I MEAN SURE, TO TALK, AND MAYBE TO DRINK, EVEN THOUGH HE SEEMS TO HAVE GIVEN THAT UP.
SUDDENLY THE HAIR BRISTLES ON THE BACK OF MY NECK.
I HEAR A GIRLISH GIGGLE AND THE COLD, OILED SOUND OF A GUN BEING COCKED BEHIND ME.
I SEE THE FACE OF A KILLER W
ISN'T YET OLD ENOUGH TO SHAVE

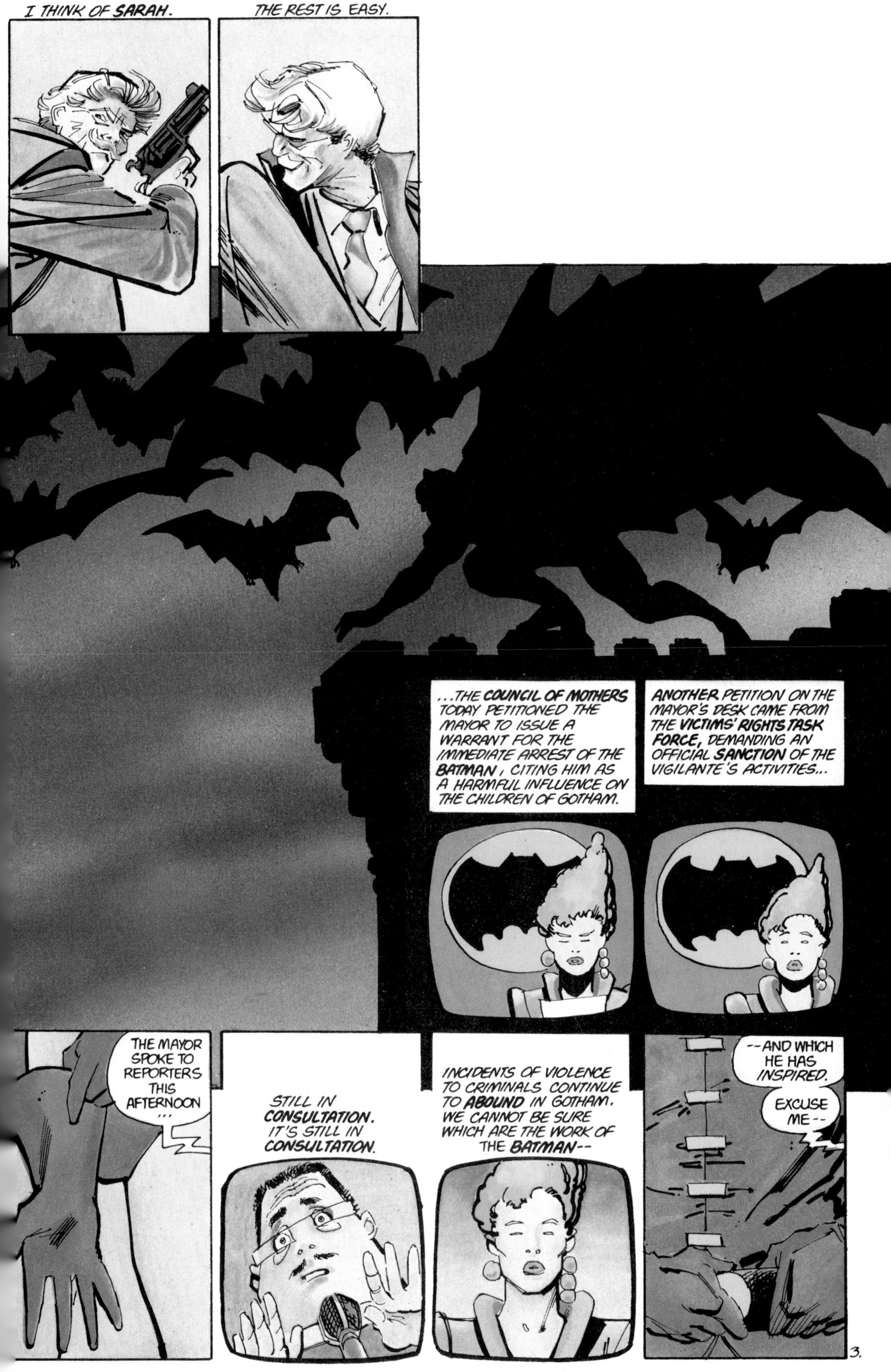
I THINK OF SARAH.
THE REST IS EASY.
...THE COUNCIL OF MOTHERS TODAY PETITIONED THE MAYOR TO ISSUE A WARRANT FOR THE IMMEDIATE ARREST OF THE BATMAN, CITING HIM AS A HARMFUL INFLUENCE ON THE CHILDREN OF GOTHAM.
ANOTHER PETITION ON THE MAYOR'S DESK CAME FROM THE VICTIMS' RIGHTS TASK FORCE, DEMANDING AN OFFICIAL SANCTION OF THE VIGILANTE'S ACTIVITIES...
THE MAYOR SPOKE TO REPORTERS THIS AFTERNOON ...
STILL IN CONSULTATION. IT'S STILL IN CONSULTATION.
INCIDENTS OF VIOLENCE TO CRIMINALS CONTINUE TO ABOUND IN GOTHAM. WE CANNOT BE SURE WHICH ARE THE WORK OF THE BATMAN--
--AND WHICH HE HAS INSPIRED.
EXCUSE ME--

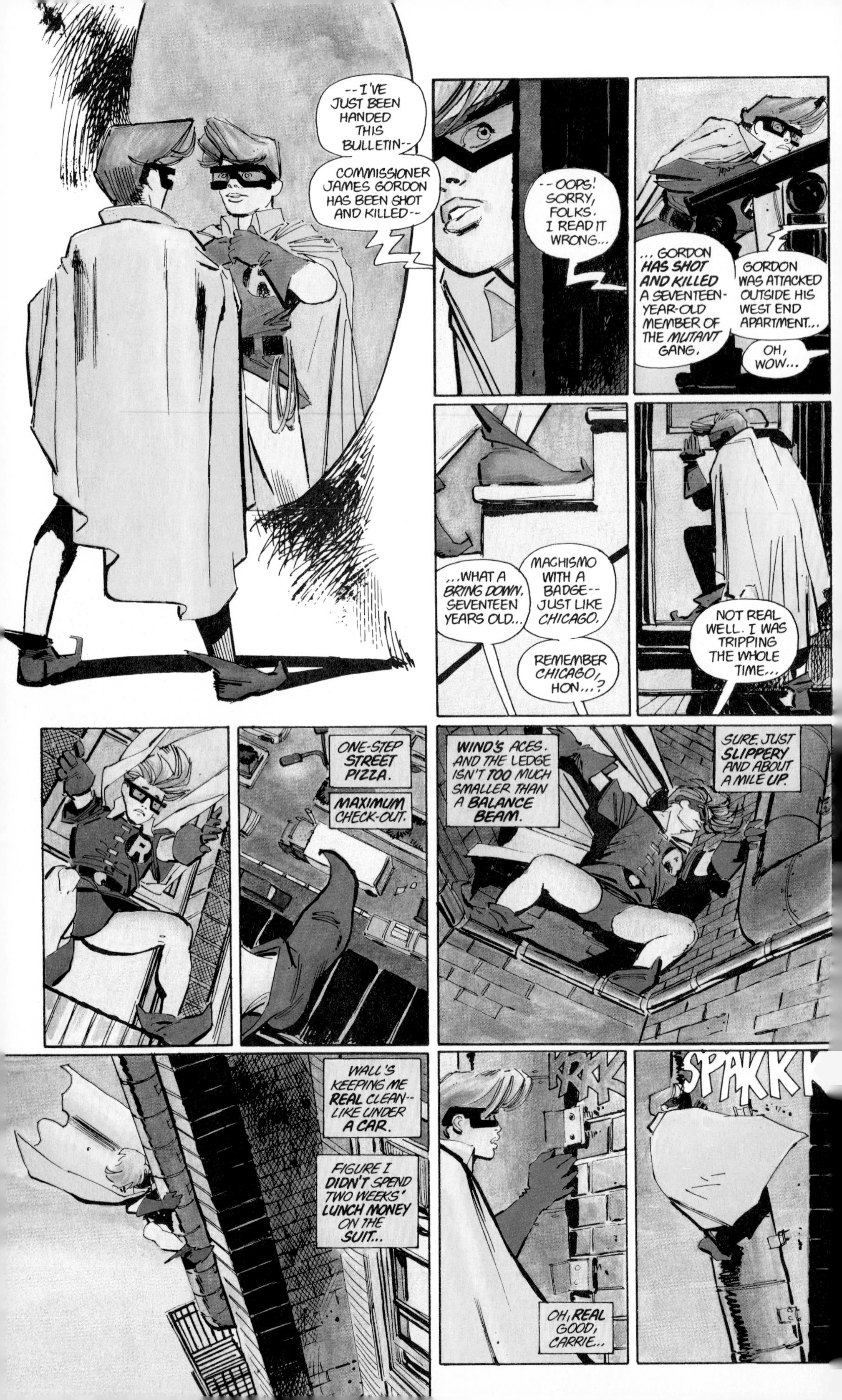

--I'VE JUST BEEN HANDED THIS BULLETIN--
COMMISSIONER JAMES GORDON HAS BEEN SHOT AND KILLED--
--OOPS! SORRY, FOLKS. I READ IT WRONG...
...GORDON HAS SHOT AND KILLED A SEVENTEEN-YEAR-OLD MEMBER OF THE MUTANT GANG.
GORDON WAS ATTACKED OUTSIDE HIS WEST END APARTMENT...
OH, WOW...
...WHAT A BRING DOWN. SEVENTEEN YEARS OLD...
MACHISMO WITH A BADGE--JUST LIKE CHICAGO.
REMEMBER CHICAGO, HON...?
NOT REAL WELL. I WAS TRIPPING THE WHOLE TIME...
ONE-STEP STREET PIZZA.
MAXIMUM CHECK-OUT.
WIND'S ACES. AND THE LEDGE ISN'T TOO MUCH SMALLER THAN A BALANCE BEAM.
SURE. JUST SLIPPERY AND ABOUT A MILE UP.
WALL'S KEEPING ME REAL CLEAN--LIKE UNDER A CAR.
FIGURE I DIDN'T SPEND TWO WEEKS' LUNCH MONEY ON THE SUIT...
KRAK
OH, REAL GOOD, CARRIE...
SPAKKK

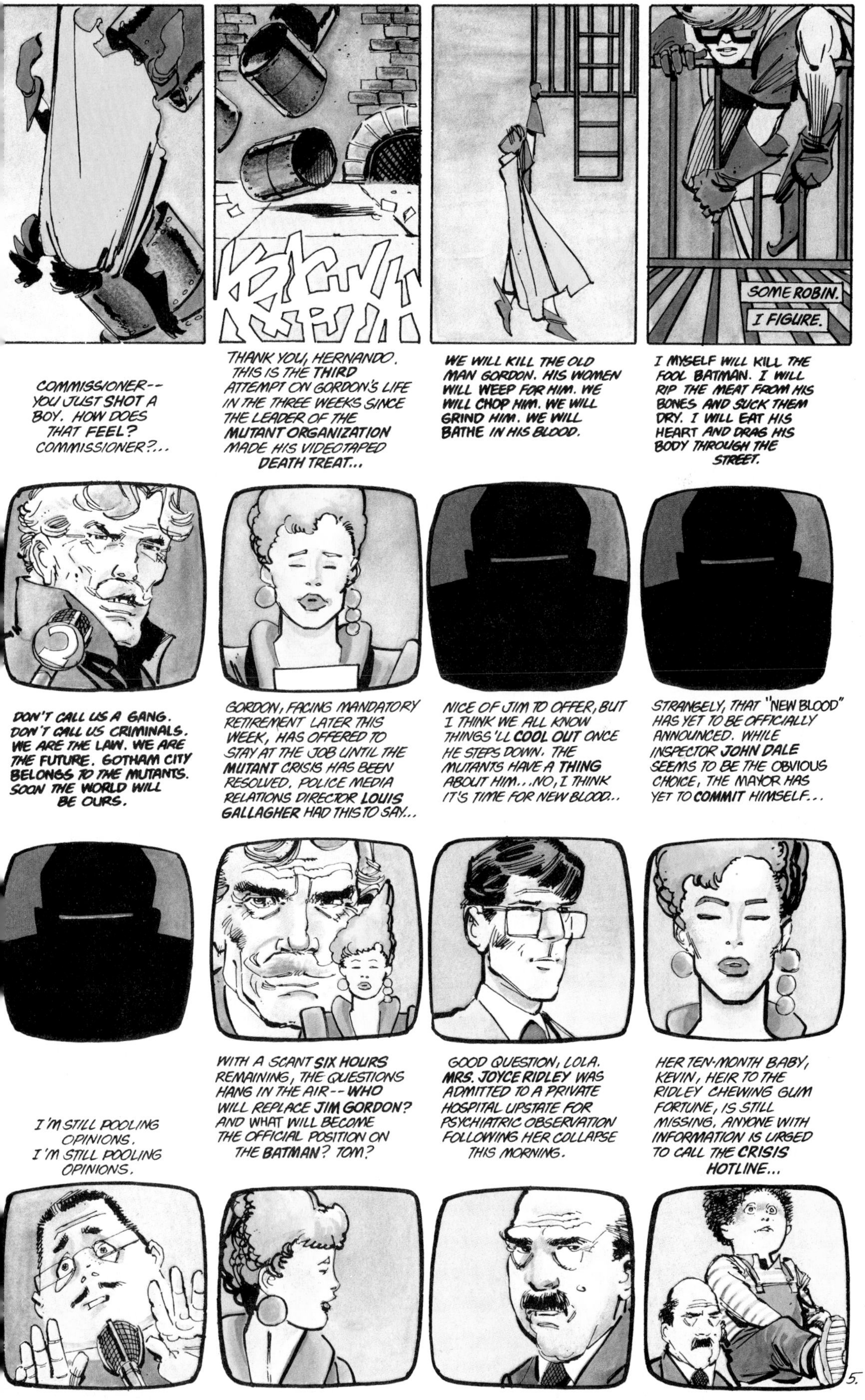
KRAK KRAK
SOME ROBIN.
I FIGURE.
COMMISSIONER-- YOU JUST SHOT A BOY. HOW DOES THAT FEEL? COMMISSIONER?...
THANK YOU, HERNANDO. THIS IS THE THIRD ATTEMPT ON GORDON'S LIFE IN THE THREE WEEKS SINCE THE LEADER OF THE MUTANT ORGANIZATION MADE HIS VIDEOTAPED DEATH TREAT...
WE WILL KILL THE OLD MAN GORDON. HIS WOMEN WILL WEEP FOR HIM. WE WILL CHOP HIM. WE WILL GRIND HIM. WE WILL BATHE IN HIS BLOOD.
I MYSELF WILL KILL THE FOOL BATMAN. I WILL RIP THE MEAT FROM HIS BONES AND SUCK THEM DRY. I WILL EAT HIS HEART AND DRAG HIS BODY THROUGH THE STREET.
DON'T CALL US A GANG. DON'T CALL US CRIMINALS. WE ARE THE LAW. WE ARE THE FUTURE. GOTHAM CITY BELONGS TO THE MUTANTS. SOON THE WORLD WILL BE OURS.
GORDON, FACING MANDATORY RETIREMENT LATER THIS WEEK, HAS OFFERED TO STAY AT THE JOB UNTIL THE MUTANT CRISIS HAS BEEN RESOLVED. POLICE MEDIA RELATIONS DIRECTOR LOUIS GALLAGHER HAD THIS TO SAY...
NICE OF JIM TO OFFER, BUT I THINK WE ALL KNOW THINGS'LL COOL OUT ONCE HE STEPS DOWN. THE MUTANTS HAVE A THING ABOUT HIM... NO, I THINK IT'S TIME FOR NEW BLOOD...
STRANGELY, THAT "NEW BLOOD" HAS YET TO BE OFFICIALLY ANNOUNCED. WHILE INSPECTOR JOHN DALE SEEMS TO BE THE OBVIOUS CHOICE, THE MAYOR HAS YET TO COMMIT HIMSELF...
I'M STILL POOLING OPINIONS. I'M STILL POOLING OPINIONS.
WITH A SCANT SIX HOURS REMAINING, THE QUESTIONS HANG IN THE AIR-- WHO WILL REPLACE JIM GORDON? AND WHAT WILL BECOME THE OFFICIAL POSITION ON THE BATMAN? TOM?
GOOD QUESTION, LOLA. MRS. JOYCE RIDLEY WAS ADMITTED TO A PRIVATE HOSPITAL UPSTATE FOR PSYCHIATRIC OBSERVATION FOLLOWING HER COLLAPSE THIS MORNING.
HER TEN-MONTH BABY, KEVIN, HEIR TO THE RIDLEY CHEWING GUM FORTUNE, IS STILL MISSING. ANYONE WITH INFORMATION IS URGED TO CALL THE CRISIS HOTLINE...

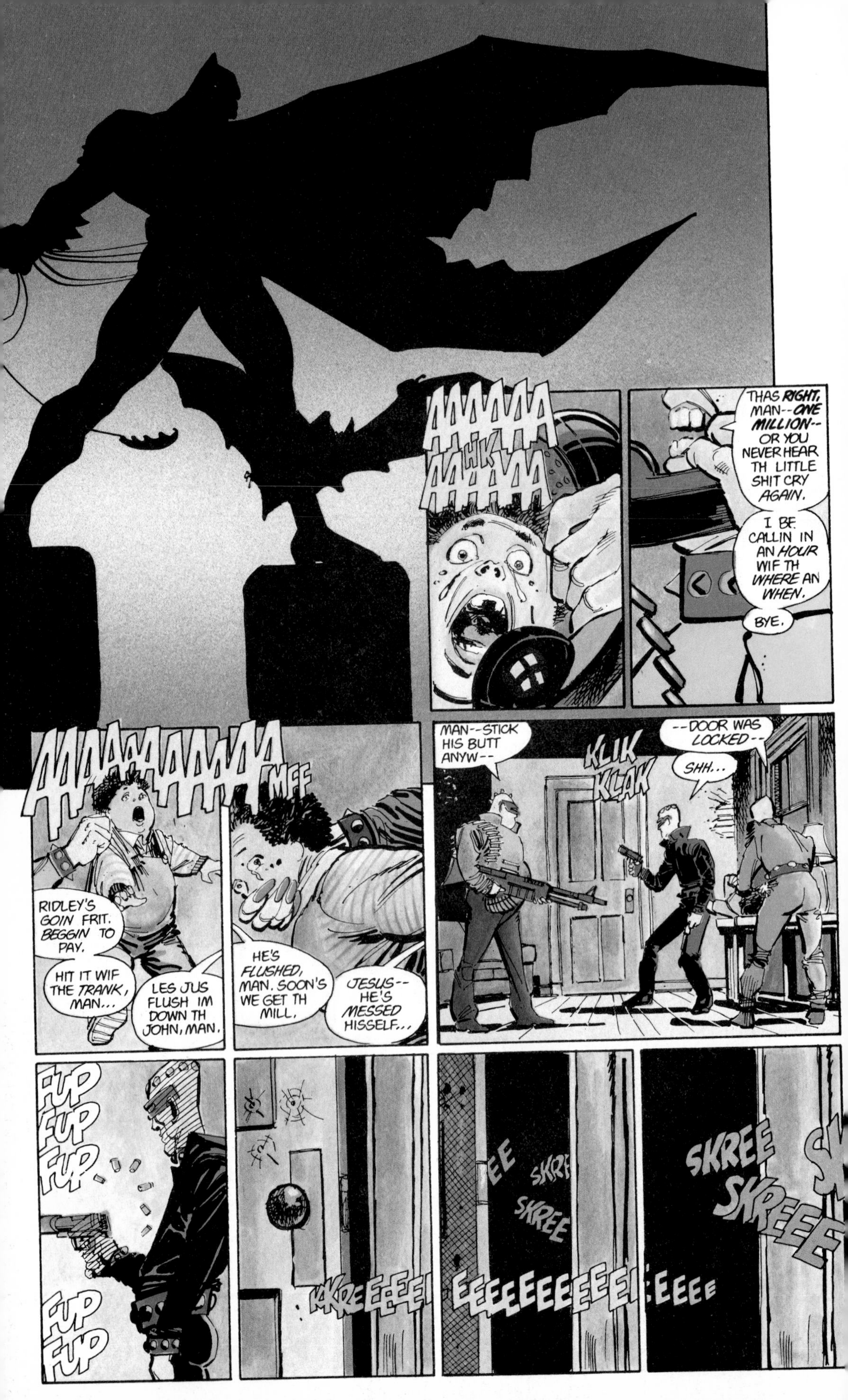
AAAAAA HK AAAAAA
THAS RIGHT, MAN--ONE MILLION--OR YOU NEVER HEAR TH LITTLE SHIT CRY AGAIN.
I BE CALLIN IN AN HOUR WIF TH WHERE AN WHEN.
BYE.
AAAAAAAAAAAA MFF
RIDLEY'S GOIN FRIT. BEGGIN TO PAY.
HIT IT WIF THE TRANK, MAN...
LES JUS FLUSH IM DOWN TH JOHN, MAN.
HE'S FLUSHED, MAN. SOON'S WE GET TH MILL.
JESUS--HE'S MESSED HISSELF...
MAN--STICK HIS BUTT ANYW--
KLIK KLAK
--DOOR WAS LOCKED--
SHH...
FUP FUP FUP
FUP FUP
KKREEEEEEEEEEEEEEEEEEEEEEE
EE SKREE SKREE
SKREE SKREE SKREEE

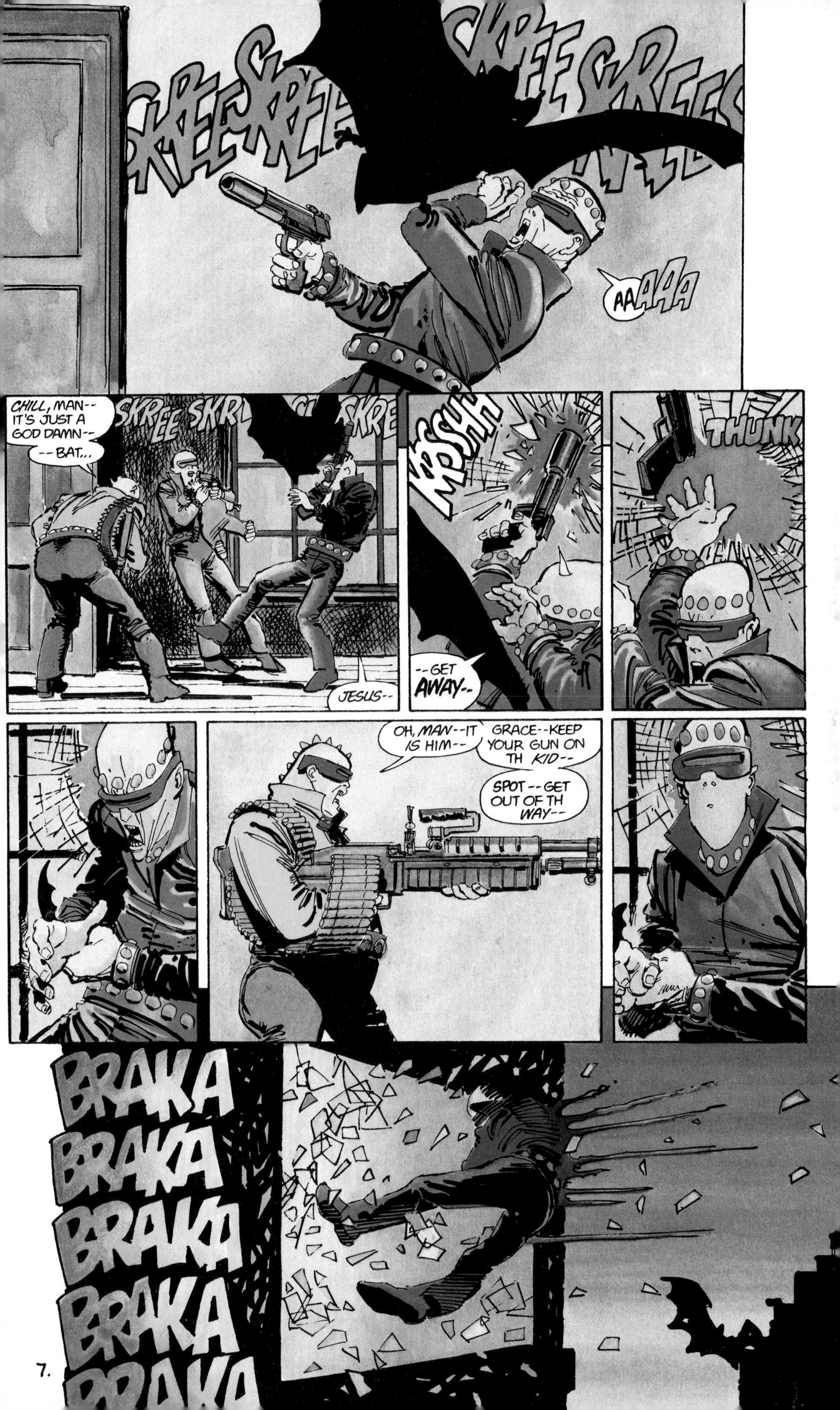
SKREE SKREE SKREE SKREE SKREE
AAAAAA
CHILL, MAN-- IT'S JUST A GOD DAMN--
--BAT...
SKREE SKRE SKRE
JESUS--
KSSSH
--GET AWAY--
THUNK
OH, MAN--IT IS HIM--
GRACE--KEEP YOUR GUN ON TH KID--
SPOT--GET OUT OF TH WAY--
BRAKA
BRAKA
BRAKA
BRAKA

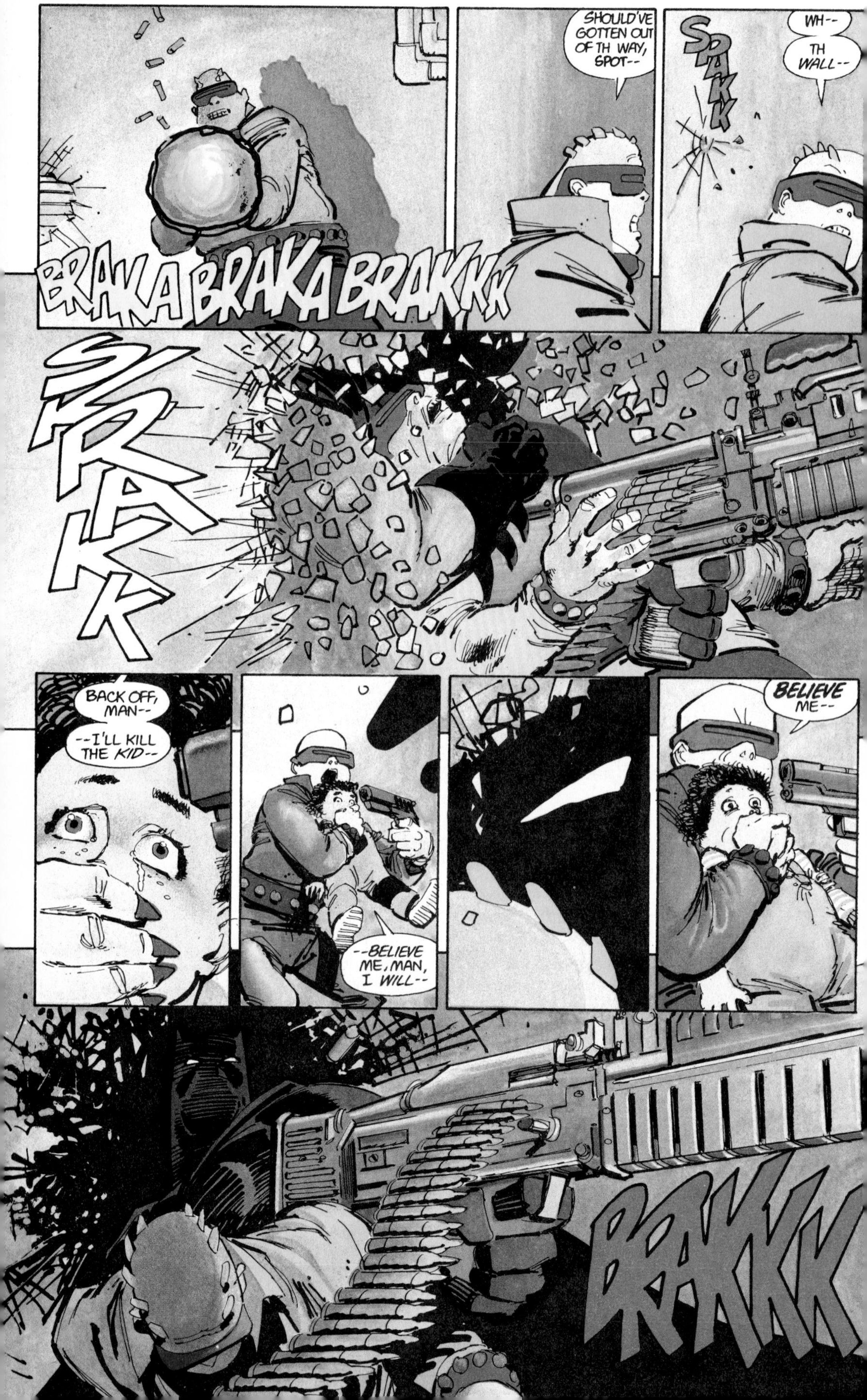
BRAKA BRAKA BRAKKK
SHOULD'VE GOTTEN OUT OF TH WAY, SPOT--
SPAKK
WH--
TH WALL--
SPRAKK
BACK OFF, MAN--
--I'LL KILL THE KID--
--BELIEVE ME, MAN, I WILL--
BELIEVE ME--
BRAKKK

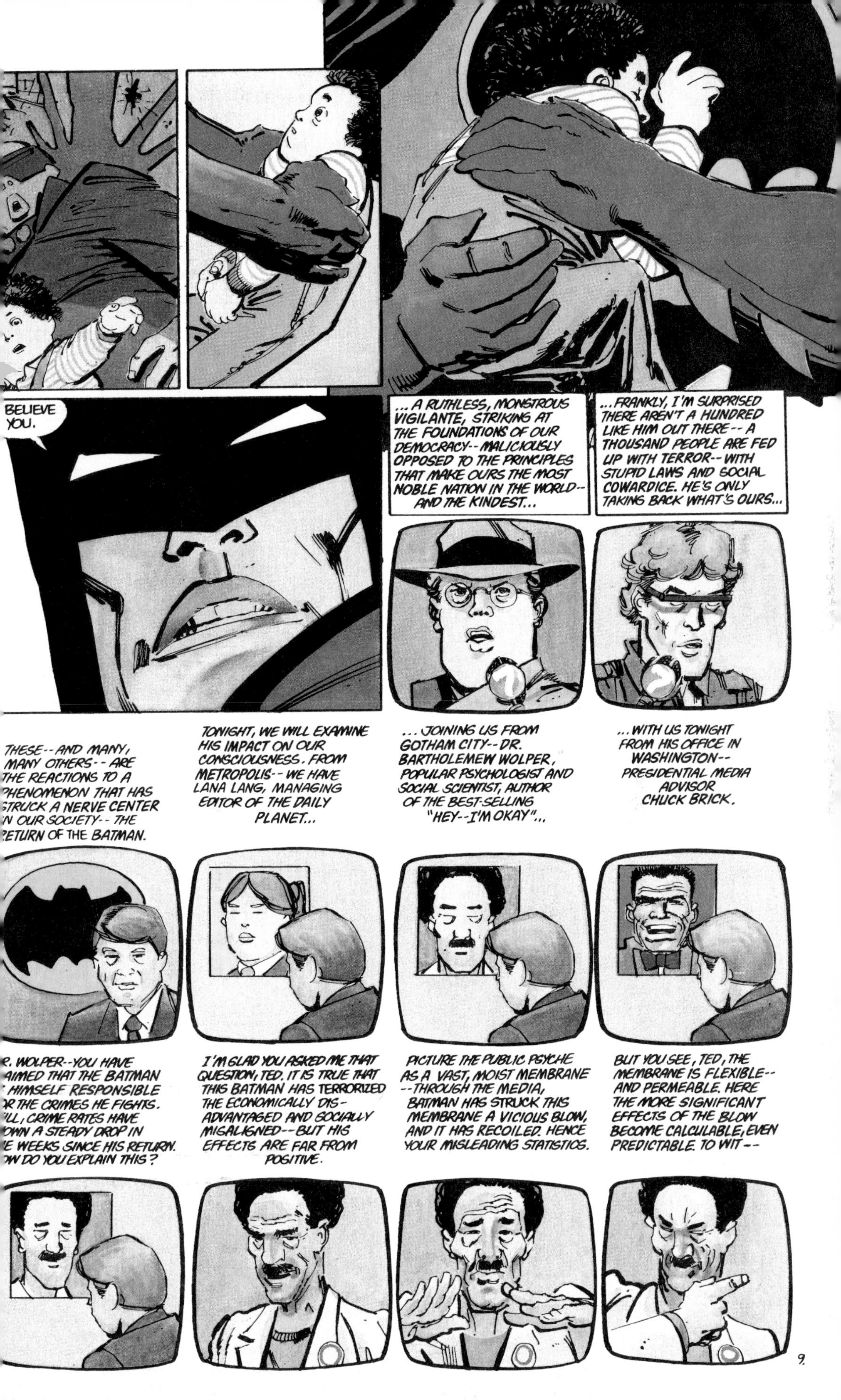

BELIEVE YOU.
... A RUTHLESS, MONSTROUS VIGILANTE, STRIKING AT THE FOUNDATIONS OF OUR DEMOCRACY-- MALICIOUSLY OPPOSED TO THE PRINCIPLES THAT MAKE OURS THE MOST NOBLE NATION IN THE WORLD-- AND THE KINDEST...
... FRANKLY, I'M SURPRISED THERE AREN'T A HUNDRED LIKE HIM OUT THERE-- A THOUSAND PEOPLE ARE FED UP WITH TERROR-- WITH STUPID LAWS AND SOCIAL COWARDICE. HE'S ONLY TAKING BACK WHAT'S OURS...
THESE-- AND MANY, MANY OTHERS-- ARE THE REACTIONS TO A PHENOMENON THAT HAS STRUCK A NERVE CENTER IN OUR SOCIETY-- THE RETURN OF THE BATMAN.
TONIGHT, WE WILL EXAMINE HIS IMPACT ON OUR CONSCIOUSNESS. FROM METROPOLIS-- WE HAVE LANA LANG, MANAGING EDITOR OF THE DAILY PLANET...
... JOINING US FROM GOTHAM CITY-- DR. BARTHOLEMEW WOLPER, POPULAR PSYCHOLOGIST AND SOCIAL SCIENTIST, AUTHOR OF THE BEST-SELLING "HEY--I'M OKAY"...
... WITH US TONIGHT FROM HIS OFFICE IN WASHINGTON-- PRESIDENTIAL MEDIA ADVISOR CHUCK BRICK.
R. WOLPER--YOU HAVE AIMED THAT THE BATMAN HIMSELF RESPONSIBLE OR THE CRIMES HE FIGHTS. ILL, CRIME RATES HAVE OWN A STEADY DROP IN E WEEKS SINCE HIS RETURN. OW DO YOU EXPLAIN THIS?
I'M GLAD YOU ASKED ME THAT QUESTION, TED. IT IS TRUE THAT THIS BATMAN HAS TERRORIZED THE ECONOMICALLY DIS-ADVANTAGED AND SOCIALLY MISALIGNED-- BUT HIS EFFECTS ARE FAR FROM POSITIVE.
PICTURE THE PUBLIC PSYCHE AS A VAST, MOIST MEMBRANE --THROUGH THE MEDIA, BATMAN HAS STRUCK THIS MEMBRANE A VICIOUS BLOW, AND IT HAS RECOILED. HENCE YOUR MISLEADING STATISTICS.
BUT YOU SEE, TED, THE MEMBRANE IS FLEXIBLE-- AND PERMEABLE. HERE THE MORE SIGNIFICANT EFFECTS OF THE BLOW BECOME CALCULABLE, EVEN PREDICTABLE. TO WIT--

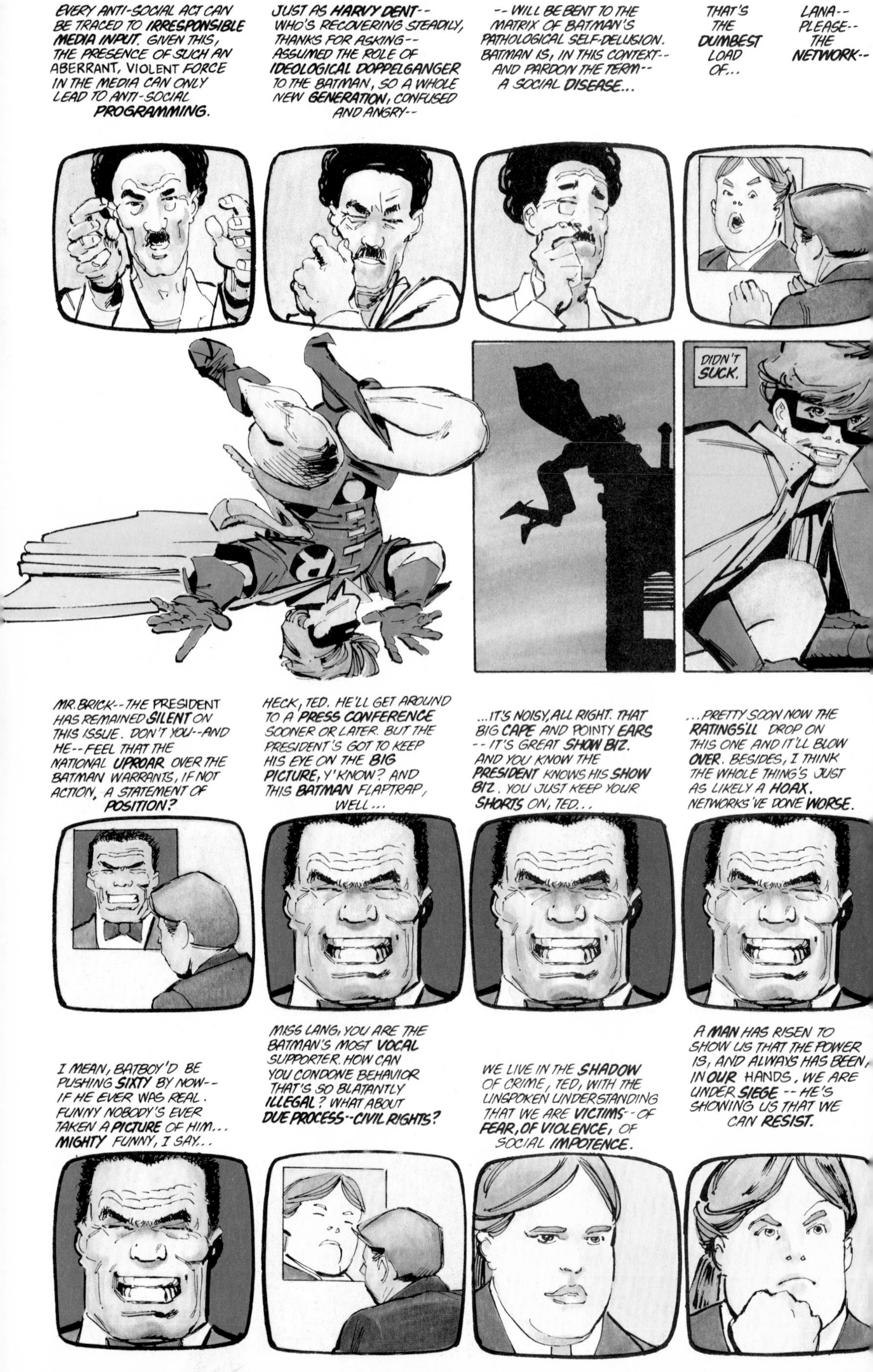
EVERY ANTI-SOCIAL ACT CAN BE TRACED TO IRRESPONSIBLE MEDIA INPUT. GIVEN THIS, THE PRESENCE OF SUCH AN ABERRANT, VIOLENT FORCE IN THE MEDIA CAN ONLY LEAD TO ANTI-SOCIAL PROGRAMMING.
JUST AS HARVY DENT-- WHO'S RECOVERING STEADILY, THANKS FOR ASKING-- ASSUMED THE ROLE OF IDEOLOGICAL DOPPELGANGER TO THE BATMAN, SO A WHOLE NEW GENERATION, CONFUSED AND ANGRY--
--WILL BE BENT TO THE MATRIX OF BATMAN'S PATHOLOGICAL SELF-DELUSION. BATMAN IS, IN THIS CONTEXT-- AND PARDON THE TERM-- A SOCIAL DISEASE...
THAT'S THE DUMBEST LOAD OF...
LANA-- PLEASE-- THE NETWORK--
DIDN'T SUCK.
MR. BRICK--THE PRESIDENT HAS REMAINED SILENT ON THIS ISSUE. DON'T YOU--AND HE--FEEL THAT THE NATIONAL UPROAR OVER THE BATMAN WARRANTS, IF NOT ACTION, A STATEMENT OF POSITION?
HECK, TED. HE'LL GET AROUND TO A PRESS CONFERENCE SOONER OR LATER. BUT THE PRESIDENT'S GOT TO KEEP HIS EYE ON THE BIG PICTURE, Y'KNOW? AND THIS BATMAN FLAPTRAP, WELL...
...IT'S NOISY, ALL RIGHT. THAT BIG CAPE AND POINTY EARS -- IT'S GREAT SHOW BIZ. AND YOU KNOW THE PRESIDENT KNOWS HIS SHOW BIZ. YOU JUST KEEP YOUR SHORTS ON, TED...
...PRETTY SOON NOW THE RATINGS'LL DROP ON THIS ONE AND IT'LL BLOW OVER. BESIDES, I THINK THE WHOLE THING'S JUST AS LIKELY A HOAX. NETWORKS'VE DONE WORSE.
I MEAN, BATBOY'D BE PUSHING SIXTY BY NOW-- IF HE EVER WAS REAL. FUNNY NOBODY'S EVER TAKEN A PICTURE OF HIM... MIGHTY FUNNY, I SAY...
MISS LANG, YOU ARE THE BATMAN'S MOST VOCAL SUPPORTER. HOW CAN YOU CONDONE BEHAVIOR THAT'S SO BLATANTLY ILLEGAL? WHAT ABOUT DUE PROCESS--CIVIL RIGHTS?
WE LIVE IN THE SHADOW OF CRIME, TED, WITH THE UNSPOKEN UNDERSTANDING THAT WE ARE VICTIMS--OF FEAR, OF VIOLENCE, OF SOCIAL IMPOTENCE.
A MAN HAS RISEN TO SHOW US THAT THE POWER IS, AND ALWAYS HAS BEEN, IN OUR HANDS. WE ARE UNDER SIEGE -- HE'S SHOWING US THAT WE CAN RESIST.

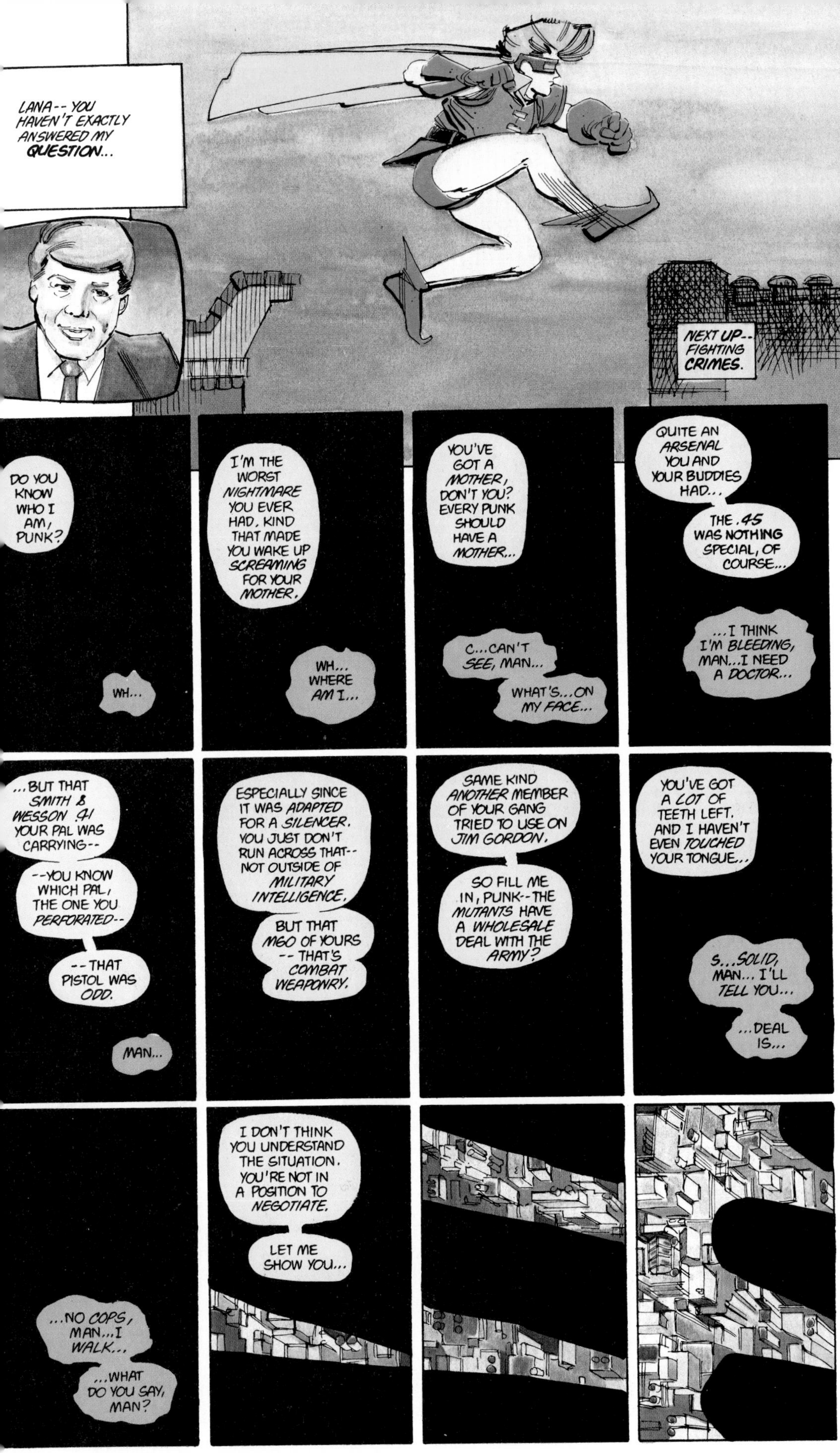

LANA-- YOU HAVEN'T EXACTLY ANSWERED MY QUESTION...
NEXT UP-- FIGHTING CRIMES.
DO YOU KNOW WHO I AM, PUNK?
WH...
I'M THE WORST NIGHTMARE YOU EVER HAD. KIND THAT MADE YOU WAKE UP SCREAMING FOR YOUR MOTHER.
WH... WHERE AM I...
YOU'VE GOT A MOTHER, DON'T YOU? EVERY PUNK SHOULD HAVE A MOTHER...
C...CAN'T SEE, MAN...
WHAT'S...ON MY FACE...
QUITE AN ARSENAL YOU AND YOUR BUDDIES HAD...
THE .45 WAS NOTHING SPECIAL, OF COURSE...
...I THINK I'M BLEEDING, MAN...I NEED A DOCTOR...
...BUT THAT SMITH & WESSON .41 YOUR PAL WAS CARRYING--
--YOU KNOW WHICH PAL, THE ONE YOU PERFORATED--
--THAT PISTOL WAS ODD.
MAN...
ESPECIALLY SINCE IT WAS ADAPTED FOR A SILENCER. YOU JUST DON'T RUN ACROSS THAT-- NOT OUTSIDE OF MILITARY INTELLIGENCE.
BUT THAT M60 OF YOURS -- THAT'S COMBAT WEAPONRY.
SAME KIND ANOTHER MEMBER OF YOUR GANG TRIED TO USE ON JIM GORDON.
SO FILL ME IN, PUNK--THE MUTANTS HAVE A WHOLESALE DEAL WITH THE ARMY?
YOU'VE GOT A LOT OF TEETH LEFT. AND I HAVEN'T EVEN TOUCHED YOUR TONGUE...
S...SOLID, MAN... I'LL TELL YOU...
...DEAL IS...
...NO COPS, MAN...I WALK...
...WHAT DO YOU SAY, MAN?
I DON'T THINK YOU UNDERSTAND THE SITUATION. YOU'RE NOT IN A POSITION TO NEGOTIATE.
LET ME SHOW YOU...

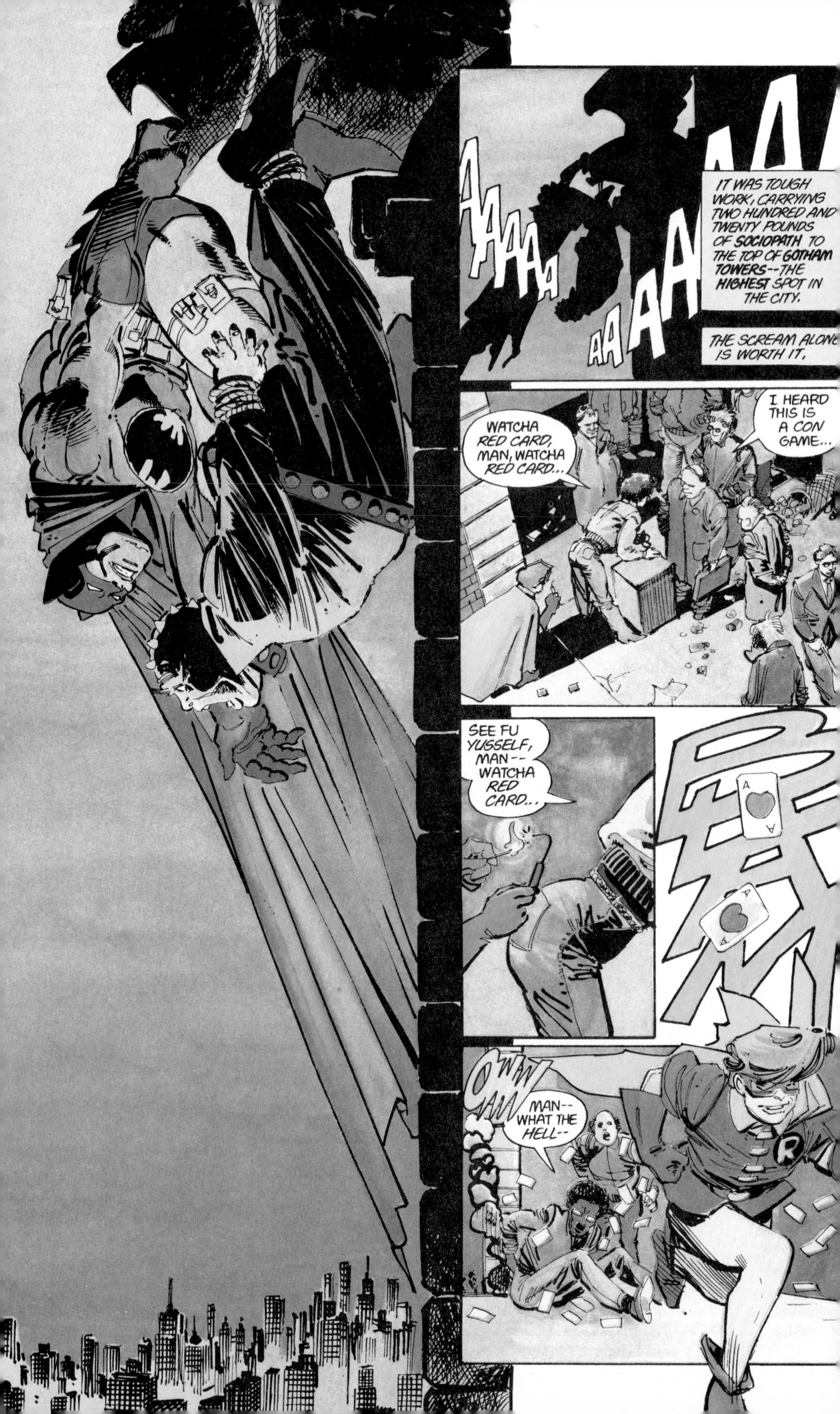
AAAAAAAAAAAAAAAAA
IT WAS TOUGH WORK, CARRYING TWO HUNDRED AND TWENTY POUNDS OF SOCIOPATH TO THE TOP OF GOTHAM TOWERS--THE HIGHEST SPOT IN THE CITY.
THE SCREAM ALONE IS WORTH IT.
WATCHA RED CARD, MAN, WATCHA RED CARD...
I HEARD THIS IS A CON GAME...
SEE FU YUSSELF, MAN-- WATCHA RED CARD...
OWAW
MAN-- WHAT THE HELL--

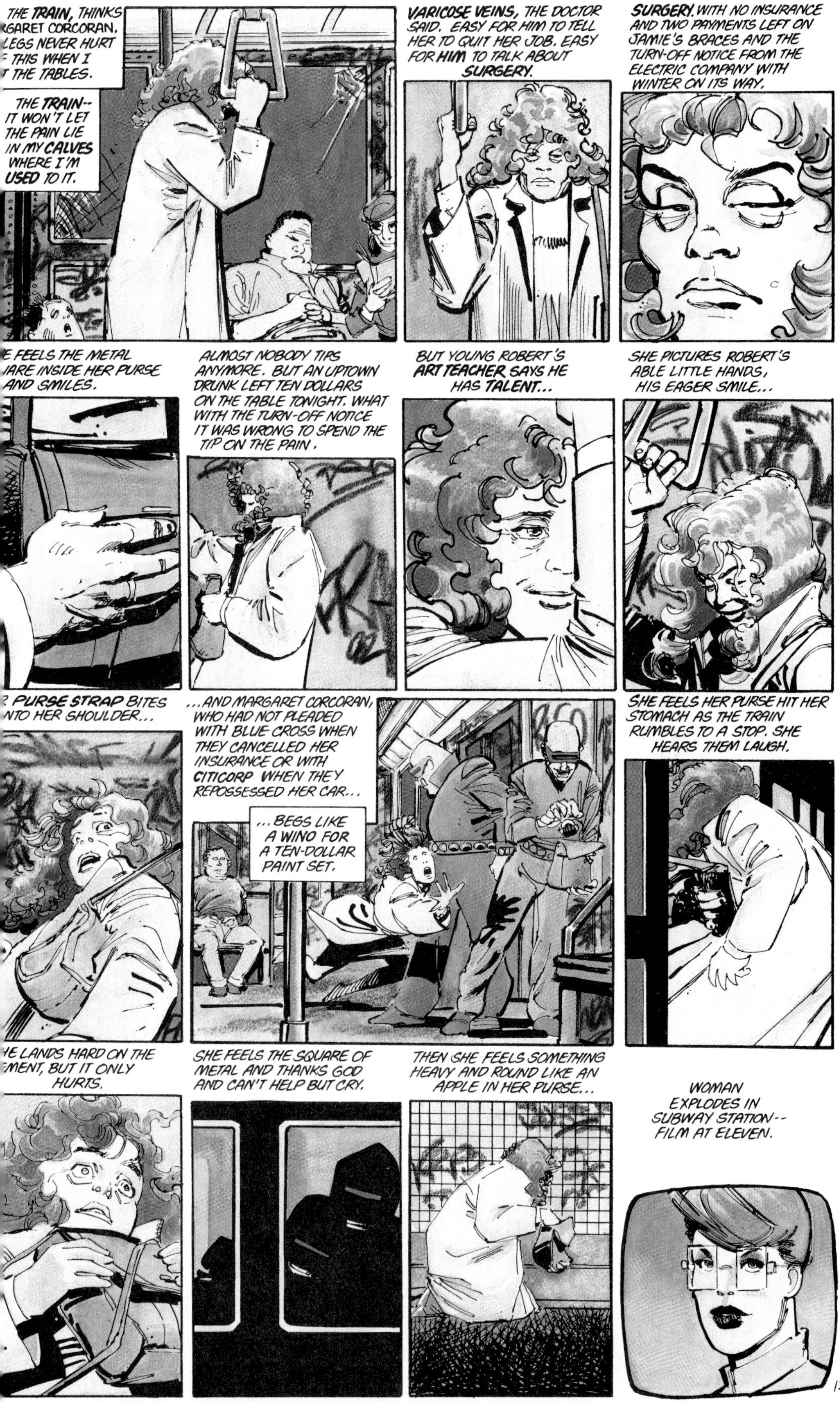

THE TRAIN, THINKS
ARGARET CORCORAN.
LEGS NEVER HURT
THIS WHEN I
THE TABLES.
THE TRAIN-- IT WON'T LET THE PAIN LIE IN MY CALVES WHERE I'M USED TO IT.
VARICOSE VEINS, THE DOCTOR SAID. EASY FOR HIM TO TELL HER TO QUIT HER JOB. EASY FOR HIM TO TALK ABOUT SURGERY.
SURGERY. WITH NO INSURANCE AND TWO PAYMENTS LEFT ON JAMIE'S BRACES AND THE TURN-OFF NOTICE FROM THE ELECTRIC COMPANY WITH WINTER ON ITS WAY.
E FEELS THE METAL
UARE INSIDE HER PURSE
AND SMILES.
ALMOST NOBODY TIPS ANYMORE. BUT AN UPTOWN DRUNK LEFT TEN DOLLARS ON THE TABLE TONIGHT. WHAT WITH THE TURN-OFF NOTICE IT WAS WRONG TO SPEND THE TIP ON THE PAIN.
BUT YOUNG ROBERT'S ART TEACHER SAYS HE HAS TALENT...
SHE PICTURES ROBERT'S ABLE LITTLE HANDS, HIS EAGER SMILE...
PURSE STRAP BITES
NTO HER SHOULDER...
...AND MARGARET CORCORAN, WHO HAD NOT PLEADED WITH BLUE CROSS WHEN THEY CANCELLED HER INSURANCE OR WITH CITICORP WHEN THEY REPOSSESSED HER CAR...
...BEGS LIKE A WINO FOR A TEN-DOLLAR PAINT SET.
SHE FEELS HER PURSE HIT HER STOMACH AS THE TRAIN RUMBLES TO A STOP. SHE HEARS THEM LAUGH.
HE LANDS HARD ON THE
EMENT, BUT IT ONLY
HURTS.
SHE FEELS THE SQUARE OF METAL AND THANKS GOD AND CAN'T HELP BUT CRY.
THEN SHE FEELS SOMETHING HEAVY AND ROUND LIKE AN APPLE IN HER PURSE...
WOMAN EXPLODES IN SUBWAY STATION-- FILM AT ELEVEN.

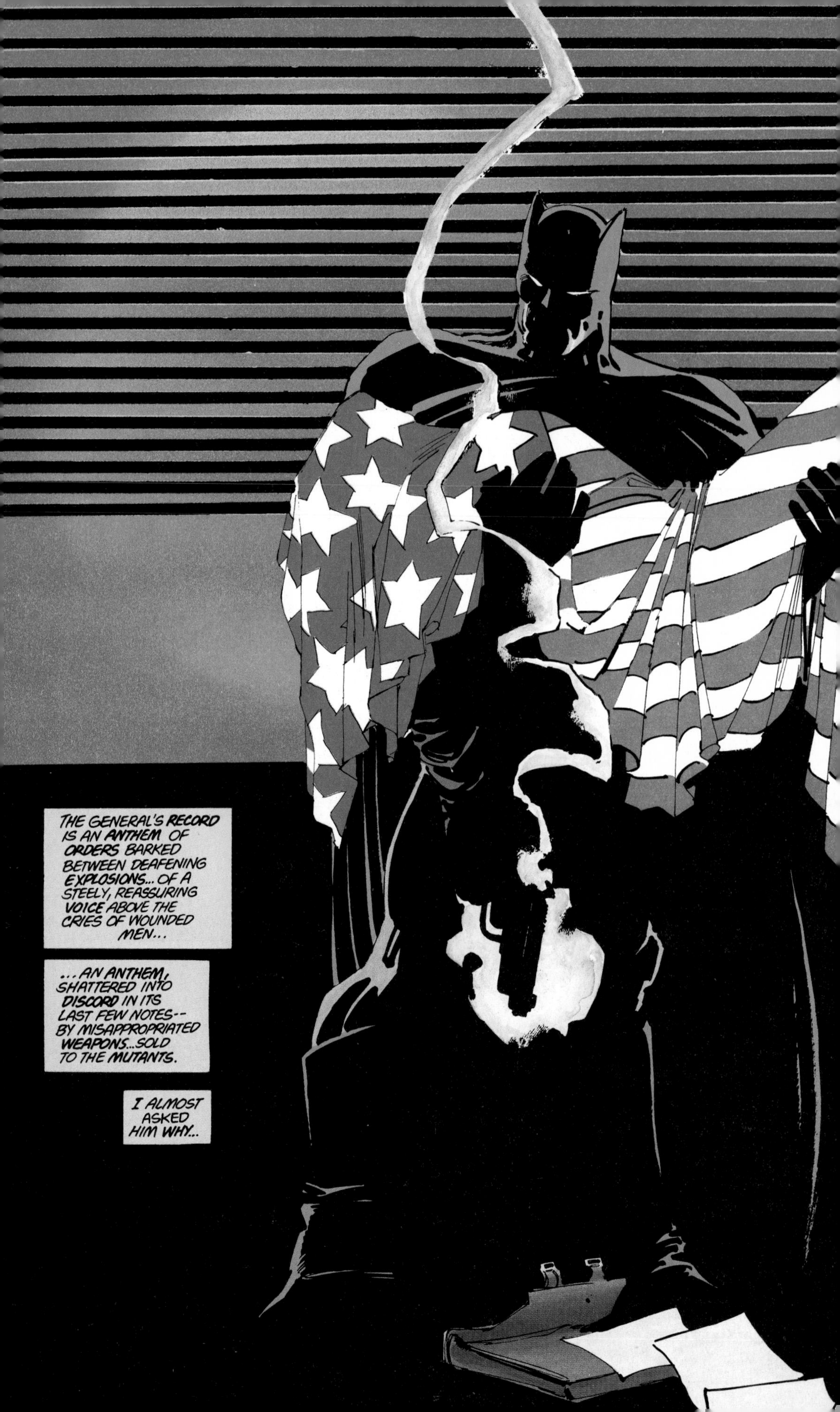
THE GENERAL'S RECORD IS AN ANTHEM OF ORDERS BARKED BETWEEN DEAFENING EXPLOSIONS... OF A STEELY, REASSURING VOICE ABOVE THE CRIES OF WOUNDED MEN...
...AN ANTHEM, SHATTERED INTO DISCORD IN ITS LAST FEW NOTES-- BY MISAPPROPRIATED WEAPONS...SOLD TO THE MUTANTS.
I ALMOST ASKED HIM WHY...

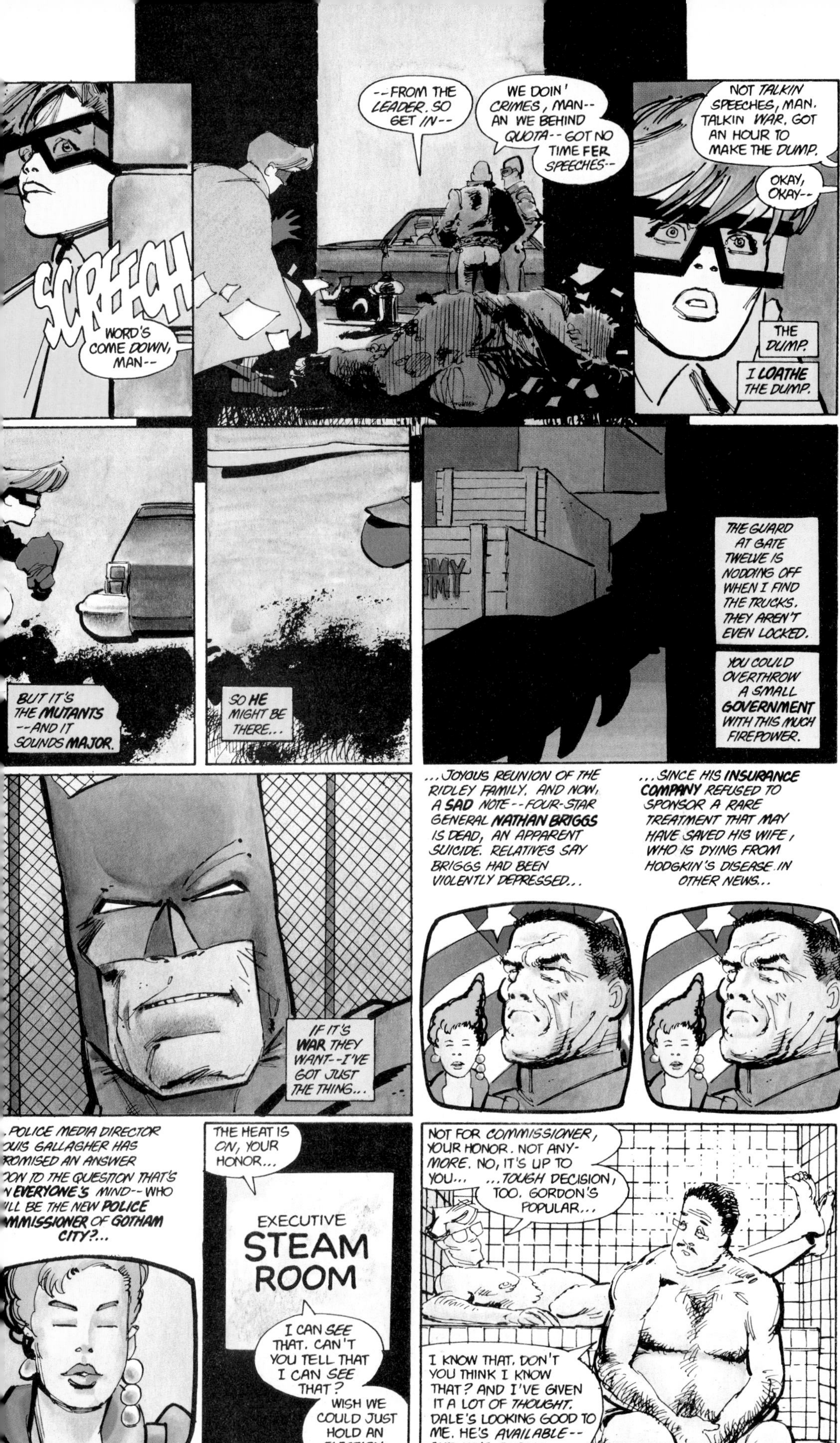
SCREECH
WORD'S COME DOWN, MAN--
--FROM THE LEADER. SO GET IN--
WE DOIN' CRIMES, MAN-- AN WE BEHIND QUOTA-- GOT NO TIME FER SPEECHES--
NOT TALKIN SPEECHES, MAN. TALKIN WAR. GOT AN HOUR TO MAKE THE DUMP.
OKAY, OKAY--
THE DUMP.
I LOATHE THE DUMP.
BUT IT'S THE MUTANTS --AND IT SOUNDS MAJOR.
SO HE MIGHT BE THERE...
THE GUARD AT GATE TWELVE IS NODDING OFF WHEN I FIND THE TRUCKS. THEY AREN'T EVEN LOCKED.
YOU COULD OVERTHROW A SMALL GOVERNMENT WITH THIS MUCH FIREPOWER.
IF IT'S WAR THEY WANT--I'VE GOT JUST THE THING...
...JOYOUS REUNION OF THE RIDLEY FAMILY. AND NOW, A SAD NOTE--FOUR-STAR GENERAL NATHAN BRIGGS IS DEAD, AN APPARENT SUICIDE. RELATIVES SAY BRIGGS HAD BEEN VIOLENTLY DEPRESSED...
...SINCE HIS INSURANCE COMPANY REFUSED TO SPONSOR A RARE TREATMENT THAT MAY HAVE SAVED HIS WIFE, WHO IS DYING FROM HODGKIN'S DISEASE. IN OTHER NEWS...
..POLICE MEDIA DIRECTOR OUIS GALLAGHER HAS ROMISED AN ANSWER OON TO THE QUESTION THAT'S N EVERYONE'S MIND-- WHO ILL BE THE NEW POLICE MMISSIONER OF GOTHAM CITY?...
THE HEAT IS ON, YOUR HONOR...
EXECUTIVE STEAM ROOM
I CAN SEE THAT. CAN'T YOU TELL THAT I CAN SEE THAT?
WISH WE COULD JUST HOLD AN ELECTION...
NOT FOR COMMISSIONER, YOUR HONOR. NOT ANY-MORE. NO, IT'S UP TO YOU... ...TOUGH DECISION, TOO. GORDON'S POPULAR...
I KNOW THAT. DON'T YOU THINK I KNOW THAT? AND I'VE GIVEN IT A LOT OF THOUGHT. DALE'S LOOKING GOOD TO ME. HE'S AVAILABLE-- AND HE'S BLACK...

BLACK'S *PASSÉ*, YOUR HONOR. BESIDES, DALE'S *NEUTRAL* ON THE *BATMAN* THING. AND YOU KNOW WHAT YOUR OWN NEUTRALITY IS *COSTING* YOU...

I'M NOT *NEUTRAL.* WHO SAYS I'M *NEUTRAL?* I'M *CONFLICTED.*

SEEMS TO ME THAT THIS IS YOUR BIG *CHANCE*, YOUR HONOR-- TO SHOW WHAT A *LEADER* YOU ARE-- TO MAKE A BOLD *DECISION* ABOUT BATMAN...

DECISIONS-- YOU'D THINK ALL THERE IS TO RUNNING A CITY IS MAKING *DECISIONS*...

WELL, ALL *RIGHT,* GALLAGHER-- I'LL MAKE A *DECISION.* I'LL *SHOW* THEM WHO'S BOSS. ON MY OWN PRIVATE AUTHORITY-- --I ASSIGN YOU THE TASK OF FINDING ME A POLICE COMMISSIONER.

I ALREADY *HAVE,* SIR.

MASTER BRUCE?

WHO *ELSE,* ALFRED?

OF COURSE, SIR. IT'S JUST THAT THE SIGNAL IS COMING FROM INSIDE THE--

THAT'S *RIGHT,* ALFRED, I'M TAKING HER *OUT.*

I HIT THE *ENGINE.* SHE RESPONDS LIKE IT WAS *YESTERDAY.*

IT *IS* YESTERDAY...

I AM EXCITED--NO, *THRILLED*--CAN'T YOU TELL I'M THRILLED?--TO GIVE YOU THE NEXT *POLICE COMMISSIONER* OF GOTHAM CITY...

...CAPTAIN ELLEN YINDEL.

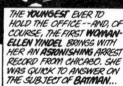

THE *YOUNGEST* EVER TO HOLD THE OFFICE--AND, OF COURSE, THE FIRST *WOMAN*-- ELLEN YINDEL BRINGS WITH HER AN *ASTONISHING* ARREST RECORD FROM CHICAGO. SHE WAS QUICK TO ANSWER ON THE SUBJECT OF *BATMAN*...

I'M SURPRISED THERE *IS* A CONTROVERSY. HIS ACTIONS ARE CATEGORICALLY *CRIMINAL.* I WILL HAVE HIM BROUGHT TO TRIAL. EXCUSE ME?...

...YES. I'LL BE SPECIFIC. MY FIRST ACT AS *POLICE COMMISSIONER* WILL BE TO ISSUE AN *ARREST WARRANT* FOR THE BATMAN ON CHARGES OF *ASSAULT,* *BREAKING AND ENTERING,* *CREATING A PUBLIC HAZARD*...

LITTLE MORE THAN *HALF* THE AGE OF THE MAN SHE'S *REPLACING*, ELLEN YINDEL IS--

A WOMAN. CHRIST ALMIGHTY...

KLIK

DID YOU SAY SOMETHING, JIM?

...NOTHING, SWEETHEART...

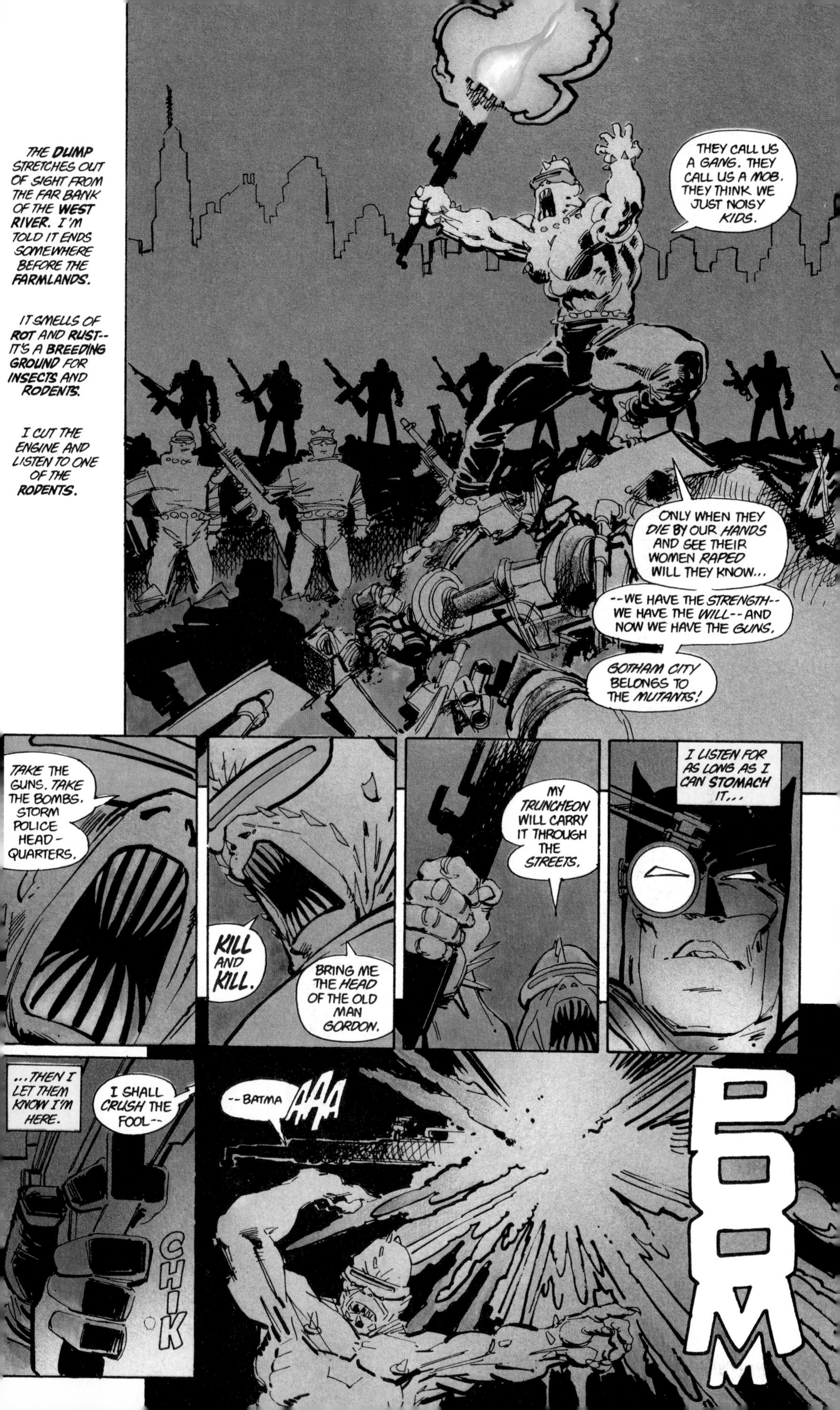
THE DUMP STRETCHES OUT OF SIGHT FROM THE FAR BANK OF THE WEST RIVER. I'M TOLD IT ENDS SOMEWHERE BEFORE THE FARMLANDS.
IT SMELLS OF ROT AND RUST-- IT'S A BREEDING GROUND FOR INSECTS AND RODENTS.
I CUT THE ENGINE AND LISTEN TO ONE OF THE RODENTS.
THEY CALL US A GANG. THEY CALL US A MOB. THEY THINK WE JUST NOISY KIDS.
ONLY WHEN THEY DIE BY OUR HANDS AND SEE THEIR WOMEN RAPED WILL THEY KNOW...
--WE HAVE THE STRENGTH-- WE HAVE THE WILL--AND NOW WE HAVE THE GUNS.
GOTHAM CITY BELONGS TO THE MUTANTS!
TAKE THE GUNS. TAKE THE BOMBS. STORM POLICE HEAD-QUARTERS.
KILL AND KILL.
BRING ME THE HEAD OF THE OLD MAN GORDON.
MY TRUNCHEON WILL CARRY IT THROUGH THE STREETS.
I LISTEN FOR AS LONG AS I CAN STOMACH IT...
...THEN I LET THEM KNOW I'M HERE.
I SHALL CRUSH THE FOOL--
CHIK
--BATMAAAA
BOOOM

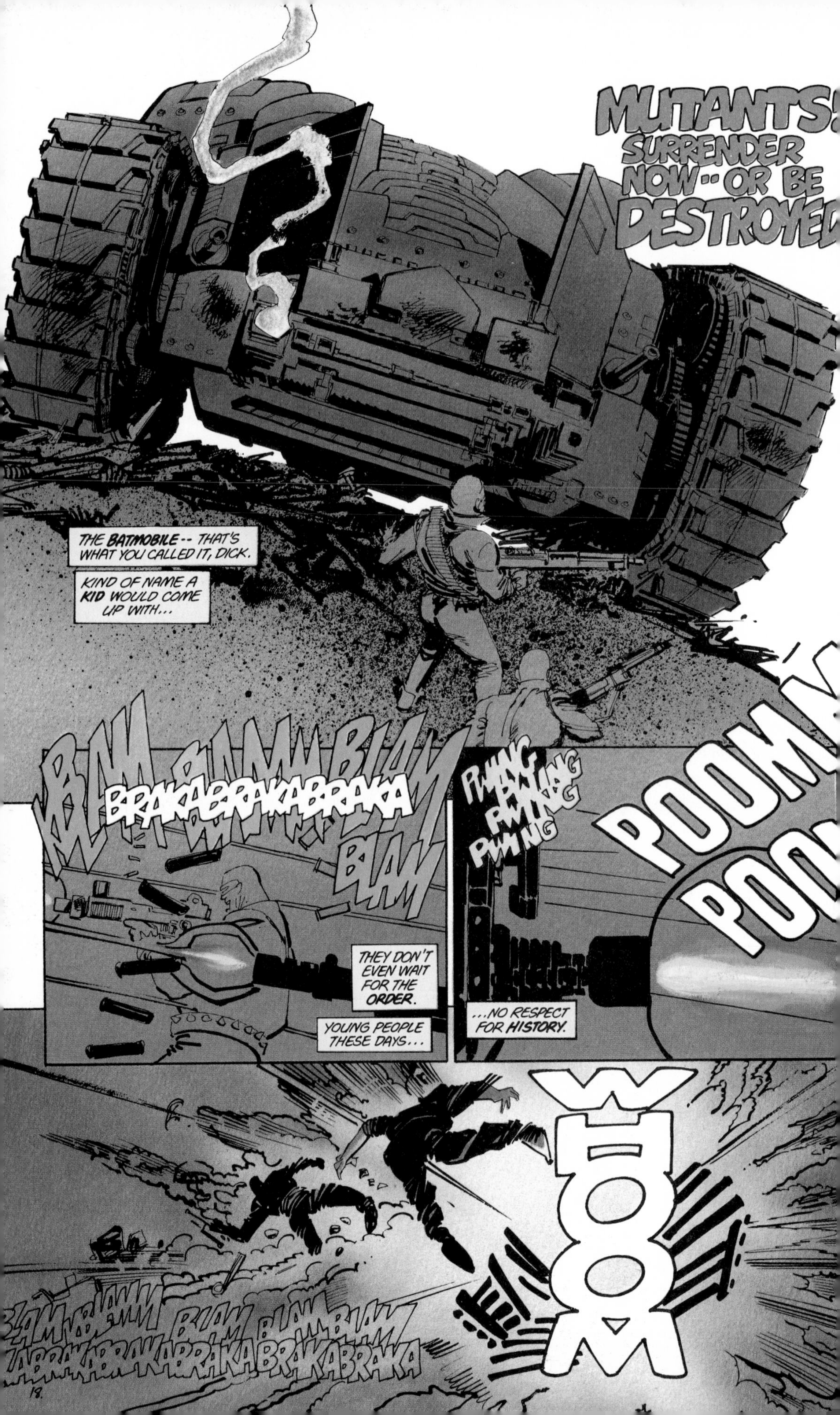

MUTANTS! SURRENDER NOW-- OR BE DESTROYED
THE BATMOBILE-- THAT'S WHAT YOU CALLED IT, DICK.
KIND OF NAME A KID WOULD COME UP WITH...
BLAM BLAM BLAM BLAM
BRAKABRAKABRAKA
THEY DON'T EVEN WAIT FOR THE ORDER.
YOUNG PEOPLE THESE DAYS...
PWING PWING PWING PWING
POOM POOM
...NO RESPECT FOR HISTORY.
WHOOM
BLAM BLAM BLAM BLAM BLAM
BRAKABRAKABRAKABRAKABRAKA

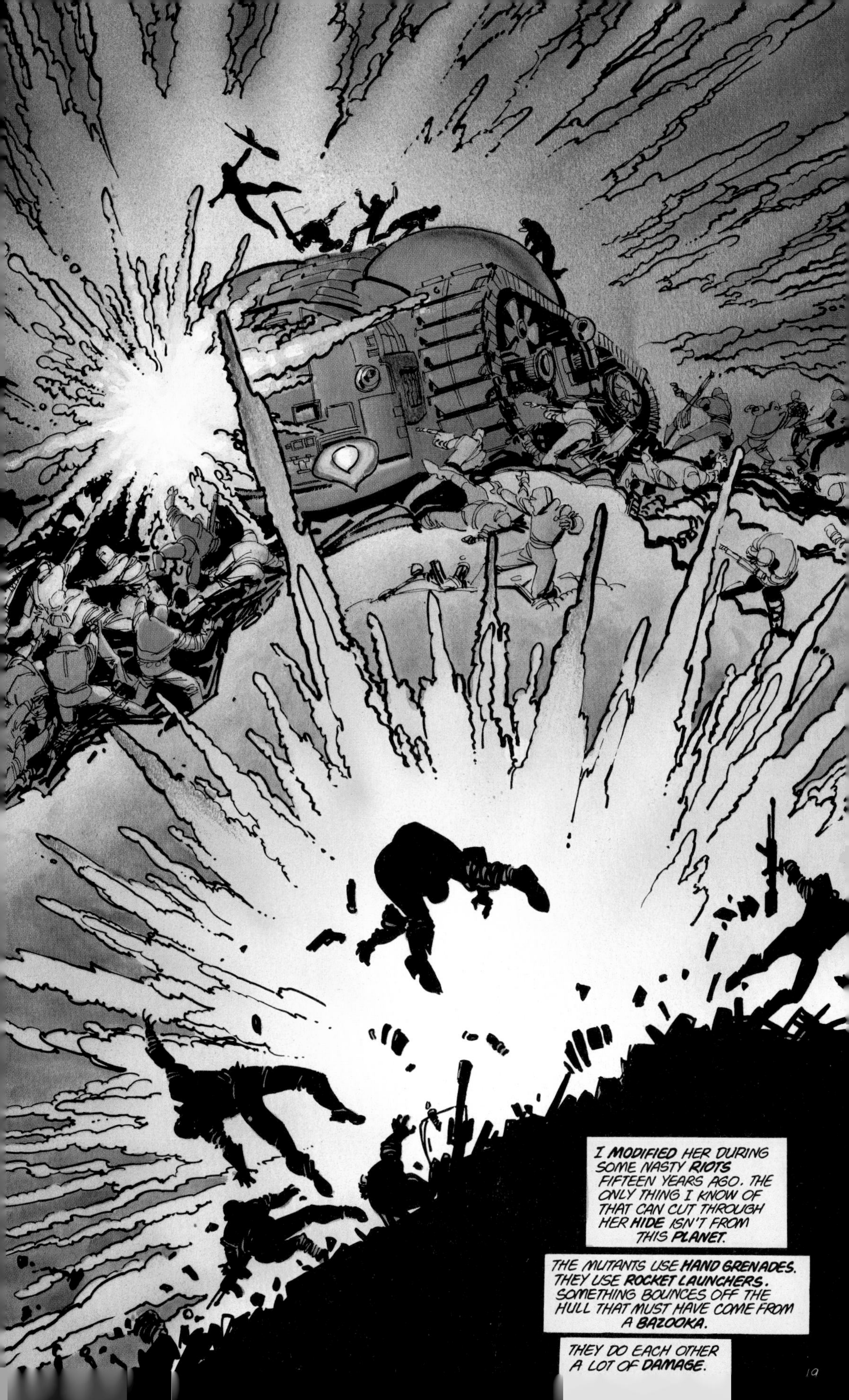
I MODIFIED HER DURING SOME NASTY RIOTS FIFTEEN YEARS AGO. THE ONLY THING I KNOW OF THAT CAN CUT THROUGH HER HIDE ISN'T FROM THIS PLANET.
THE MUTANTS USE HAND GRENADES. THEY USE ROCKET LAUNCHERS. SOMETHING BOUNCES OFF THE HULL THAT MUST HAVE COME FROM A BAZOOKA.
THEY DO EACH OTHER A LOT OF DAMAGE.

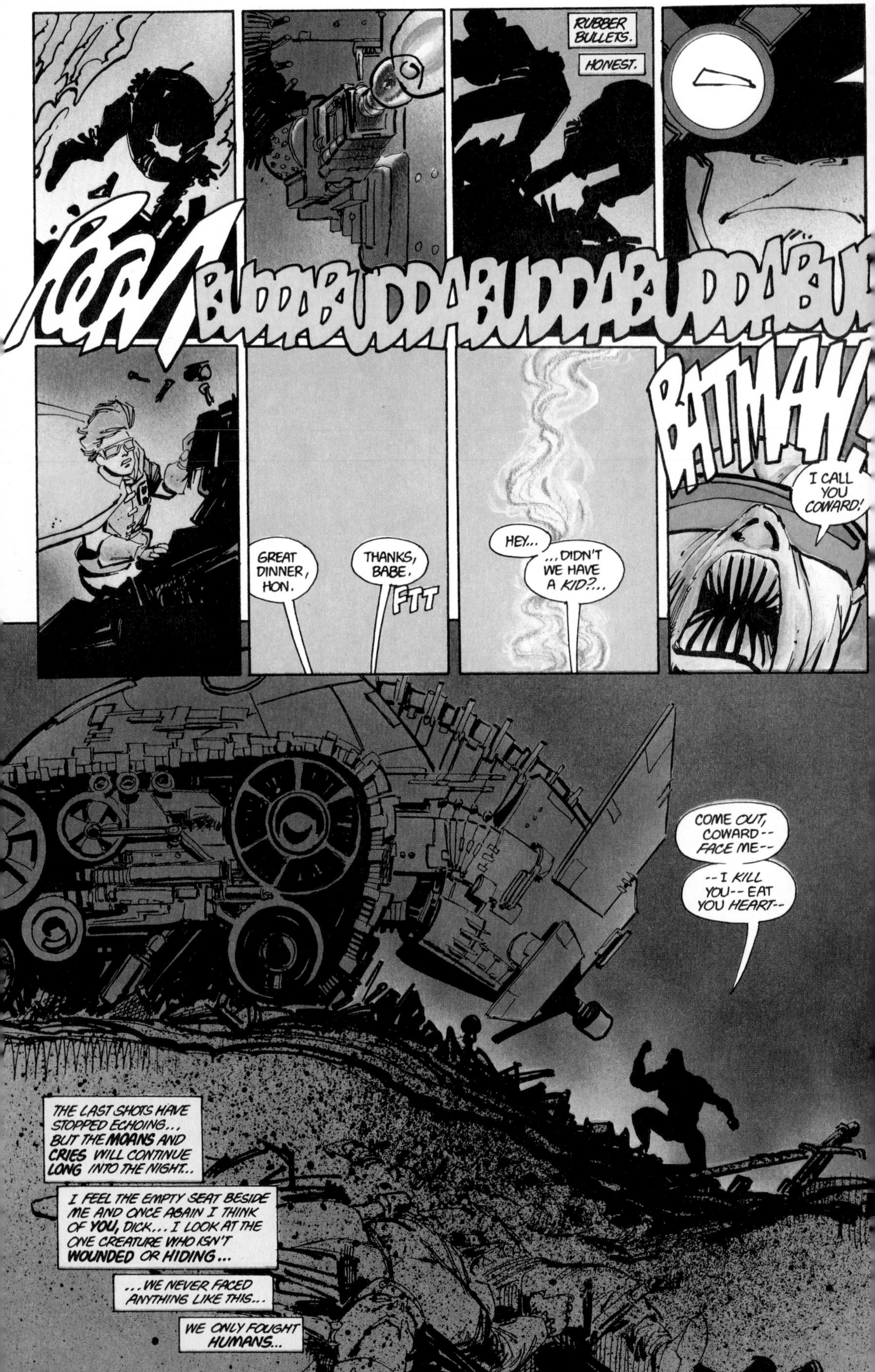

RUBBER BULLETS.
HONEST.
POM
BUDDABUDDABUDDABUDDABUDDABU
GREAT DINNER, HON.
THANKS, BABE.
FTT
HEY...
...DIDN'T WE HAVE A KID?...
BATMAN
I CALL YOU COWARD!
COME OUT, COWARD-- FACE ME--
--I KILL YOU-- EAT YOU HEART--
THE LAST SHOTS HAVE STOPPED ECHOING... BUT THE MOANS AND CRIES WILL CONTINUE LONG INTO THE NIGHT...
I FEEL THE EMPTY SEAT BESIDE ME AND ONCE AGAIN I THINK OF YOU, DICK... I LOOK AT THE ONE CREATURE WHO ISN'T WOUNDED OR HIDING...
...WE NEVER FACED ANYTHING LIKE THIS...
WE ONLY FOUGHT HUMANS...

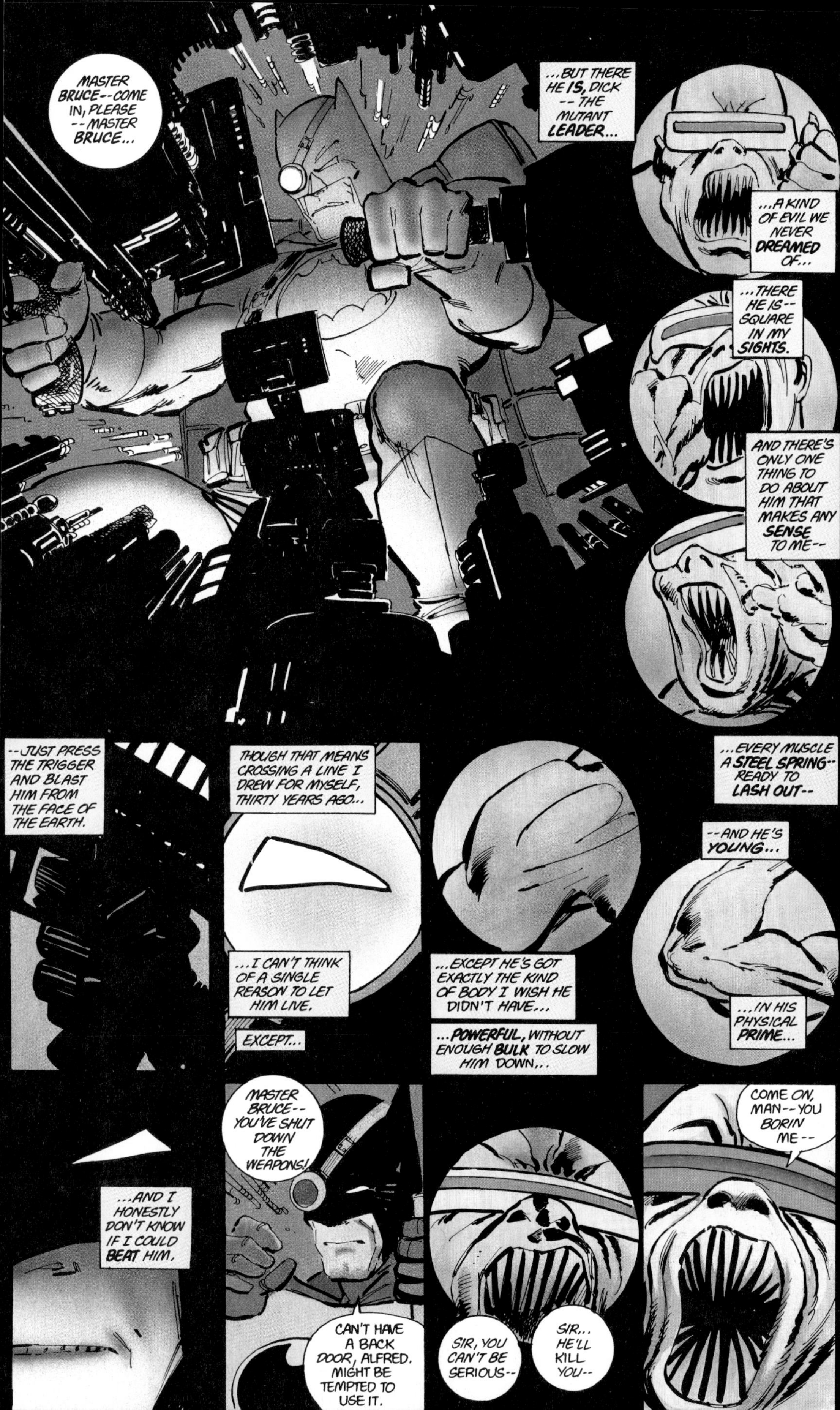

MASTER BRUCE--COME IN, PLEASE --MASTER BRUCE...
...BUT THERE HE IS, DICK -- THE MUTANT LEADER...
...A KIND OF EVIL WE NEVER DREAMED OF...
...THERE HE IS--SQUARE IN MY SIGHTS.
AND THERE'S ONLY ONE THING TO DO ABOUT HIM THAT MAKES ANY SENSE TO ME--
--JUST PRESS THE TRIGGER AND BLAST HIM FROM THE FACE OF THE EARTH.
THOUGH THAT MEANS CROSSING A LINE I DREW FOR MYSELF, THIRTY YEARS AGO...
...I CAN'T THINK OF A SINGLE REASON TO LET HIM LIVE.
EXCEPT...
...EXCEPT HE'S GOT EXACTLY THE KIND OF BODY I WISH HE DIDN'T HAVE...
...POWERFUL, WITHOUT ENOUGH BULK TO SLOW HIM DOWN...
...EVERY MUSCLE A STEEL SPRING-- READY TO LASH OUT--
--AND HE'S YOUNG...
...IN HIS PHYSICAL PRIME...
...AND I HONESTLY DON'T KNOW IF I COULD BEAT HIM.
MASTER BRUCE-- YOU'VE SHUT DOWN THE WEAPONS!
CAN'T HAVE A BACK DOOR, ALFRED. MIGHT BE TEMPTED TO USE IT.
SIR, YOU CAN'T BE SERIOUS--
SIR... HE'LL KILL YOU--
COME ON, MAN--YOU BORIN ME--

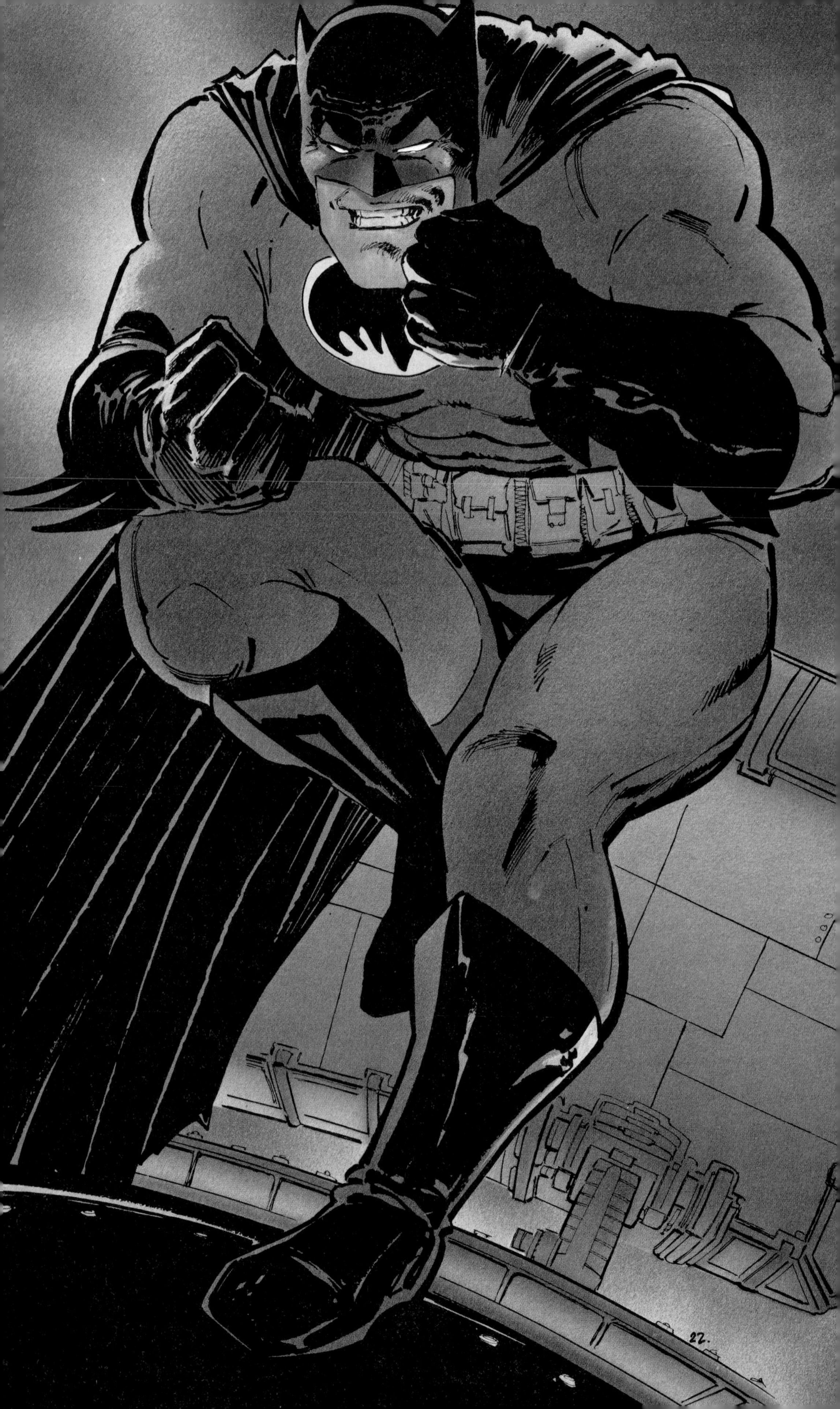
22.

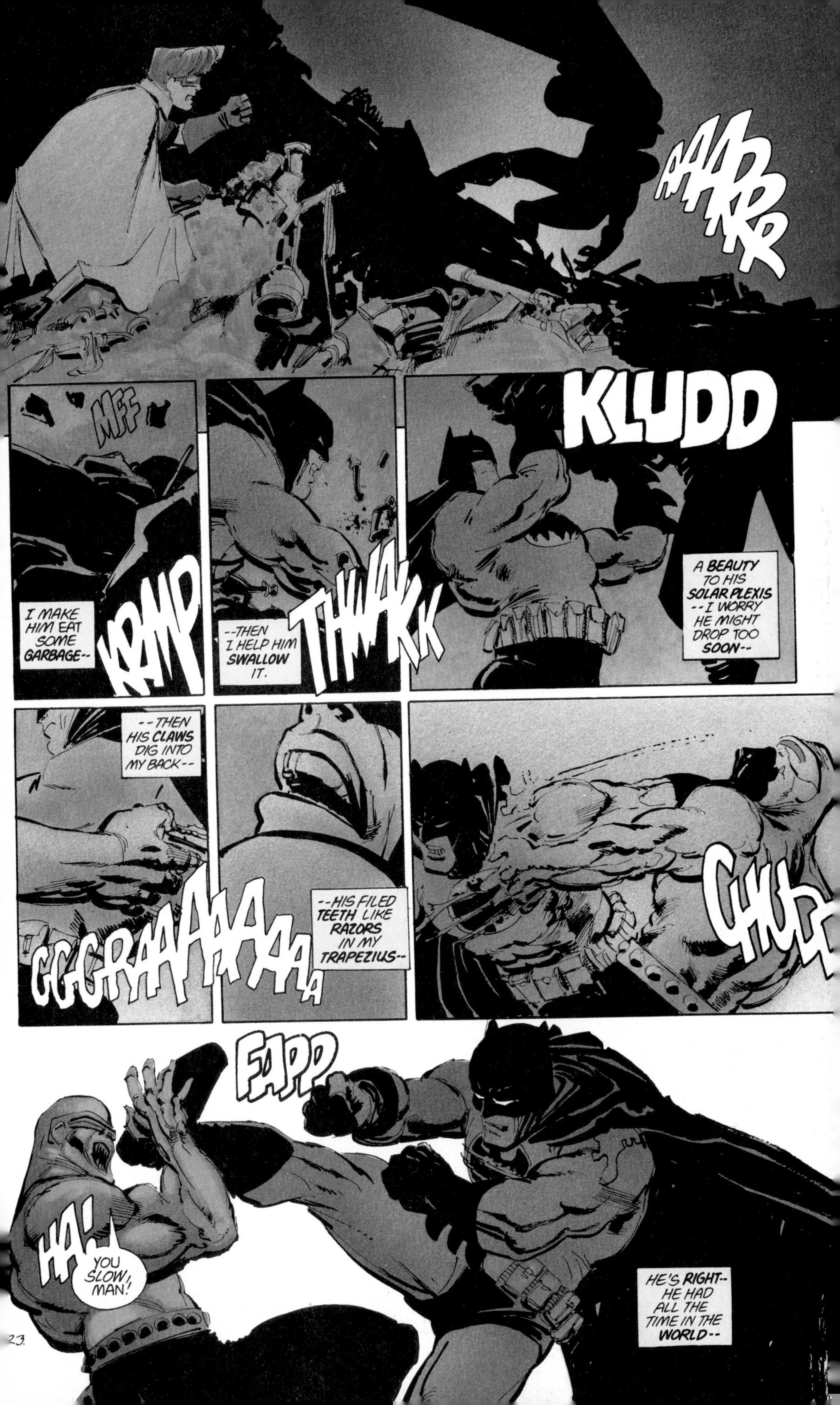
AAAARRRR
MFF
I MAKE HIM EAT SOME GARBAGE--
KRAMP
--THEN I HELP HIM SWALLOW IT.
THWAKK
KLUDD
A BEAUTY TO HIS SOLAR PLEXIS --I WORRY HE MIGHT DROP TOO SOON--
--THEN HIS CLAWS DIG INTO MY BACK--
GGGRAAAAAAAAAA
--HIS FILED TEETH LIKE RAZORS IN MY TRAPEZIUS--
FAPP
HA!
YOU SLOW, MAN!
HE'S RIGHT-- HE HAD ALL THE TIME IN THE WORLD--

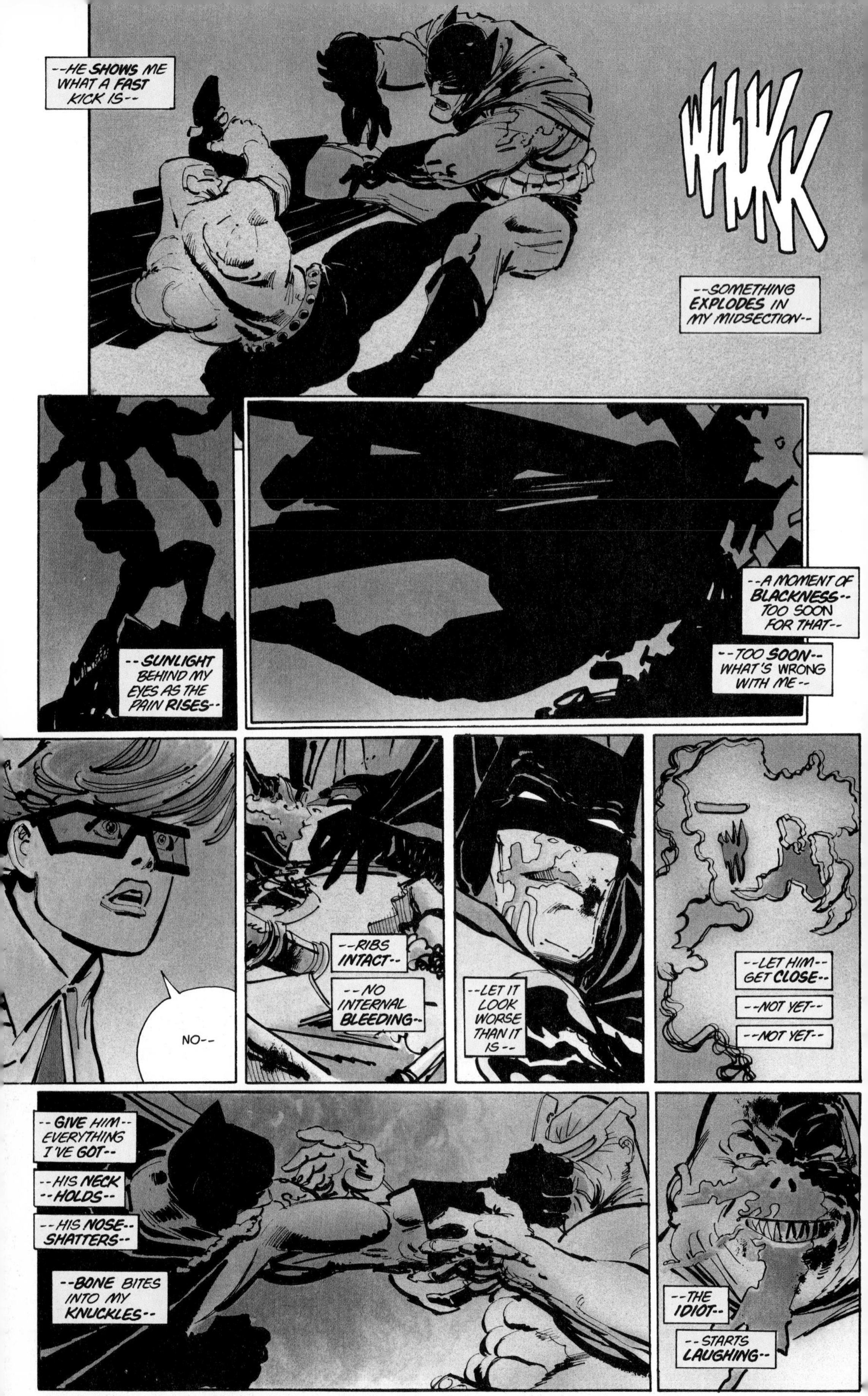

--HE SHOWS ME WHAT A FAST KICK IS--
WHUMK
--SOMETHING EXPLODES IN MY MIDSECTION--
--SUNLIGHT BEHIND MY EYES AS THE PAIN RISES--
--A MOMENT OF BLACKNESS-- TOO SOON FOR THAT--
--TOO SOON-- WHAT'S WRONG WITH ME--
NO--
--RIBS INTACT--
--NO INTERNAL BLEEDING--
--LET IT LOOK WORSE THAN IT IS--
--LET HIM-- GET CLOSE--
--NOT YET--
--NOT YET--
--GIVE HIM-- EVERYTHING I'VE GOT--
--HIS NECK --HOLDS--
--HIS NOSE-- SHATTERS--
--BONE BITES INTO MY KNUCKLES--
--THE IDIOT--
--STARTS LAUGHING--

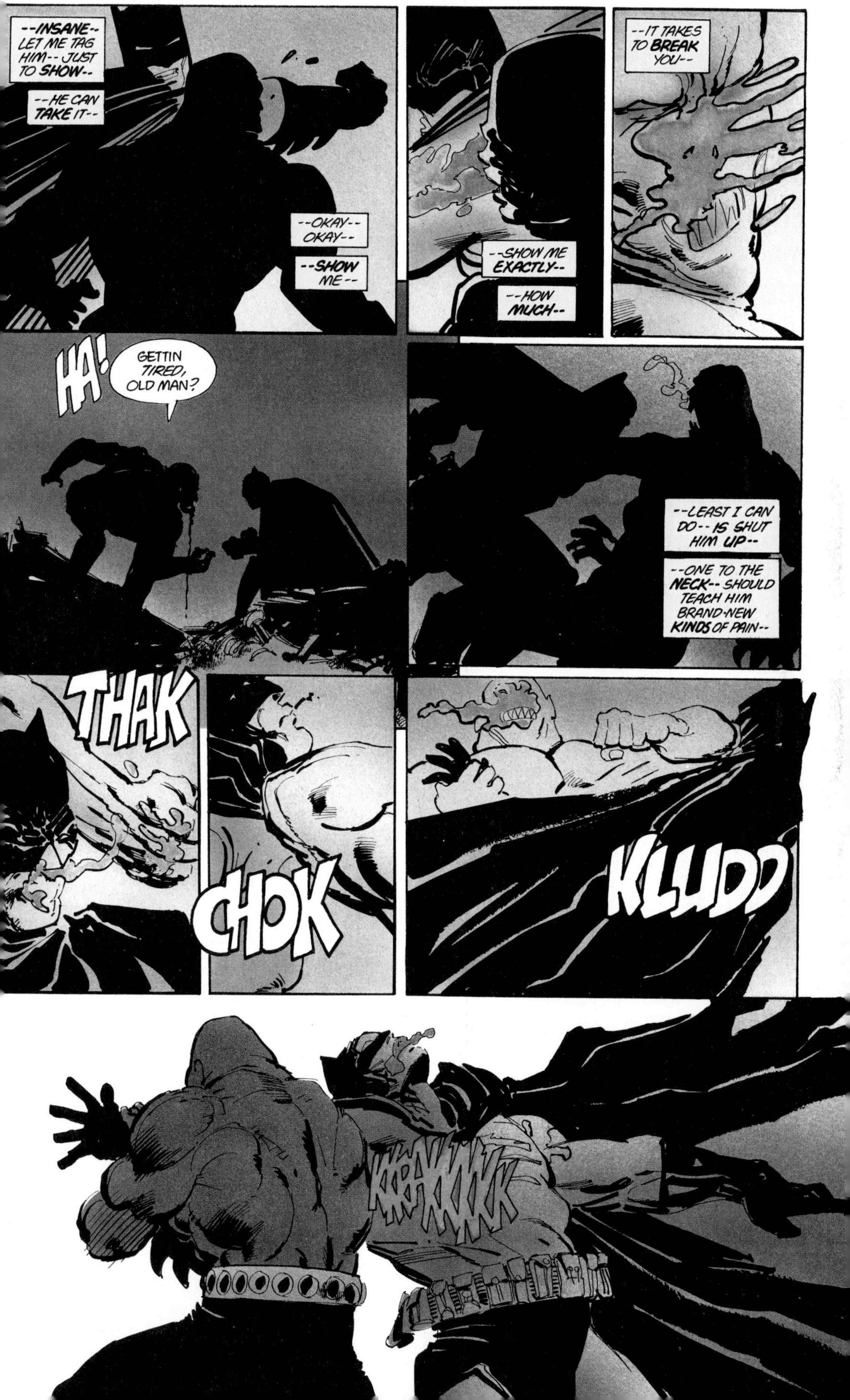
--INSANE-- LET ME TAG HIM-- JUST TO SHOW--
--HE CAN TAKE IT--
--OKAY-- OKAY--
--SHOW ME--
--SHOW ME EXACTLY--
--HOW MUCH--
--IT TAKES TO BREAK YOU--
HA!
GETTIN TIRED, OLD MAN?
--LEAST I CAN DO-- IS SHUT HIM UP--
--ONE TO THE NECK-- SHOULD TEACH HIM BRAND-NEW KINDS OF PAIN--
THAK
CHOK
KLUDD
KKRAKKKKK

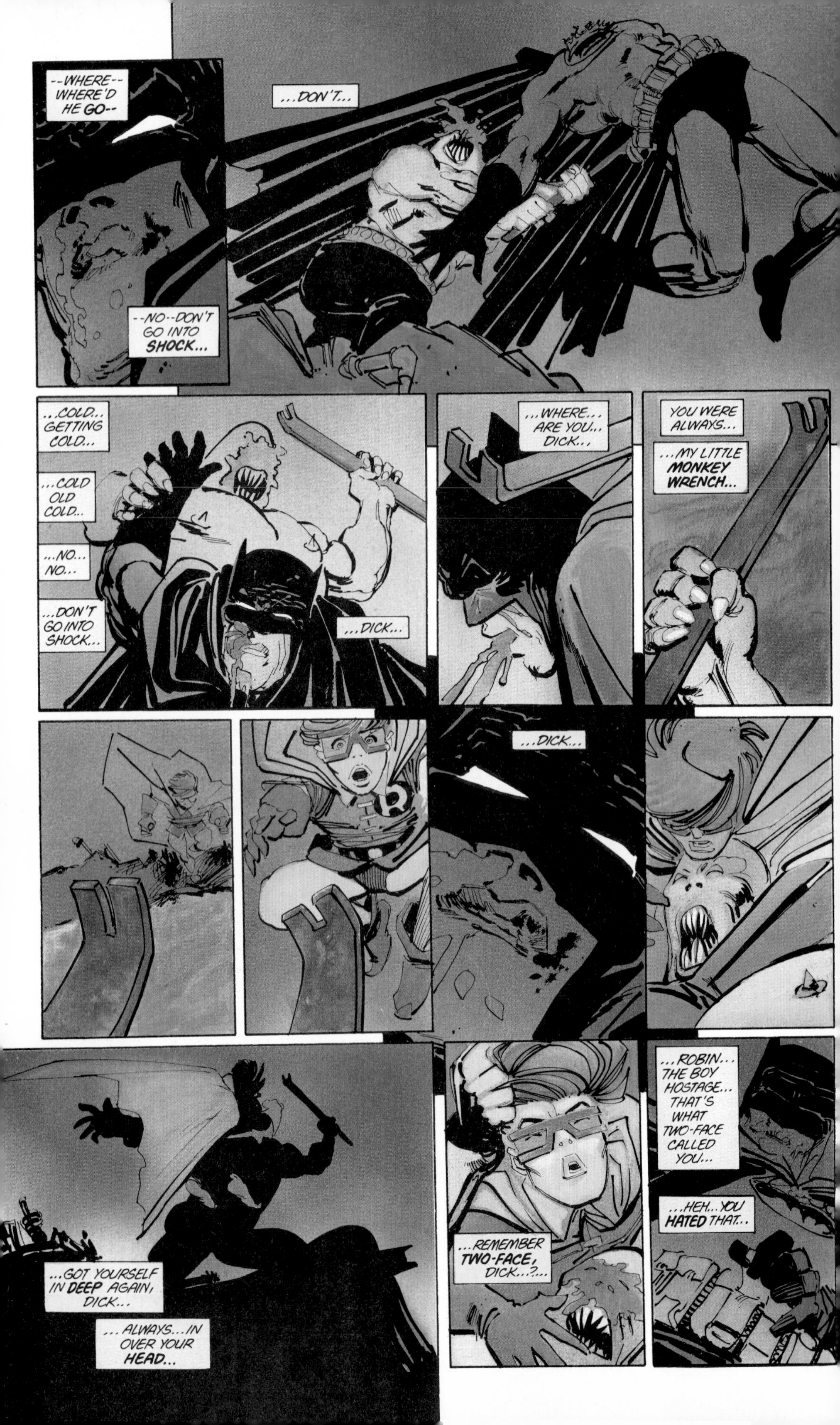
--WHERE--
WHERE'D
HE GO--
...DON'T...
--NO--DON'T
GO INTO
SHOCK...
...COLD...
GETTING
COLD...
...COLD
OLD
COLD...
...NO...
NO...
...DON'T
GO INTO
SHOCK...
...DICK...
...WHERE...
ARE YOU...
DICK...
YOU WERE
ALWAYS...
...MY LITTLE
MONKEY
WRENCH...
...DICK...
...GOT YOURSELF
IN DEEP AGAIN,
DICK...
...ALWAYS...IN
OVER YOUR
HEAD...
...REMEMBER
TWO-FACE,
DICK...?...
...ROBIN...
THE BOY
HOSTAGE...
THAT'S
WHAT
TWO-FACE
CALLED
YOU...
...HEH...YOU
HATED THAT...

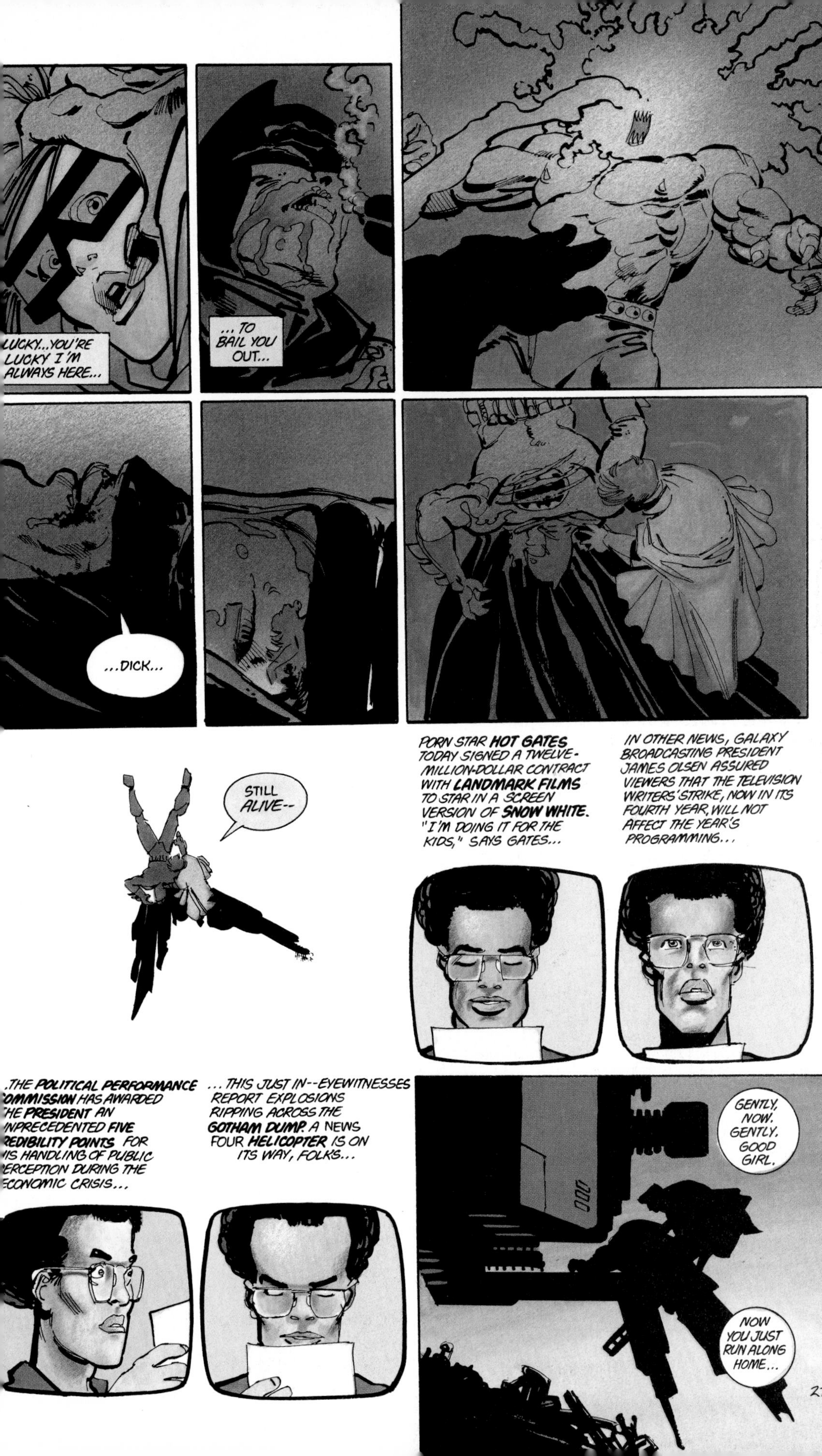
LUCKY...YOU'RE LUCKY I'M ALWAYS HERE...
...TO BAIL YOU OUT...
...DICK...
STILL ALIVE--
PORN STAR HOT GATES TODAY SIGNED A TWELVE-MILLION-DOLLAR CONTRACT WITH LANDMARK FILMS TO STAR IN A SCREEN VERSION OF SNOW WHITE. "I'M DOING IT FOR THE KIDS," SAYS GATES...
IN OTHER NEWS, GALAXY BROADCASTING PRESIDENT JAMES OLSEN ASSURED VIEWERS THAT THE TELEVISION WRITERS' STRIKE, NOW IN ITS FOURTH YEAR, WILL NOT AFFECT THE YEAR'S PROGRAMMING...
.THE POLITICAL PERFORMANCE COMMISSION HAS AWARDED THE PRESIDENT AN UNPRECEDENTED FIVE CREDIBILITY POINTS FOR HIS HANDLING OF PUBLIC PERCEPTION DURING THE ECONOMIC CRISIS...
...THIS JUST IN--EYEWITNESSES REPORT EXPLOSIONS RIPPING ACROSS THE GOTHAM DUMP. A NEWS FOUR HELICOPTER IS ON ITS WAY, FOLKS...
GENTLY, NOW. GENTLY. GOOD GIRL.
NOW YOU JUST RUN ALONG HOME...

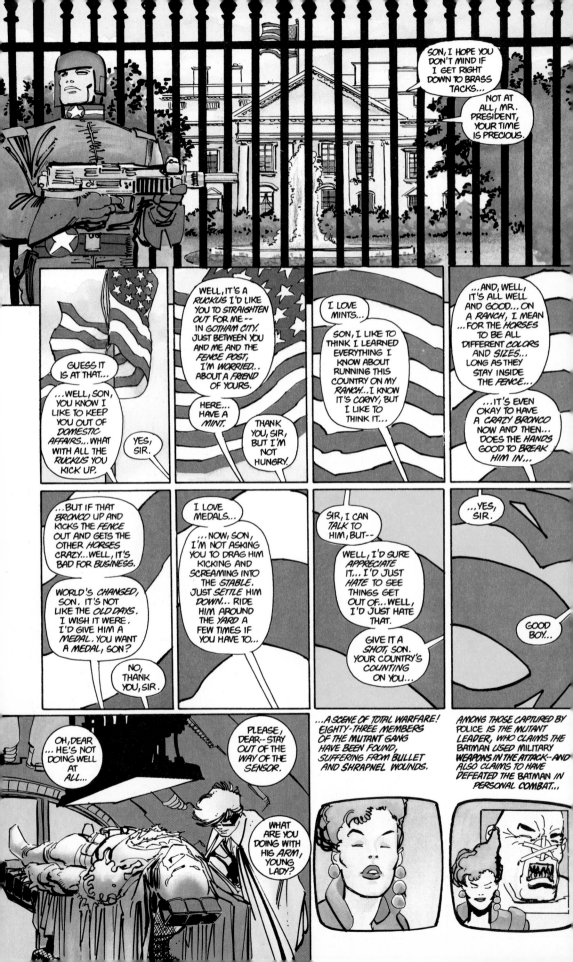

BATMAN **IS** A **COWARD**. I **BROKE** HIS BONES. I **CONQUERED** THE FOOL. I MADE HIM **BEG** FOR MERCY. ONLY BY **CHEATING** DID HE ESCAPE ALIVE.

LET HIM GO TO HIS **WOMEN**. LET HIM **LICK** HIS WOUNDS. HIS DAY IS **DONE**. GOTHAM CITY BELONGS TO THE **MUTANTS**.

CAREFUL, MAN--YOU'RE BOUNCING AROUND TOO--

NO... ...NOT... BOUNCING ME...DON'T WORRY...

SKREECH

STRETCHER'S... ON A GYROSCOPE... STAYS LEVEL... NO MATTER WHAT...

THAT'S KEEN.

NOW DON'T YOU **STRAIN** YOURSELF, SIR. YOU'VE QUITE A LOT OF INTERNAL BLEEDING.

THIS YOUNG LADY WAS KIND ENOUGH TO HELP YOU ABOARD...

I...KNOW WHAT SHE DID, ALFRED.

WHERE...DID YOU LEARN TO SET AN *ARM*... MAKE A *SPLINT*...?

GIRL SCOUTS.

WHAT'S... YOUR NAME...

CARRIE. CARRIE KELLEY.

ROBIN.

MINE'S BRUCE...

SIR! YOU'RE DELIRIOUS, SIR. YOU JUST **REST** NOW--DON'T TRY TO SPEAK--

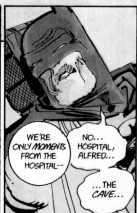

WE'RE ONLY *MOMENTS* FROM THE HOSPITAL--

NO... HOSPITAL, ALFRED...

...THE CAVE...

BUT SIR--

THE CAVE...

...AND ROBIN... COMES WITH US...

SOON MY ARMY WILL **STORM** GOTHAM CITY. SOON THE HEAD OF **GORDON** WILL BE CARRIED THROUGH THE **STREETS**. THEN I WILL HUNT YOUR **NEW** COP--YOUR **WOMAN** COP--AND I WILL ⁜

29.

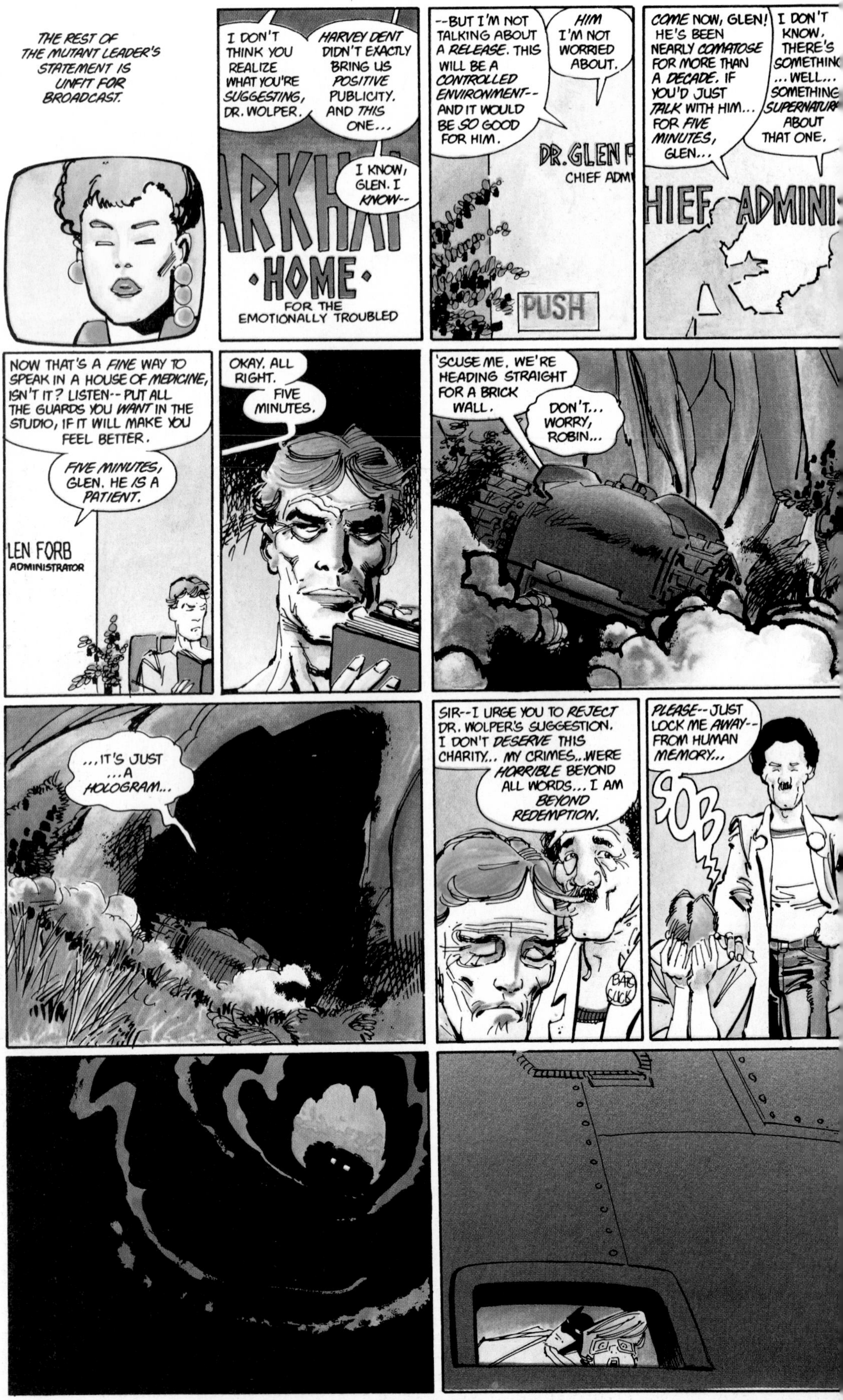
THE REST OF THE MUTANT LEADER'S STATEMENT IS UNFIT FOR BROADCAST.
I DON'T THINK YOU REALIZE WHAT YOU'RE SUGGESTING, DR. WOLPER.
HARVEY DENT DIDN'T EXACTLY BRING US POSITIVE PUBLICITY. AND THIS ONE...
I KNOW, GLEN. I KNOW--
ARKHAM HOME FOR THE EMOTIONALLY TROUBLED
--BUT I'M NOT TALKING ABOUT A RELEASE. THIS WILL BE A CONTROLLED ENVIRONMENT--AND IT WOULD BE SO GOOD FOR HIM.
HIM I'M NOT WORRIED ABOUT.
DR. GLEN F
CHIEF ADM
PUSH
COME NOW, GLEN! HE'S BEEN NEARLY COMATOSE FOR MORE THAN A DECADE. IF YOU'D JUST TALK WITH HIM... FOR FIVE MINUTES, GLEN...
I DON'T KNOW. THERE'S SOMETHING... WELL... SOMETHING SUPERNATURAL ABOUT THAT ONE.
HIEF ADMINI
NOW THAT'S A FINE WAY TO SPEAK IN A HOUSE OF MEDICINE, ISN'T IT? LISTEN--PUT ALL THE GUARDS YOU WANT IN THE STUDIO, IF IT WILL MAKE YOU FEEL BETTER.
FIVE MINUTES, GLEN. HE IS A PATIENT.
LEN FORB
ADMINISTRATOR
OKAY. ALL RIGHT. FIVE MINUTES.
'SCUSE ME. WE'RE HEADING STRAIGHT FOR A BRICK WALL.
DON'T... WORRY, ROBIN...
...IT'S JUST ...A HOLOGRAM...
SIR--I URGE YOU TO REJECT DR. WOLPER'S SUGGESTION. I DON'T DESERVE THIS CHARITY... MY CRIMES...WERE HORRIBLE BEYOND ALL WORDS... I AM BEYOND REDEMPTION.
PLEASE--JUST LOCK ME AWAY--FROM HUMAN MEMORY...
SOB

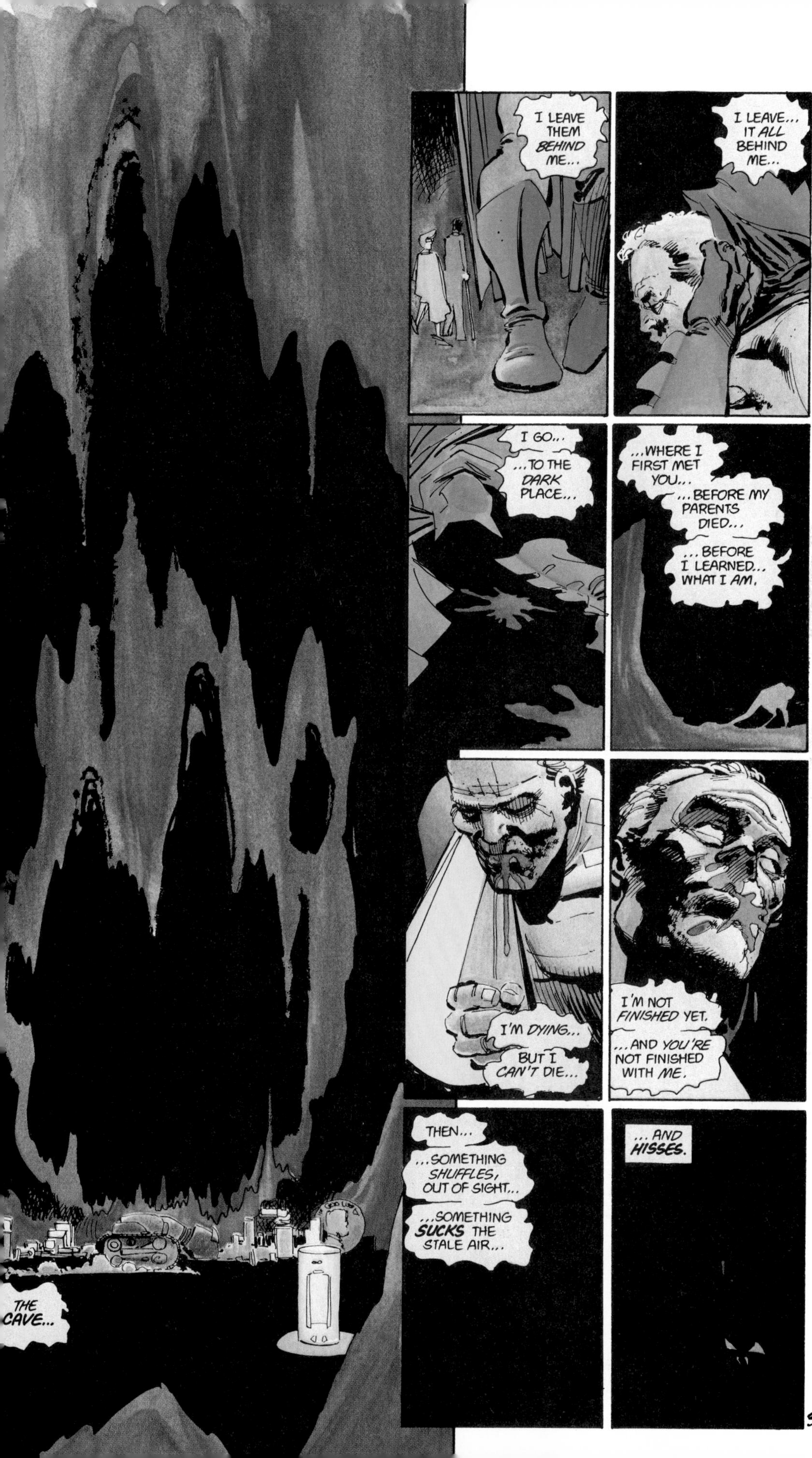
I LEAVE THEM BEHIND ME...
I LEAVE... IT ALL BEHIND ME...
I GO...
...TO THE DARK PLACE...
...WHERE I FIRST MET YOU...
...BEFORE MY PARENTS DIED...
...BEFORE I LEARNED... WHAT I AM.
I'M DYING...
BUT I CAN'T DIE...
I'M NOT FINISHED YET.
...AND YOU'RE NOT FINISHED WITH ME.
THE CAVE...
THEN...
...SOMETHING SHUFFLES, OUT OF SIGHT...
...SOMETHING SUCKS THE STALE AIR...
...AND HISSES.

EYES *GLEAMING,* UNTOUCHED BY LOVE OR JOY OR SORROW...

BREATH HOT WITH THE TASTE OF FALLEN FOES... THE STENCH OF DEAD THINGS, *DAMNED* THINGS...

GLIDING WITH *ANCIENT* GRACE...

SURELY THE FIERCEST SURVIVOR ...THE *PUREST* WARRIOR...

GLARING, *HATING...*

...CLAIMING ME AS YOUR *OWN.*

WE WILL COME FOR OUR LEADER. WE WILL *RAZE* GOTHAM. WE WILL *RAPE* GOTHAM. WE WILL TASTE GOTHAM'S *BLOOD.*

ON HEARING THIS MESSAGE FROM THE MUTANTS, COMMISSIONER GORDON PUT HIMSELF AND HIS MEN ON TWENTY-FOUR HOUR ALERT--WHILE THE MAYOR WAS QUICK TO SPEAK OUT...

THIS WHOLE SITUATION IS THE RESULT OF GORDON'S *INCOMPETENCE*--AND OF THE TERRORIST ACTIONS OF THE *BATMAN.* I WISH TO SIT DOWN WITH THE MUTANT LEADER,...TO NEGOTIATE A *SETTLEMENT...*

WHAT DO YOU THINK, TRISH? HIS HONOR GONE *NUTS?*

NOT AT ALL, BILL. FRANKLY I EXPECT THE MAYOR'S CREDIBILITY RATING TO GO THROUGH THE *ROOF,* *ESPECIALLY* IF HE'S *SUCCESSFUL* IN THE NEGOTIATIONS.

THIS, COMBINED WITH HIS STRONG STAND ON *BATMAN*-- AND MAKING A WOMAN THE NEXT POLICE COMMISSIONER-- WELL, I THINK WE'VE GOT A WHOLE NEW *MAYOR* ON OUR HANDS--

--PUBLIC PERCEPTION- WISE, THAT IS.

ALL THIS AND BRAINS TOO!

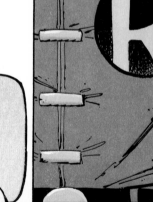

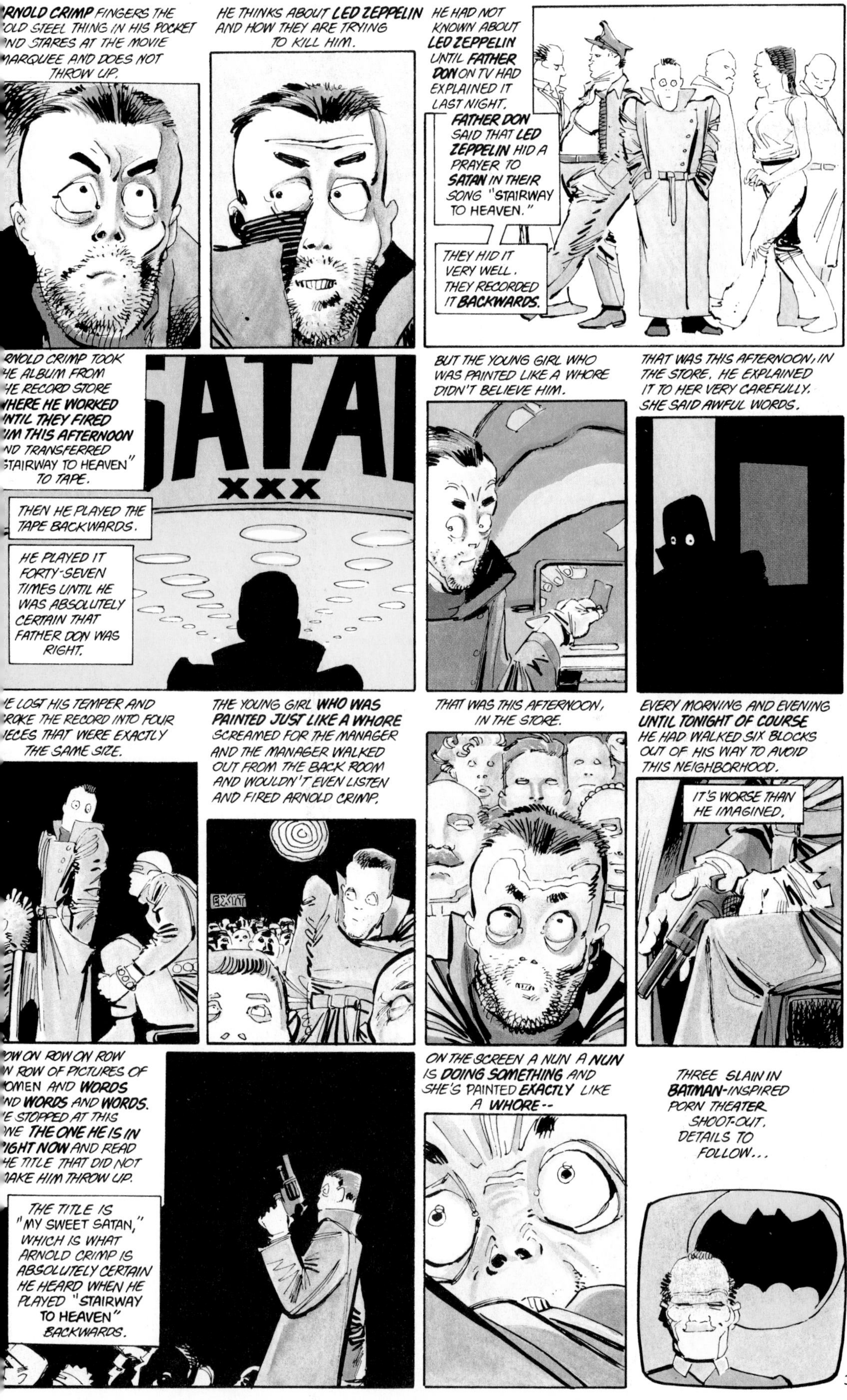

RNOLD CRIMP FINGERS THE OLD STEEL THING IN HIS POCKET ND STARES AT THE MOVIE MARQUEE AND DOES NOT THROW UP.
HE THINKS ABOUT LED ZEPPELIN AND HOW THEY ARE TRYING TO KILL HIM.
HE HAD NOT KNOWN ABOUT LED ZEPPELIN UNTIL FATHER DON ON TV HAD EXPLAINED IT LAST NIGHT.
FATHER DON SAID THAT LED ZEPPELIN HID A PRAYER TO SATAN IN THEIR SONG "STAIRWAY TO HEAVEN."
THEY HID IT VERY WELL. THEY RECORDED IT BACKWARDS.
RNOLD CRIMP TOOK HE ALBUM FROM HE RECORD STORE WHERE HE WORKED UNTIL THEY FIRED IM THIS AFTERNOON ND TRANSFERRED STAIRWAY TO HEAVEN" TO TAPE.
SATA
XXX
THEN HE PLAYED THE TAPE BACKWARDS.
HE PLAYED IT FORTY-SEVEN TIMES UNTIL HE WAS ABSOLUTELY CERTAIN THAT FATHER DON WAS RIGHT.
BUT THE YOUNG GIRL WHO WAS PAINTED LIKE A WHORE DIDN'T BELIEVE HIM.
THAT WAS THIS AFTERNOON, IN THE STORE. HE EXPLAINED IT TO HER VERY CAREFULLY. SHE SAID AWFUL WORDS.
E LOST HIS TEMPER AND ROKE THE RECORD INTO FOUR IECES THAT WERE EXACTLY THE SAME SIZE.
THE YOUNG GIRL WHO WAS PAINTED JUST LIKE A WHORE SCREAMED FOR THE MANAGER AND THE MANAGER WALKED OUT FROM THE BACK ROOM AND WOULDN'T EVEN LISTEN AND FIRED ARNOLD CRIMP.
EXIT
THAT WAS THIS AFTERNOON, IN THE STORE.
EVERY MORNING AND EVENING UNTIL TONIGHT OF COURSE HE HAD WALKED SIX BLOCKS OUT OF HIS WAY TO AVOID THIS NEIGHBORHOOD.
IT'S WORSE THAN HE IMAGINED.
OW ON ROW ON ROW N ROW OF PICTURES OF OMEN AND WORDS ND WORDS AND WORDS. E STOPPED AT THIS NE THE ONE HE IS IN IGHT NOW AND READ HE TITLE THAT DID NOT MAKE HIM THROW UP.
THE TITLE IS "MY SWEET SATAN," WHICH IS WHAT ARNOLD CRIMP IS ABSOLUTELY CERTAIN HE HEARD WHEN HE PLAYED "STAIRWAY TO HEAVEN" BACKWARDS.
ON THE SCREEN A NUN A NUN IS DOING SOMETHING AND SHE'S PAINTED EXACTLY LIKE A WHORE--
THREE SLAIN IN BATMAN-INSPIRED PORN THEATER SHOOT-OUT. DETAILS TO FOLLOW...

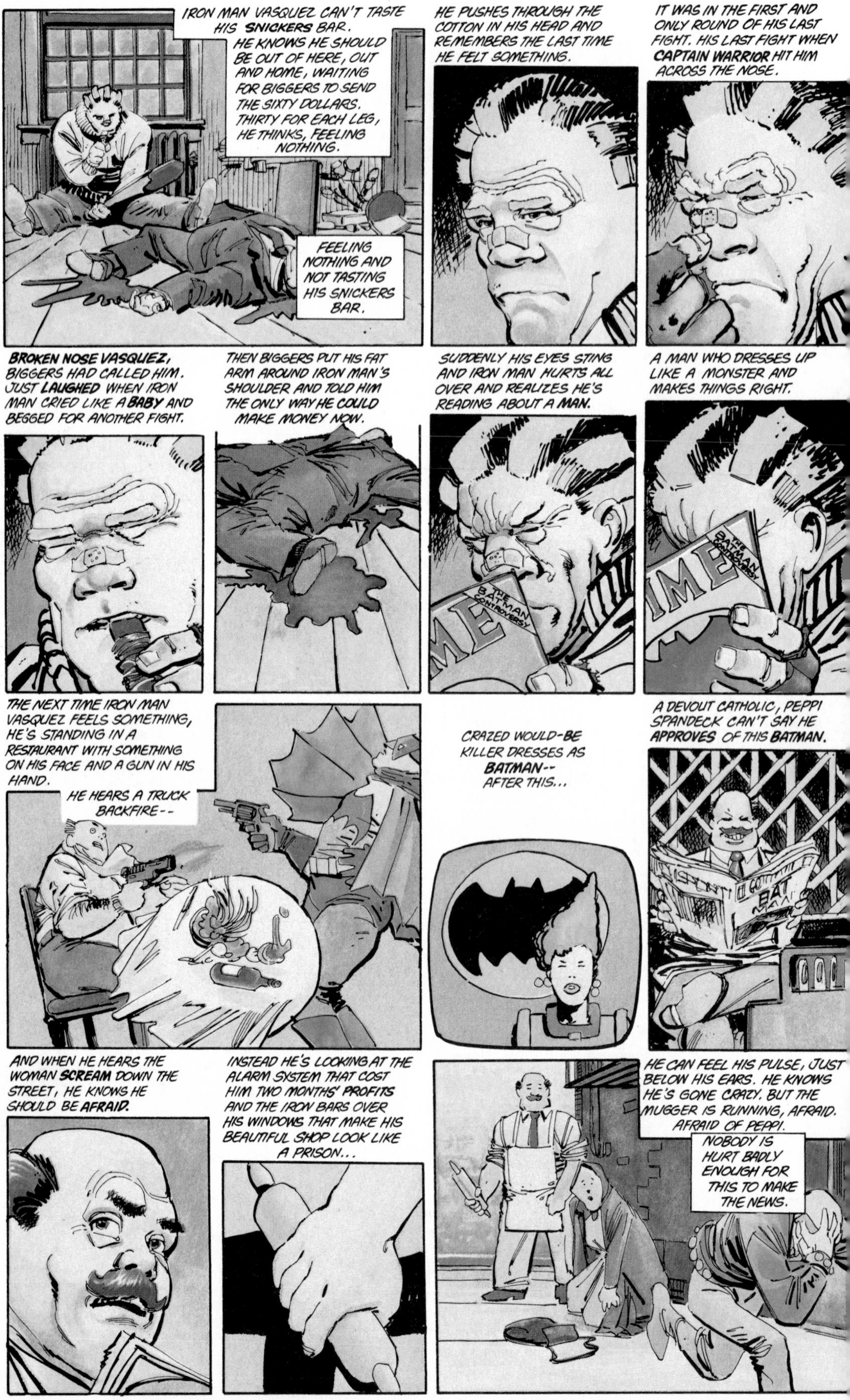
IRON MAN VASQUEZ CAN'T TASTE HIS SNICKERS BAR.
HE KNOWS HE SHOULD BE OUT OF HERE, OUT AND HOME, WAITING FOR BIGGERS TO SEND THE SIXTY DOLLARS. THIRTY FOR EACH LEG, HE THINKS, FEELING NOTHING.
FEELING NOTHING AND NOT TASTING HIS SNICKERS BAR.
HE PUSHES THROUGH THE COTTON IN HIS HEAD AND REMEMBERS THE LAST TIME HE FELT SOMETHING.
IT WAS IN THE FIRST AND ONLY ROUND OF HIS LAST FIGHT. HIS LAST FIGHT WHEN CAPTAIN WARRIOR HIT HIM ACROSS THE NOSE.
BROKEN NOSE VASQUEZ, BIGGERS HAD CALLED HIM. JUST LAUGHED WHEN IRON MAN CRIED LIKE A BABY AND BEGGED FOR ANOTHER FIGHT.
THEN BIGGERS PUT HIS FAT ARM AROUND IRON MAN'S SHOULDER AND TOLD HIM THE ONLY WAY HE COULD MAKE MONEY NOW.
SUDDENLY HIS EYES STING AND IRON MAN HURTS ALL OVER AND REALIZES HE'S READING ABOUT A MAN.
THE BATMAN CONTROVERSY
A MAN WHO DRESSES UP LIKE A MONSTER AND MAKES THINGS RIGHT.
THE BATMAN CONTROVERSY
THE NEXT TIME IRON MAN VASQUEZ FEELS SOMETHING, HE'S STANDING IN A RESTAURANT WITH SOMETHING ON HIS FACE AND A GUN IN HIS HAND.
HE HEARS A TRUCK BACKFIRE--
CRAZED WOULD-BE KILLER DRESSES AS BATMAN-- AFTER THIS...
A DEVOUT CATHOLIC, PEPPI SPANDECK CAN'T SAY HE APPROVES OF THIS BATMAN.
BAT
AND WHEN HE HEARS THE WOMAN SCREAM DOWN THE STREET, HE KNOWS HE SHOULD BE AFRAID.
INSTEAD HE'S LOOKING AT THE ALARM SYSTEM THAT COST HIM TWO MONTHS' PROFITS AND THE IRON BARS OVER HIS WINDOWS THAT MAKE HIS BEAUTIFUL SHOP LOOK LIKE A PRISON...
HE CAN FEEL HIS PULSE, JUST BELOW HIS EARS. HE KNOWS HE'S GONE CRAZY. BUT THE MUGGER IS RUNNING, AFRAID. AFRAID OF PEPPI.
NOBODY IS HURT BADLY ENOUGH FOR THIS TO MAKE THE NEWS.

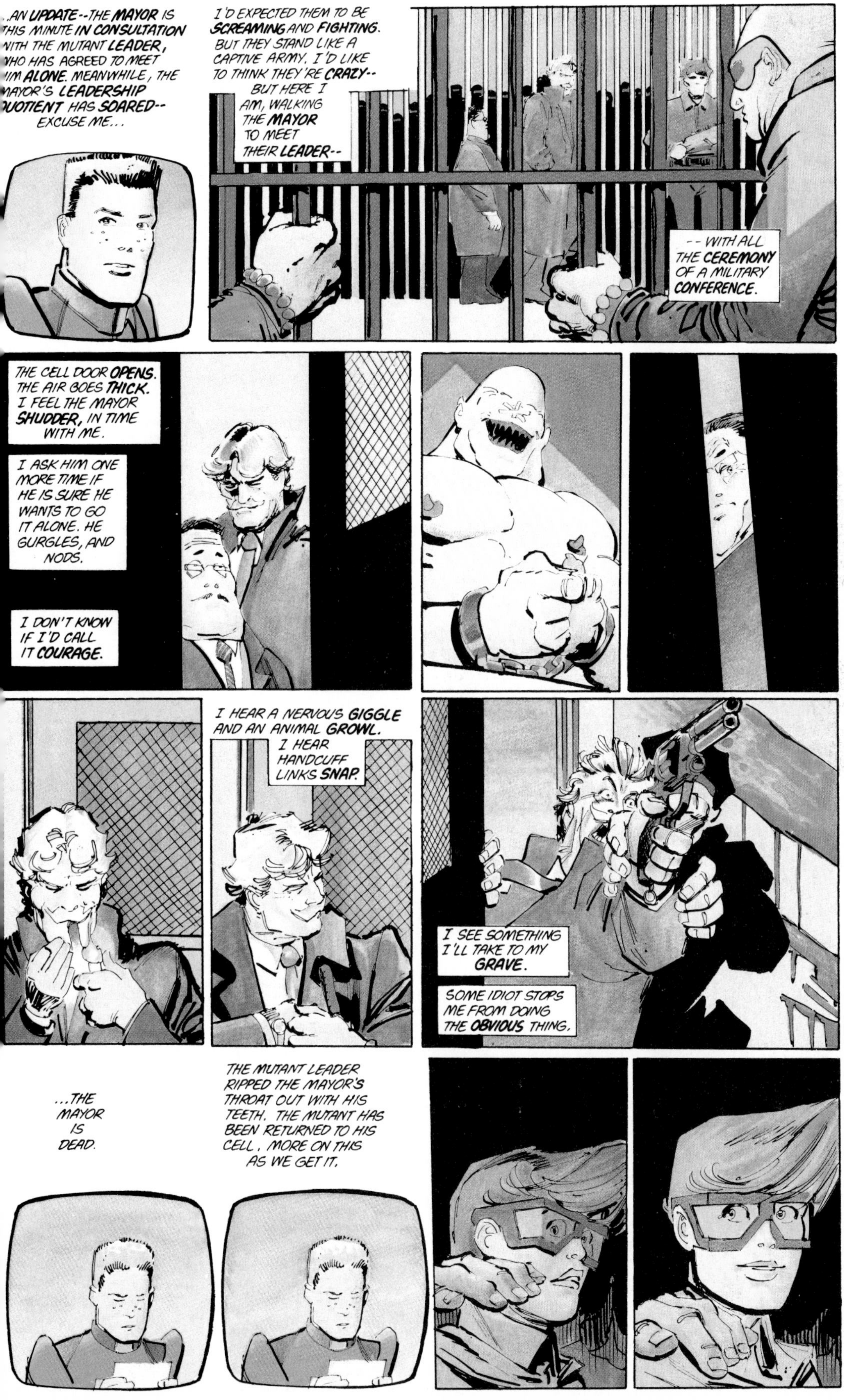
..AN UPDATE--THE MAYOR IS THIS MINUTE IN CONSULTATION WITH THE MUTANT LEADER, WHO HAS AGREED TO MEET HIM ALONE. MEANWHILE, THE MAYOR'S LEADERSHIP QUOTIENT HAS SOARED-- EXCUSE ME...
I'D EXPECTED THEM TO BE SCREAMING AND FIGHTING. BUT THEY STAND LIKE A CAPTIVE ARMY. I'D LIKE TO THINK THEY'RE CRAZY--
BUT HERE I AM, WALKING THE MAYOR TO MEET THEIR LEADER--
--WITH ALL THE CEREMONY OF A MILITARY CONFERENCE.
THE CELL DOOR OPENS. THE AIR GOES THICK. I FEEL THE MAYOR SHUDDER, IN TIME WITH ME.
I ASK HIM ONE MORE TIME IF HE IS SURE HE WANTS TO GO IT ALONE. HE GURGLES, AND NODS.
I DON'T KNOW IF I'D CALL IT COURAGE.
I HEAR A NERVOUS GIGGLE AND AN ANIMAL GROWL.
I HEAR HANDCUFF LINKS SNAP.
I SEE SOMETHING I'LL TAKE TO MY GRAVE.
SOME IDIOT STOPS ME FROM DOING THE OBVIOUS THING.
...THE MAYOR IS DEAD.
THE MUTANT LEADER RIPPED THE MAYOR'S THROAT OUT WITH HIS TEETH. THE MUTANT HAS BEEN RETURNED TO HIS CELL, MORE ON THIS AS WE GET IT.

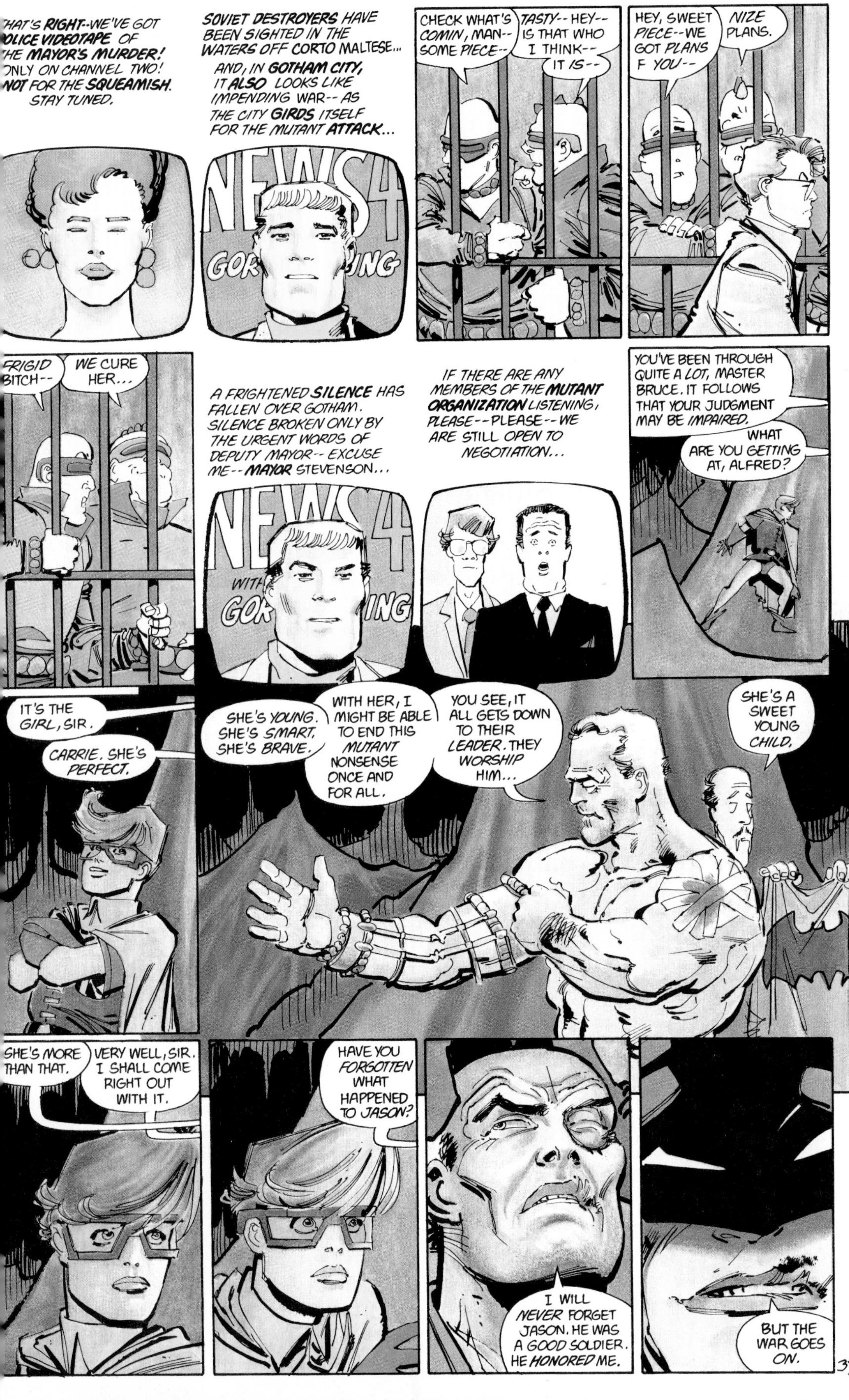
HAT'S RIGHT--WE'VE GOT OLICE VIDEOTAPE OF HE MAYOR'S MURDER! ONLY ON CHANNEL TWO! NOT FOR THE SQUEAMISH. STAY TUNED.
SOVIET DESTROYERS HAVE BEEN SIGHTED IN THE WATERS OFF CORTO MALTESE...
AND, IN GOTHAM CITY, IT ALSO LOOKS LIKE IMPENDING WAR-- AS THE CITY GIRDS ITSELF FOR THE MUTANT ATTACK...
NEWS 4
GOR ING
CHECK WHAT'S COMIN, MAN-- SOME PIECE--
TASTY-- HEY-- IS THAT WHO I THINK-- IT IS--
HEY, SWEET PIECE--WE GOT PLANS F YOU--
NIZE PLANS.
FRIGID BITCH--
WE CURE HER...
A FRIGHTENED SILENCE HAS FALLEN OVER GOTHAM. SILENCE BROKEN ONLY BY THE URGENT WORDS OF DEPUTY MAYOR-- EXCUSE ME-- MAYOR STEVENSON...
NEWS 4
WITH
GOR ING
IF THERE ARE ANY MEMBERS OF THE MUTANT ORGANIZATION LISTENING, PLEASE--PLEASE-- WE ARE STILL OPEN TO NEGOTIATION...
YOU'VE BEEN THROUGH QUITE A LOT, MASTER BRUCE. IT FOLLOWS THAT YOUR JUDGMENT MAY BE IMPAIRED.
WHAT ARE YOU GETTING AT, ALFRED?
IT'S THE GIRL, SIR.
CARRIE. SHE'S PERFECT.
SHE'S YOUNG. SHE'S SMART. SHE'S BRAVE.
WITH HER, I MIGHT BE ABLE TO END THIS MUTANT NONSENSE ONCE AND FOR ALL.
YOU SEE, IT ALL GETS DOWN TO THEIR LEADER. THEY WORSHIP HIM...
SHE'S A SWEET YOUNG CHILD.
SHE'S MORE THAN THAT.
VERY WELL, SIR. I SHALL COME RIGHT OUT WITH IT.
HAVE YOU FORGOTTEN WHAT HAPPENED TO JASON?
I WILL NEVER FORGET JASON. HE WAS A GOOD SOLDIER. HE HONORED ME.
BUT THE WAR GOES ON.

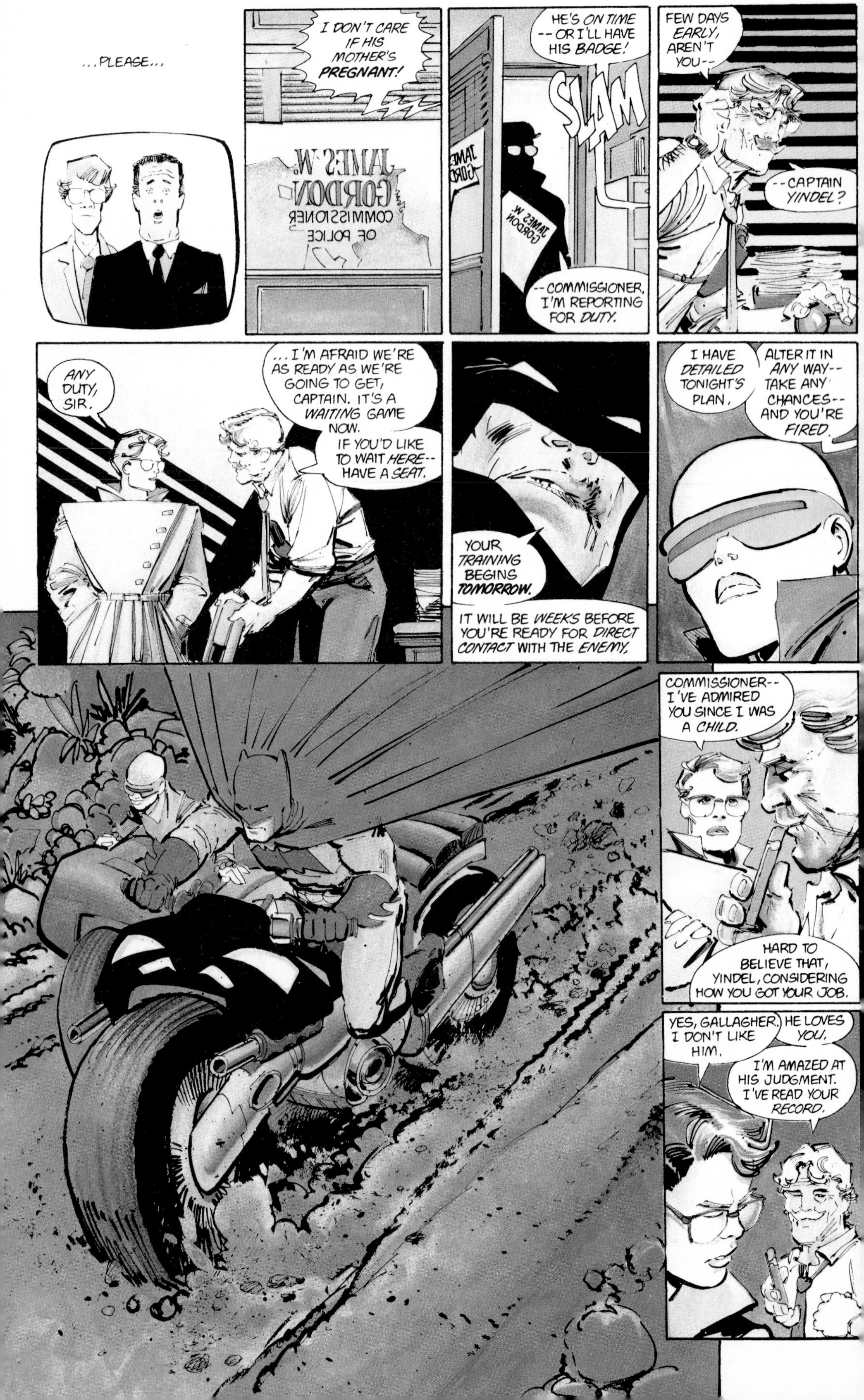
...PLEASE...
I DON'T CARE IF HIS MOTHER'S PREGNANT!
JAMES W. GORDON COMMISSIONER OF POLICE
HE'S ON TIME -- OR I'LL HAVE HIS BADGE!
SLAM
--COMMISSIONER, I'M REPORTING FOR DUTY.
FEW DAYS EARLY, AREN'T YOU--
--CAPTAIN YINDEL?
ANY DUTY, SIR.
...I'M AFRAID WE'RE AS READY AS WE'RE GOING TO GET, CAPTAIN. IT'S A WAITING GAME NOW.
IF YOU'D LIKE TO WAIT HERE-- HAVE A SEAT.
YOUR TRAINING BEGINS TOMORROW.
IT WILL BE WEEKS BEFORE YOU'RE READY FOR DIRECT CONTACT WITH THE ENEMY.
I HAVE DETAILED TONIGHT'S PLAN.
ALTER IT IN ANY WAY-- TAKE ANY CHANCES-- AND YOU'RE FIRED.
COMMISSIONER-- I'VE ADMIRED YOU SINCE I WAS A CHILD.
HARD TO BELIEVE THAT, YINDEL, CONSIDERING HOW YOU GOT YOUR JOB.
YES, GALLAGHER. I DON'T LIKE HIM.
HE LOVES YOU.
I'M AMAZED AT HIS JUDGMENT. I'VE READ YOUR RECORD.

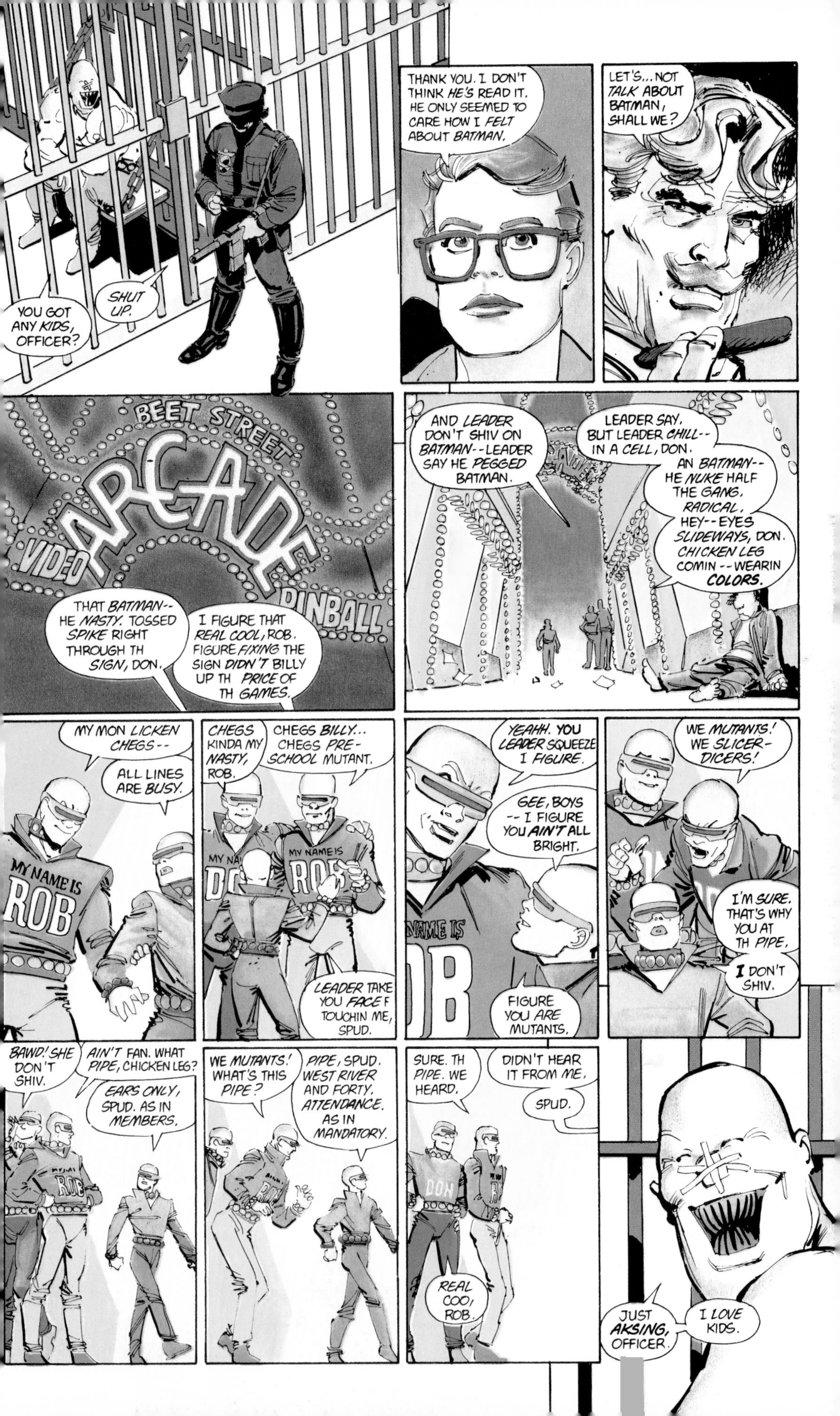
YOU GOT ANY KIDS, OFFICER?
SHUT UP.
THANK YOU. I DON'T THINK HE'S READ IT. HE ONLY SEEMED TO CARE HOW I FELT ABOUT BATMAN.
LET'S... NOT TALK ABOUT BATMAN, SHALL WE?
BEET STREET VIDEO ARCADE PINBALL
THAT BATMAN-- HE NASTY. TOSSED SPIKE RIGHT THROUGH TH SIGN, DON.
I FIGURE THAT REAL COOL, ROB. FIGURE FIXING THE SIGN DIDN'T BILLY UP TH PRICE OF TH GAMES.
AND LEADER DON'T SHIV ON BATMAN--LEADER SAY HE PEGGED BATMAN.
LEADER SAY, BUT LEADER CHILL-- IN A CELL, DON.
AN BATMAN-- HE NUKE HALF THE GANG. RADICAL. HEY--EYES SLIDEWAYS, DON. CHICKEN LEG COMIN--WEARIN COLORS.
MY MON LICKEN CHEGS--
ALL LINES ARE BUSY.
MY NAME IS ROB
CHEGS KINDA MY NASTY, ROB.
CHEGS BILLY... CHEGS PRE-SCHOOL MUTANT.
LEADER TAKE YOU FACE F TOUCHIN ME, SPUD.
YEAHH. YOU LEADER SQUEEZE I FIGURE.
GEE, BOYS --I FIGURE YOU AIN'T ALL BRIGHT.
FIGURE YOU ARE MUTANTS.
WE MUTANTS! WE SLICER-DICERS!
I'M SURE. THAT'S WHY YOU AT TH PIPE.
I DON'T SHIV.
BAWD! SHE DON'T SHIV.
AIN'T FAN. WHAT PIPE, CHICKEN LEG?
EARS ONLY, SPUD. AS IN MEMBERS.
WE MUTANTS! WHAT'S THIS PIPE?
PIPE, SPUD. WEST RIVER AND FORTY. ATTENDANCE. AS IN MANDATORY.
SURE. TH PIPE. WE HEARD.
DIDN'T HEAR IT FROM ME,
SPUD.
REAL COO, ROB.
JUST AKSING, OFFICER.
I LOVE KIDS.

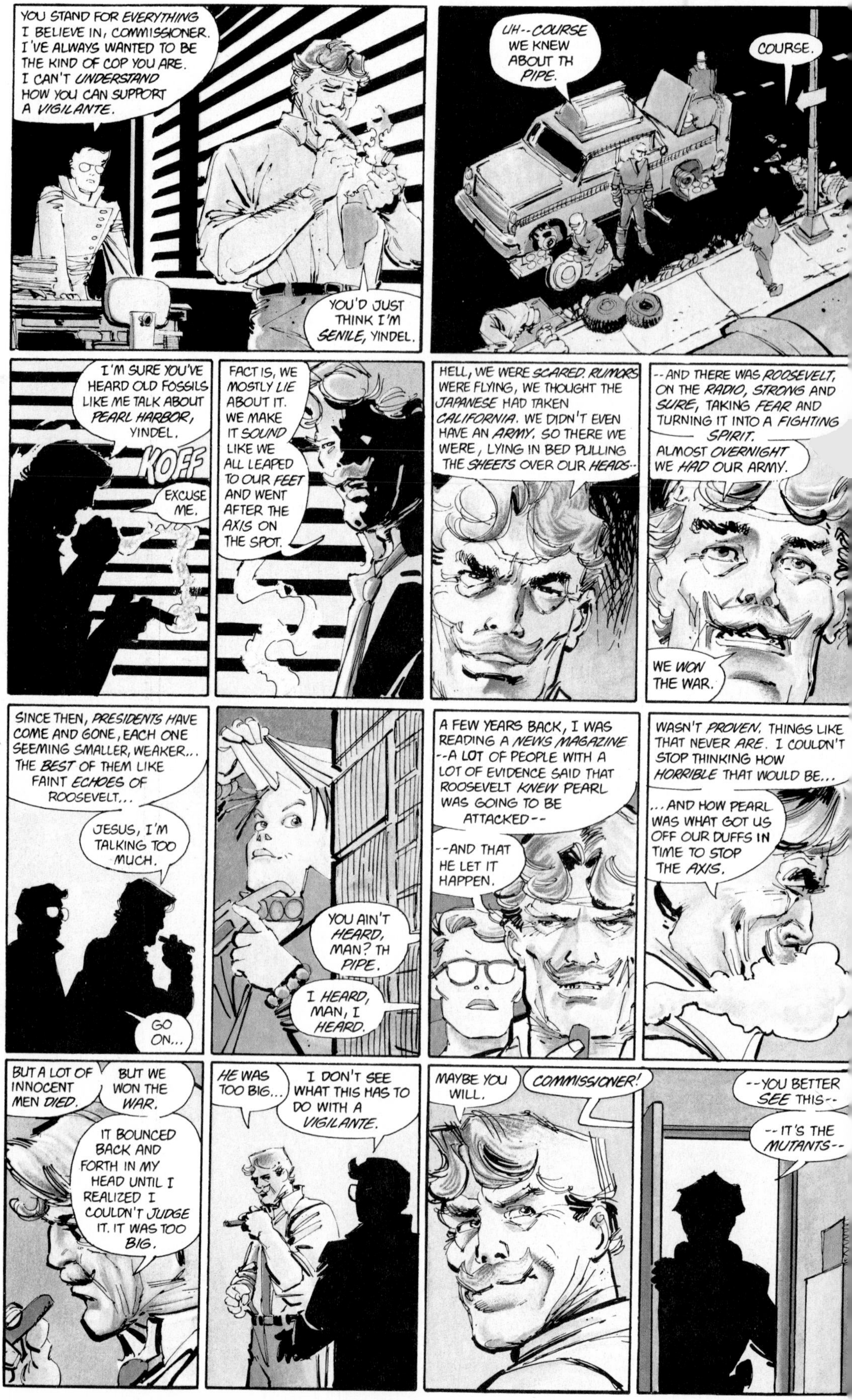
YOU STAND FOR EVERYTHING I BELIEVE IN, COMMISSIONER. I'VE ALWAYS WANTED TO BE THE KIND OF COP YOU ARE. I CAN'T UNDERSTAND HOW YOU CAN SUPPORT A VIGILANTE.
YOU'D JUST THINK I'M SENILE, YINDEL.
UH--COURSE WE KNEW ABOUT TH PIPE.
COURSE.
I'M SURE YOU'VE HEARD OLD FOSSILS LIKE ME TALK ABOUT PEARL HARBOR, YINDEL.
KOFF
EXCUSE ME.
FACT IS, WE MOSTLY LIE ABOUT IT. WE MAKE IT SOUND LIKE WE ALL LEAPED TO OUR FEET AND WENT AFTER THE AXIS ON THE SPOT.
HELL, WE WERE SCARED. RUMORS WERE FLYING, WE THOUGHT THE JAPANESE HAD TAKEN CALIFORNIA. WE DIDN'T EVEN HAVE AN ARMY. SO THERE WE WERE, LYING IN BED PULLING THE SHEETS OVER OUR HEADS--
--AND THERE WAS ROOSEVELT, ON THE RADIO, STRONG AND SURE, TAKING FEAR AND TURNING IT INTO A FIGHTING SPIRIT.
ALMOST OVERNIGHT WE HAD OUR ARMY.
WE WON THE WAR.
SINCE THEN, PRESIDENTS HAVE COME AND GONE, EACH ONE SEEMING SMALLER, WEAKER... THE BEST OF THEM LIKE FAINT ECHOES OF ROOSEVELT...
JESUS, I'M TALKING TOO MUCH.
GO ON...
YOU AIN'T HEARD, MAN? TH PIPE.
I HEARD, MAN, I HEARD.
A FEW YEARS BACK, I WAS READING A NEWS MAGAZINE --A LOT OF PEOPLE WITH A LOT OF EVIDENCE SAID THAT ROOSEVELT KNEW PEARL WAS GOING TO BE ATTACKED--
--AND THAT HE LET IT HAPPEN.
WASN'T PROVEN. THINGS LIKE THAT NEVER ARE. I COULDN'T STOP THINKING HOW HORRIBLE THAT WOULD BE...
...AND HOW PEARL WAS WHAT GOT US OFF OUR DUFFS IN TIME TO STOP THE AXIS.
BUT A LOT OF INNOCENT MEN DIED.
BUT WE WON THE WAR.
IT BOUNCED BACK AND FORTH IN MY HEAD UNTIL I REALIZED I COULDN'T JUDGE IT. IT WAS TOO BIG.
HE WAS TOO BIG...
I DON'T SEE WHAT THIS HAS TO DO WITH A VIGILANTE.
MAYBE YOU WILL.
COMMISSIONER!
--YOU BETTER SEE THIS--
--IT'S THE MUTANTS--

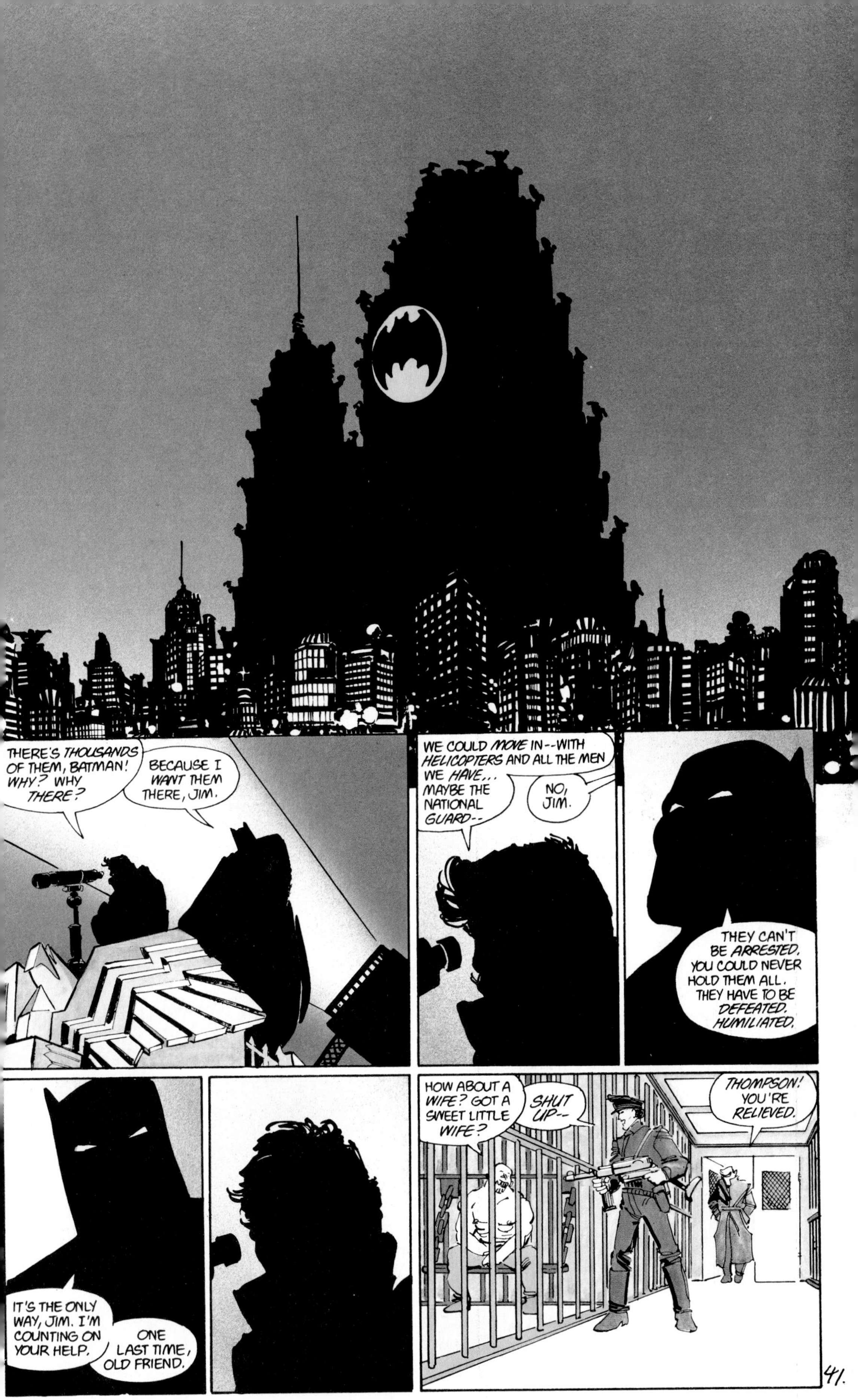
THERE'S THOUSANDS OF THEM, BATMAN! WHY? WHY THERE?
BECAUSE I WANT THEM THERE, JIM.
WE COULD MOVE IN--WITH HELICOPTERS AND ALL THE MEN WE HAVE... MAYBE THE NATIONAL GUARD--
NO, JIM.
THEY CAN'T BE ARRESTED. YOU COULD NEVER HOLD THEM ALL. THEY HAVE TO BE DEFEATED. HUMILIATED.
IT'S THE ONLY WAY, JIM. I'M COUNTING ON YOUR HELP.
ONE LAST TIME, OLD FRIEND.
HOW ABOUT A WIFE? GOT A SWEET LITTLE WIFE?
SHUT UP--
THOMPSON! YOU'RE RELIEVED.

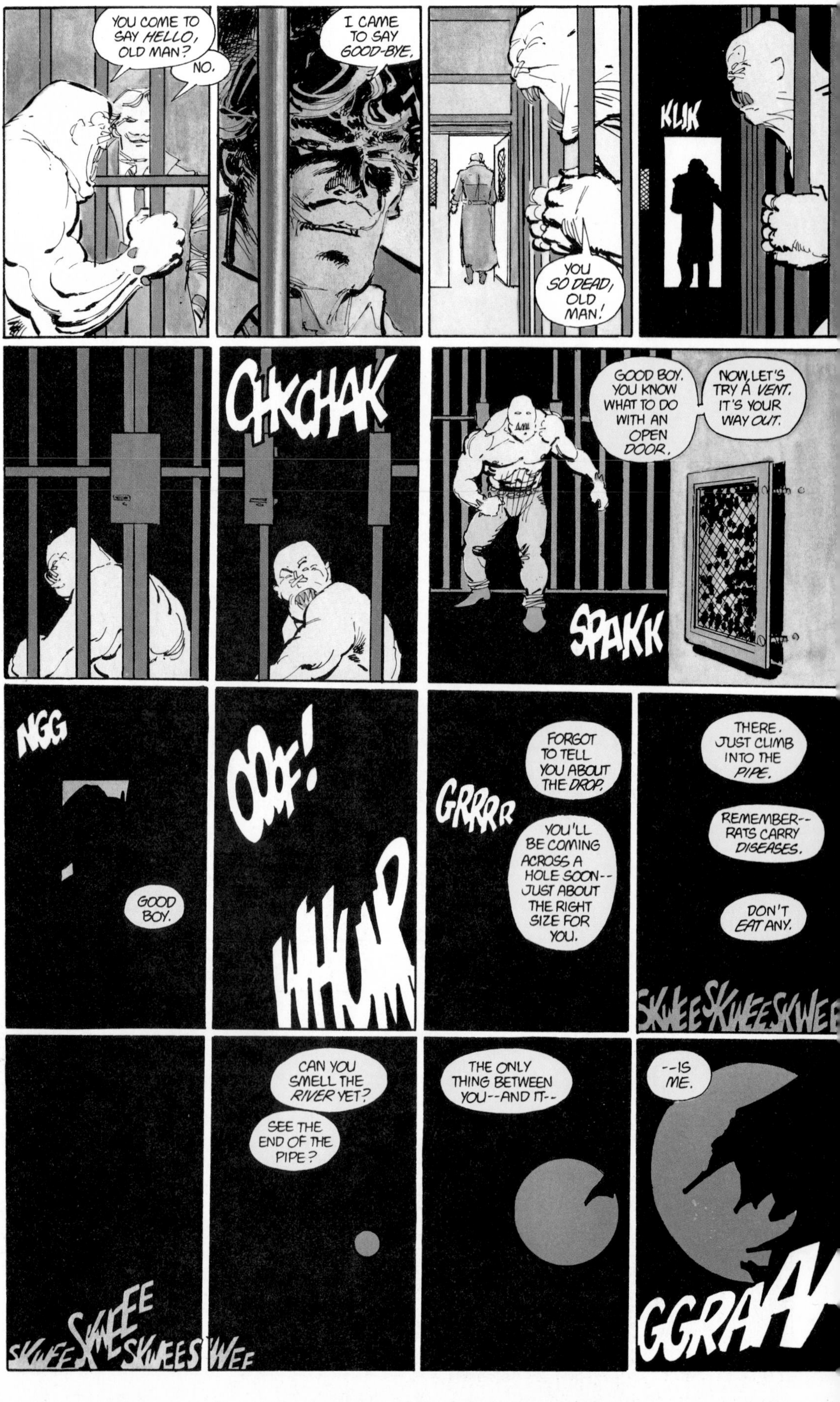

YOU COME TO SAY HELLO, OLD MAN?
NO.
I CAME TO SAY GOOD-BYE.
YOU SO DEAD, OLD MAN!
KLIK
CHKCHAK
GOOD BOY. YOU KNOW WHAT TO DO WITH AN OPEN DOOR.
NOW, LET'S TRY A VENT. IT'S YOUR WAY OUT.
SPAKK
NGG
GOOD BOY.
OOOF!
WHUMP
GRRRR
FORGOT TO TELL YOU ABOUT THE DROP.
YOU'LL BE COMING ACROSS A HOLE SOON-- JUST ABOUT THE RIGHT SIZE FOR YOU.
THERE. JUST CLIMB INTO THE PIPE.
REMEMBER-- RATS CARRY DISEASES.
DON'T EAT ANY.
SKWEE SKWEE SKWEE
SKWEE SKWEE SKWEE SKWEE
CAN YOU SMELL THE RIVER YET?
SEE THE END OF THE PIPE?
THE ONLY THING BETWEEN YOU--AND IT--
--IS ME.
GGRAA

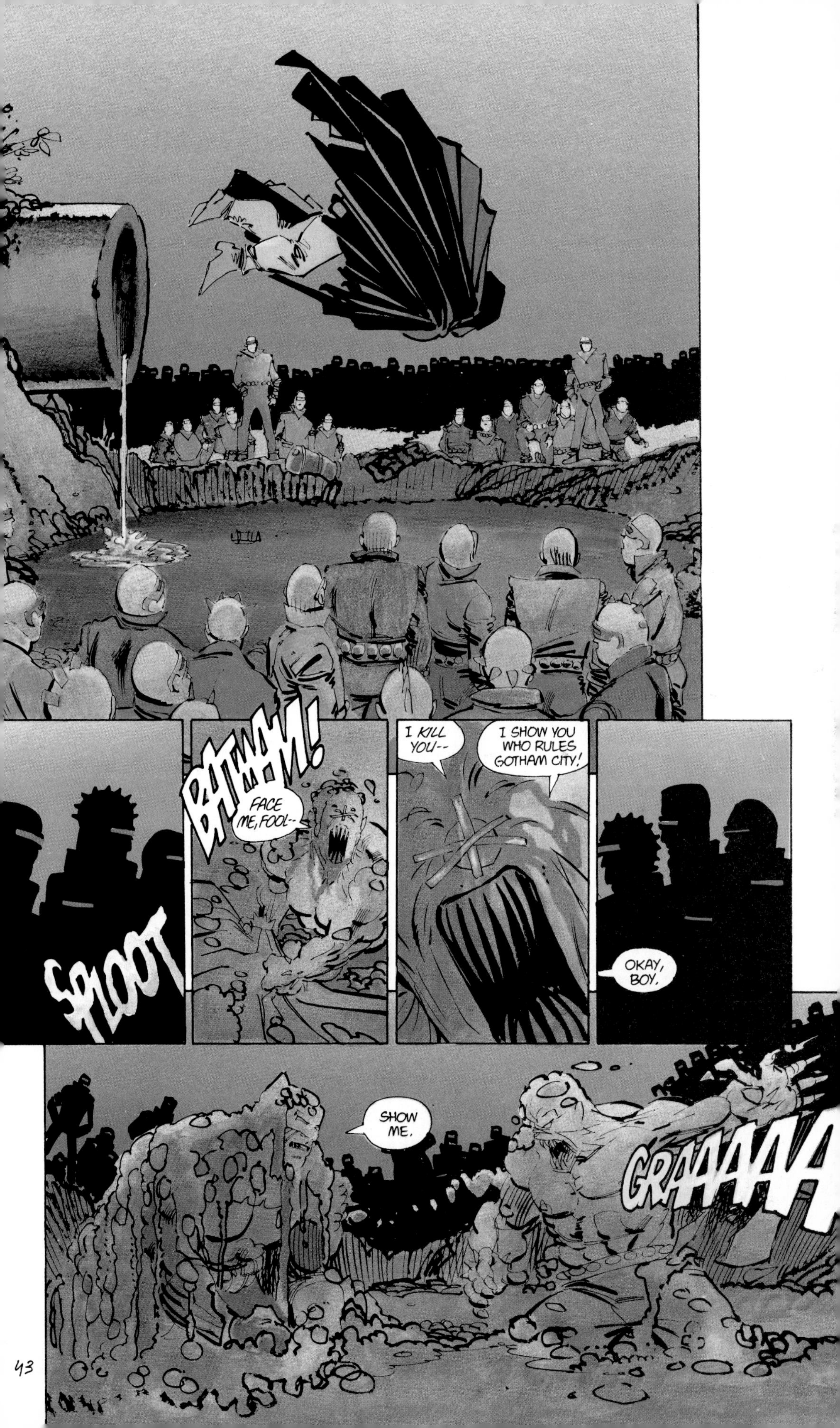
SPLOOT
BATMAN!
FACE ME, FOOL--
I KILL YOU--
I SHOW YOU WHO RULES GOTHAM CITY!
OKAY, BOY.
SHOW ME.
GRAAAAA

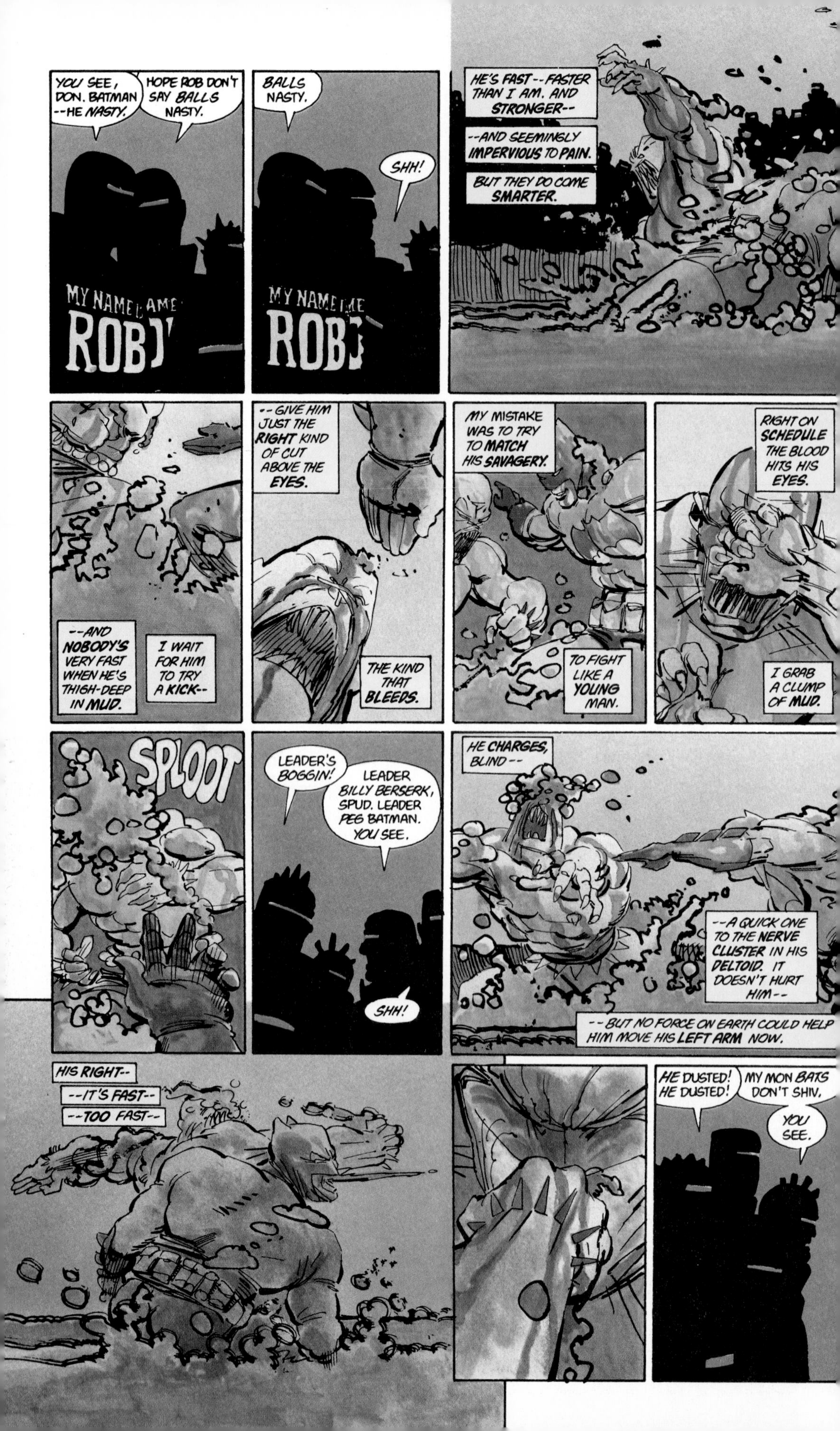

YOU SEE, DON. BATMAN --HE NASTY.
HOPE ROB DON'T SAY BALLS NASTY.
MY NAME ROB
BALLS NASTY.
SHH!
HE'S FAST--FASTER THAN I AM. AND STRONGER--
--AND SEEMINGLY IMPERVIOUS TO PAIN.
BUT THEY DO COME SMARTER.
--AND NOBODY'S VERY FAST WHEN HE'S THIGH-DEEP IN MUD.
I WAIT FOR HIM TO TRY A KICK--
--GIVE HIM JUST THE RIGHT KIND OF CUT ABOVE THE EYES.
THE KIND THAT BLEEDS.
MY MISTAKE WAS TO TRY TO MATCH HIS SAVAGERY.
TO FIGHT LIKE A YOUNG MAN.
RIGHT ON SCHEDULE THE BLOOD HITS HIS EYES.
I GRAB A CLUMP OF MUD.
SPLOOT
LEADER'S BOGGIN'!
LEADER BILLY BERSERK, SPUD. LEADER PEG BATMAN. YOU SEE.
SHH!
HE CHARGES, BLIND--
--A QUICK ONE TO THE NERVE CLUSTER IN HIS DELTOID. IT DOESN'T HURT HIM--
--BUT NO FORCE ON EARTH COULD HELP HIM MOVE HIS LEFT ARM NOW.
HIS RIGHT--
--IT'S FAST--
--TOO FAST--
HE DUSTED! HE DUSTED!
MY MON BATS DON'T SHIV.
YOU SEE.

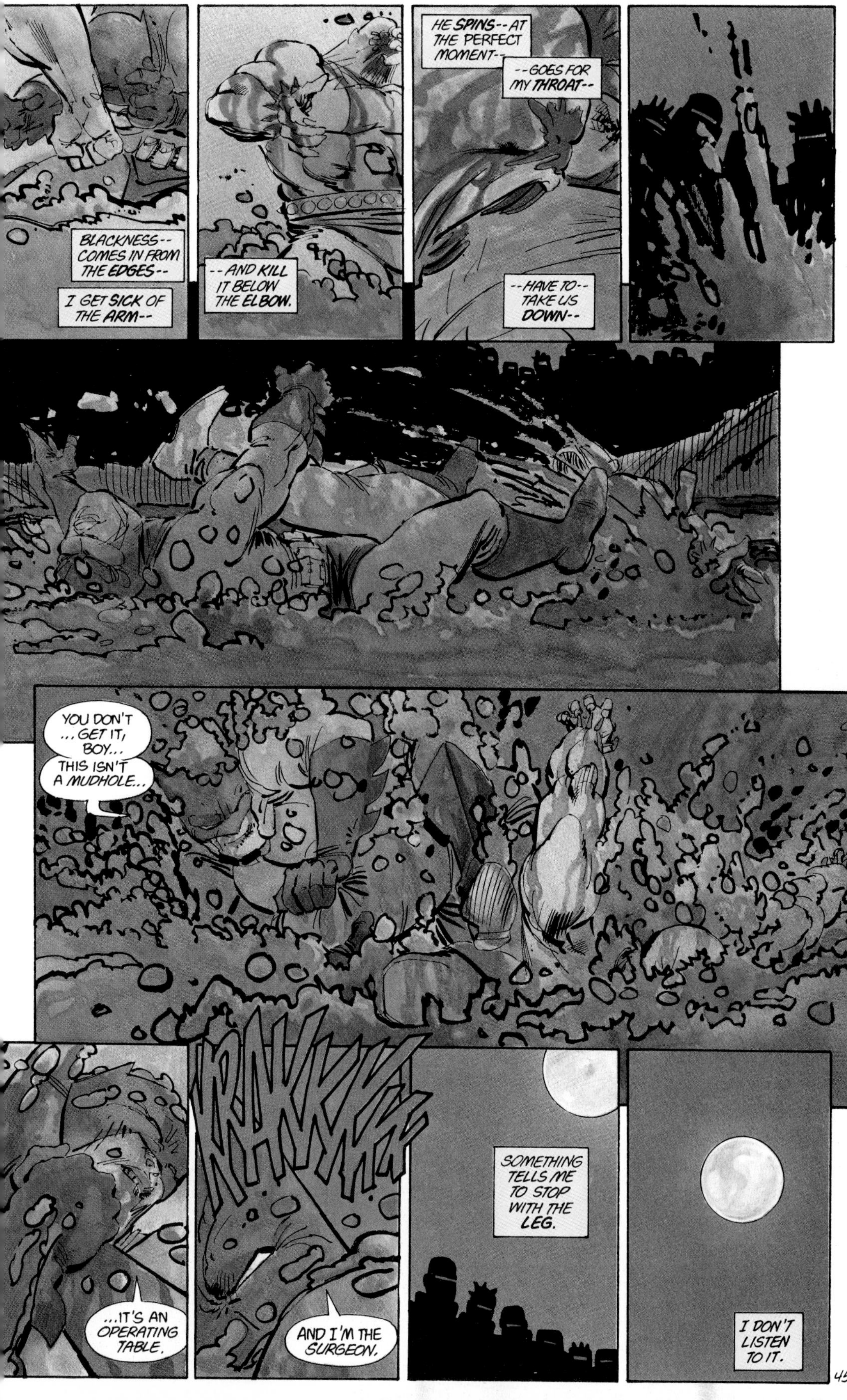
BLACKNESS--
COMES IN FROM
THE EDGES--
I GET SICK OF
THE ARM--
--AND KILL
IT BELOW
THE ELBOW.
HE SPINS--AT
THE PERFECT
MOMENT--
--GOES FOR
MY THROAT--
--HAVE TO--
TAKE US
DOWN--
YOU DON'T
...GET IT,
BOY...
THIS ISN'T
A MUDHOLE...
...IT'S AN
OPERATING
TABLE.
AND I'M THE
SURGEON.
SOMETHING
TELLS ME
TO STOP
WITH THE
LEG.
I DON'T
LISTEN
TO IT.

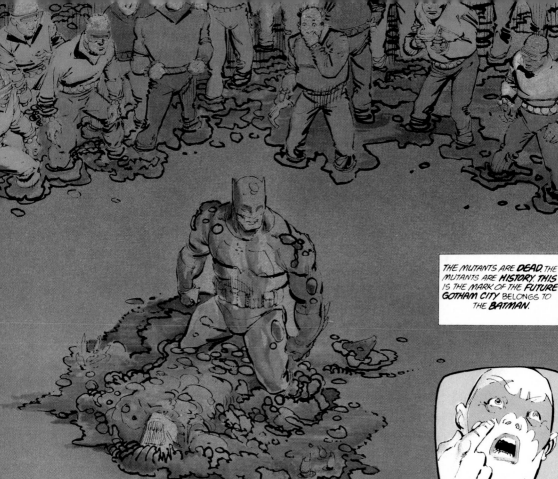

THE MUTANTS ARE **DEAD**. THE MUTANTS ARE **HISTORY**. THIS IS THE MARK OF THE **FUTURE**. **GOTHAM CITY** BELONGS TO THE **BATMAN**.

JUST AS I PREDICTED--THE BATMAN HAS **INFECTED** THE YOUTH OF GOTHAM-- **POISONED** THEM WITH AN INSIDIOUS **EXCUSE** FOR THE MOST VIOLENTLY ANTI-SOCIAL BEHAVIOR.

WE'RE NOT TALKING ABOUT LETTING THE MUTANT LEADER GO. ONCE HE IS **MOBILE** HE WILL BE **ARRAIGNED**-- TO SEE IF HE IS FIT TO STAND TRIAL , OR THE **VICTIM** OF **MENTAL ILLNESS**.

BATMAN? I'M PLAIN TIRED OF **HEARING** ABOUT HIM. HIM AND HOW HE DOESN'T LET THINGS **STOP** HIM OR JUST LET THINGS **GO** THE WAY US **HUMANS** DO. WE COUNT **TOO**.

THOUGH SURROUNDED BY SINFULNESS AND **TERROR**, WE MUST NOT BECOME SO **EMBITTERED** THAT WE TAKE SATAN'S METHODS AS OUR OWN.

DO NOT **EXPECT** ANY FURTHER **STATEMENTS**. THE SONS OF THE **BATMAN** DO NOT **TALK**. WE **ACT**. LET GOTHAM'S CRIMINALS **BEWARE**. THEY ARE ABOUT TO ENTER **HELL**.

SO A BUNCH OF **PSYCHOPATHS** TURN ON **CRIMINALS**, INSTEAD OF INNOCENTS. FOR THIS YOU WANT TO **BLAME** BATMAN?

THE PRESIDENT IS CONCERNED, YOU CAN **BANK** ON THAT, PAL . BUT DON'T EXPECT HIM TO GO JUMPING IN ON GOTHAM'S OWN FINE MAYOR AND GOVERNOR. NO, SIR. THIS IS **AMERICA**.

I SAID **NO COMMENT**.

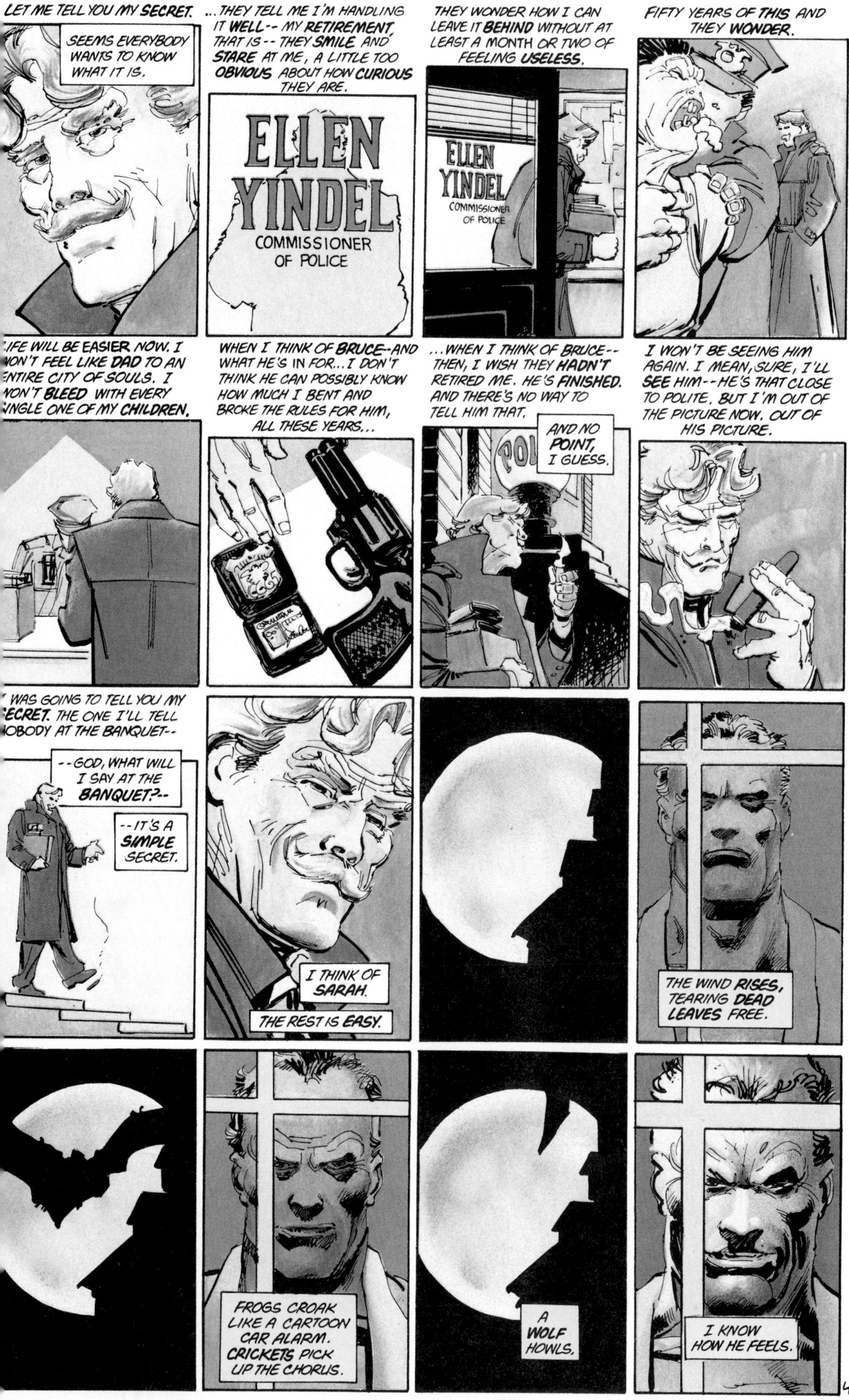

LET ME TELL YOU MY SECRET.
SEEMS EVERYBODY WANTS TO KNOW WHAT IT IS.
...THEY TELL ME I'M HANDLING IT WELL-- MY RETIREMENT, THAT IS-- THEY SMILE AND STARE AT ME, A LITTLE TOO OBVIOUS ABOUT HOW CURIOUS THEY ARE.
ELLEN YINDEL COMMISSIONER OF POLICE
THEY WONDER HOW I CAN LEAVE IT BEHIND WITHOUT AT LEAST A MONTH OR TWO OF FEELING USELESS.
ELLEN YINDEL COMMISSIONER OF POLICE
FIFTY YEARS OF THIS AND THEY WONDER.
IFE WILL BE EASIER NOW. I ON'T FEEL LIKE DAD TO AN NTIRE CITY OF SOULS. I ON'T BLEED WITH EVERY INGLE ONE OF MY CHILDREN.
WHEN I THINK OF BRUCE--AND WHAT HE'S IN FOR...I DON'T THINK HE CAN POSSIBLY KNOW HOW MUCH I BENT AND BROKE THE RULES FOR HIM, ALL THESE YEARS...
...WHEN I THINK OF BRUCE-- THEN, I WISH THEY HADN'T RETIRED ME. HE'S FINISHED. AND THERE'S NO WAY TO TELL HIM THAT.
AND NO POINT, I GUESS.
I WON'T BE SEEING HIM AGAIN. I MEAN, SURE, I'LL SEE HIM--HE'S THAT CLOSE TO POLITE. BUT I'M OUT OF THE PICTURE NOW. OUT OF HIS PICTURE.
WAS GOING TO TELL YOU MY ECRET. THE ONE I'LL TELL OBODY AT THE BANQUET--
--GOD, WHAT WILL I SAY AT THE BANQUET?--
--IT'S A SIMPLE SECRET.
I THINK OF SARAH.
THE REST IS EASY.
THE WIND RISES, TEARING DEAD LEAVES FREE.
FROGS CROAK LIKE A CARTOON CAR ALARM. CRICKETS PICK UP THE CHORUS.
A WOLF HOWLS.
I KNOW HOW HE FEELS.

BOOK THREE

HUNT THE DARK KNIGHT

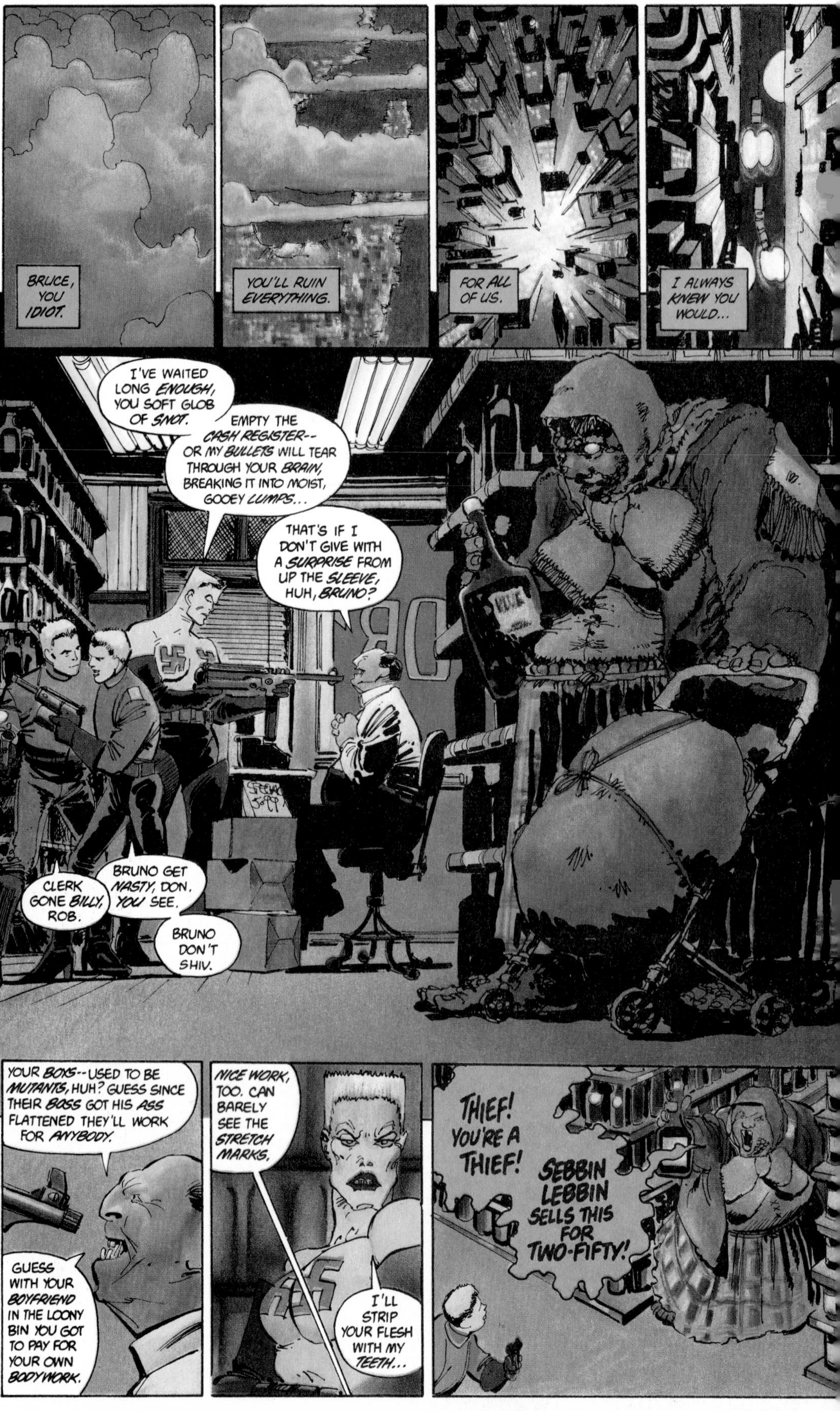
BRUCE, YOU IDIOT.
YOU'LL RUIN EVERYTHING.
FOR ALL OF US.
I ALWAYS KNEW YOU WOULD...
I'VE WAITED LONG ENOUGH, YOU SOFT GLOB OF SNOT.
EMPTY THE CASH REGISTER-- OR MY BULLETS WILL TEAR THROUGH YOUR BRAIN, BREAKING IT INTO MOIST, GOOEY LUMPS...
THAT'S IF I DON'T GIVE WITH A SURPRISE FROM UP THE SLEEVE, HUH, BRUNO?
CLERK GONE BILLY, ROB.
BRUNO GET NASTY, DON. YOU SEE.
BRUNO DON'T SHIV.
YOUR BOYS--USED TO BE MUTANTS, HUH? GUESS SINCE THEIR BOSS GOT HIS ASS FLATTENED THEY'LL WORK FOR ANYBODY.
GUESS WITH YOUR BOYFRIEND IN THE LOONY BIN YOU GOT TO PAY FOR YOUR OWN BODYWORK.
NICE WORK, TOO. CAN BARELY SEE THE STRETCH MARKS.
I'LL STRIP YOUR FLESH WITH MY TEETH...
THIEF! YOU'RE A THIEF!
SEBBIN LEBBIN SELLS THIS FOR TWO-FIFTY!

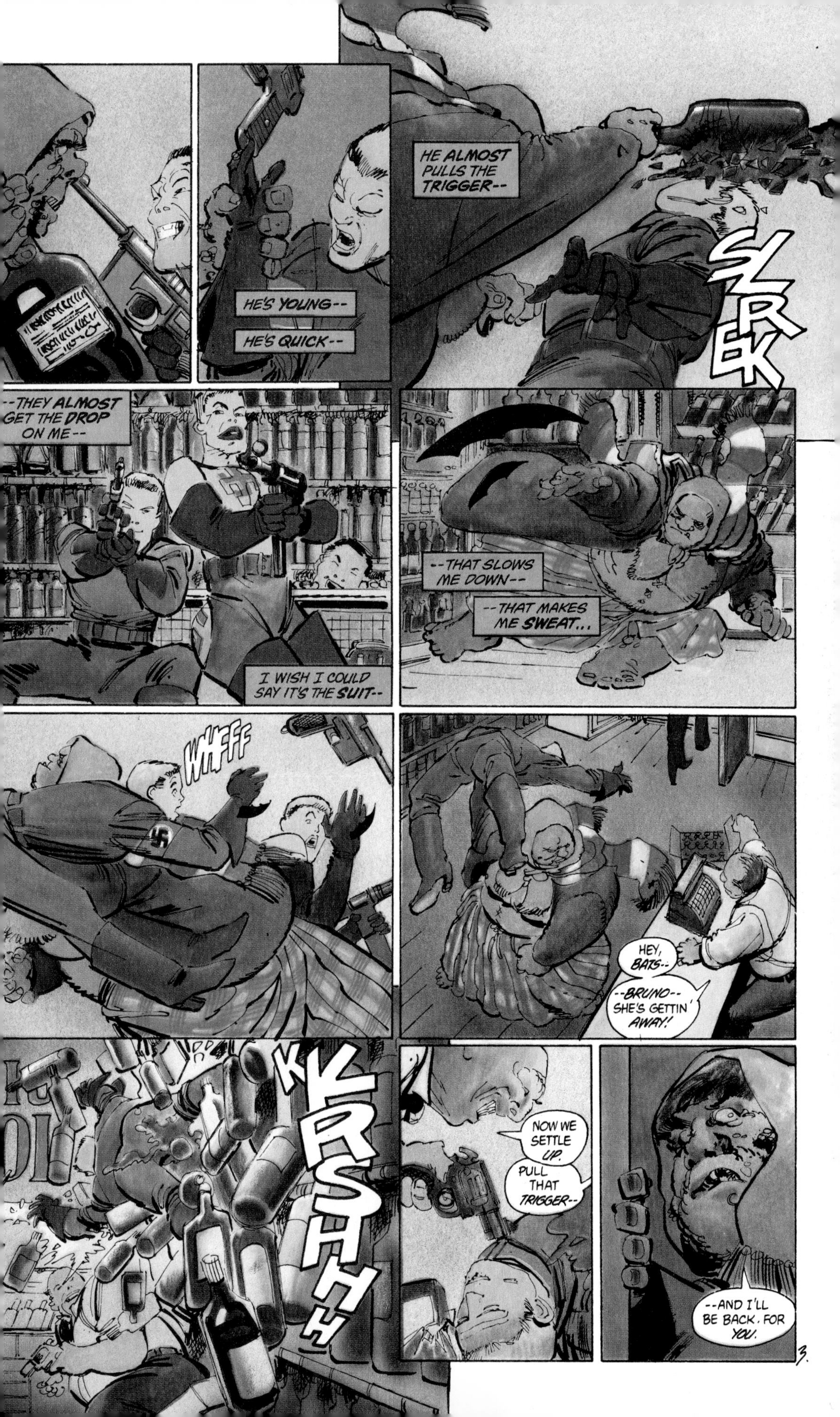
HE'S YOUNG--
HE'S QUICK--
HE ALMOST PULLS THE TRIGGER--
SLREK
--THEY ALMOST GET THE DROP ON ME--
I WISH I COULD SAY IT'S THE SUIT--
--THAT SLOWS ME DOWN--
--THAT MAKES ME SWEAT...
WHFFF
HEY, BATS--
--BRUNO-- SHE'S GETTIN' AWAY!
KKRSHHH
NOW WE SETTLE UP.
PULL THAT TRIGGER--
--AND I'LL BE BACK. FOR YOU.

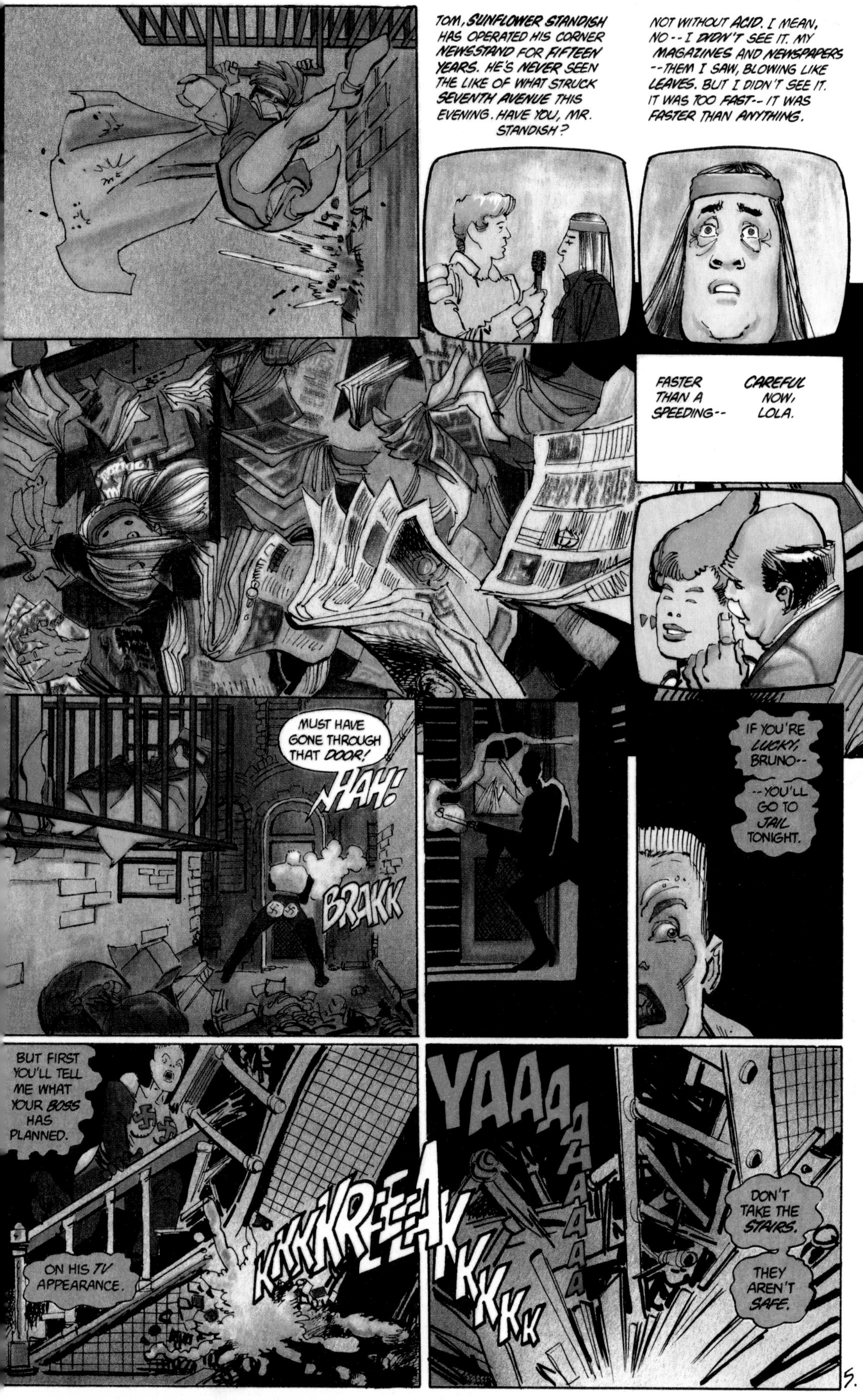
TOM, SUNFLOWER STANDISH HAS OPERATED HIS CORNER NEWSSTAND FOR FIFTEEN YEARS. HE'S NEVER SEEN THE LIKE OF WHAT STRUCK SEVENTH AVENUE THIS EVENING. HAVE YOU, MR. STANDISH?
NOT WITHOUT ACID. I MEAN, NO -- I DIDN'T SEE IT. MY MAGAZINES AND NEWSPAPERS -- THEM I SAW, BLOWING LIKE LEAVES. BUT I DIDN'T SEE IT. IT WAS TOO FAST -- IT WAS FASTER THAN ANYTHING.
FASTER THAN A SPEEDING--
CAREFUL NOW, LOLA.
MUST HAVE GONE THROUGH THAT DOOR!
HAH!
BRAKK
IF YOU'RE LUCKY, BRUNO--
--YOU'LL GO TO JAIL TONIGHT.
BUT FIRST YOU'LL TELL ME WHAT YOUR BOSS HAS PLANNED.
ON HIS TV APPEARANCE.
KKKKREEEAKKKKK
YAAAAAAAAAA
DON'T TAKE THE STAIRS.
THEY AREN'T SAFE.

NEVER MEANT-- TO GIVE HER TIME--

CH-CHAKK

--TO COCK THAT THING--

BRAPP

THIS-- WOULD BE A STUPID DEATH...

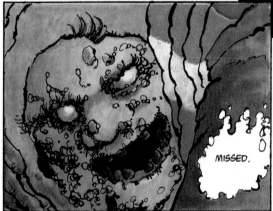

MISSED.

LUCKY--

--LUCKY OLD MAN...

ANOTHER *BIZARRE* INCIDENT--THIS ONE IN THE SOUTH STREET *SUBWAY STATION.* ADVERTISING AGENT *BYRON BRASSBALLS* TOLD REPORTERS...

I DIDN'T DO ANYTHING *WRONG.* I WAS JUST TRYING TO *PROTECT* MYSELF. THE SUBWAYS ARE DANGEROUS. YOU DON'T NEED ME TO TELL YOU THAT. SO THERE I WAS, ALONE IN THE STATION EXCEPT FOR THIS "BEGGAR"-- I WANT THAT IN *QUOTES*--

--WHAT?...HOW WAS I TO KNOW HE DIDN'T HAVE A GUN? THEY NEVER *SHOW* YOU THAT UNTIL THEY'RE READY TO KILL YOU-- WHAT?...OH, SURE. THE *CRUTCHES.* A LOT OF THEM USE *CRUTCHES,* YOU KNOW WHAT I MEAN.

HEY--HE STARTED IT. AND IT WAS *HIS* CRUTCHES THAT TRIPPED HIM UP, BABE-- WHAT?... YOU BET HE YELLED. WANTED ME TO JUMP DOWN AND DIE *WITH* HIM. OF *COURSE* I RAN. WHO *WOULDN'T?* THEN SOMETHING HIT ME HARD--IN THE CHEST--

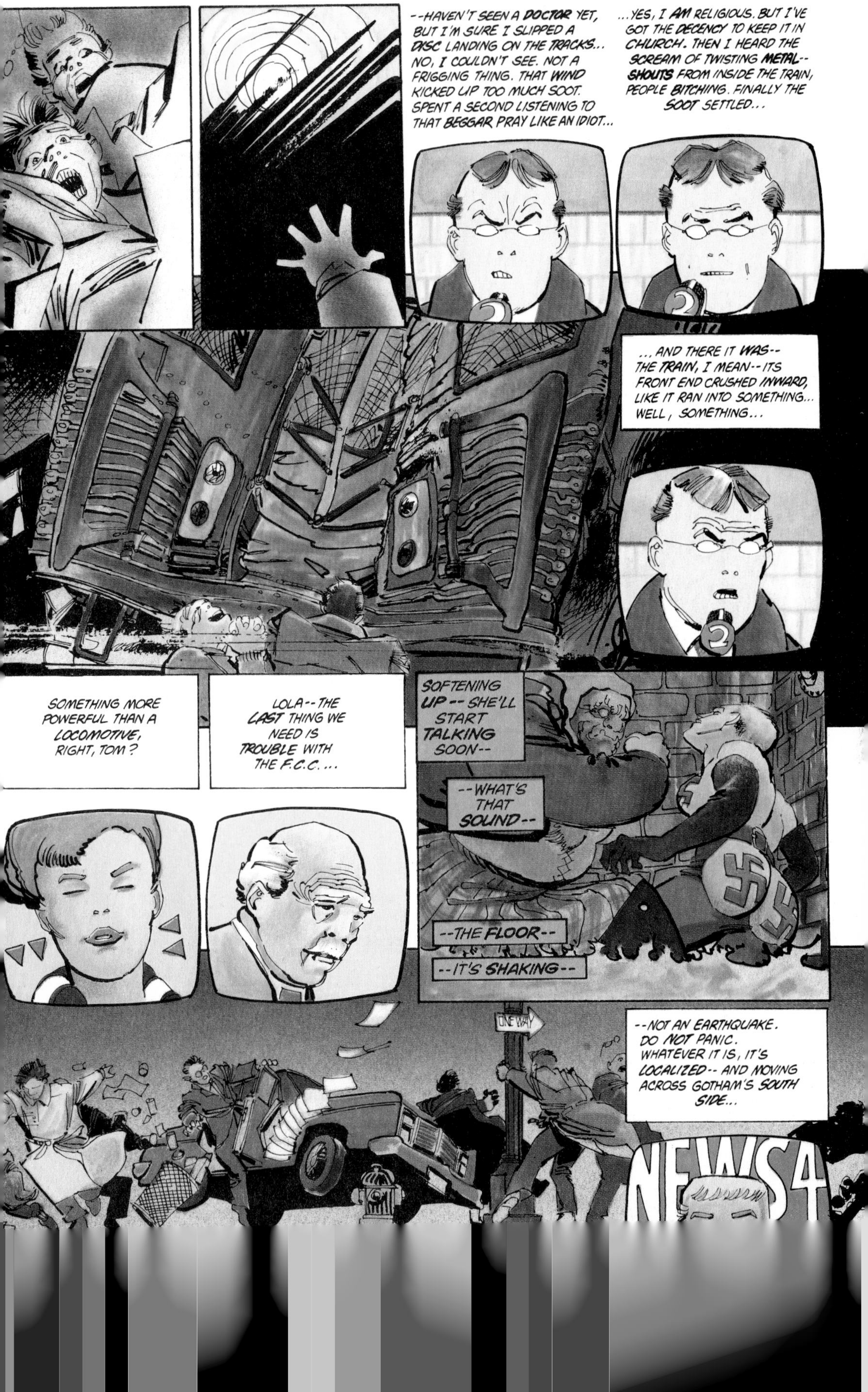
--HAVEN'T SEEN A DOCTOR YET, BUT I'M SURE I SLIPPED A DISC LANDING ON THE TRACKS... NO, I COULDN'T SEE. NOT A FRIGGING THING. THAT WIND KICKED UP TOO MUCH SOOT. SPENT A SECOND LISTENING TO THAT BEGGAR PRAY LIKE AN IDIOT...
...YES, I AM RELIGIOUS. BUT I'VE GOT THE DECENCY TO KEEP IT IN CHURCH. THEN I HEARD THE SCREAM OF TWISTING METAL--SHOUTS FROM INSIDE THE TRAIN, PEOPLE BITCHING. FINALLY THE SOOT SETTLED...
..., AND THERE IT WAS--THE TRAIN, I MEAN--ITS FRONT END CRUSHED INWARD, LIKE IT RAN INTO SOMETHING... WELL, SOMETHING...
SOMETHING MORE POWERFUL THAN A LOCOMOTIVE, RIGHT, TOM?
LOLA--THE LAST THING WE NEED IS TROUBLE WITH THE F.C.C. ...
SOFTENING UP--SHE'LL START TALKING SOON--
--WHAT'S THAT SOUND--
--THE FLOOR--
--IT'S SHAKING--
ONE WAY
--NOT AN EARTHQUAKE. DO NOT PANIC. WHATEVER IT IS, IT'S LOCALIZED--AND MOVING ACROSS GOTHAM'S SOUTH SIDE...
NEWS4

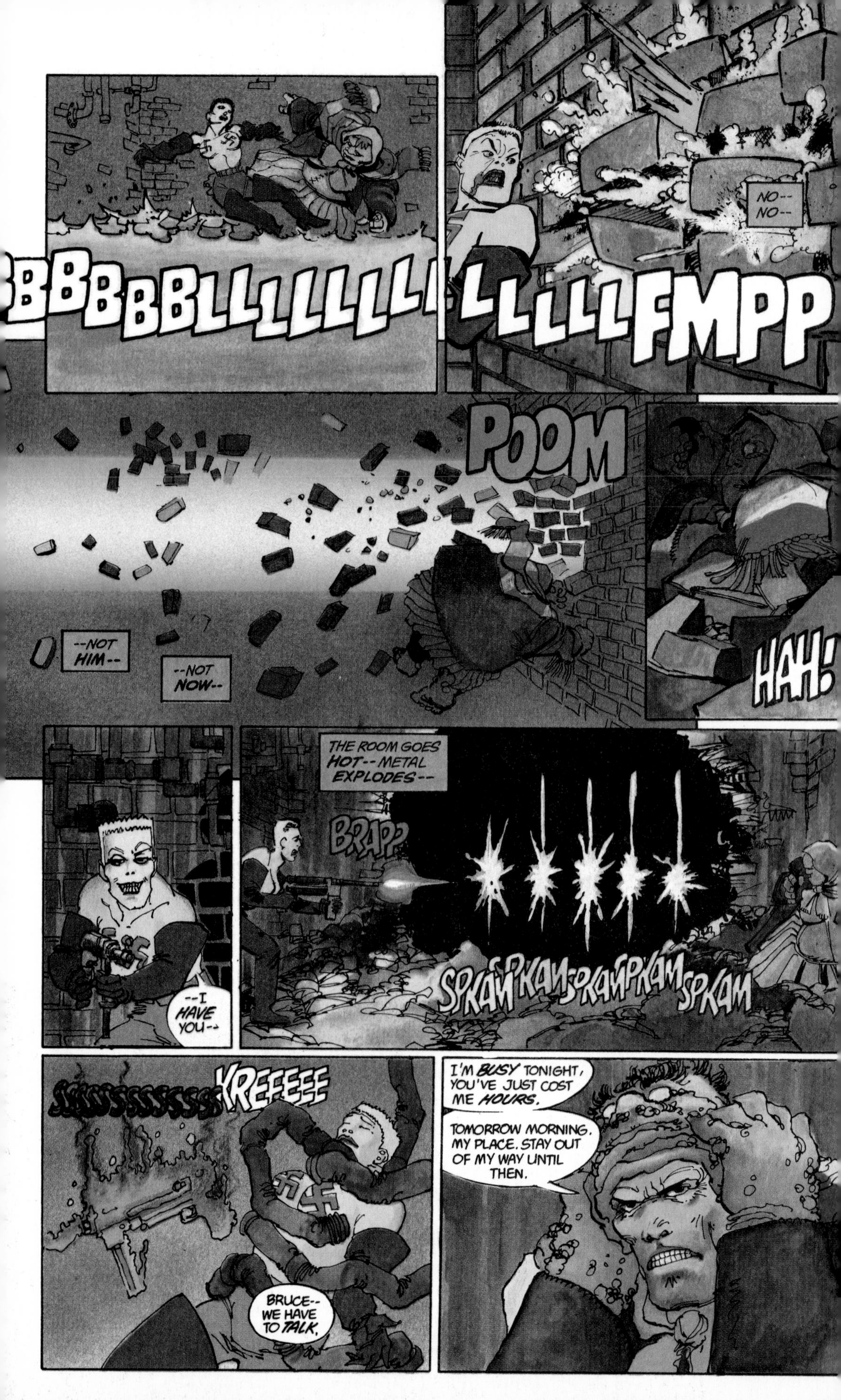
NO--
NO--
BBBBBLLLLLLLLLLLLFMPP
POOM
--NOT HIM--
--NOT NOW--
HAH!
--I HAVE YOU--
THE ROOM GOES HOT--METAL EXPLODES--
BRAPP
SPKAM SPKAM SPKAM SPKAM SPKAM
SSSSSSSSSSSKREEEEE
BRUCE-- WE HAVE TO TALK.
I'M BUSY TONIGHT, YOU'VE JUST COST ME HOURS.
TOMORROW MORNING. MY PLACE. STAY OUT OF MY WAY UNTIL THEN.

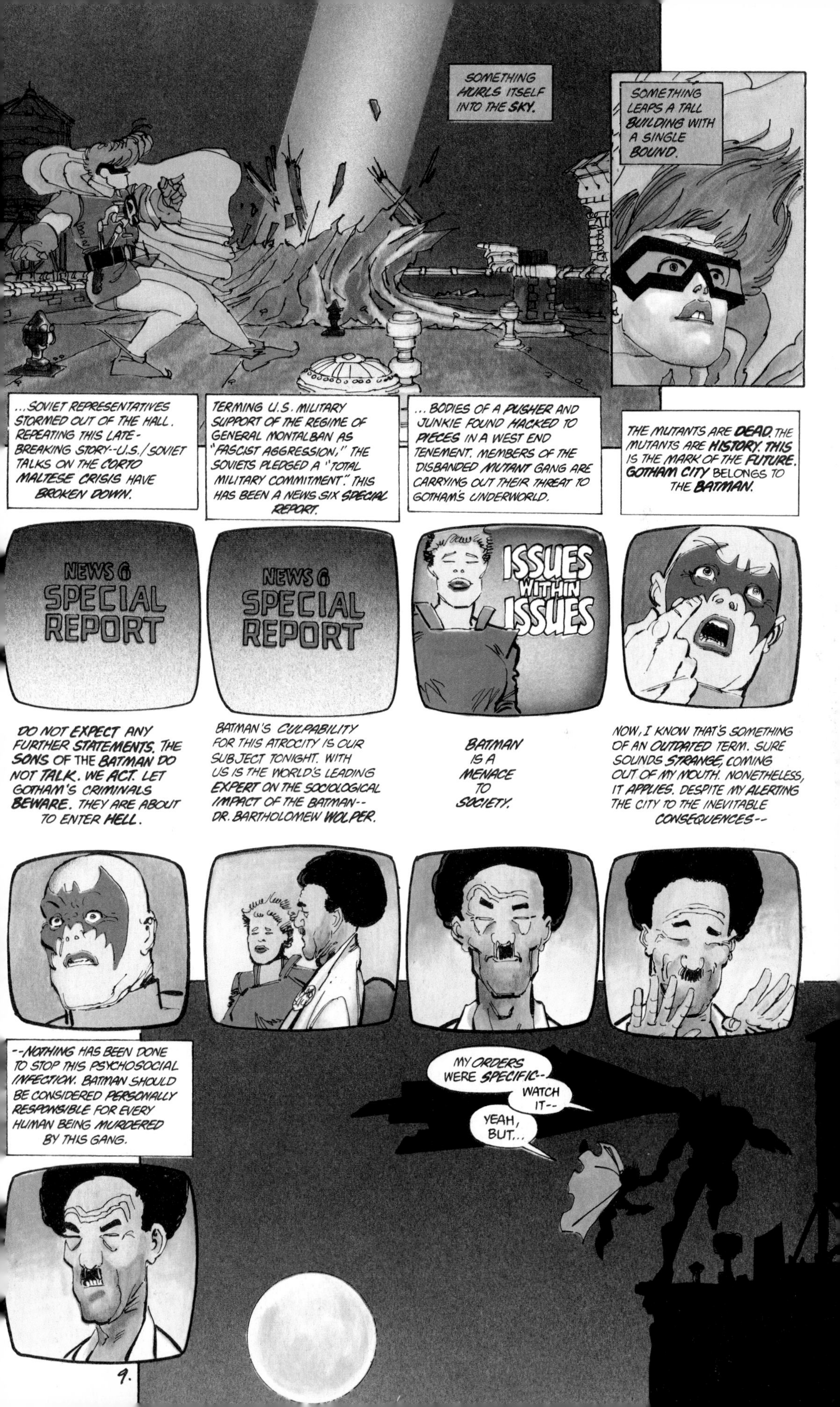
SOMETHING HURLS ITSELF INTO THE SKY.
SOMETHING LEAPS A TALL BUILDING WITH A SINGLE BOUND.
...SOVIET REPRESENTATIVES STORMED OUT OF THE HALL. REPEATING THIS LATE-BREAKING STORY--U.S./SOVIET TALKS ON THE CORTO MALTESE CRISIS HAVE BROKEN DOWN.
TERMING U.S. MILITARY SUPPORT OF THE REGIME OF GENERAL MONTALBAN AS "FASCIST AGGRESSION," THE SOVIETS PLEDGED A "TOTAL MILITARY COMMITMENT." THIS HAS BEEN A NEWS SIX SPECIAL REPORT.
...BODIES OF A PUSHER AND JUNKIE FOUND HACKED TO PIECES IN A WEST END TENEMENT. MEMBERS OF THE DISBANDED MUTANT GANG ARE CARRYING OUT THEIR THREAT TO GOTHAM'S UNDERWORLD.
THE MUTANTS ARE DEAD. THE MUTANTS ARE HISTORY. THIS IS THE MARK OF THE FUTURE. GOTHAM CITY BELONGS TO THE BATMAN.
NEWS 6 SPECIAL REPORT
NEWS 6 SPECIAL REPORT
ISSUES WITHIN ISSUES
DO NOT EXPECT ANY FURTHER STATEMENTS. THE SONS OF THE BATMAN DO NOT TALK. WE ACT. LET GOTHAM'S CRIMINALS BEWARE. THEY ARE ABOUT TO ENTER HELL.
BATMAN'S CULPABILITY FOR THIS ATROCITY IS OUR SUBJECT TONIGHT. WITH US IS THE WORLD'S LEADING EXPERT ON THE SOCIOLOGICAL IMPACT OF THE BATMAN-- DR. BARTHOLOMEW WOLPER.
BATMAN IS A MENACE TO SOCIETY.
NOW, I KNOW THAT'S SOMETHING OF AN OUTDATED TERM. SURE SOUNDS STRANGE, COMING OUT OF MY MOUTH. NONETHELESS, IT APPLIES. DESPITE MY ALERTING THE CITY TO THE INEVITABLE CONSEQUENCES--
--NOTHING HAS BEEN DONE TO STOP THIS PSYCHOSOCIAL INFECTION. BATMAN SHOULD BE CONSIDERED PERSONALLY RESPONSIBLE FOR EVERY HUMAN BEING MURDERED BY THIS GANG.
MY ORDERS WERE SPECIFIC--
WATCH IT--
YEAH, BUT...
9.

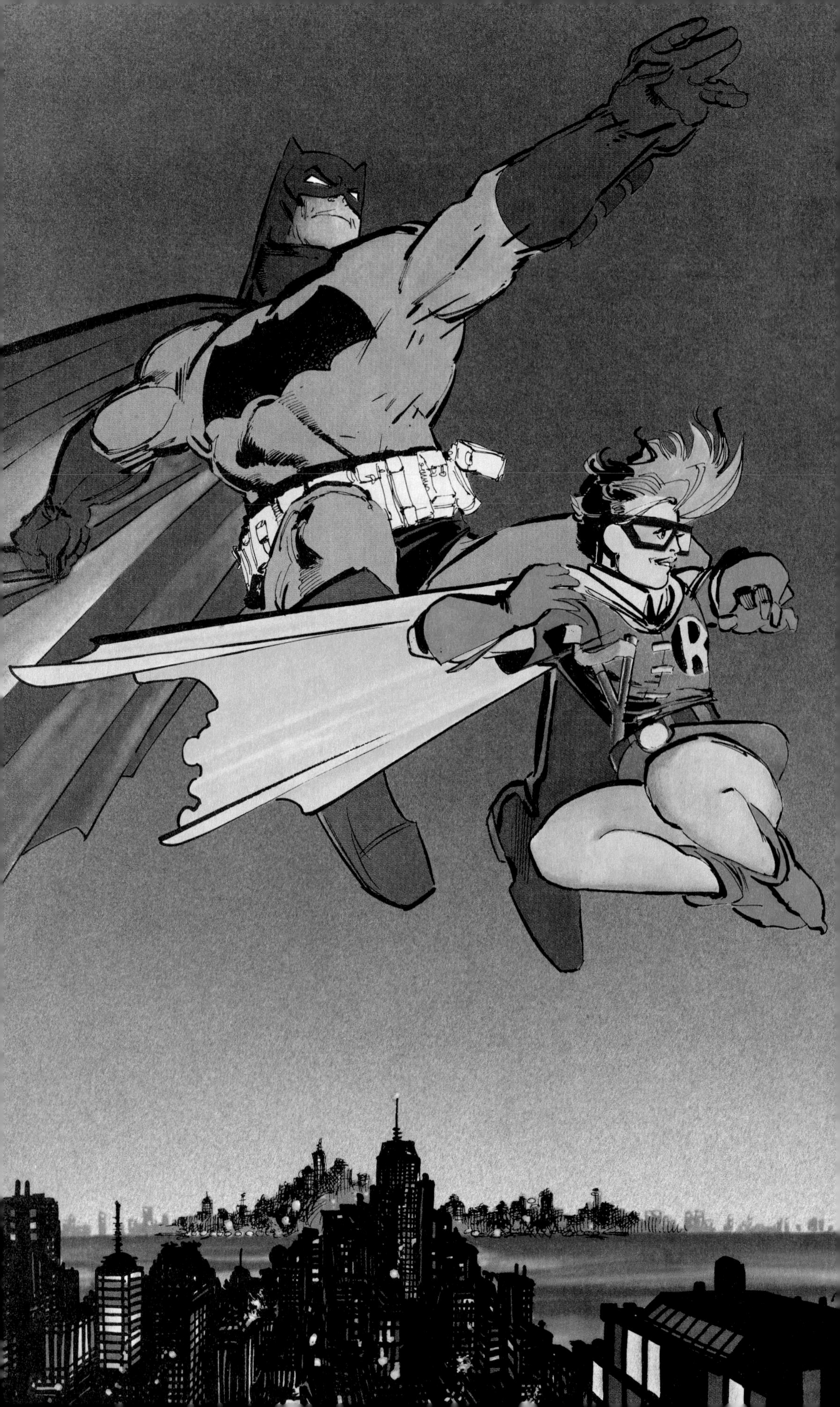

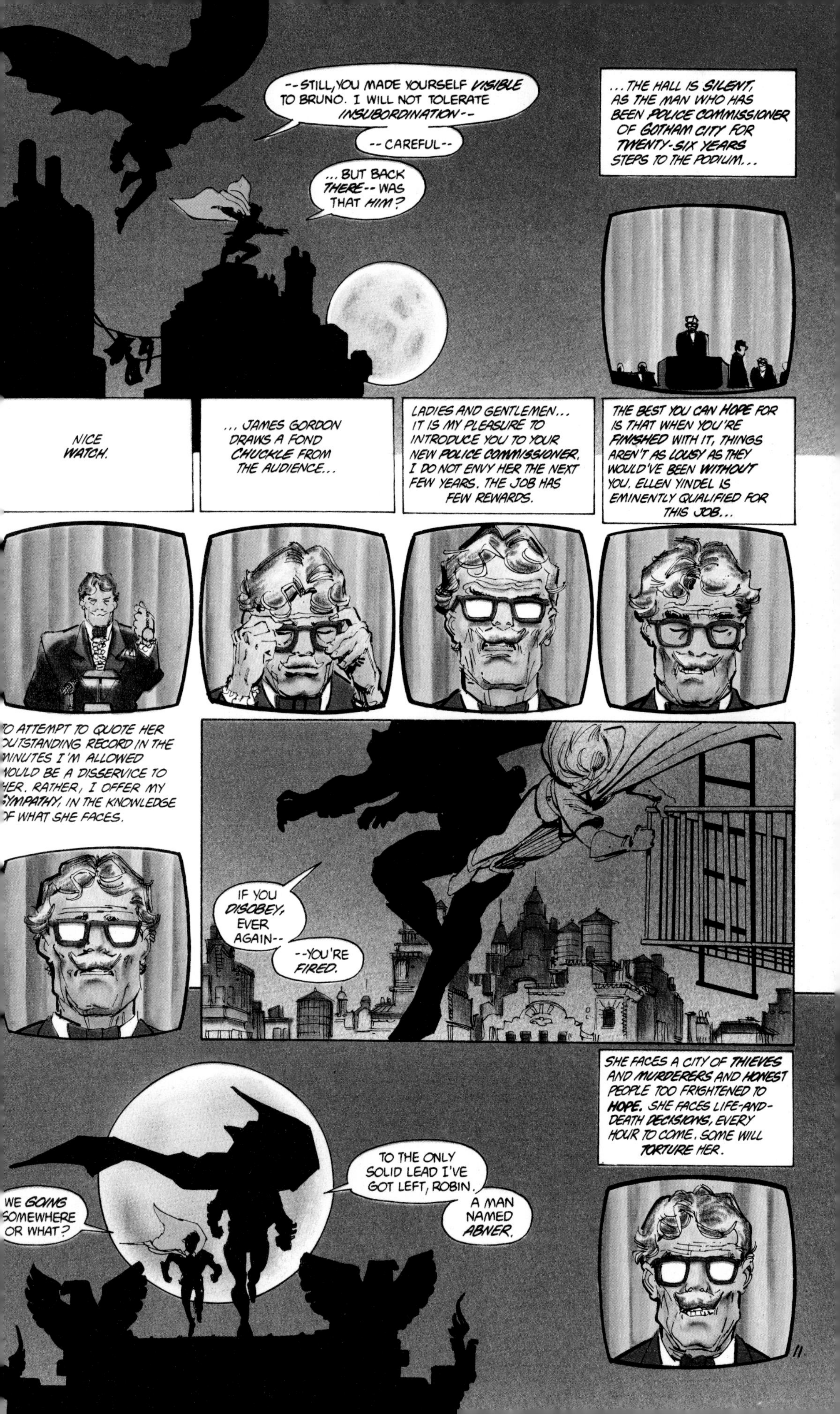

--STILL, YOU MADE YOURSELF VISIBLE TO BRUNO. I WILL NOT TOLERATE INSUBORDINATION--
--CAREFUL--
...BUT BACK THERE-- WAS THAT HIM?
...THE HALL IS SILENT, AS THE MAN WHO HAS BEEN POLICE COMMISSIONER OF GOTHAM CITY FOR TWENTY-SIX YEARS STEPS TO THE PODIUM...
NICE WATCH.
...JAMES GORDON DRAWS A FOND CHUCKLE FROM THE AUDIENCE...
LADIES AND GENTLEMEN... IT IS MY PLEASURE TO INTRODUCE YOU TO YOUR NEW POLICE COMMISSIONER. I DO NOT ENVY HER THE NEXT FEW YEARS. THE JOB HAS FEW REWARDS.
THE BEST YOU CAN HOPE FOR IS THAT WHEN YOU'RE FINISHED WITH IT, THINGS AREN'T AS LOUSY AS THEY WOULD'VE BEEN WITHOUT YOU. ELLEN YINDEL IS EMINENTLY QUALIFIED FOR THIS JOB...
TO ATTEMPT TO QUOTE HER OUTSTANDING RECORD IN THE MINUTES I'M ALLOWED WOULD BE A DISSERVICE TO HER. RATHER, I OFFER MY SYMPATHY, IN THE KNOWLEDGE OF WHAT SHE FACES.
IF YOU DISOBEY, EVER AGAIN--
--YOU'RE FIRED.
SHE FACES A CITY OF THIEVES AND MURDERERS AND HONEST PEOPLE TOO FRIGHTENED TO HOPE. SHE FACES LIFE-AND-DEATH DECISIONS, EVERY HOUR TO COME. SOME WILL TORTURE HER.
WE GOING SOMEWHERE OR WHAT?
TO THE ONLY SOLID LEAD I'VE GOT LEFT, ROBIN.
A MAN NAMED ABNER.

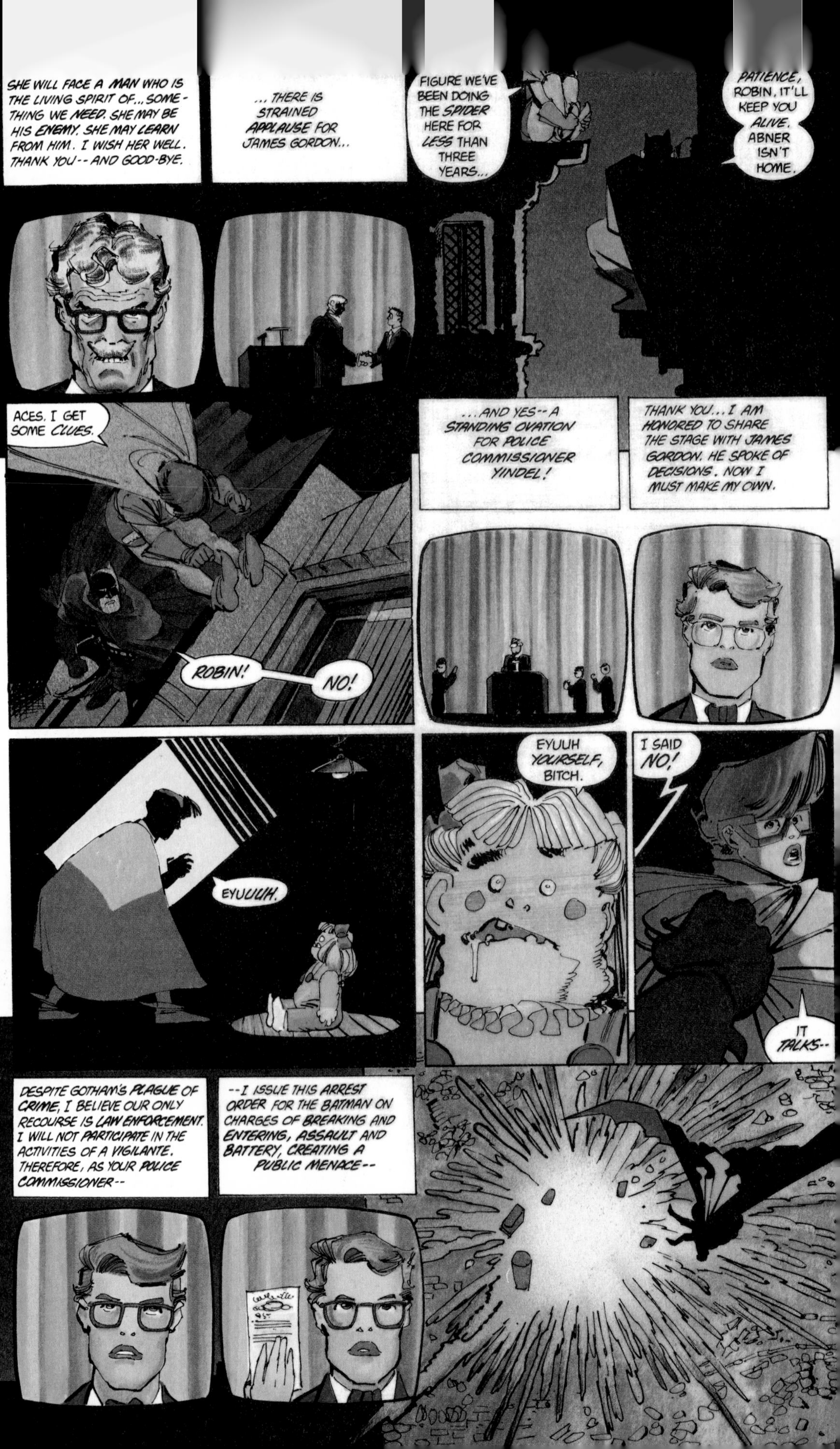

SHE WILL FACE A MAN WHO IS THE LIVING SPIRIT OF... SOMETHING WE NEED. SHE MAY BE HIS ENEMY. SHE MAY LEARN FROM HIM. I WISH HER WELL. THANK YOU-- AND GOOD-BYE.
... THERE IS STRAINED APPLAUSE FOR JAMES GORDON...
FIGURE WE'VE BEEN DOING THE SPIDER HERE FOR LESS THAN THREE YEARS...
PATIENCE, ROBIN. IT'LL KEEP YOU ALIVE. ABNER ISN'T HOME.
ACES. I GET SOME CLUES.
ROBIN!
NO!
...AND YES-- A STANDING OVATION FOR POLICE COMMISSIONER YINDEL!
THANK YOU... I AM HONORED TO SHARE THE STAGE WITH JAMES GORDON. HE SPOKE OF DECISIONS. NOW I MUST MAKE MY OWN.
EYUUUH.
EYUUH YOURSELF, BITCH.
I SAID NO!
IT TALKS--
DESPITE GOTHAM'S PLAGUE OF CRIME, I BELIEVE OUR ONLY RECOURSE IS LAW ENFORCEMENT. I WILL NOT PARTICIPATE IN THE ACTIVITIES OF A VIGILANTE. THEREFORE, AS YOUR POLICE COMMISSIONER--
--I ISSUE THIS ARREST ORDER FOR THE BATMAN ON CHARGES OF BREAKING AND ENTERING, ASSAULT AND BATTERY, CREATING A PUBLIC MENACE--

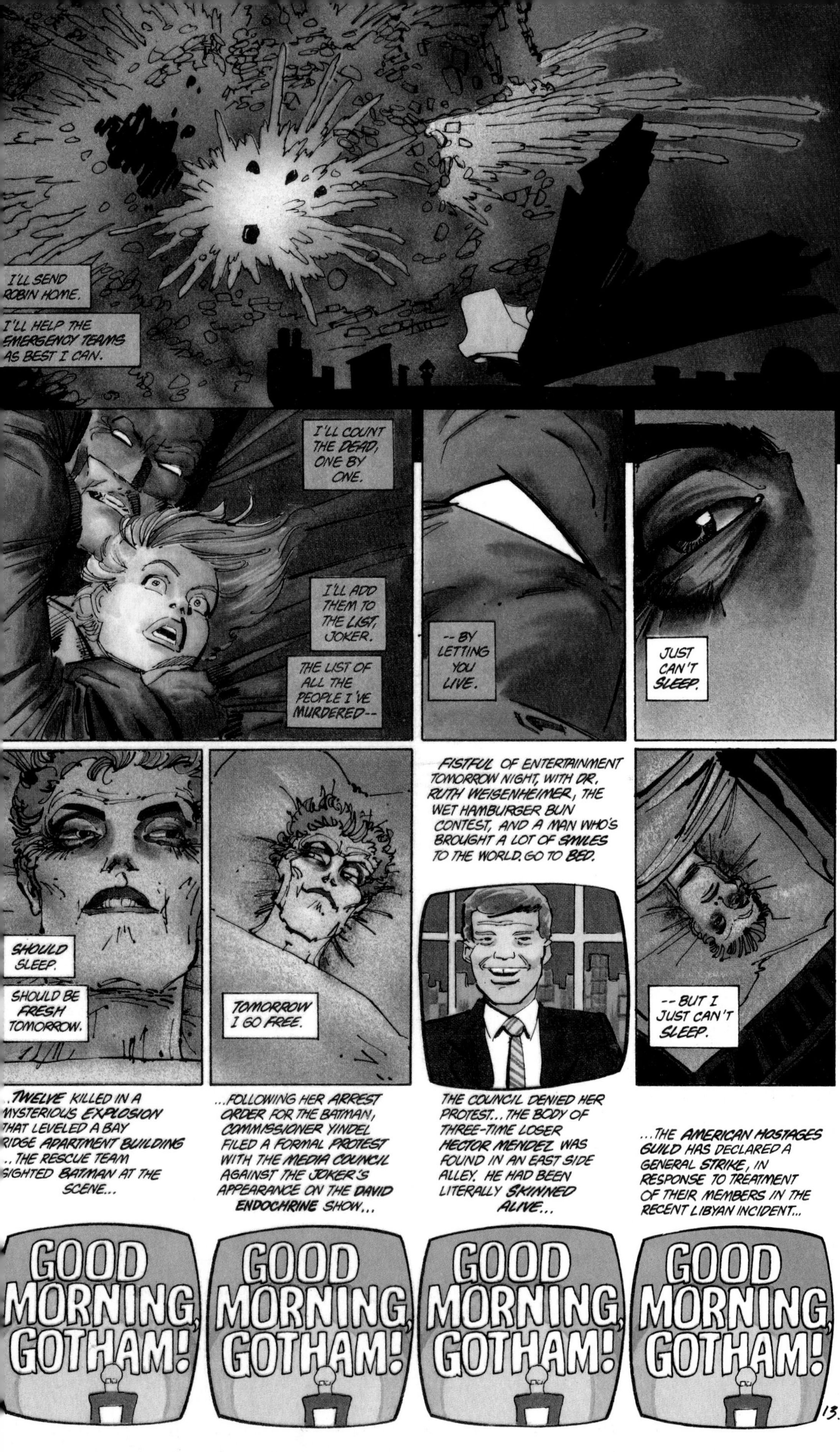

I'LL SEND ROBIN HOME.
I'LL HELP THE EMERGENCY TEAMS AS BEST I CAN.
I'LL COUNT THE DEAD, ONE BY ONE.
I'LL ADD THEM TO THE LIST, JOKER.
THE LIST OF ALL THE PEOPLE I'VE MURDERED--
--BY LETTING YOU LIVE.
JUST CAN'T SLEEP.
SHOULD SLEEP.
SHOULD BE FRESH TOMORROW.
TOMORROW I GO FREE.
--FISTFUL OF ENTERTAINMENT TOMORROW NIGHT, WITH DR. RUTH WEISENHEIMER, THE WET HAMBURGER BUN CONTEST, AND A MAN WHO'S BROUGHT A LOT OF SMILES TO THE WORLD. GO TO BED.
--BUT I JUST CAN'T SLEEP.
...TWELVE KILLED IN A MYSTERIOUS EXPLOSION THAT LEVELED A BAY RIDGE APARTMENT BUILDING ...THE RESCUE TEAM SIGHTED BATMAN AT THE SCENE...
...FOLLOWING HER ARREST ORDER FOR THE BATMAN, COMMISSIONER YINDEL FILED A FORMAL PROTEST WITH THE MEDIA COUNCIL AGAINST THE JOKER'S APPEARANCE ON THE DAVID ENDOCHRINE SHOW...
THE COUNCIL DENIED HER PROTEST... THE BODY OF THREE-TIME LOSER HECTOR MENDEZ WAS FOUND IN AN EAST SIDE ALLEY. HE HAD BEEN LITERALLY SKINNED ALIVE...
...THE AMERICAN HOSTAGES GUILD HAS DECLARED A GENERAL STRIKE, IN RESPONSE TO TREATMENT OF THEIR MEMBERS IN THE RECENT LIBYAN INCIDENT...
GOOD MORNING, GOTHAM!
GOOD MORNING, GOTHAM!
GOOD MORNING, GOTHAM!
GOOD MORNING, GOTHAM!

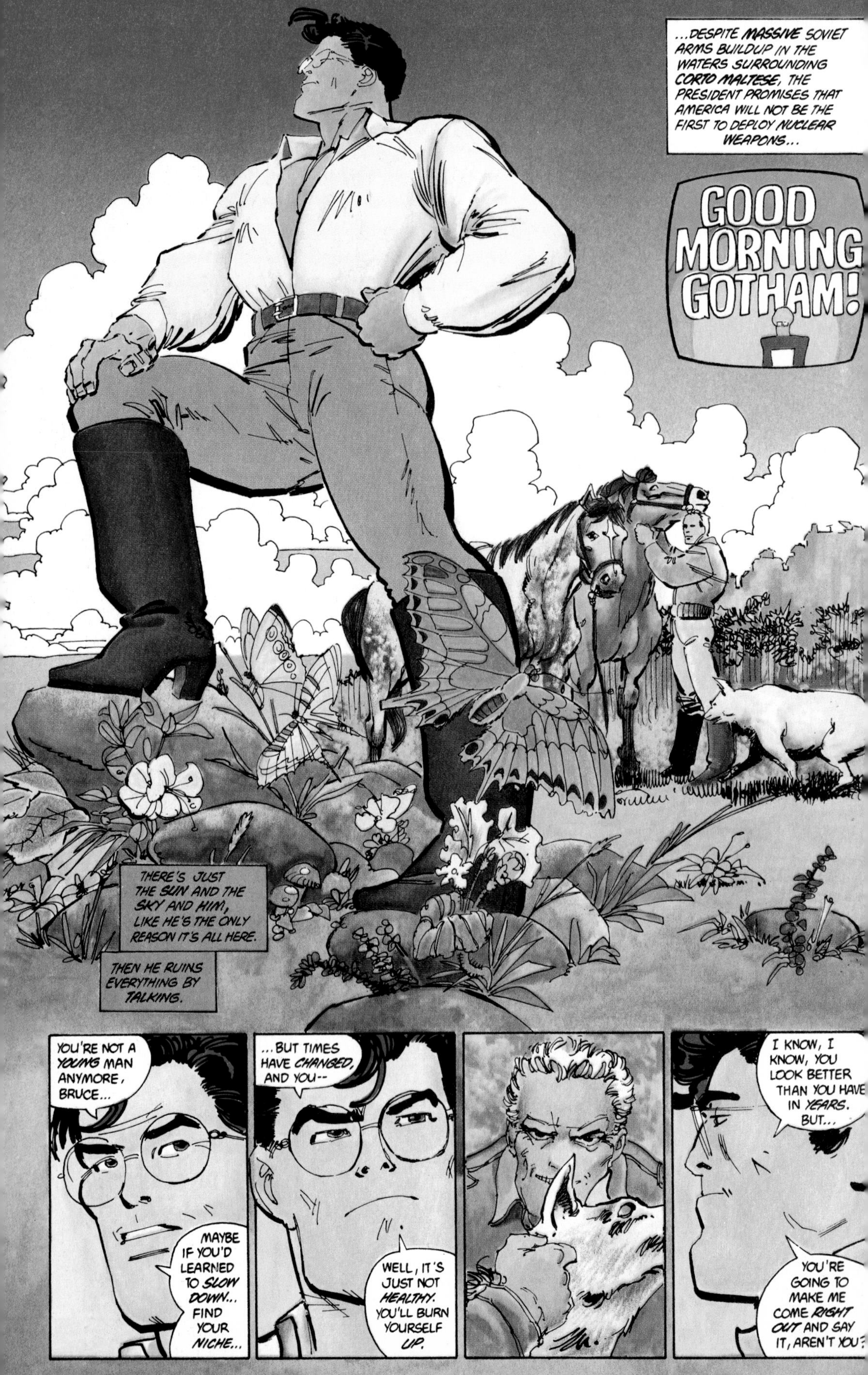
...DESPITE MASSIVE SOVIET ARMS BUILDUP IN THE WATERS SURROUNDING CORTO MALTESE, THE PRESIDENT PROMISES THAT AMERICA WILL NOT BE THE FIRST TO DEPLOY NUCLEAR WEAPONS...
GOOD MORNING GOTHAM!
THERE'S JUST THE SUN AND THE SKY AND HIM, LIKE HE'S THE ONLY REASON IT'S ALL HERE.
THEN HE RUINS EVERYTHING BY TALKING.
YOU'RE NOT A YOUNG MAN ANYMORE, BRUCE...
MAYBE IF YOU'D LEARNED TO SLOW DOWN... FIND YOUR NICHE...
...BUT TIMES HAVE CHANGED, AND YOU--
WELL, IT'S JUST NOT HEALTHY. YOU'LL BURN YOURSELF UP.
I KNOW, I KNOW, YOU LOOK BETTER THAN YOU HAVE IN YEARS. BUT...
YOU'RE GOING TO MAKE ME COME RIGHT OUT AND SAY IT, AREN'T YOU?

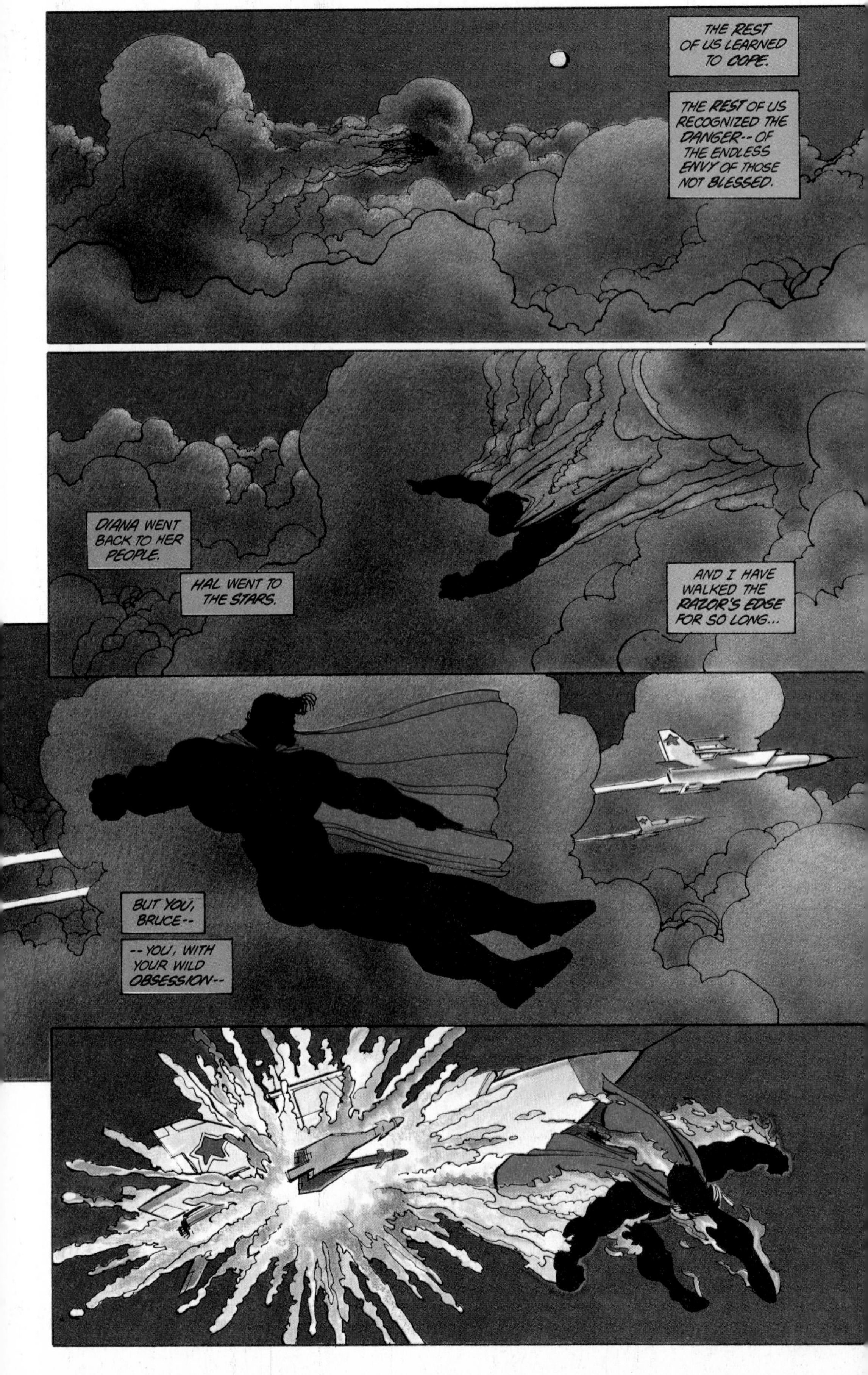
THE REST OF US LEARNED TO COPE.
THE REST OF US RECOGNIZED THE DANGER-- OF THE ENDLESS ENVY OF THOSE NOT BLESSED.
DIANA WENT BACK TO HER PEOPLE.
HAL WENT TO THE STARS.
AND I HAVE WALKED THE RAZOR'S EDGE FOR SO LONG...
BUT YOU, BRUCE--
--YOU, WITH YOUR WILD OBSESSION--

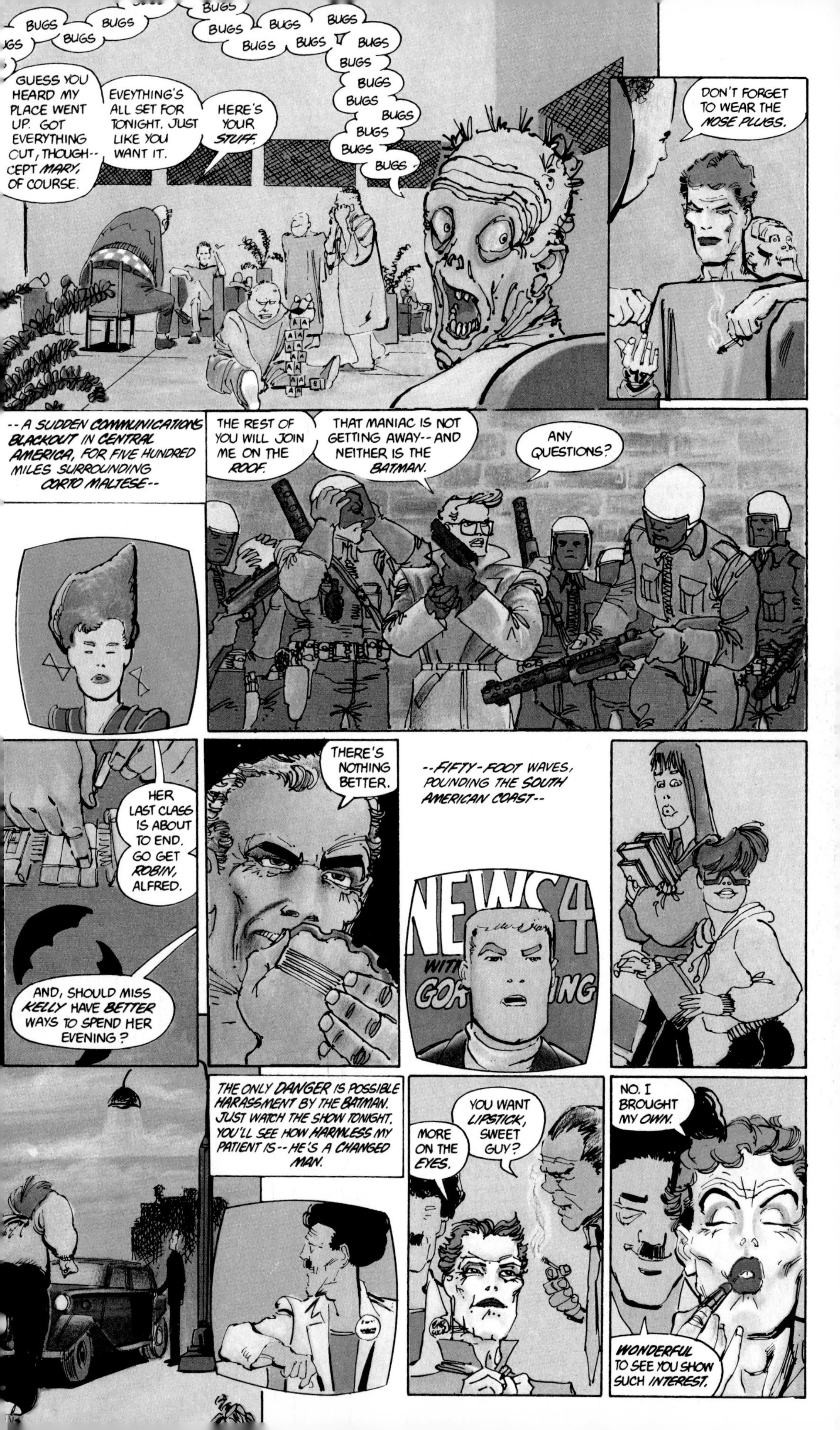
BUGS BUGS BUGS BUGS BUGS BUGS BUGS BUGS BUGS BUGS BUGS BUGS BUGS BUGS BUGS BUGS
GUESS YOU HEARD MY PLACE WENT UP. GOT EVERYTHING OUT, THOUGH--'CEPT MARY, OF COURSE.
EVEYTHING'S ALL SET FOR TONIGHT, JUST LIKE YOU WANT IT.
HERE'S YOUR STUFF.
DON'T FORGET TO WEAR THE NOSE PLUGS.
--A SUDDEN COMMUNICATIONS BLACKOUT IN CENTRAL AMERICA, FOR FIVE HUNDRED MILES SURROUNDING CORTO MALTESE--
THE REST OF YOU WILL JOIN ME ON THE ROOF.
THAT MANIAC IS NOT GETTING AWAY--AND NEITHER IS THE BATMAN.
ANY QUESTIONS?
HER LAST CLASS IS ABOUT TO END. GO GET ROBIN, ALFRED.
AND, SHOULD MISS KELLY HAVE BETTER WAYS TO SPEND HER EVENING?
THERE'S NOTHING BETTER.
--FIFTY-FOOT WAVES, POUNDING THE SOUTH AMERICAN COAST--
NEWS 4
THE ONLY DANGER IS POSSIBLE HARASSMENT BY THE BATMAN. JUST WATCH THE SHOW TONIGHT. YOU'LL SEE HOW HARMLESS MY PATIENT IS--HE'S A CHANGED MAN.
MORE ON THE EYES.
YOU WANT LIPSTICK, SWEET GUY?
NO. I BROUGHT MY OWN.
WONDERFUL TO SEE YOU SHOW SUCH INTEREST.

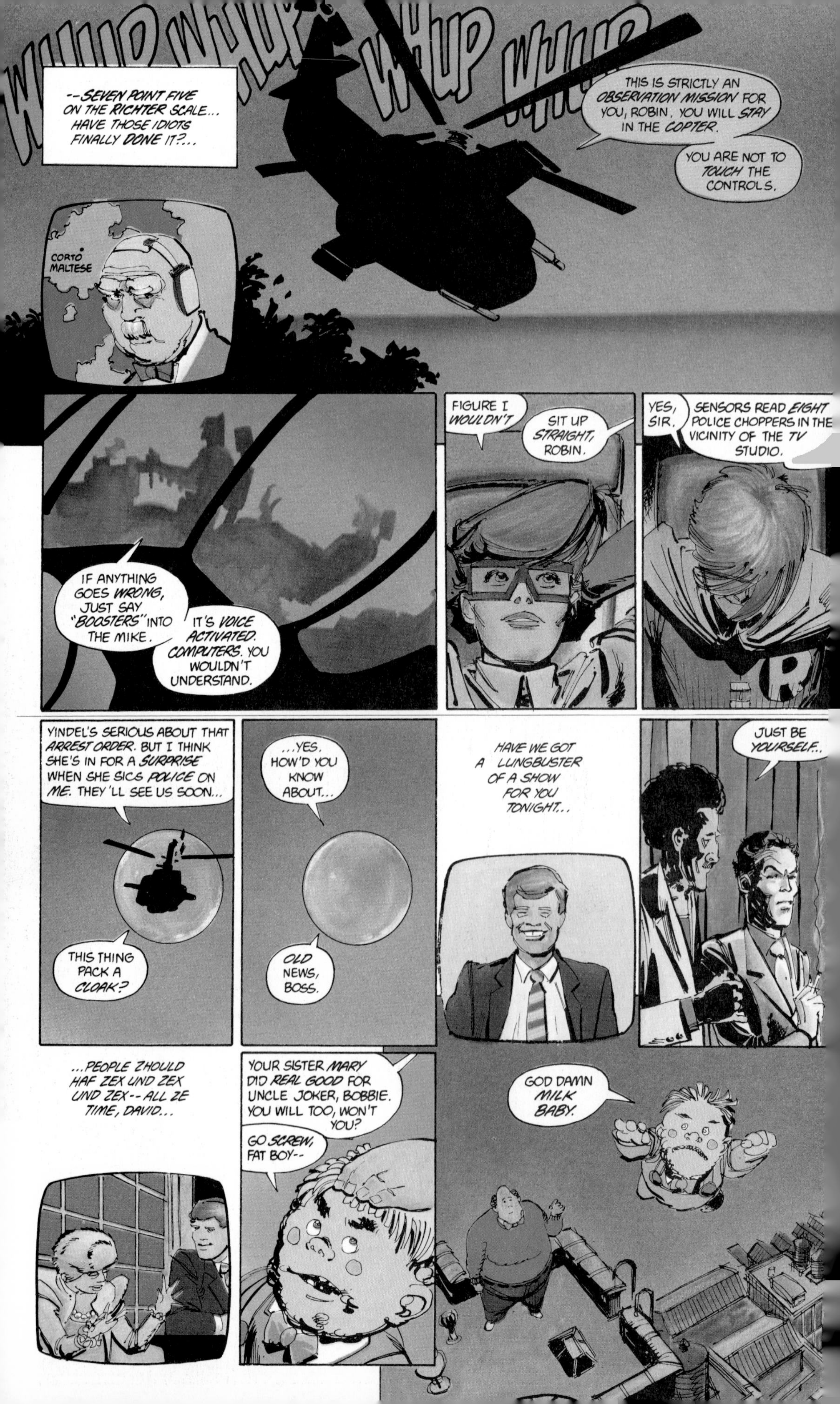
WHUP WHUP WHUP WHUP
--SEVEN POINT FIVE ON THE RICHTER SCALE... HAVE THOSE IDIOTS FINALLY DONE IT?...
THIS IS STRICTLY AN OBSERVATION MISSION FOR YOU, ROBIN. YOU WILL STAY IN THE COPTER.
YOU ARE NOT TO TOUCH THE CONTROLS.
CORTO MALTESE
IF ANYTHING GOES WRONG, JUST SAY "BOOSTERS" INTO THE MIKE.
IT'S VOICE ACTIVATED. COMPUTERS. YOU WOULDN'T UNDERSTAND.
FIGURE I WOULDN'T
SIT UP STRAIGHT, ROBIN.
YES, SIR.
SENSORS READ EIGHT POLICE CHOPPERS IN THE VICINITY OF THE TV STUDIO.
YINDEL'S SERIOUS ABOUT THAT ARREST ORDER. BUT I THINK SHE'S IN FOR A SURPRISE WHEN SHE SICS POLICE ON ME. THEY'LL SEE US SOON...
THIS THING PACK A CLOAK?
...YES. HOW'D YOU KNOW ABOUT...
OLD NEWS, BOSS.
HAVE WE GOT A LUNGBUSTER OF A SHOW FOR YOU TONIGHT...
JUST BE YOURSELF...
...PEOPLE ZHOULD HAF ZEX UND ZEX UND ZEX--ALL ZE TIME, DAVID...
YOUR SISTER MARY DID REAL GOOD FOR UNCLE JOKER, BOBBIE. YOU WILL TOO, WON'T YOU?
GO SCREW, FAT BOY--
GOD DAMN MILK BABY.

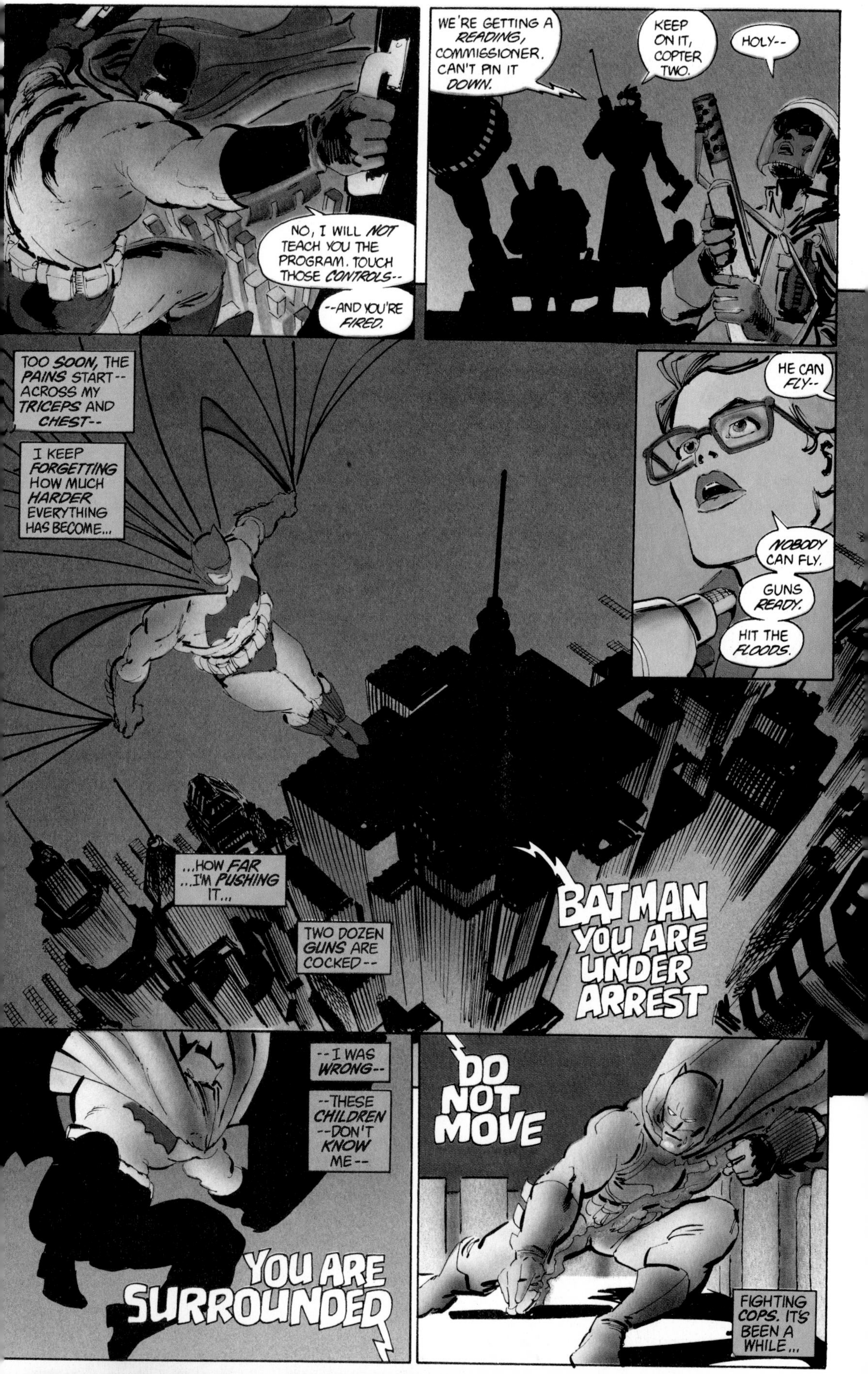
NO, I WILL NOT TEACH YOU THE PROGRAM. TOUCH THOSE CONTROLS--
--AND YOU'RE FIRED.
WE'RE GETTING A READING, COMMISSIONER. CAN'T PIN IT DOWN.
KEEP ON IT, COPTER TWO.
HOLY--
TOO SOON, THE PAINS START-- ACROSS MY TRICEPS AND CHEST--
I KEEP FORGETTING HOW MUCH HARDER EVERYTHING HAS BECOME...
HE CAN FLY--
NOBODY CAN FLY.
GUNS READY.
HIT THE FLOODS.
...HOW FAR ...I'M PUSHING IT...
TWO DOZEN GUNS ARE COCKED--
BATMAN YOU ARE UNDER ARREST
--I WAS WRONG--
--THESE CHILDREN --DON'T KNOW ME--
YOU ARE SURROUNDED
DO NOT MOVE
FIGHTING COPS. IT'S BEEN A WHILE...

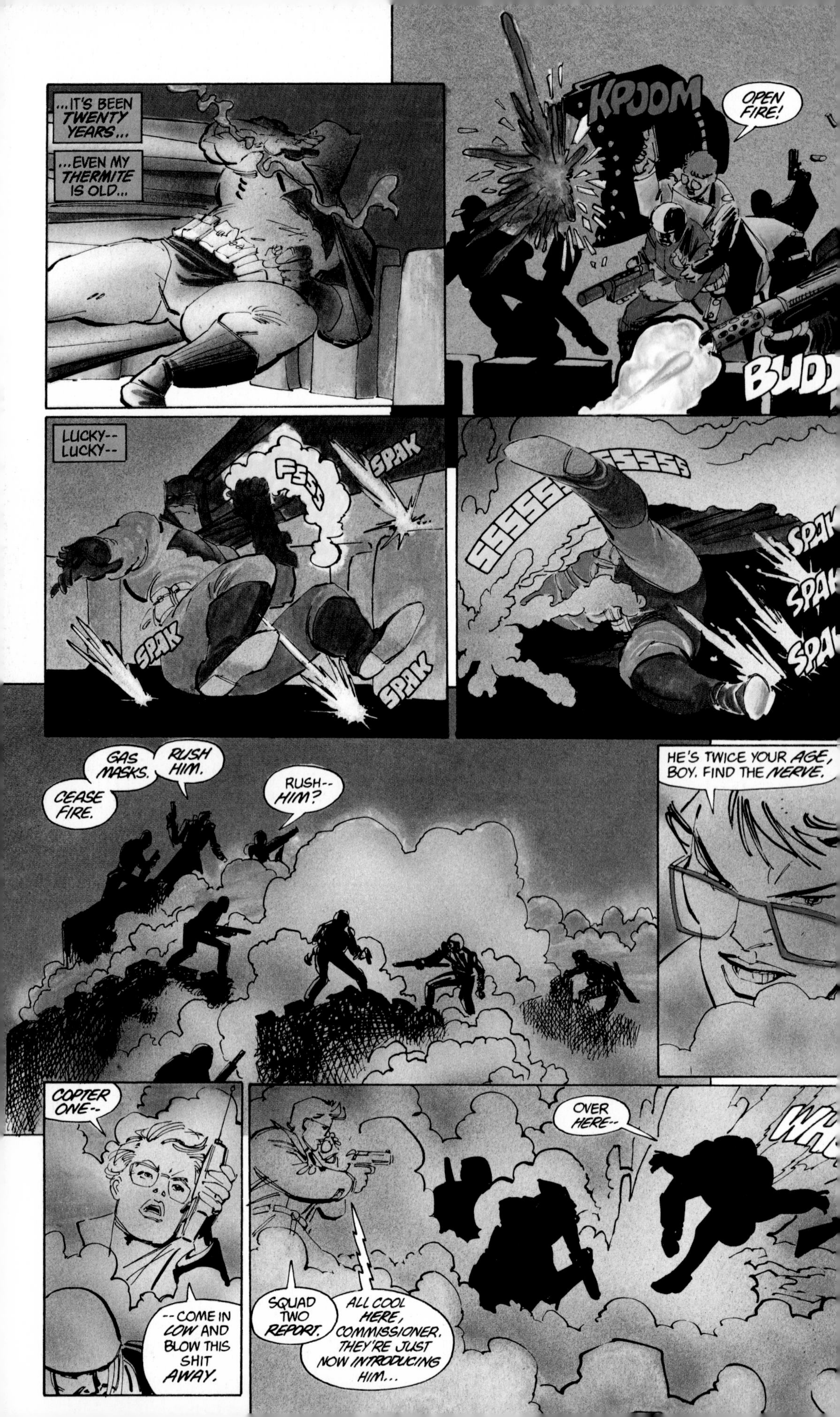
...IT'S BEEN TWENTY YEARS...
...EVEN MY THERMITE IS OLD...
KPJOOM
OPEN FIRE!
BUDD
LUCKY-- LUCKY--
FSSS
SPAK
SPAK
SPAK
SSSSSSSSSSS
SPAK
SPAK
SPAK
GAS MASKS.
RUSH HIM.
CEASE FIRE.
RUSH-- HIM?
HE'S TWICE YOUR AGE, BOY. FIND THE NERVE.
COPTER ONE--
--COME IN LOW AND BLOW THIS SHIT AWAY.
SQUAD TWO REPORT.
ALL COOL HERE, COMMISSIONER. THEY'RE JUST NOW INTRODUCING HIM...
OVER HERE--

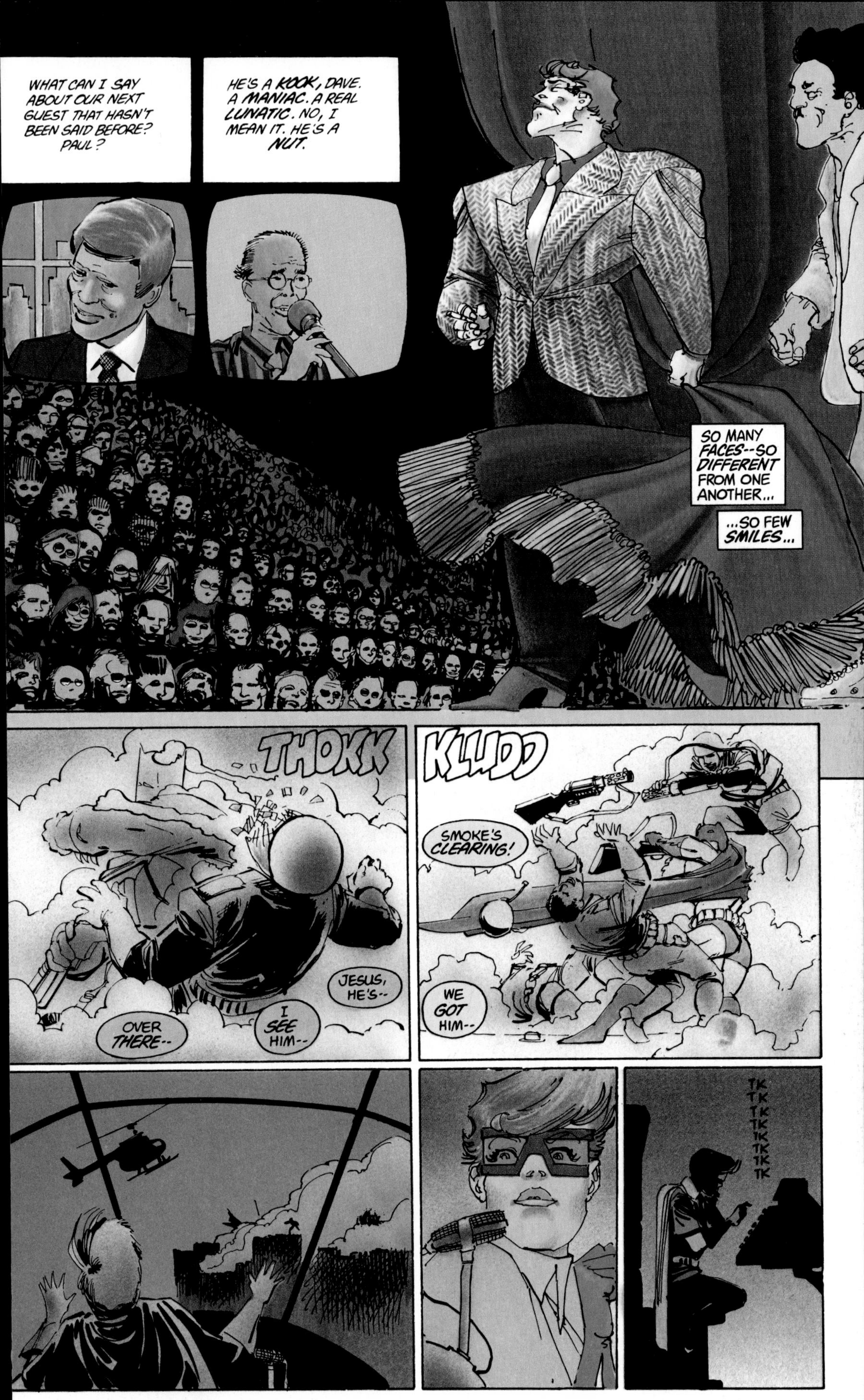
WHAT CAN I SAY ABOUT OUR NEXT GUEST THAT HASN'T BEEN SAID BEFORE? PAUL?
HE'S A KOOK, DAVE. A MANIAC. A REAL LUNATIC. NO, I MEAN IT. HE'S A NUT.
SO MANY FACES--SO DIFFERENT FROM ONE ANOTHER...
...SO FEW SMILES...
THOKK
JESUS, HE'S--
I SEE HIM--
OVER THERE--
KLUDD
SMOKE'S CLEARING!
WE GOT HIM--
TK TK TK TK TK TK TK TK TK TK TK TK TK

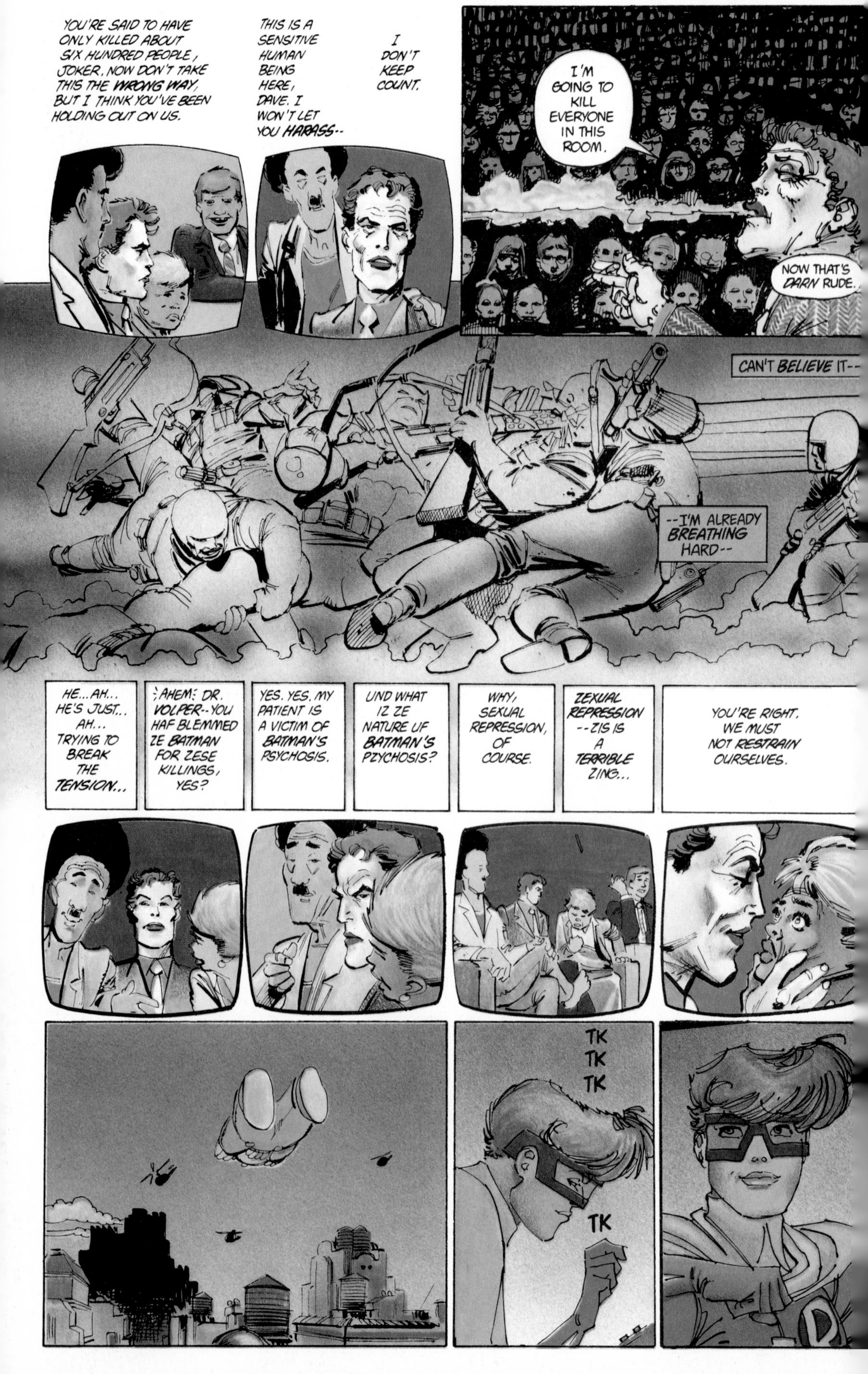

YOU'RE SAID TO HAVE ONLY KILLED ABOUT SIX HUNDRED PEOPLE, JOKER. NOW DON'T TAKE THIS THE WRONG WAY, BUT I THINK YOU'VE BEEN HOLDING OUT ON US.
THIS IS A SENSITIVE HUMAN BEING HERE, DAVE. I WON'T LET YOU HARASS--
I DON'T KEEP COUNT.
I'M GOING TO KILL EVERYONE IN THIS ROOM.
NOW THAT'S DARN RUDE.
CAN'T BELIEVE IT--
--I'M ALREADY BREATHING HARD--
HE...AH... HE'S JUST... AH... TRYING TO BREAK THE TENSION...
:AHEM: DR. VOLPER--YOU HAF BLEMMED ZE BATMAN FOR ZESE KILLINGS, YES?
YES. YES, MY PATIENT IS A VICTIM OF BATMAN'S PSYCHOSIS.
UND WHAT IZ ZE NATURE UF BATMAN'S PZYCHOSIS?
WHY, SEXUAL REPRESSION, OF COURSE.
ZEXUAL REPRESSION --ZIS IS A TERRIBLE ZING...
YOU'RE RIGHT. WE MUST NOT RESTRAIN OURSELVES.
TK
TK
TK
TK

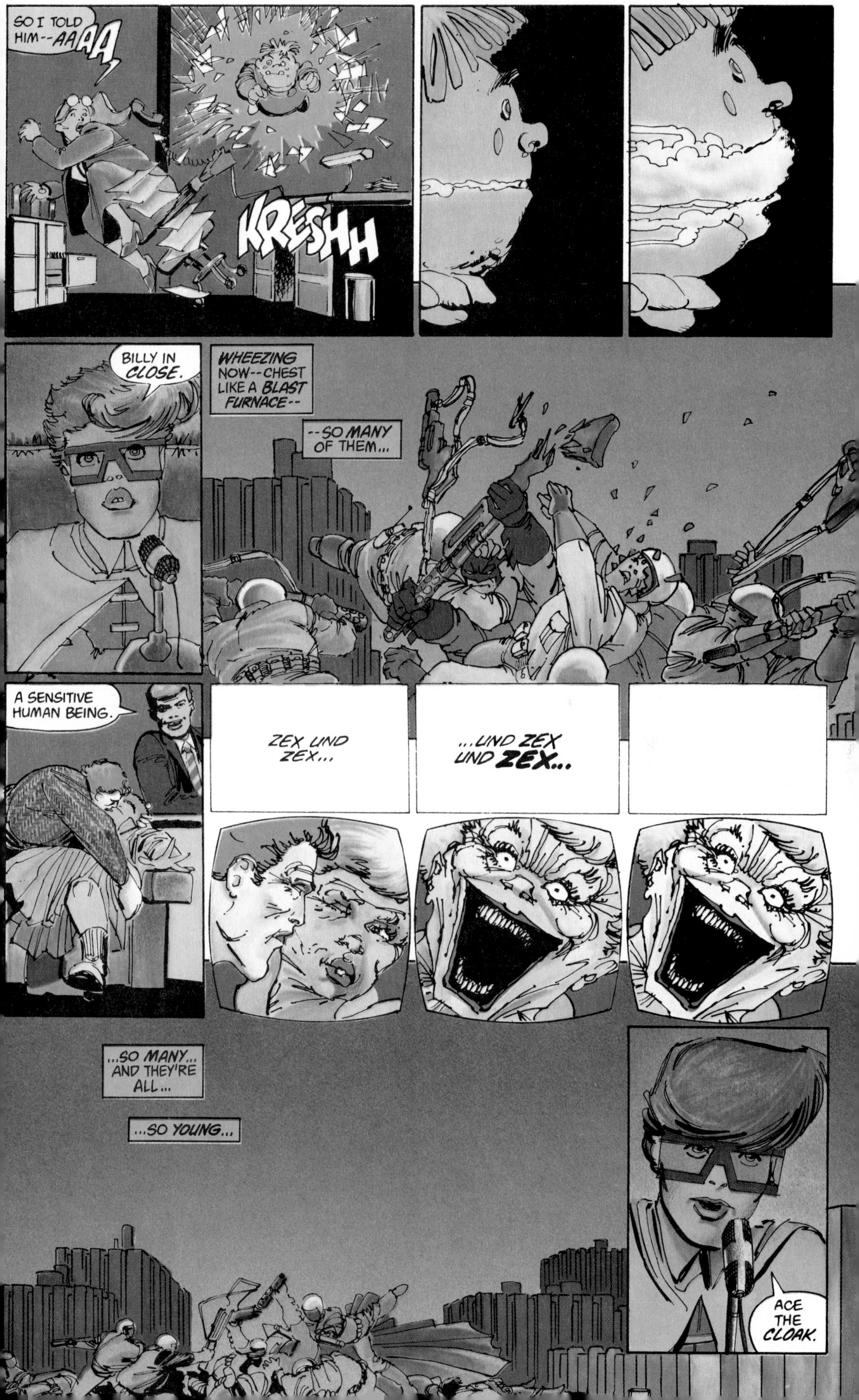
SO I TOLD HIM--AAAA
KRESHH
BILLY IN CLOSE.
WHEEZING NOW--CHEST LIKE A BLAST FURNACE--
--SO MANY OF THEM...
A SENSITIVE HUMAN BEING.
ZEX UND ZEX...
...UND ZEX UND ZEX...
...SO MANY... AND THEY'RE ALL...
...SO YOUNG...
ACE THE CLOAK.

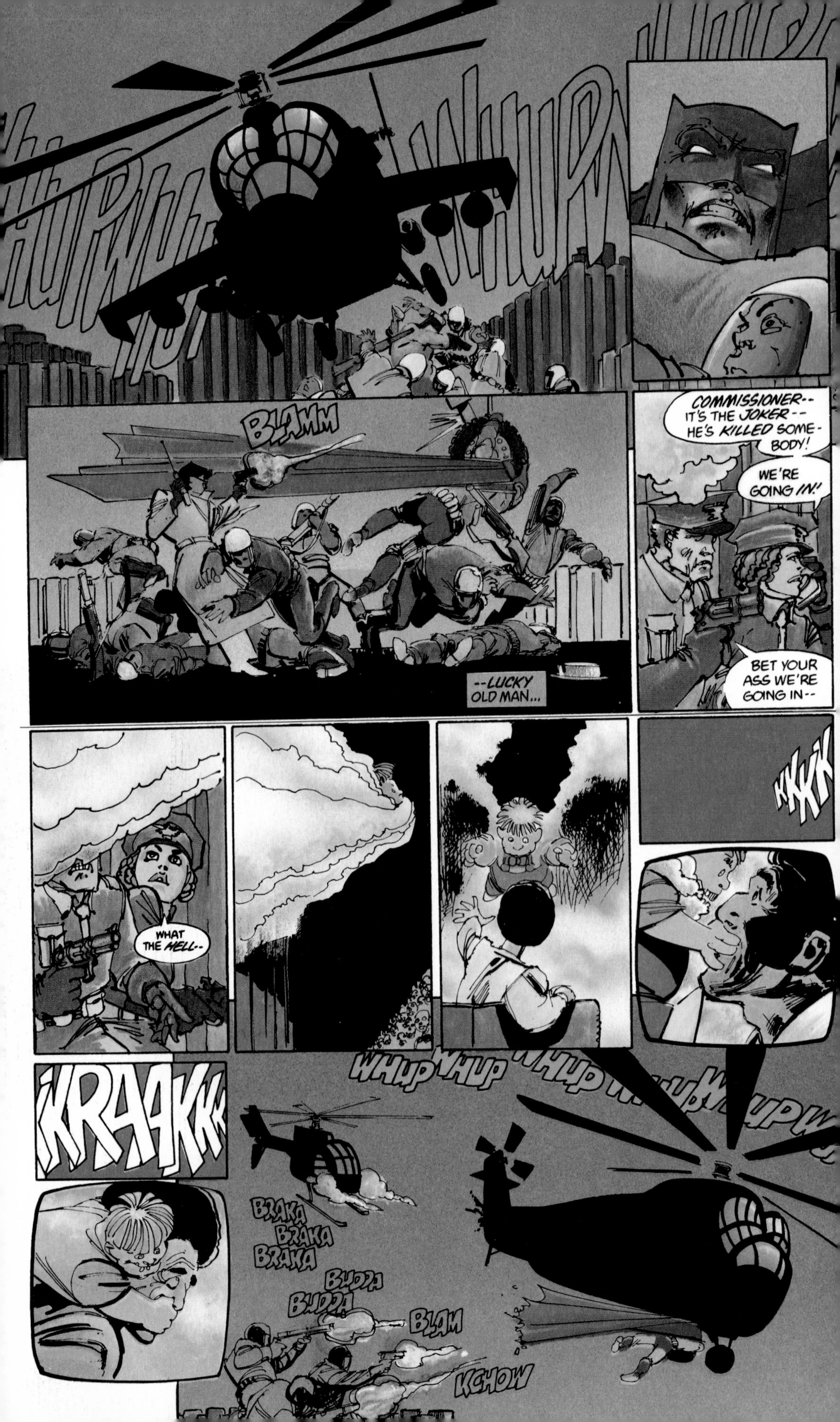
WHUPWHUPWHUP
BLAMM
COMMISSIONER-- IT'S THE JOKER-- HE'S KILLED SOME-BODY!
WE'RE GOING IN!
--LUCKY OLD MAN...
BET YOUR ASS WE'RE GOING IN--
WHAT THE HELL--
KKKK
KRAAKKK
WHUP WHUP WHUP
BRAKA BRAKA BRAKA
BUDDA BUDDA
BLAM
KCHOW

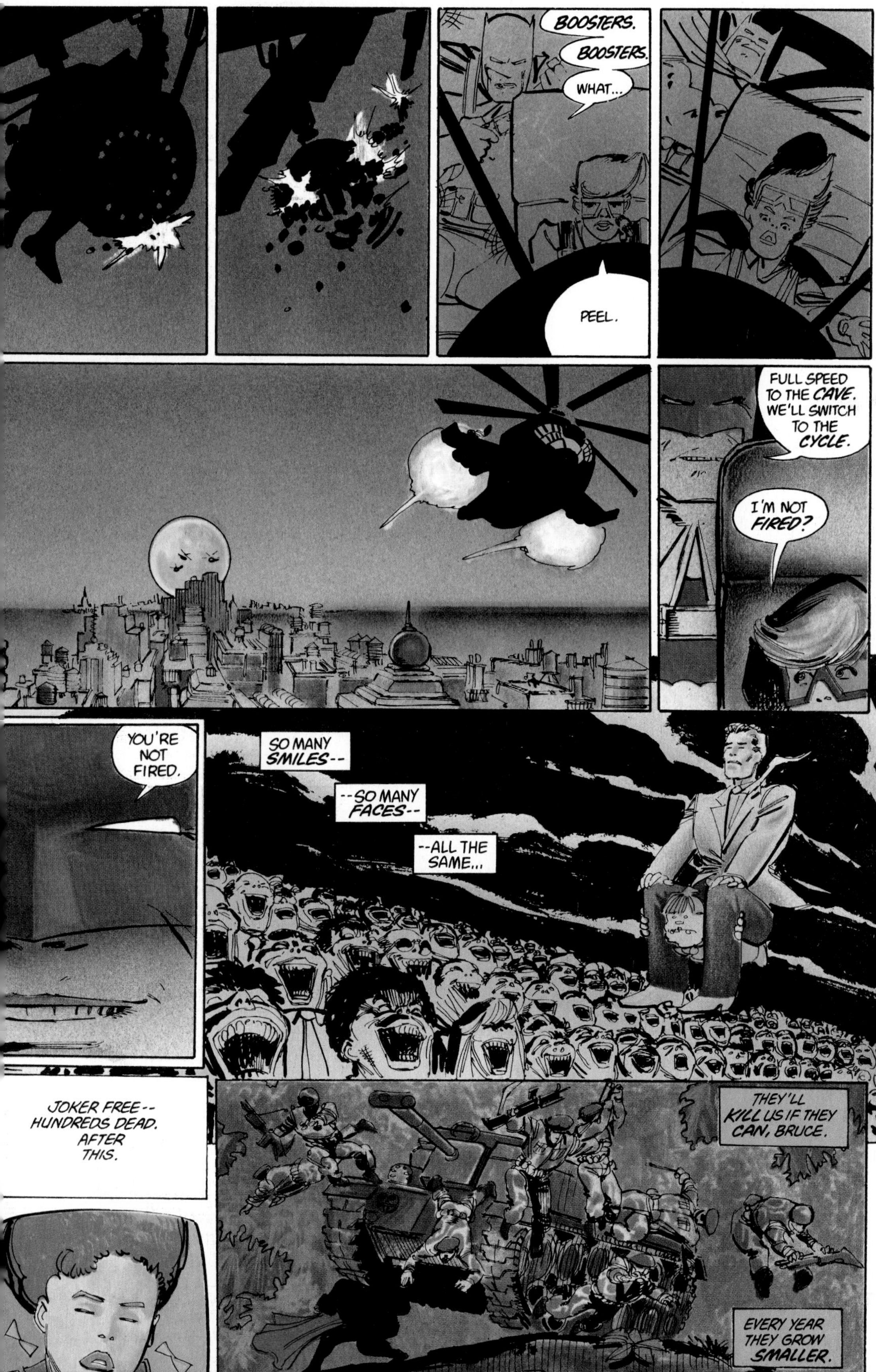

BOOSTERS.
BOOSTERS.
WHAT...
PEEL.
FULL SPEED TO THE CAVE. WE'LL SWITCH TO THE CYCLE.
I'M NOT FIRED?
YOU'RE NOT FIRED.
SO MANY SMILES--
--SO MANY FACES--
--ALL THE SAME...
JOKER FREE-- HUNDREDS DEAD. AFTER THIS.
THEY'LL KILL US IF THEY CAN, BRUCE.
EVERY YEAR THEY GROW SMALLER.
EVERY YEAR THEY HATE US MORE.

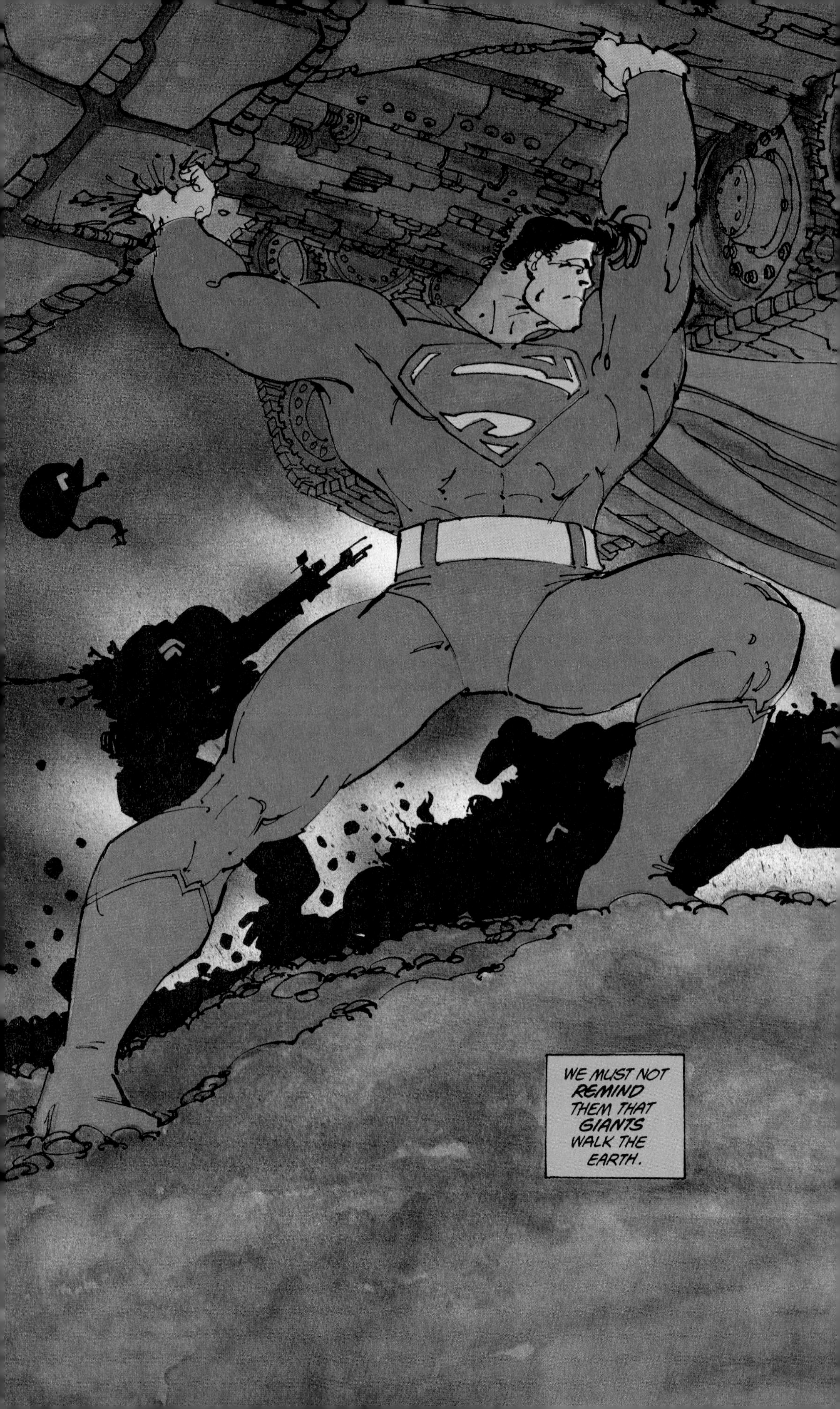
WE MUST NOT REMIND THEM THAT GIANTS WALK THE EARTH.

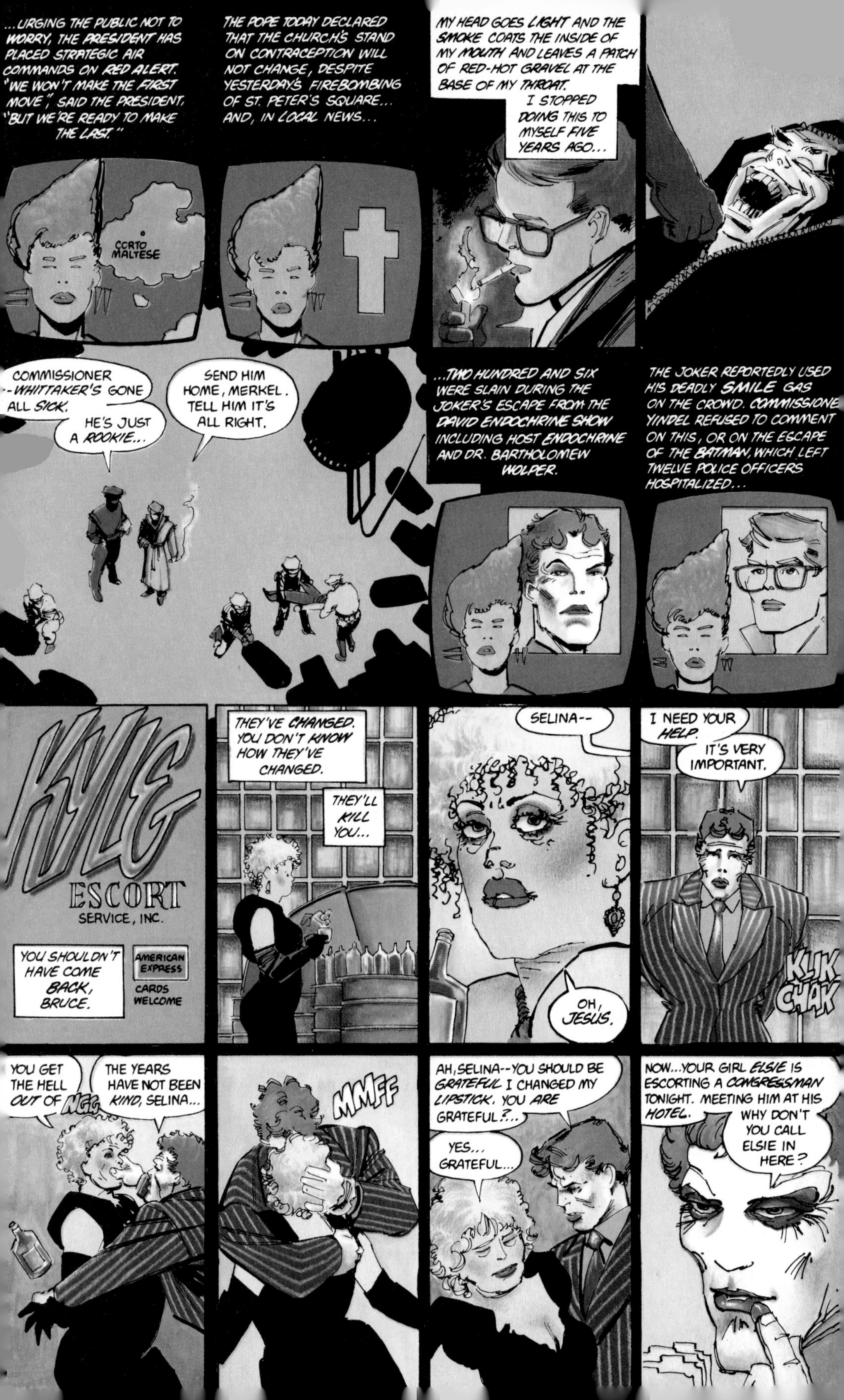
...URGING THE PUBLIC NOT TO WORRY, THE PRESIDENT HAS PLACED STRATEGIC AIR COMMANDS ON RED ALERT. "WE WON'T MAKE THE FIRST MOVE," SAID THE PRESIDENT. "BUT WE'RE READY TO MAKE THE LAST."
CORTO MALTESE
THE POPE TODAY DECLARED THAT THE CHURCH'S STAND ON CONTRACEPTION WILL NOT CHANGE, DESPITE YESTERDAY'S FIREBOMBING OF ST. PETER'S SQUARE... AND, IN LOCAL NEWS...
MY HEAD GOES LIGHT AND THE SMOKE COATS THE INSIDE OF MY MOUTH AND LEAVES A PATCH OF RED-HOT GRAVEL AT THE BASE OF MY THROAT.
I STOPPED DOING THIS TO MYSELF FIVE YEARS AGO...
COMMISSIONER --WHITTAKER'S GONE ALL SICK.
HE'S JUST A ROOKIE...
SEND HIM HOME, MERKEL. TELL HIM IT'S ALL RIGHT.
...TWO HUNDRED AND SIX WERE SLAIN DURING THE JOKER'S ESCAPE FROM THE DAVID ENDOCHRINE SHOW INCLUDING HOST ENDOCHRINE AND DR. BARTHOLOMEW WOLPER.
THE JOKER REPORTEDLY USED HIS DEADLY SMILE GAS ON THE CROWD. COMMISSIONE YINDEL REFUSED TO COMMENT ON THIS, OR ON THE ESCAPE OF THE BATMAN, WHICH LEFT TWELVE POLICE OFFICERS HOSPITALIZED...
KYLE
ESCORT
SERVICE, INC.
YOU SHOULDN'T HAVE COME BACK, BRUCE.
AMERICAN EXPRESS
CARDS WELCOME
THEY'VE CHANGED. YOU DON'T KNOW HOW THEY'VE CHANGED.
THEY'LL KILL YOU...
SELINA--
OH, JESUS.
I NEED YOUR HELP.
IT'S VERY IMPORTANT.
KLIK
CHAK
YOU GET THE HELL OUT OF NGG
THE YEARS HAVE NOT BEEN KIND, SELINA...
MMFF
AH, SELINA--YOU SHOULD BE GRATEFUL I CHANGED MY LIPSTICK. YOU ARE GRATEFUL?...
YES... GRATEFUL...
NOW...YOUR GIRL ELSIE IS ESCORTING A CONGRESSMAN TONIGHT. MEETING HIM AT HIS HOTEL.
WHY DON'T YOU CALL ELSIE IN HERE?

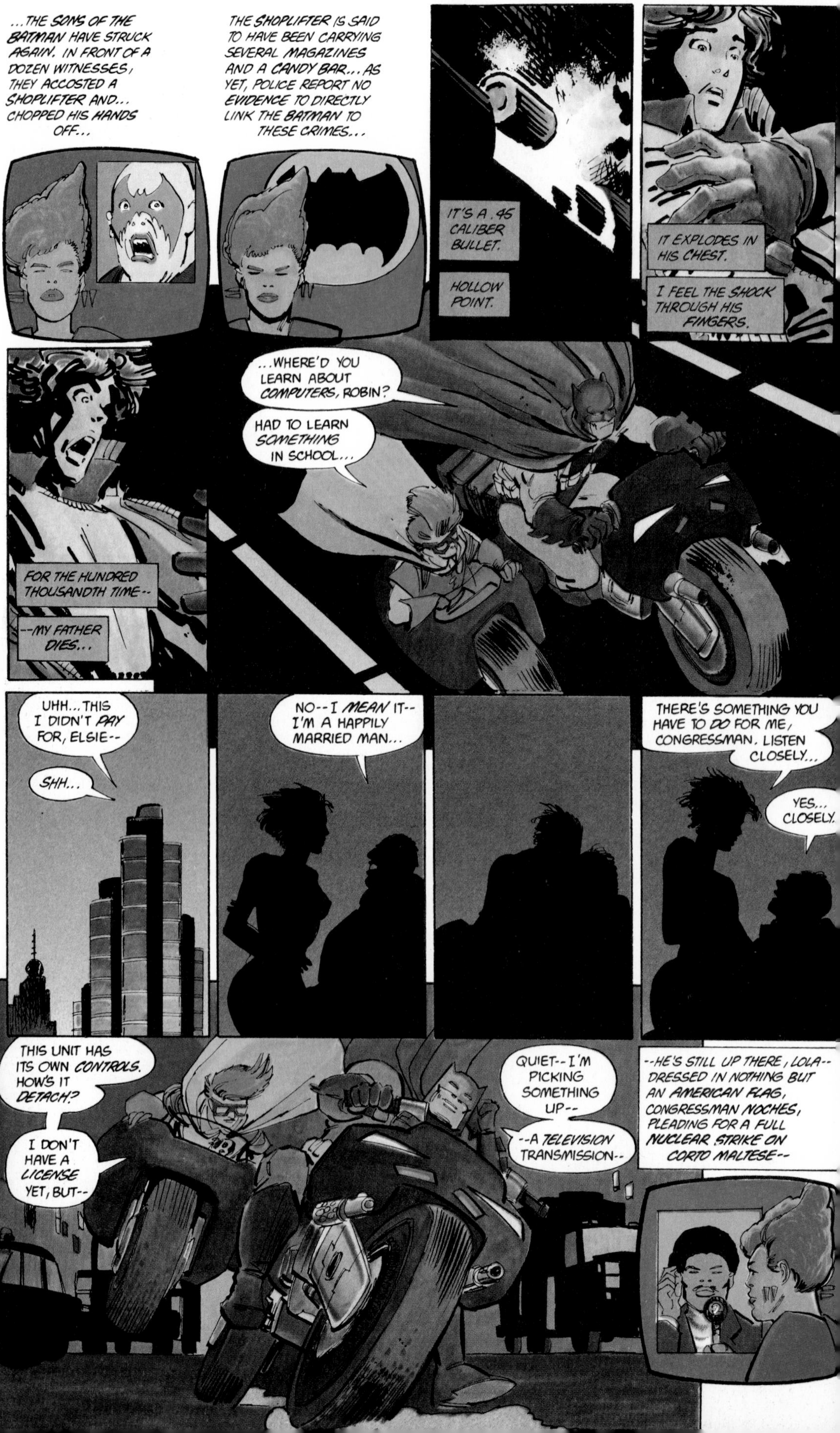
...THE SONS OF THE BATMAN HAVE STRUCK AGAIN. IN FRONT OF A DOZEN WITNESSES, THEY ACCOSTED A SHOPLIFTER AND... CHOPPED HIS HANDS OFF...
THE SHOPLIFTER IS SAID TO HAVE BEEN CARRYING SEVERAL MAGAZINES AND A CANDY BAR... AS YET, POLICE REPORT NO EVIDENCE TO DIRECTLY LINK THE BATMAN TO THESE CRIMES...
IT'S A .45 CALIBER BULLET.
HOLLOW POINT.
IT EXPLODES IN HIS CHEST.
I FEEL THE SHOCK THROUGH HIS FINGERS.
FOR THE HUNDRED THOUSANDTH TIME--
--MY FATHER DIES...
...WHERE'D YOU LEARN ABOUT COMPUTERS, ROBIN?
HAD TO LEARN SOMETHING IN SCHOOL...
UHH... THIS I DIDN'T PAY FOR, ELSIE--
SHH...
NO--I MEAN IT--I'M A HAPPILY MARRIED MAN...
THERE'S SOMETHING YOU HAVE TO DO FOR ME, CONGRESSMAN. LISTEN CLOSELY...
YES... CLOSELY.
THIS UNIT HAS ITS OWN CONTROLS. HOW'S IT DETACH?
I DON'T HAVE A LICENSE YET, BUT--
QUIET--I'M PICKING SOMETHING UP--
--A TELEVISION TRANSMISSION--
--HE'S STILL UP THERE, LOLA--DRESSED IN NOTHING BUT AN AMERICAN FLAG, CONGRESSMAN NOCHES, PLEADING FOR A FULL NUCLEAR STRIKE ON CORTO MALTESE--

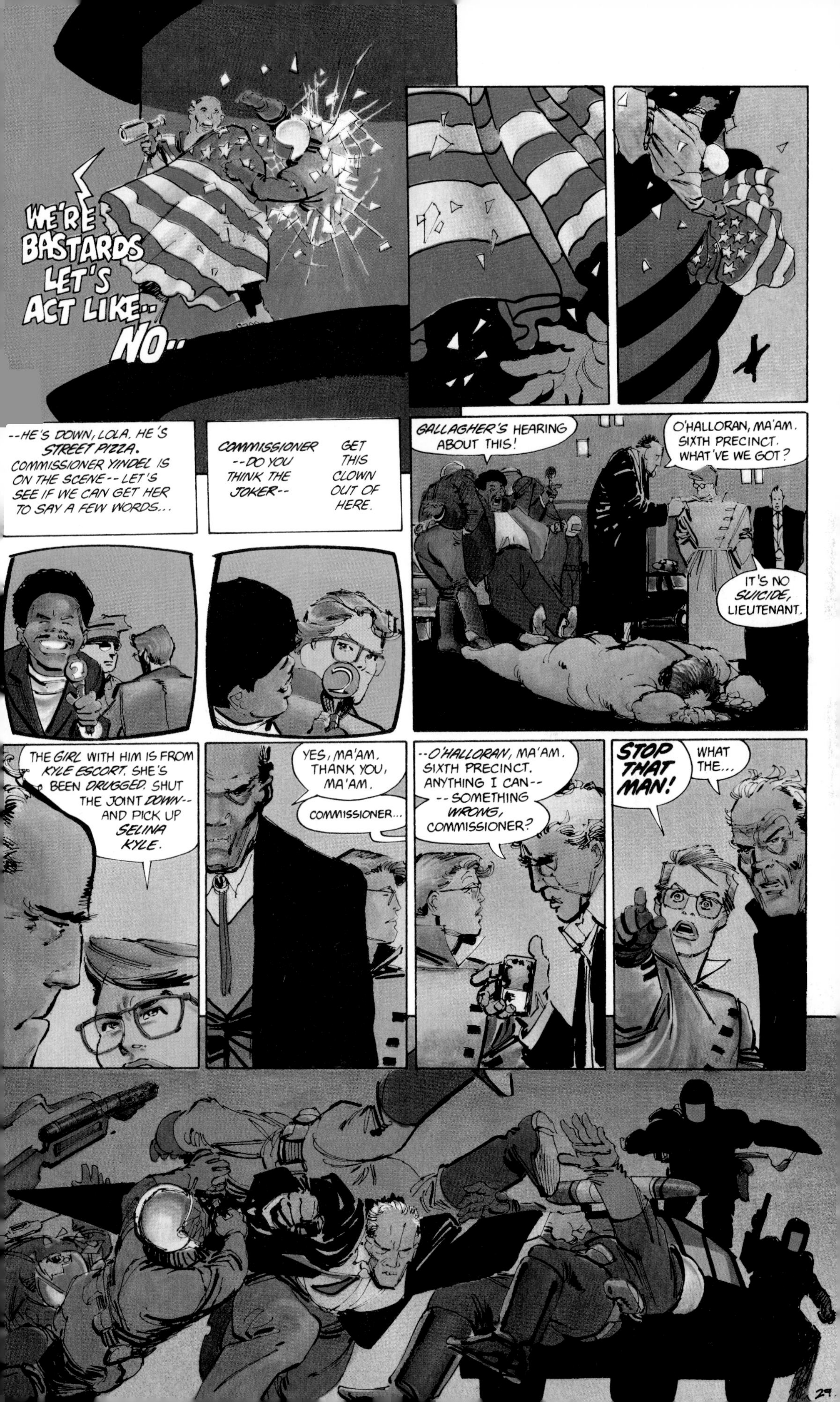
WE'RE BASTARDS LET'S ACT LIKE..
NO..
--HE'S DOWN, LOLA. HE'S STREET PIZZA. COMMISSIONER YINDEL IS ON THE SCENE--LET'S SEE IF WE CAN GET HER TO SAY A FEW WORDS...
COMMISSIONER --DO YOU THINK THE JOKER--
GET THIS CLOWN OUT OF HERE.
GALLAGHER'S HEARING ABOUT THIS!
O'HALLORAN, MA'AM. SIXTH PRECINCT. WHAT'VE WE GOT?
IT'S NO SUICIDE, LIEUTENANT.
THE GIRL WITH HIM IS FROM KYLE ESCORT. SHE'S BEEN DRUGGED. SHUT THE JOINT DOWN-- AND PICK UP SELINA KYLE.
YES, MA'AM. THANK YOU, MA'AM.
COMMISSIONER...
--O'HALLORAN, MA'AM. SIXTH PRECINCT. ANYTHING I CAN-- --SOMETHING WRONG, COMMISSIONER?
STOP THAT MAN!
WHAT THE...

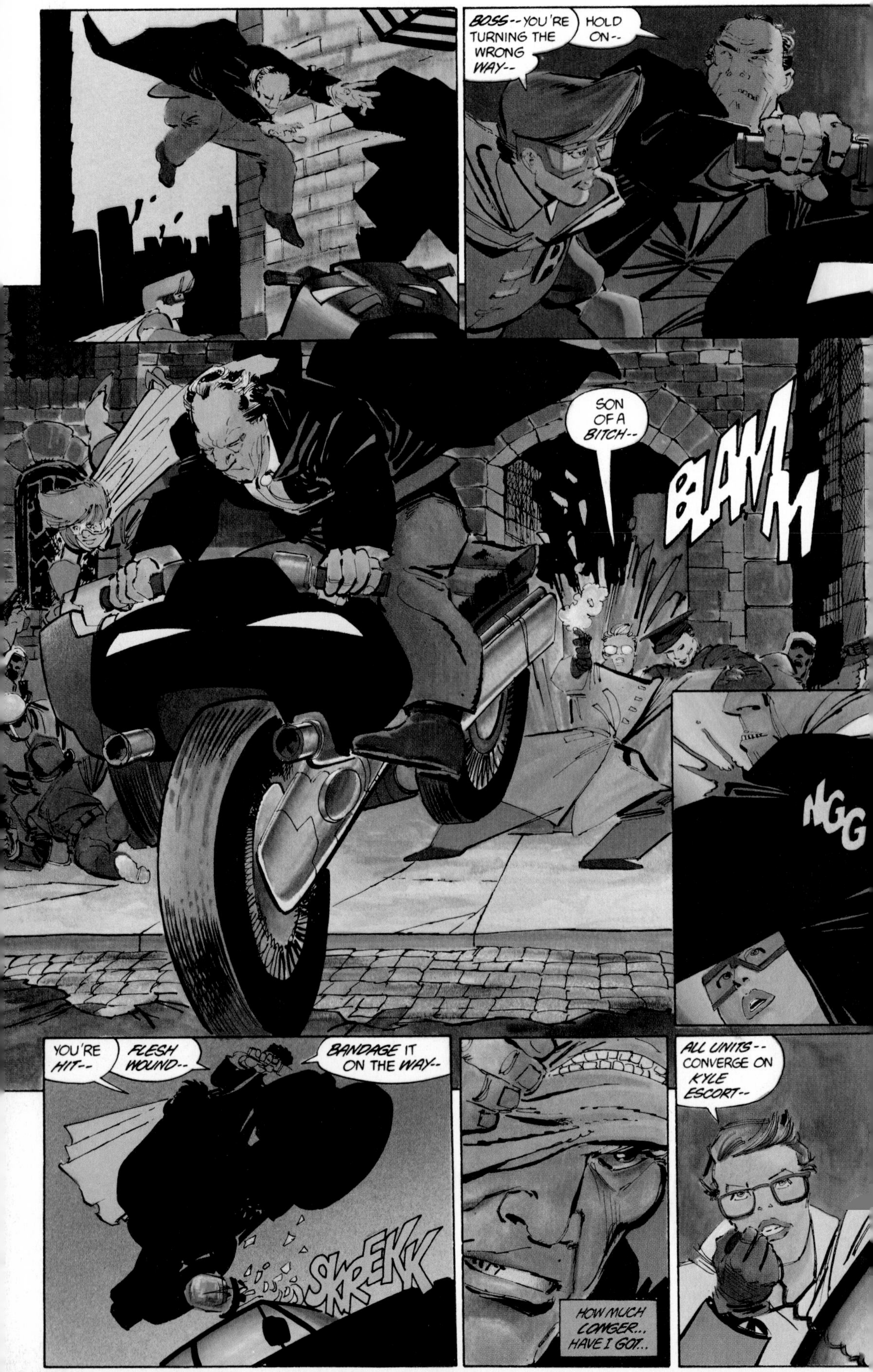
BOSS--YOU'RE TURNING THE WRONG WAY--
HOLD ON--
SON OF A BITCH--
BLAMM
NGG
YOU'RE HIT--
FLESH WOUND--
BANDAGE IT ON THE WAY--
SKREEKK
HOW MUCH LONGER... HAVE I GOT...
ALL UNITS--CONVERGE ON KYLE ESCORT--

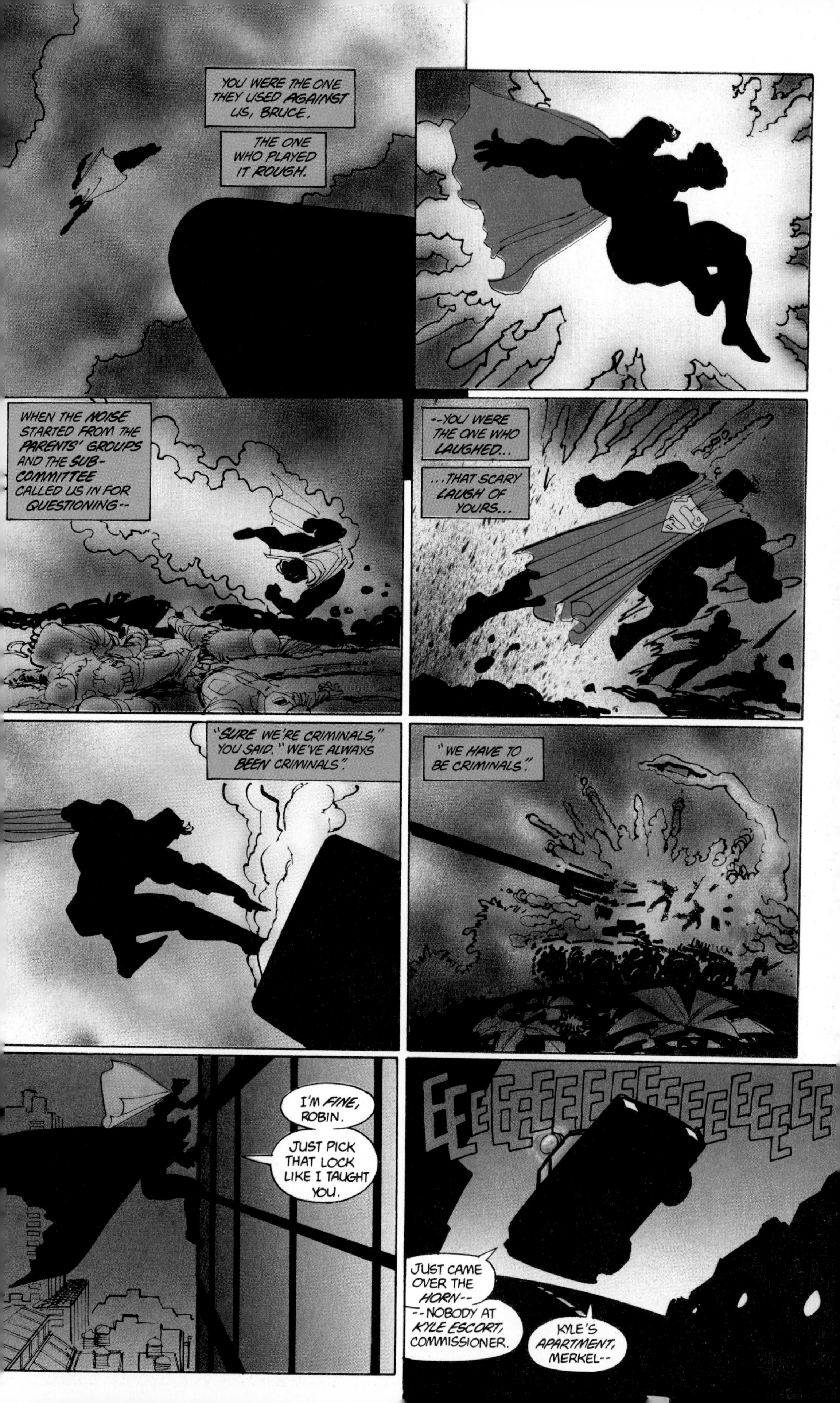
YOU WERE THE ONE THEY USED AGAINST US, BRUCE.
THE ONE WHO PLAYED IT ROUGH.
WHEN THE NOISE STARTED FROM THE PARENTS' GROUPS AND THE SUB-COMMITTEE CALLED US IN FOR QUESTIONING--
--YOU WERE THE ONE WHO LAUGHED...
...THAT SCARY LAUGH OF YOURS...
"SURE WE'RE CRIMINALS," YOU SAID. "WE'VE ALWAYS BEEN CRIMINALS".
"WE HAVE TO BE CRIMINALS".
I'M FINE, ROBIN.
JUST PICK THAT LOCK LIKE I TAUGHT YOU.
EEEEEEEEEEEEEEEEEEEEE
JUST CAME OVER THE HORN--
--NOBODY AT KYLE ESCORT, COMMISSIONER.
KYLE'S APARTMENT, MERKEL--

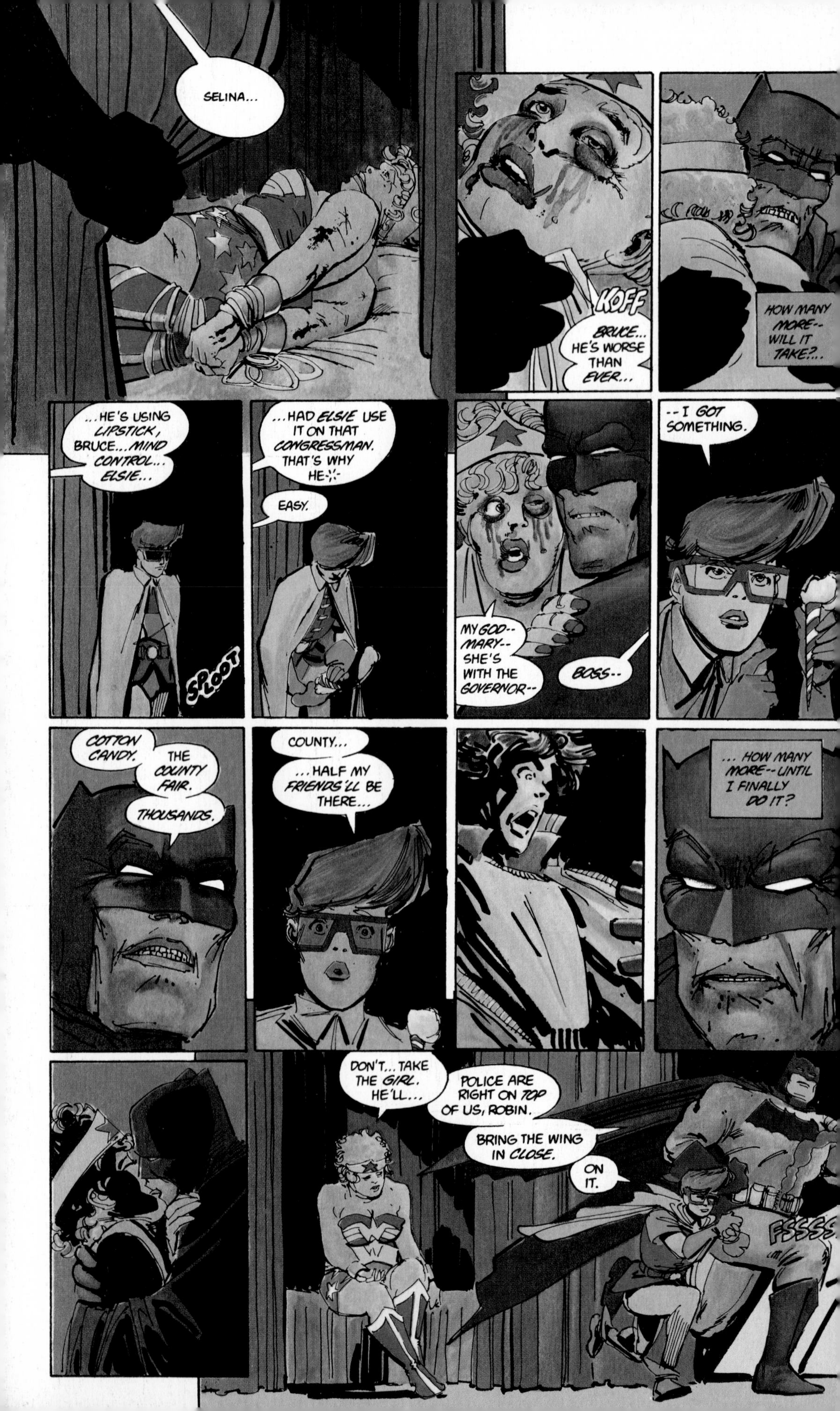
SELINA...
KOFF
BRUCE... HE'S WORSE THAN EVER...
HOW MANY MORE-- WILL IT TAKE?..
...HE'S USING LIPSTICK, BRUCE...MIND CONTROL... ELSIE...
SPLOOT
...HAD ELSIE USE IT ON THAT CONGRESSMAN. THAT'S WHY HE-
EASY.
MY GOD-- MARY-- SHE'S WITH THE GOVERNOR--
BOSS--
--I GOT SOMETHING.
COTTON CANDY.
THE COUNTY FAIR.
THOUSANDS.
COUNTY...
...HALF MY FRIENDS'LL BE THERE...
... HOW MANY MORE--UNTIL I FINALLY DO IT?
DON'T... TAKE THE GIRL. HE'LL...
POLICE ARE RIGHT ON TOP OF US, ROBIN.
BRING THE WING IN CLOSE.
ON IT.
FSSSS

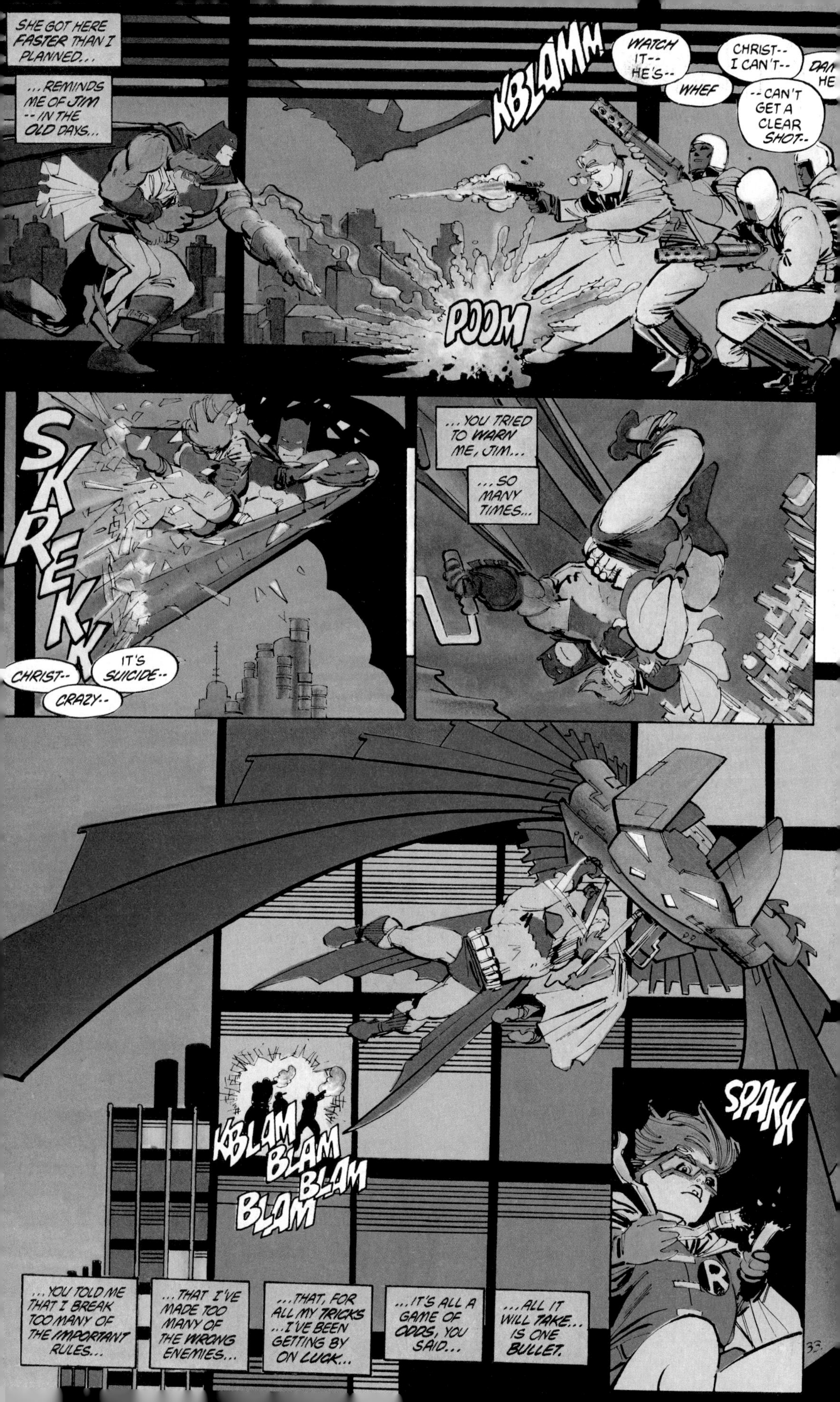

SHE GOT HERE FASTER THAN I PLANNED...
...REMINDS ME OF JIM --IN THE OLD DAYS...
KBLOMM
WATCH IT-- HE'S--
WHEF
CHRIST-- I CAN'T--
--CAN'T GET A CLEAR SHOT--
POOM
SKREKK
CHRIST--
IT'S SUICIDE--
CRAZY--
...YOU TRIED TO WARN ME, JIM...
...SO MANY TIMES...
KBLAM BLAM BLAM BLAM
SPAKK
...YOU TOLD ME THAT I BREAK TOO MANY OF THE IMPORTANT RULES...
...THAT I'VE MADE TOO MANY OF THE WRONG ENEMIES...
...THAT, FOR ALL MY TRICKS ...I'VE BEEN GETTING BY ON LUCK...
...IT'S ALL A GAME OF ODDS, YOU SAID...
...ALL IT WILL TAKE... IS ONE BULLET.

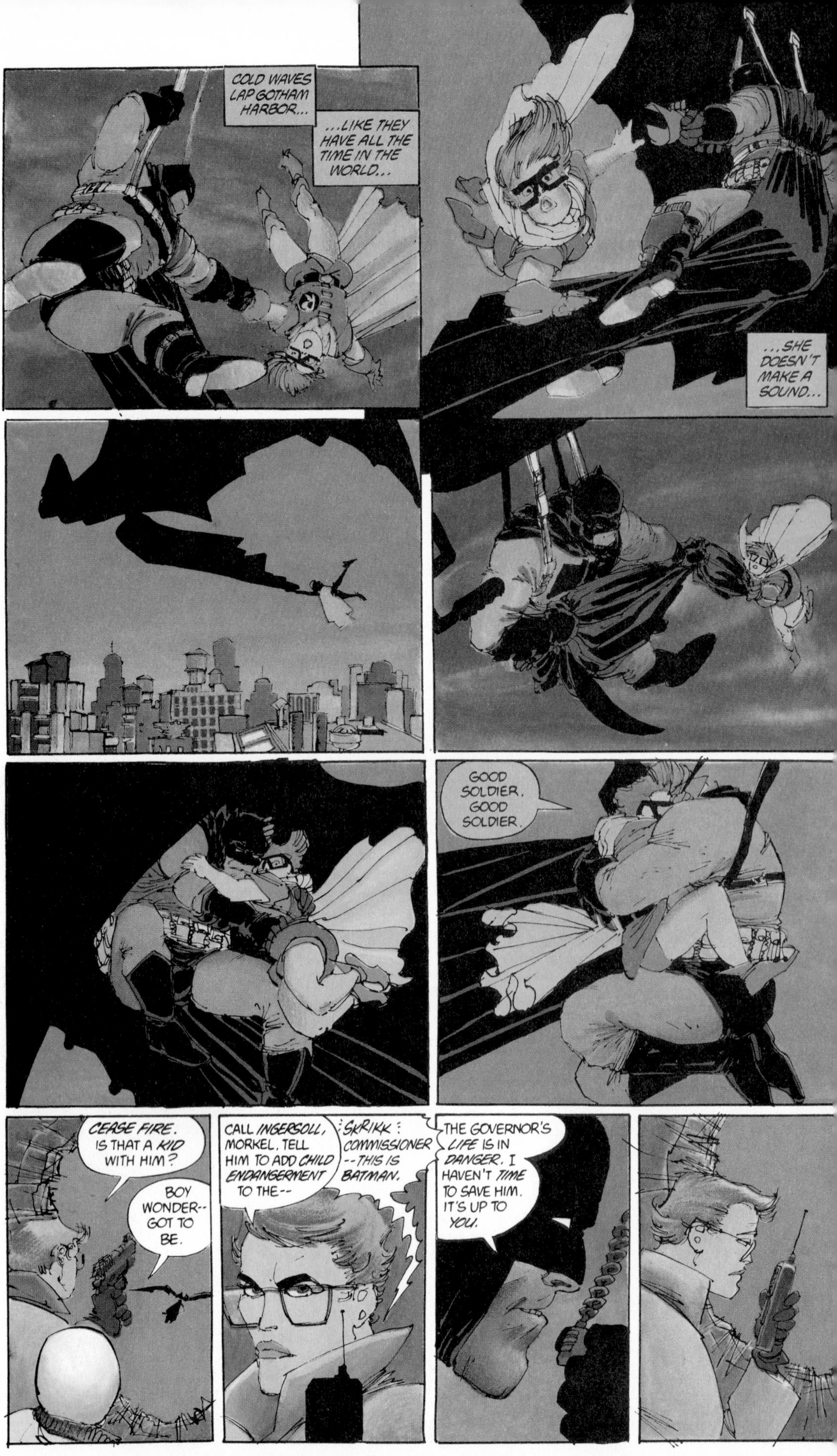
COLD WAVES LAP GOTHAM HARBOR...
...LIKE THEY HAVE ALL THE TIME IN THE WORLD...
...SHE DOESN'T MAKE A SOUND...
GOOD SOLDIER. GOOD SOLDIER.
CEASE FIRE. IS THAT A KID WITH HIM?
BOY WONDER-- GOT TO BE.
CALL INGERSOLL, MORKEL. TELL HIM TO ADD CHILD ENDANGERMENT TO THE--
SKRIKK
COMMISSIONER --THIS IS BATMAN.
THE GOVERNOR'S LIFE IS IN DANGER. I HAVEN'T TIME TO SAVE HIM. IT'S UP TO YOU.

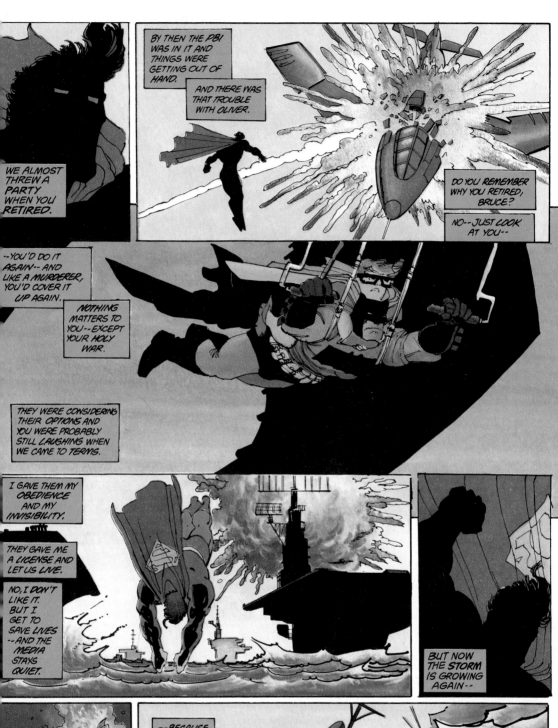

BY THEN THE PBI WAS IN IT AND THINGS WERE GETTING OUT OF HAND.

AND THERE WAS THAT TROUBLE WITH OLIVER.

WE ALMOST THREW A PARTY WHEN YOU RETIRED.

DO YOU REMEMBER WHY YOU RETIRED, BRUCE?

NO-- JUST LOOK AT YOU--

--YOU'D DO IT AGAIN-- AND LIKE A MURDERER, YOU'D COVER IT UP AGAIN.

NOTHING MATTERS TO YOU-- EXCEPT YOUR HOLY WAR.

THEY WERE CONSIDERING THEIR OPTIONS AND YOU WERE PROBABLY STILL LAUGHING WHEN WE CAME TO TERMS.

I GAVE THEM MY OBEDIENCE AND MY INVISIBILITY.

THEY GAVE ME A LICENSE AND LET US LIVE.

NO, I DON'T LIKE IT. BUT I GET TO SAVE LIVES --AND THE MEDIA STAYS QUIET.

BUT NOW THE STORM IS GROWING AGAIN--

--THEY'LL HUNT US DOWN AGAIN--

--BECAUSE OF YOU.

35.

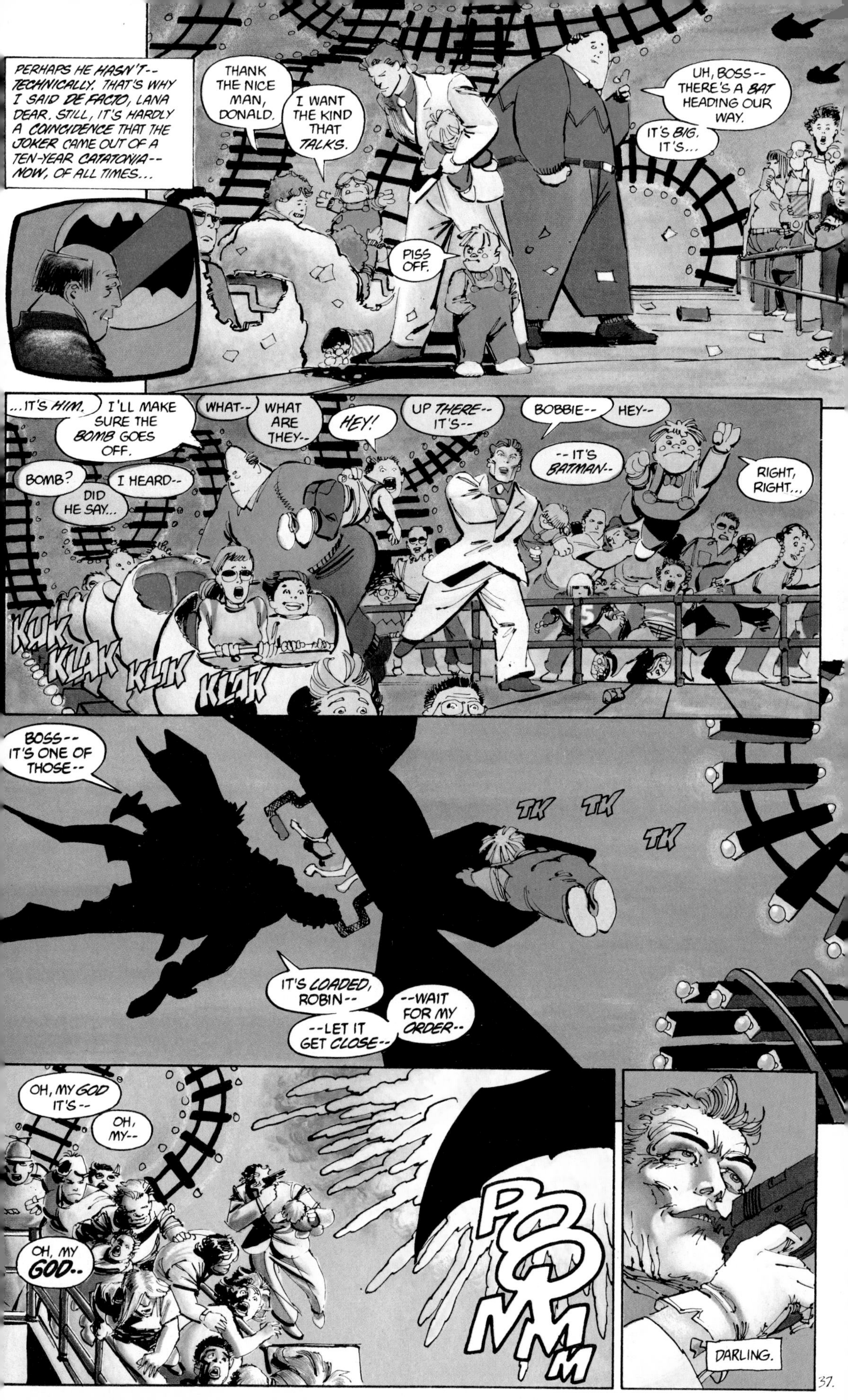
PERHAPS HE HASN'T-- TECHNICALLY. THAT'S WHY I SAID DE FACTO, LANA DEAR. STILL, IT'S HARDLY A COINCIDENCE THAT THE JOKER CAME OUT OF A TEN-YEAR CATATONIA-- NOW, OF ALL TIMES...
THANK THE NICE MAN, DONALD.
I WANT THE KIND THAT TALKS.
UH, BOSS-- THERE'S A BAT HEADING OUR WAY.
IT'S BIG. IT'S...
PISS OFF.
...IT'S HIM.
I'LL MAKE SURE THE BOMB GOES OFF.
WHAT--
WHAT ARE THEY--
HEY!
UP THERE-- IT'S--
BOBBIE--
HEY--
--IT'S BATMAN--
RIGHT, RIGHT...
BOMB?
DID HE SAY...
I HEARD--
KLIK
KLAK
KLIK
KLAK
BOSS-- IT'S ONE OF THOSE--
TK
TK
TK
IT'S LOADED, ROBIN--
--LET IT GET CLOSE--
--WAIT FOR MY ORDER--
OH, MY GOD IT'S--
OH, MY--
OH, MY GOD..
POMM
DARLING.

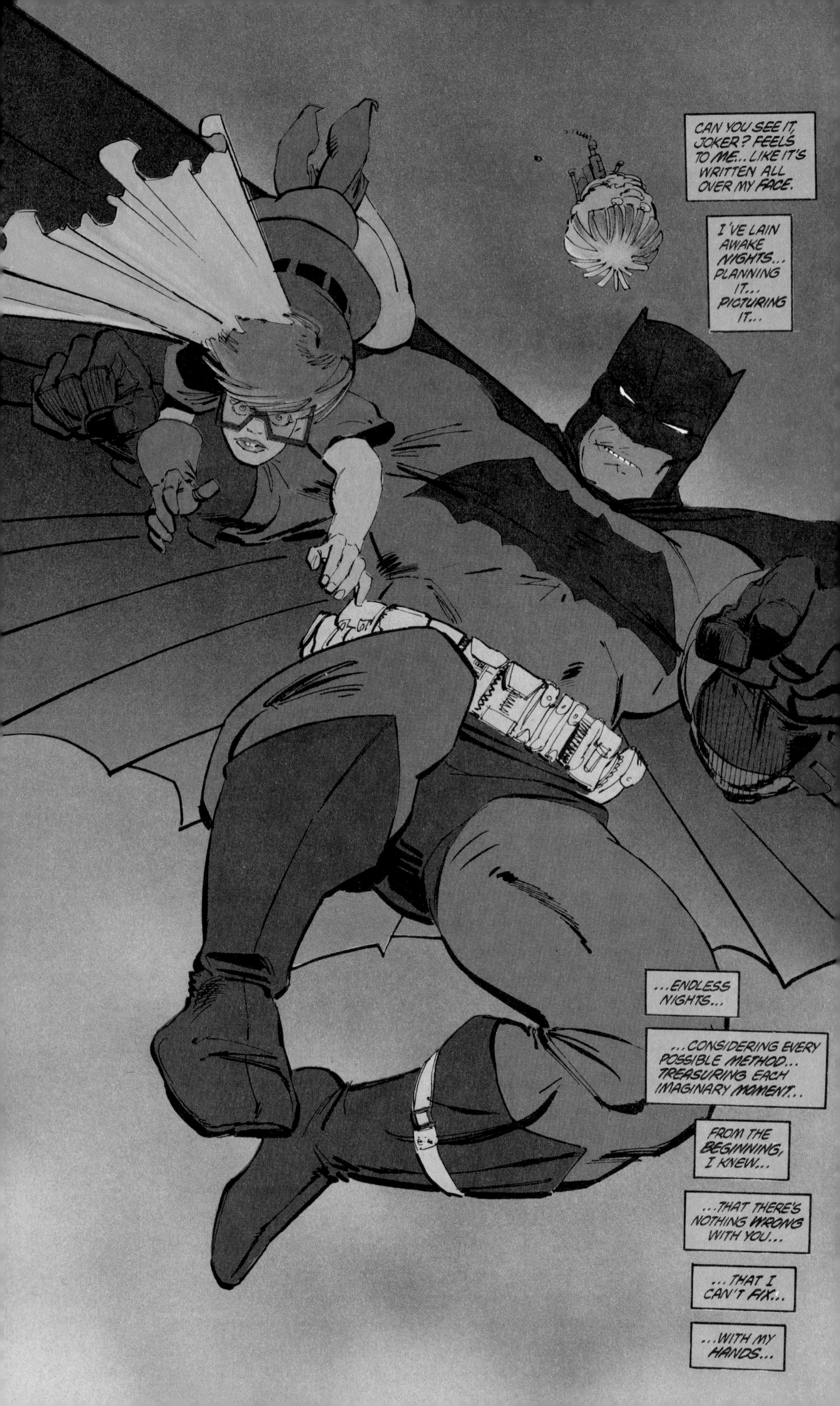
CAN YOU SEE IT, JOKER? FEELS TO ME... LIKE IT'S WRITTEN ALL OVER MY FACE.
I'VE LAIN AWAKE NIGHTS... PLANNING IT... PICTURING IT...
...ENDLESS NIGHTS...
...CONSIDERING EVERY POSSIBLE METHOD... TREASURING EACH IMAGINARY MOMENT...
FROM THE BEGINNING, I KNEW...
...THAT THERE'S NOTHING WRONG WITH YOU...
...THAT I CAN'T FIX...
...WITH MY HANDS...

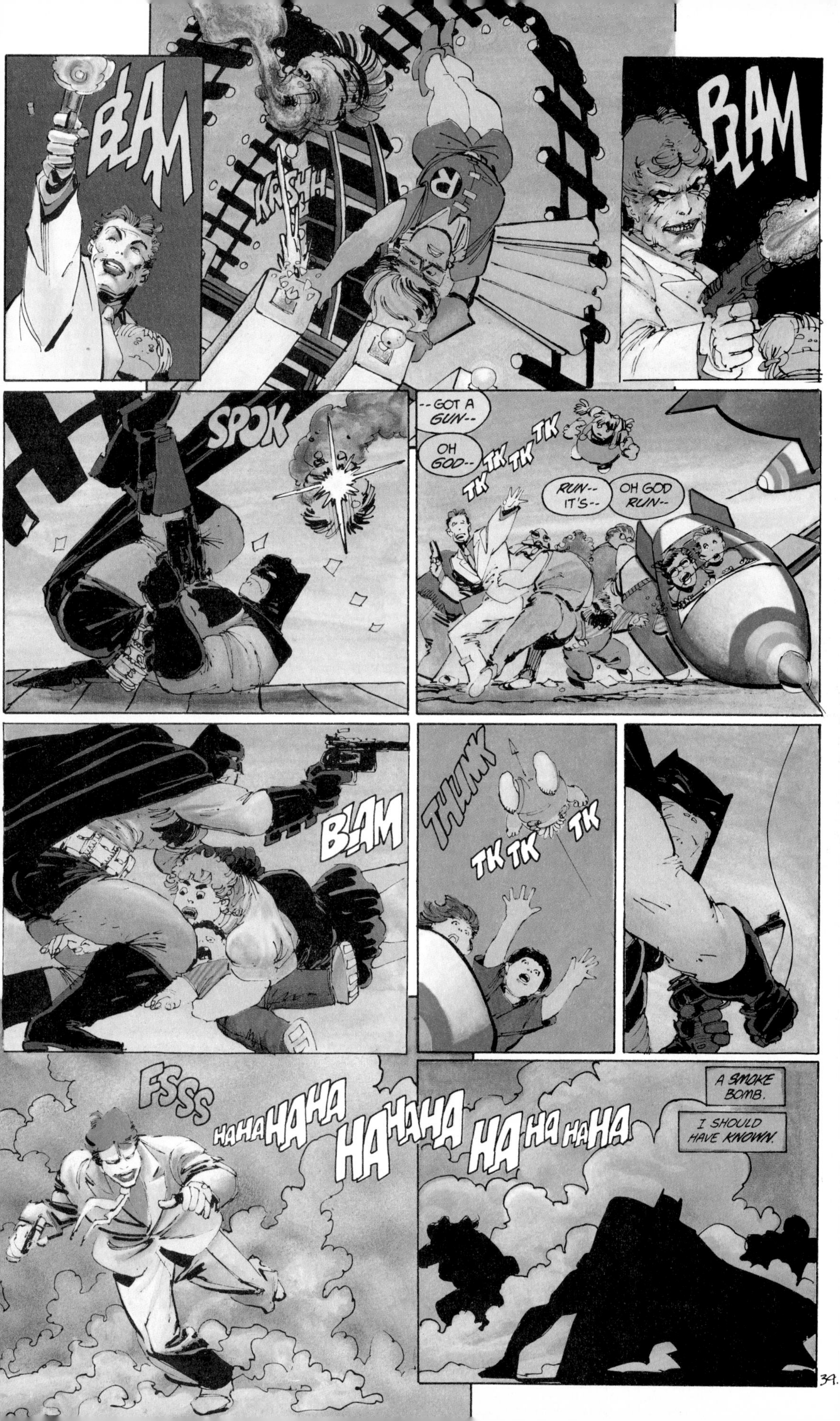
BLAM
KRSHH
BLAM
SPOK
--GOT A GUN--
OH GOD--
TK TK TK TK
RUN-- IT'S--
OH GOD RUN--
BLAM
THUNK
TK TK TK
FSSS
HAHAHAHA HAHAHA HAHAHAHA
A SMOKE BOMB.
I SHOULD HAVE KNOWN.

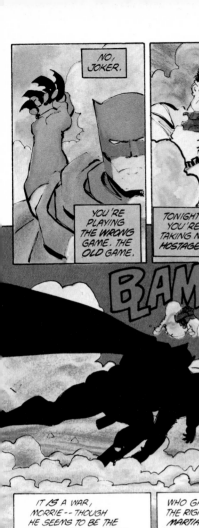

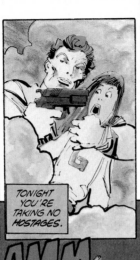

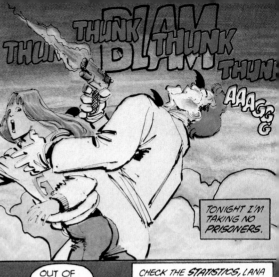

NO, JOKER.
YOU'RE PLAYING THE WRONG GAME. THE OLD GAME.
TONIGHT YOU'RE TAKING NO HOSTAGES.
THUNK BLAM THUNK THUNK BLAM THUNK
AAAGGG
TONIGHT I'M TAKING NO PRISONERS.
BAMM
OUT OF YOUR MIND--
CHECK THE STATISTICS, LANA DEAR--HECK, IF YOU TOSS IN THE VICTIMS OF HIS FAN CLUB, THE BATMAN-RELATED BODY COUNT IS UP THERE WITH A MINOR WAR.
IT IS A WAR, MORRIE--THOUGH HE SEEMS TO BE THE ONLY ONE WITH BALLS ENOUGH TO FIGHT IT.
WHO GAVE THIS THUG THE RIGHT TO DECLARE MARTIAL LAW, HM? LAST I HEARD, THAT TAKES AN ACT OF CONGRESS.
BILLY
GONE BILLY
CAN'T
BELIEVE
I'M
DOING
THIS--
OH, REAL COO--
--LIKE ALL FAN--
BLAM
KPWEE
--BEFORE THE DOLL--
--WON'T DUST ME--
--LIKE GOODYEAR THERE--
KLIK KLAK
KLIK KLAK
KLIK KLAK
TK TK TK
--DOES THE MAXIMUM FLASH--
KLIK KLAK
BLAM
KLIK KLAK

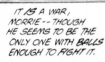

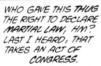

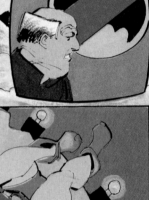

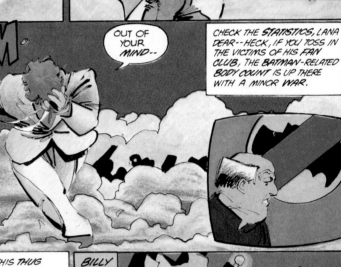

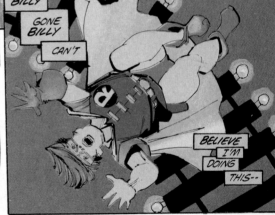

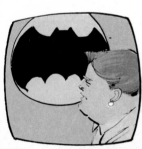

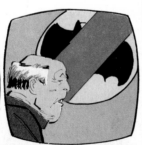

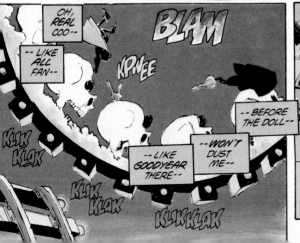

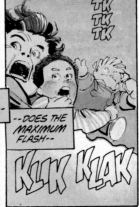

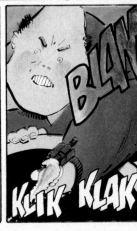

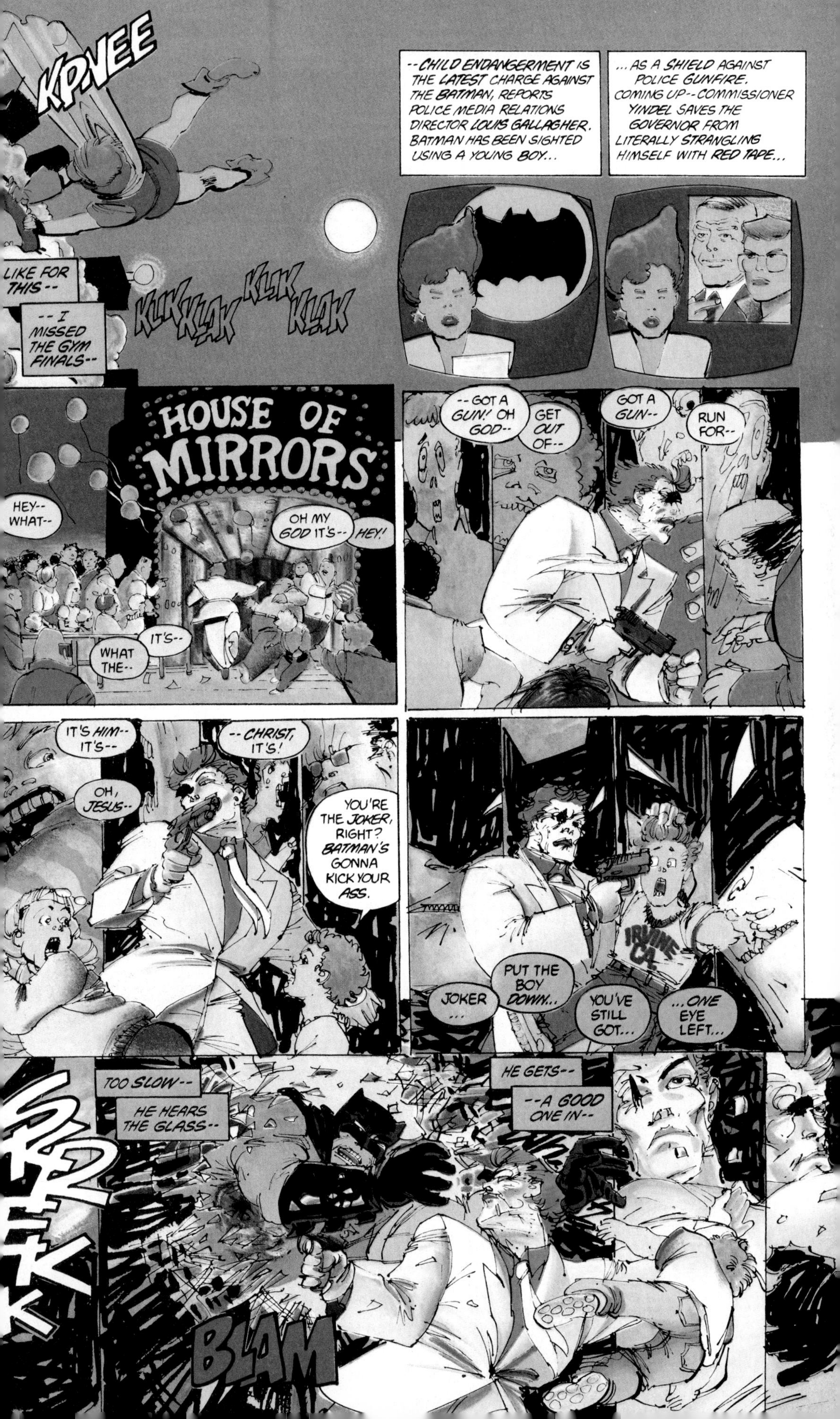

KPWEE
--CHILD ENDANGERMENT IS THE LATEST CHARGE AGAINST THE BATMAN, REPORTS POLICE MEDIA RELATIONS DIRECTOR LOUIS GALLAGHER. BATMAN HAS BEEN SIGHTED USING A YOUNG BOY...
...AS A SHIELD AGAINST POLICE GUNFIRE. COMING UP--COMMISSIONER YINDEL SAVES THE GOVERNOR FROM LITERALLY STRANGLING HIMSELF WITH RED TAPE...
LIKE FOR THIS--
--I MISSED THE GYM FINALS--
KLIK KLAK KLIK KLAK
HOUSE OF MIRRORS
HEY-- WHAT--
OH MY GOD IT'S--
HEY!
WHAT THE--
IT'S--
--GOT A GUN! OH GOD--
GET OUT OF--
GOT A GUN--
RUN FOR--
IT'S HIM-- IT'S--
--CHRIST, IT'S!
OH, JESUS--
YOU'RE THE JOKER, RIGHT? BATMAN'S GONNA KICK YOUR ASS.
IRVINE CA
JOKER ...
PUT THE BOY DOWN...
YOU'VE STILL GOT...
...ONE EYE LEFT...
TOO SLOW--
HE HEARS THE GLASS--
HE GETS--
--A GOOD ONE IN--
SKRITKK
BLAM

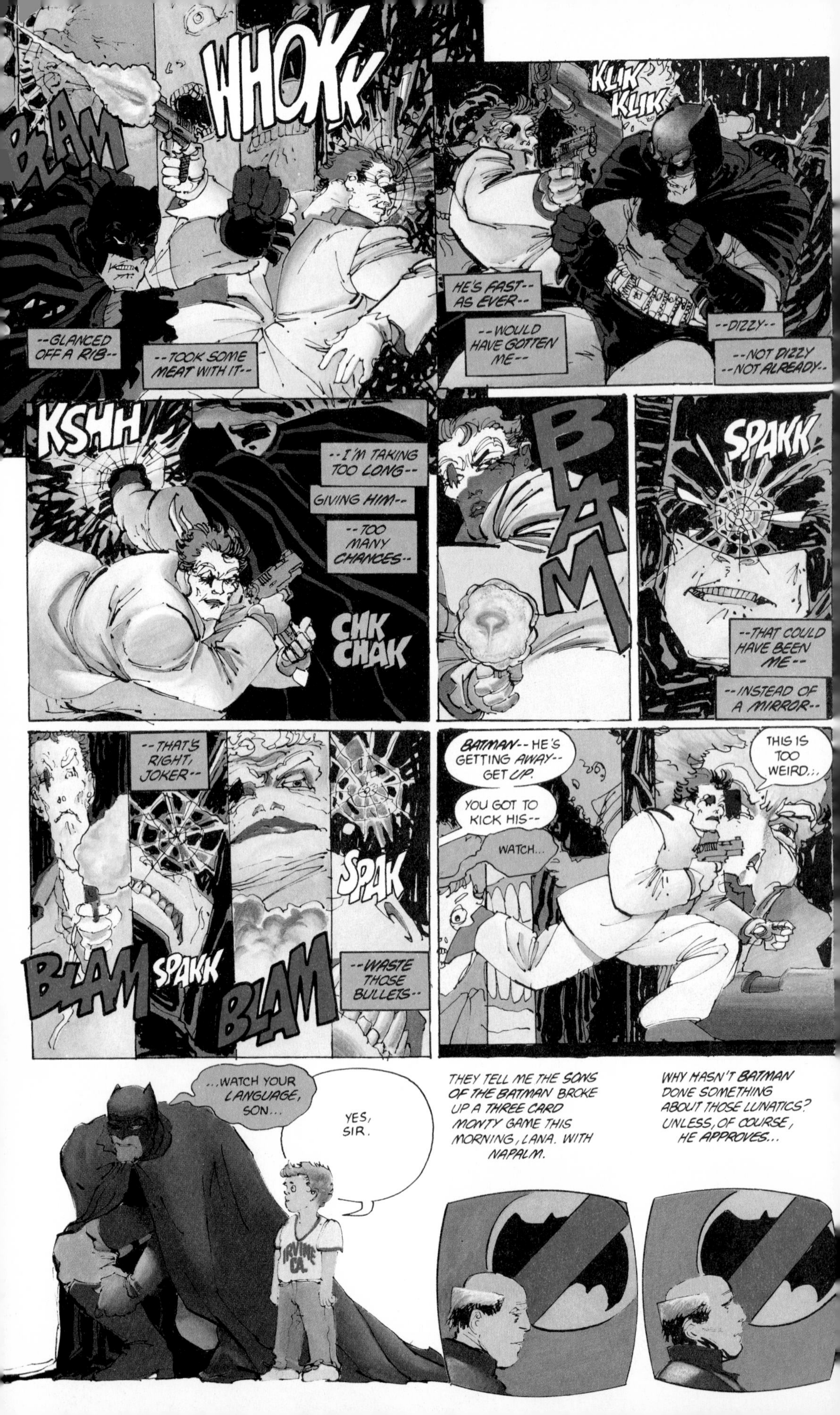

BLAM
WHOKK
--GLANCED OFF A RIB--
--TOOK SOME MEAT WITH IT--
KLIK KLIK
HE'S FAST-- AS EVER--
--WOULD HAVE GOTTEN ME--
--DIZZY--
--NOT DIZZY --NOT ALREADY--
KSHH
--I'M TAKING TOO LONG--
GIVING HIM--
--TOO MANY CHANCES--
CHK CHAK
BLAM
SPAKK
--THAT COULD HAVE BEEN ME--
--INSTEAD OF A MIRROR--
--THAT'S RIGHT, JOKER--
BLAM
SPAKK
BLAM
SPAK
--WASTE THOSE BULLETS--
BATMAN-- HE'S GETTING AWAY-- GET UP.
YOU GOT TO KICK HIS--
WATCH...
THIS IS TOO WEIRD...
...WATCH YOUR LANGUAGE, SON...
YES, SIR.
IRVINE CA.
THEY TELL ME THE SONS OF THE BATMAN BROKE UP A THREE CARD MONTY GAME THIS MORNING, LANA. WITH NAPALM.
WHY HASN'T BATMAN DONE SOMETHING ABOUT THOSE LUNATICS? UNLESS, OF COURSE, HE APPROVES...

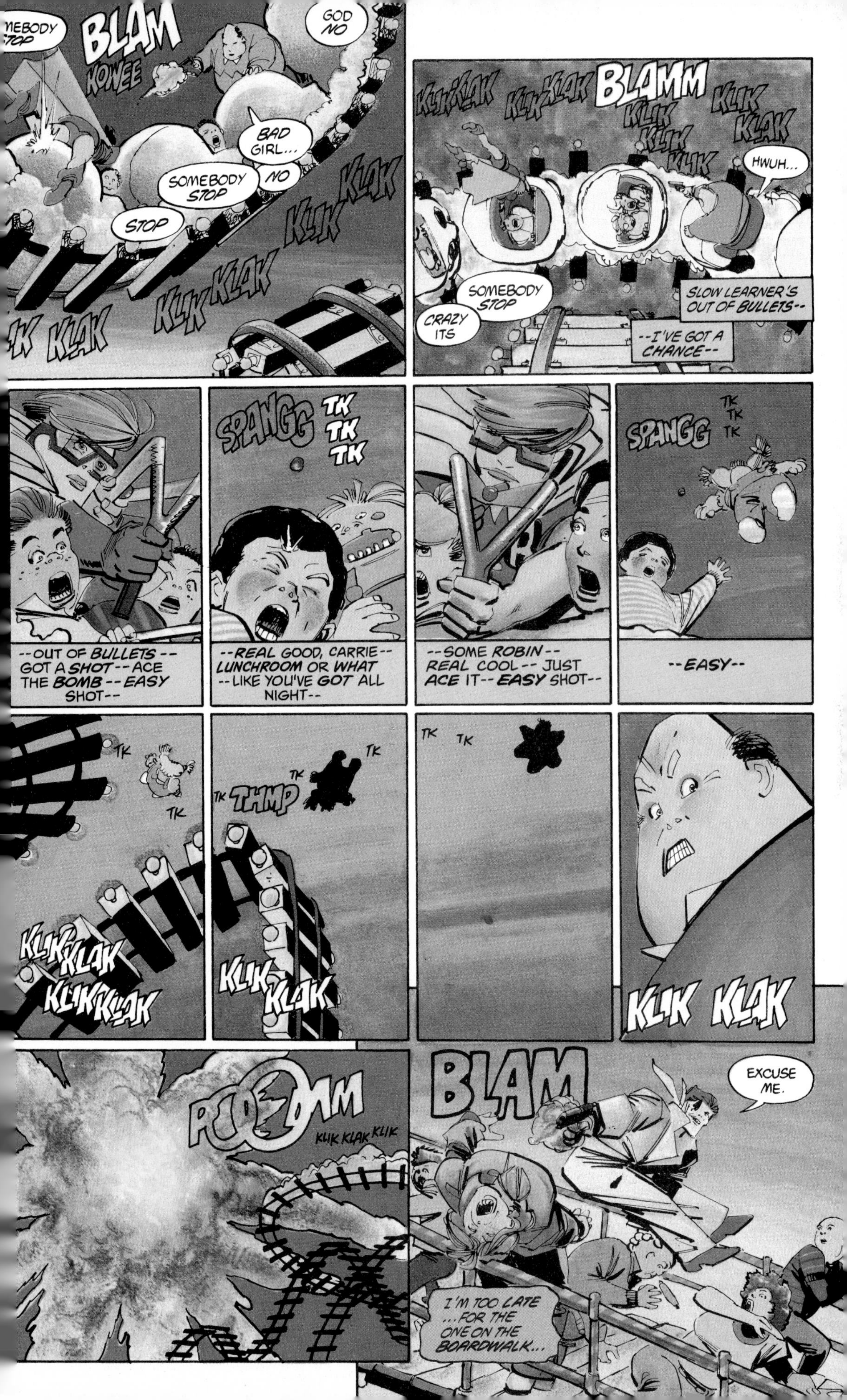

MEBODY STOP
BLAM
KOWEE
GOD NO
BAD GIRL...
NO
SOMEBODY STOP
STOP
KLIK KLAK KLIK KLAK KLIK KLAK
KLIK KLAK KLIK KLAK BLAMM KLIK KLIK KLIK KLIK KLAK
HWUH...
SOMEBODY STOP
CRAZY ITS
SLOW LEARNER'S OUT OF BULLETS--
--I'VE GOT A CHANCE--
--OUT OF BULLETS-- GOT A SHOT--ACE THE BOMB--EASY SHOT--
SPANGG TK TK TK
--REAL GOOD, CARRIE-- LUNCHROOM OR WHAT --LIKE YOU'VE GOT ALL NIGHT--
--SOME ROBIN-- REAL COOL-- JUST ACE IT--EASY SHOT--
SPANGG TK TK TK
--EASY--
TK TK
KLIK KLAK KLIK KLAK
TK TK THMP TK
KLIK KLAK
TK TK
KLIK KLAK
POOM KLIK KLAK KLIK
BLAM
EXCUSE ME.
I'M TOO LATE ...FOR THE ONE ON THE BOARDWALK...

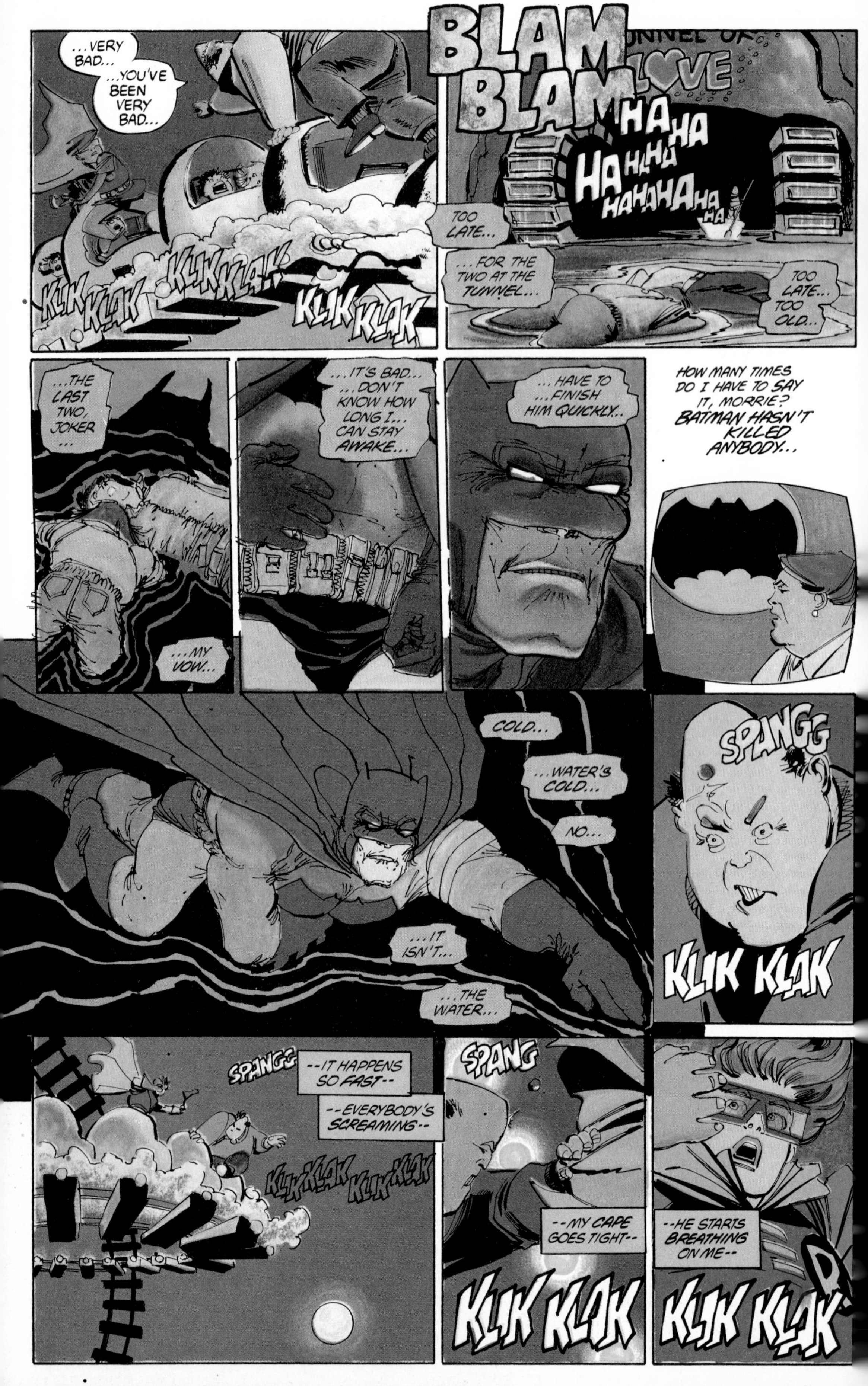

...VERY BAD... ...YOU'VE BEEN VERY BAD...
KLIK KLAK
KLIK KLAK
KLIK KLAK
BLAM
BLAM
TUNNEL OF LOVE
HA HA HA HA HA HAHAHAHAHA
TOO LATE...
...FOR THE TWO AT THE TUNNEL...
TOO LATE... TOO OLD...
...THE LAST TWO, JOKER ...
...MY VOW...
...IT'S BAD... ...DON'T KNOW HOW LONG I... CAN STAY AWAKE...
...HAVE TO ...FINISH HIM QUICKLY...
HOW MANY TIMES DO I HAVE TO SAY IT, MORRIE? BATMAN HASN'T KILLED ANYBODY...
COLD...
...WATER'S COLD...
NO...
...IT ISN'T...
...THE WATER...
SPANGG
KLIK KLAK
SPANGG
--IT HAPPENS SO FAST--
--EVERYBODY'S SCREAMING--
KLIK KLAK KLIK KLAK
SPANG
--MY CAPE GOES TIGHT--
KLIK KLAK
--HE STARTS BREATHING ON ME--
KLIK KLAK

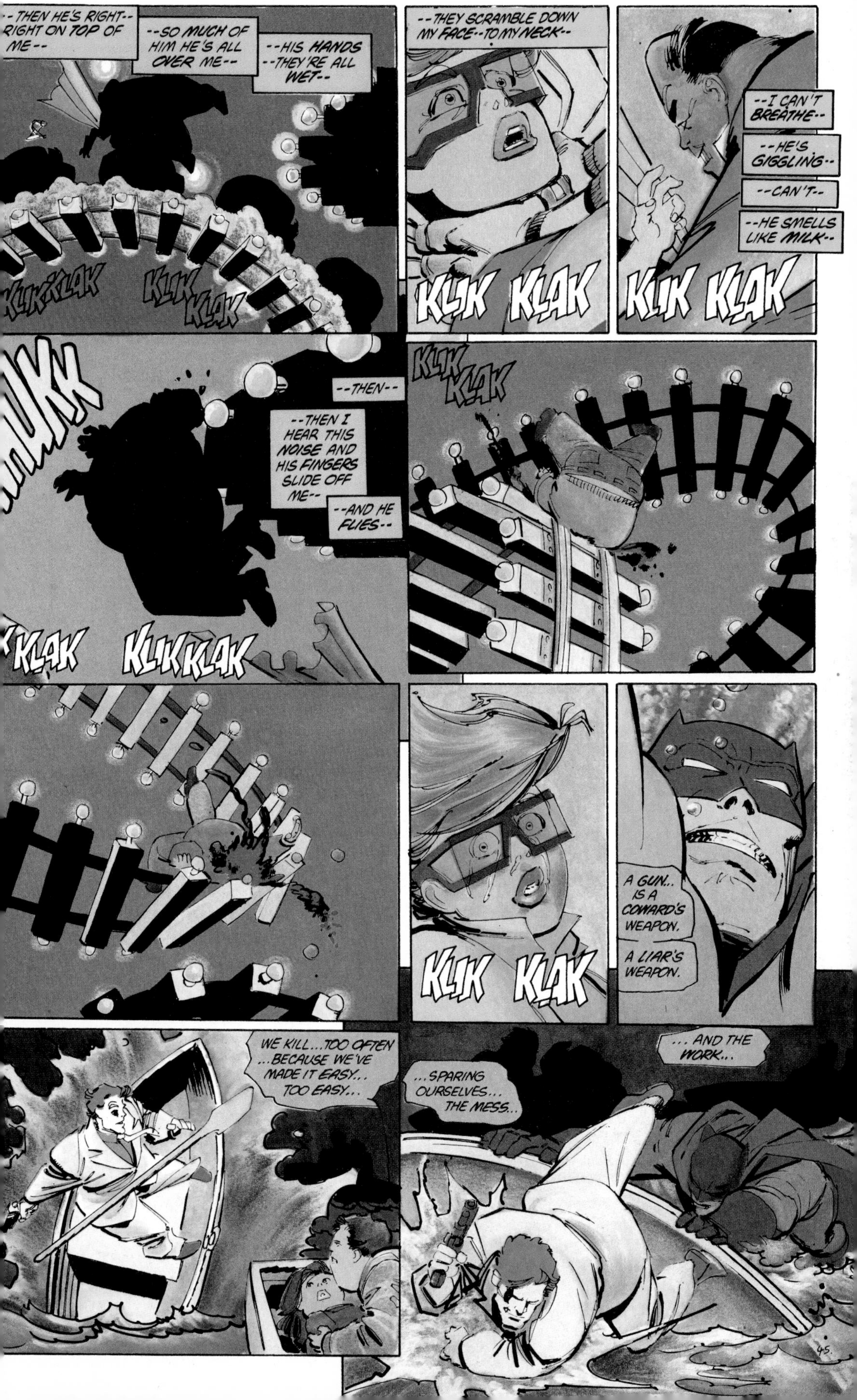
--THEN HE'S RIGHT-- RIGHT ON TOP OF ME--
--SO MUCH OF HIM HE'S ALL OVER ME--
--HIS HANDS --THEY'RE ALL WET--
KLIK KLAK
KLIK KLAK
--THEY SCRAMBLE DOWN MY FACE--TO MY NECK--
KLIK KLAK
--I CAN'T BREATHE--
--HE'S GIGGLING--
--CAN'T--
--HE SMELLS LIKE MILK--
KLIK KLAK
CHUKK
--THEN--
--THEN I HEAR THIS NOISE AND HIS FINGERS SLIDE OFF ME--
--AND HE FLIES--
KLAK
KLIK KLAK
KLIK KLAK
KLIK KLAK
A GUN... IS A COWARD'S WEAPON.
A LIAR'S WEAPON.
WE KILL...TOO OFTEN ...BECAUSE WE'VE MADE IT EASY... TOO EASY...
...SPARING OURSELVES... THE MESS...
...AND THE WORK...

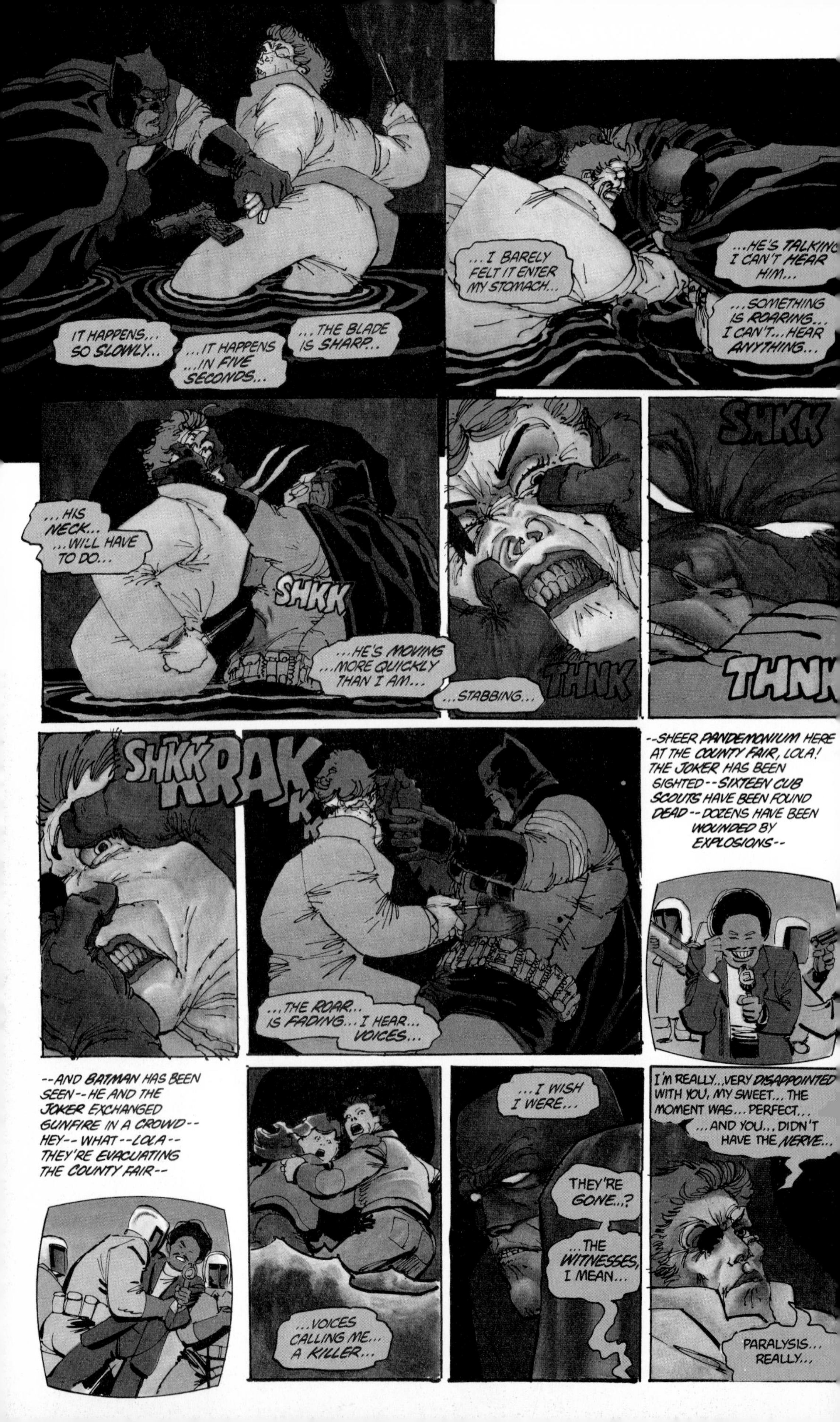
IT HAPPENS... SO SLOWLY...
...IT HAPPENS IN FIVE SECONDS...
...THE BLADE IS SHARP...
...I BARELY FELT IT ENTER MY STOMACH...
...HE'S TALKING I CAN'T HEAR HIM...
...SOMETHING IS ROARING... I CAN'T... HEAR ANYTHING...
...HIS NECK... ...WILL HAVE TO DO...
SHKK
...HE'S MOVING MORE QUICKLY THAN I AM...
...STABBING...
THNK
SHKK
THNK
SHKK
KRAK
K
K
...THE ROAR... IS FADING... I HEAR... VOICES...
--SHEER PANDEMONIUM HERE AT THE COUNTY FAIR, LOLA! THE JOKER HAS BEEN SIGHTED--SIXTEEN CUB SCOUTS HAVE BEEN FOUND DEAD--DOZENS HAVE BEEN WOUNDED BY EXPLOSIONS--
--AND BATMAN HAS BEEN SEEN--HE AND THE JOKER EXCHANGED GUNFIRE IN A CROWD--HEY--WHAT--LOLA--THEY'RE EVACUATING THE COUNTY FAIR--
...VOICES CALLING ME... A KILLER...
...I WISH I WERE...
THEY'RE GONE...?
...THE WITNESSES, I MEAN...
I'M REALLY... VERY DISAPPOINTED WITH YOU, MY SWEET... THE MOMENT WAS... PERFECT...
...AND YOU... DIDN'T HAVE THE NERVE...
PARALYSIS... REALLY...

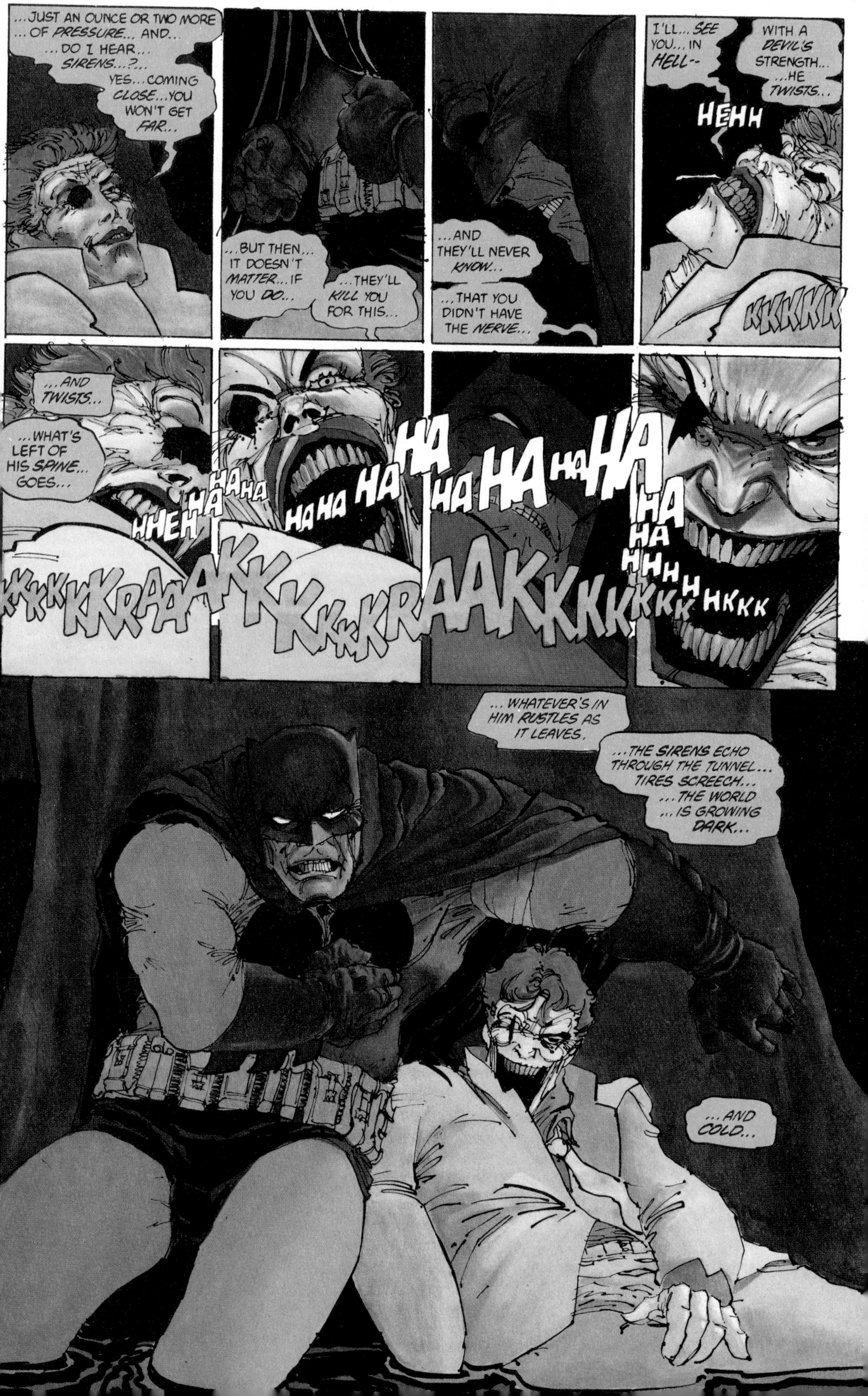
...JUST AN OUNCE OR TWO MORE ...OF PRESSURE... AND...
...DO I HEAR... ...SIRENS...?...
YES...COMING CLOSE...YOU WON'T GET FAR...
...BUT THEN... IT DOESN'T MATTER...IF YOU DO...
...THEY'LL KILL YOU FOR THIS...
...AND THEY'LL NEVER KNOW...
...THAT YOU DIDN'T HAVE THE NERVE...
I'LL... SEE YOU... IN HELL--
WITH A DEVIL'S STRENGTH... ...HE TWISTS...
HEHH
KKKKKK
...AND TWISTS...
...WHAT'S LEFT OF HIS SPINE... GOES...
HHEH HA HA HA
HA HA HA HA
HA HA HA ha HA
HA HA HHH H HKKK
KKKKKRAAAKKKKKRAAAKKKK
...WHATEVER'S IN HIM RUSTLES AS IT LEAVES.
...THE SIRENS ECHO THROUGH THE TUNNEL... TIRES SCREECH... ...THE WORLD ...IS GROWING DARK...
...AND COLD...

BOOK FOUR

THE
DARK
KNIGHT
FALLS

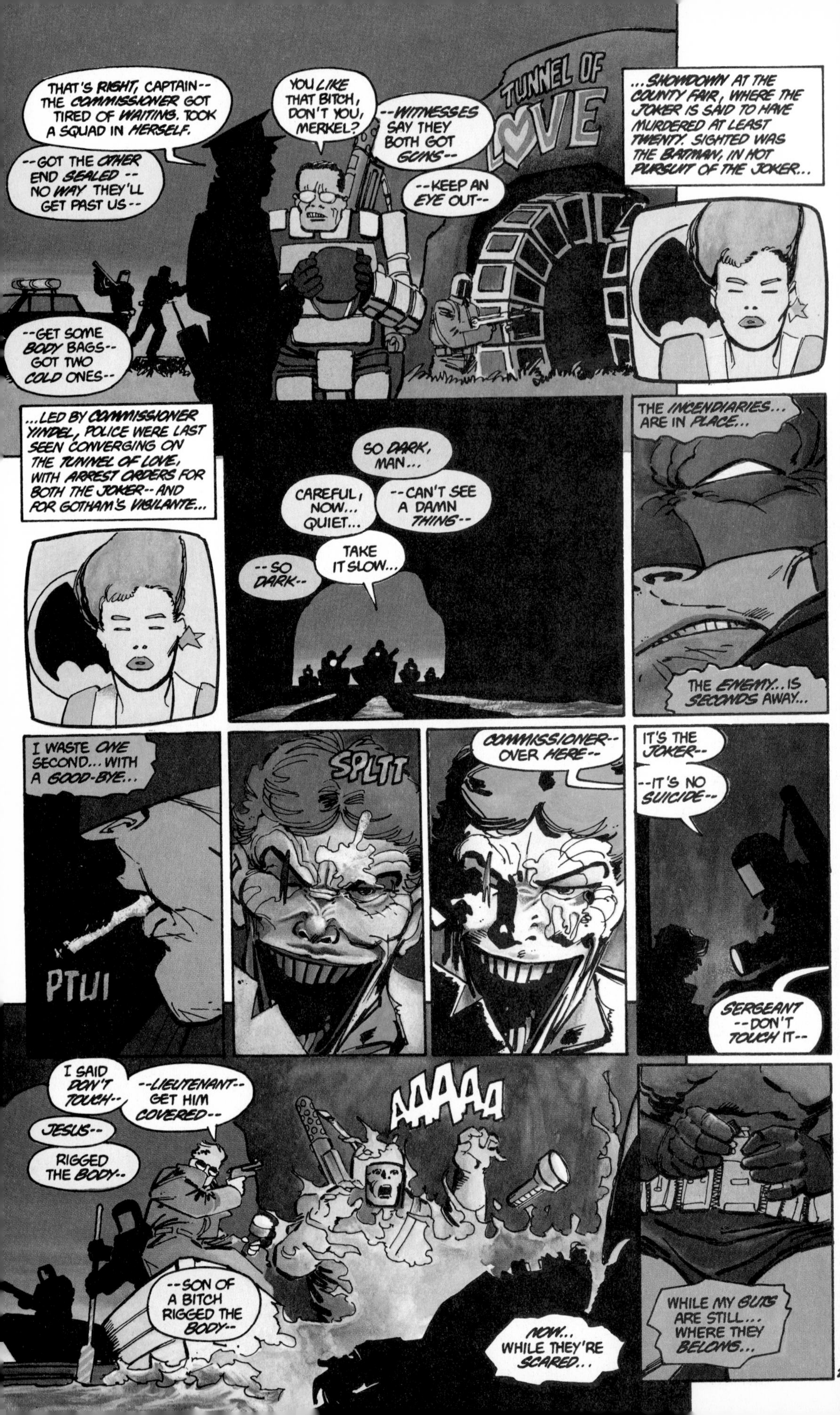
THAT'S RIGHT, CAPTAIN-- THE COMMISSIONER GOT TIRED OF WAITING. TOOK A SQUAD IN HERSELF.
--GOT THE OTHER END SEALED -- NO WAY THEY'LL GET PAST US--
YOU LIKE THAT BITCH, DON'T YOU, MERKEL?
--WITNESSES SAY THEY BOTH GOT GUNS--
--KEEP AN EYE OUT--
TUNNEL OF LOVE
...SHOWDOWN AT THE COUNTY FAIR, WHERE THE JOKER IS SAID TO HAVE MURDERED AT LEAST TWENTY. SIGHTED WAS THE BATMAN, IN HOT PURSUIT OF THE JOKER...
--GET SOME BODY BAGS-- GOT TWO COLD ONES--
...LED BY COMMISSIONER YINDEL, POLICE WERE LAST SEEN CONVERGING ON THE TUNNEL OF LOVE, WITH ARREST ORDERS FOR BOTH THE JOKER--AND FOR GOTHAM'S VIGILANTE...
SO DARK, MAN...
CAREFUL, NOW... QUIET...
--CAN'T SEE A DAMN THING--
--SO DARK--
TAKE IT SLOW...
THE INCENDIARIES... ARE IN PLACE...
THE ENEMY... IS SECONDS AWAY...
I WASTE ONE SECOND... WITH A GOOD-BYE...
PTUI
SPLTT
COMMISSIONER-- OVER HERE--
IT'S THE JOKER--
--IT'S NO SUICIDE--
SERGEANT --DON'T TOUCH IT--
I SAID DON'T TOUCH--
--LIEUTENANT-- GET HIM COVERED--
JESUS--
RIGGED THE BODY--
AAAAA
--SON OF A BITCH RIGGED THE BODY--
NOW... WHILE THEY'RE SCARED...
WHILE MY GUTS ARE STILL... WHERE THEY BELONG...

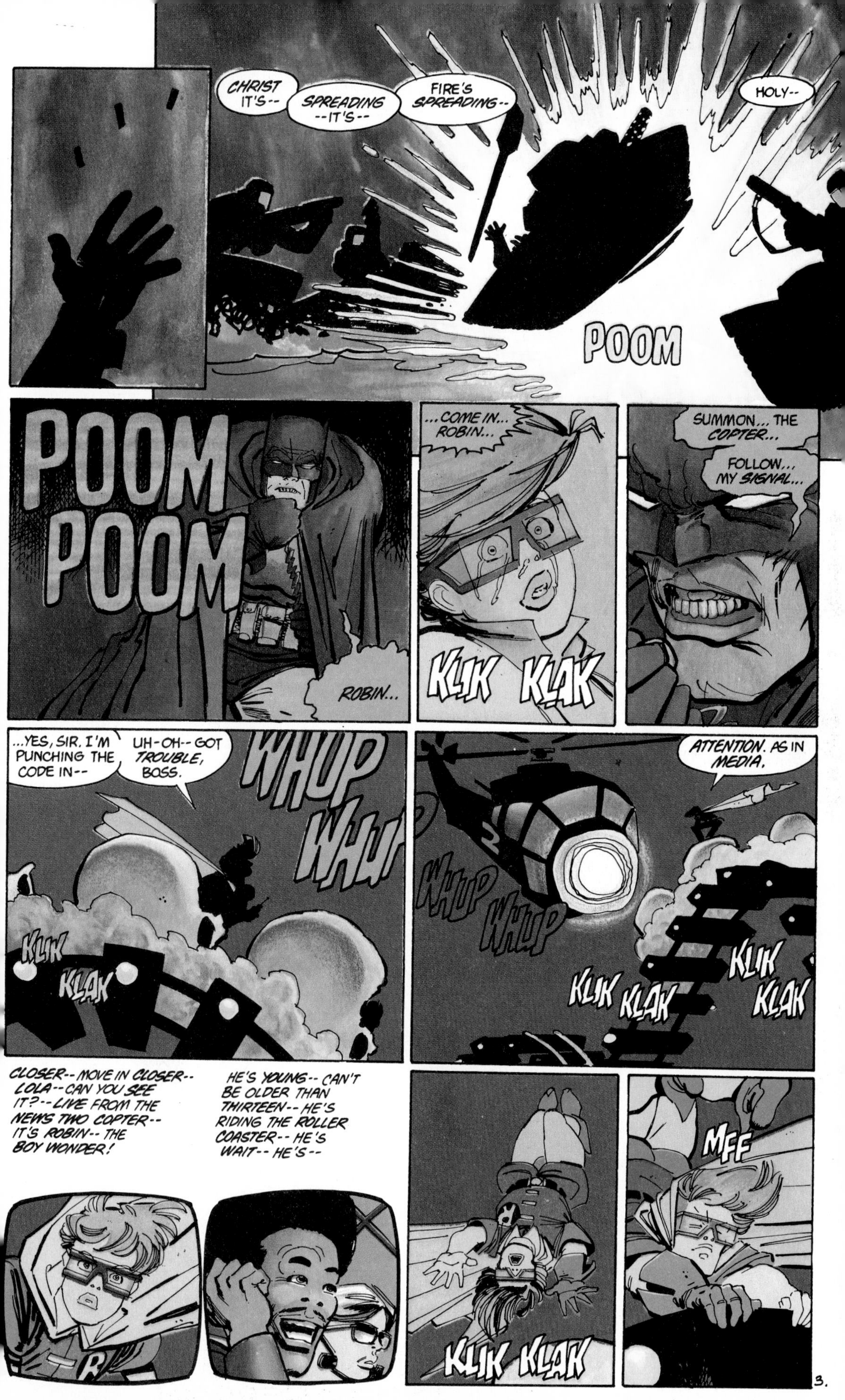
CHRIST IT'S--
SPREADING --IT'S--
FIRE'S SPREADING--
HOLY--
POOM
POOM POOM POOM
ROBIN...
...COME IN... ROBIN...
KLIK KLAK
SUMMON... THE COPTER...
FOLLOW... MY SIGNAL...
...YES, SIR. I'M PUNCHING THE CODE IN--
UH-OH--GOT TROUBLE, BOSS.
WHUP WHUP
KLIK KLAK
ATTENTION. AS IN MEDIA.
WHUP WHUP
KLIK KLAK KLIK KLAK
CLOSER--MOVE IN CLOSER-- LOLA--CAN YOU SEE IT?--LIVE FROM THE NEWS TWO COPTER-- IT'S ROBIN--THE BOY WONDER!
HE'S YOUNG--CAN'T BE OLDER THAN THIRTEEN--HE'S RIDING THE ROLLER COASTER--HE'S WAIT--HE'S--
KLIK KLAK
MFF

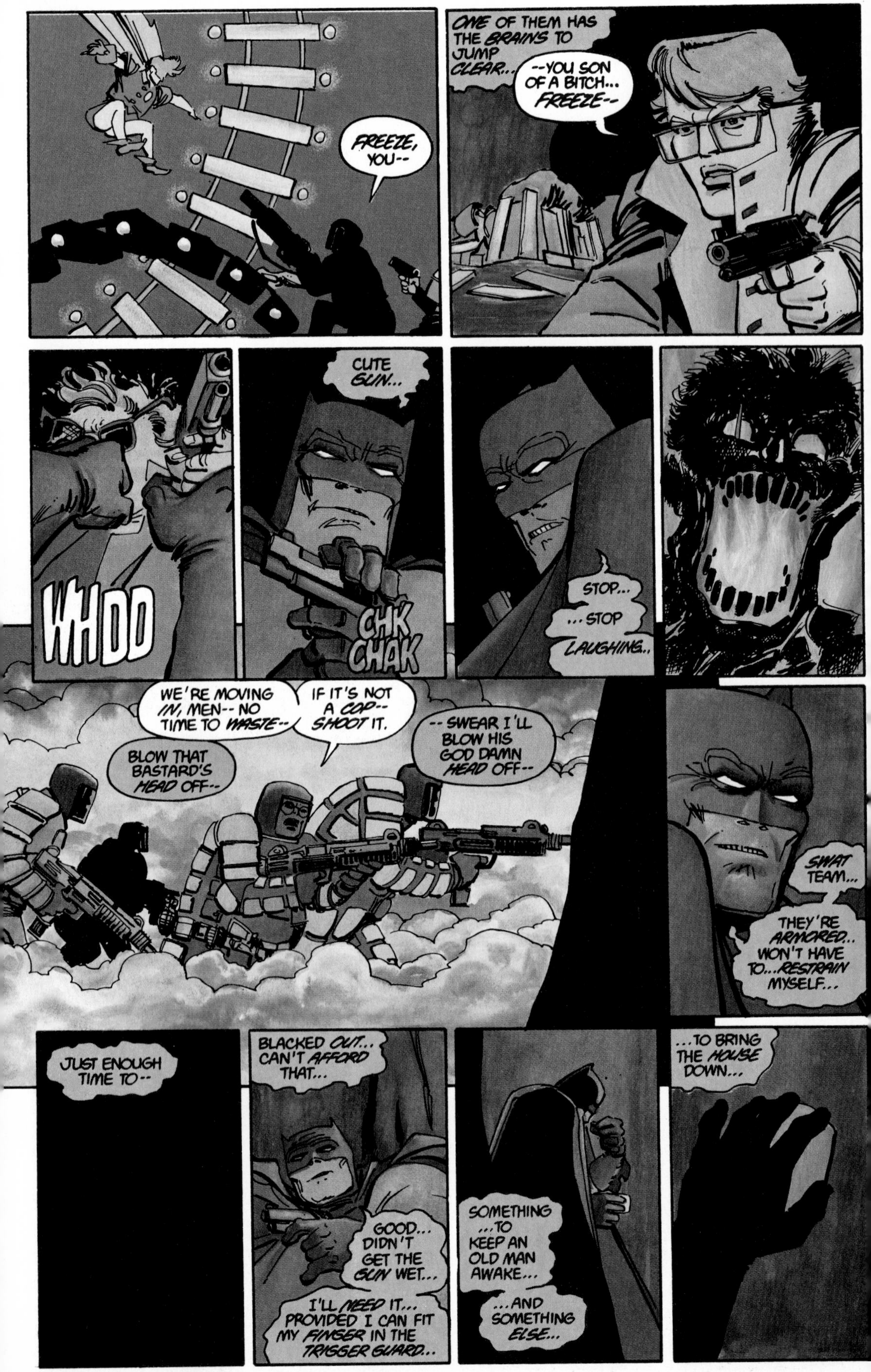
FREEZE, YOU--
ONE OF THEM HAS THE BRAINS TO JUMP CLEAR...
--YOU SON OF A BITCH... FREEZE--
WHDD
CUTE GUN...
CHK CHAK
STOP...
...STOP
LAUGHING...
WE'RE MOVING IN, MEN-- NO TIME TO WASTE--
IF IT'S NOT A COP-- SHOOT IT.
BLOW THAT BASTARD'S HEAD OFF--
-- SWEAR I'LL BLOW HIS GOD DAMN HEAD OFF--
SWAT TEAM...
THEY'RE ARMORED... WON'T HAVE TO...RESTRAIN MYSELF...
JUST ENOUGH TIME TO--
BLACKED OUT... CAN'T AFFORD THAT...
GOOD... DIDN'T GET THE GUN WET...
I'LL NEED IT... PROVIDED I CAN FIT MY FINGER IN THE TRIGGER GUARD...
SOMETHING ...TO KEEP AN OLD MAN AWAKE...
...AND SOMETHING ELSE...
...TO BRING THE HOUSE DOWN...

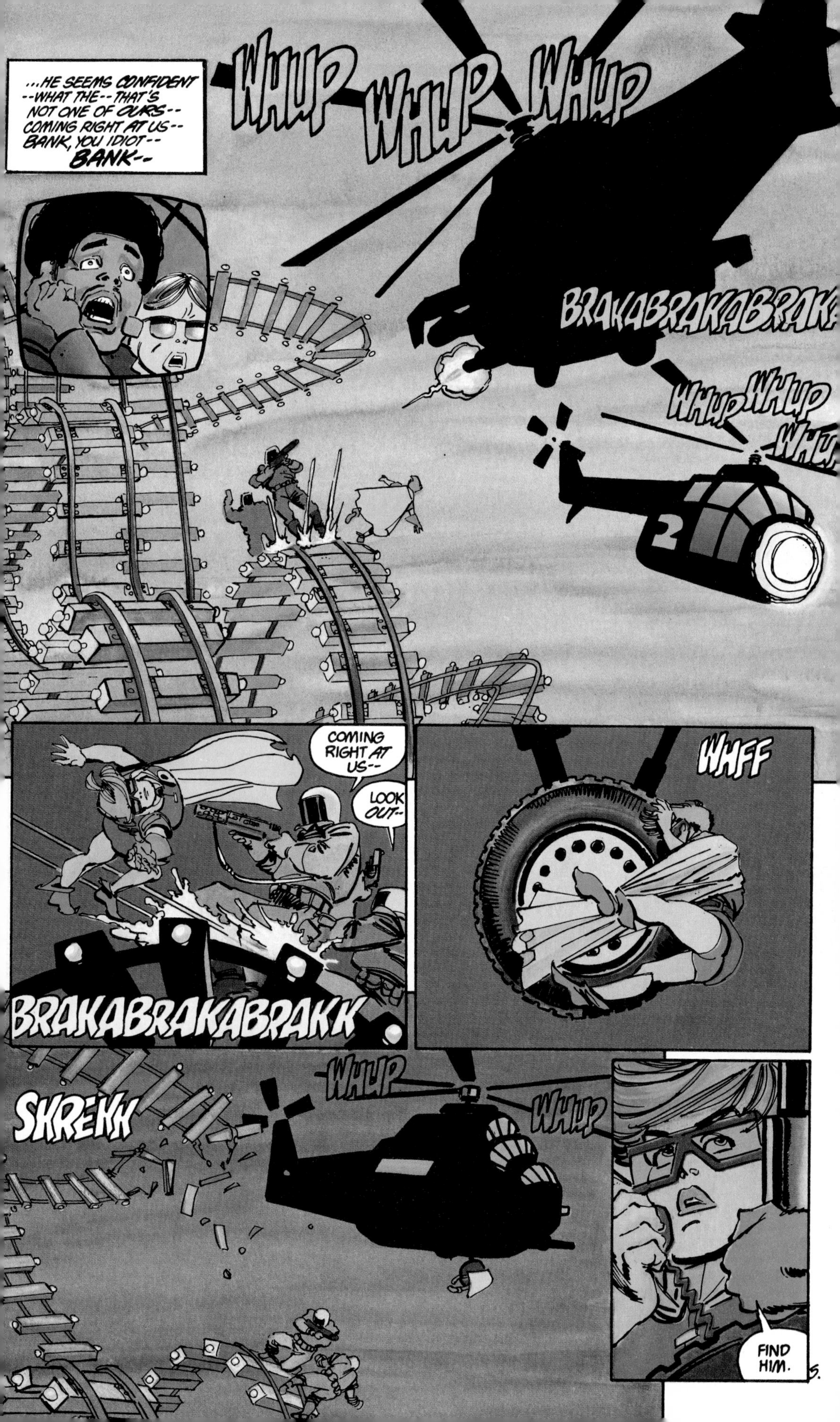
...HE SEEMS CONFIDENT --WHAT THE--THAT'S NOT ONE OF OURS--COMING RIGHT AT US--BANK, YOU IDIOT--BANK--
WHUP WHUP WHUP
BRAKABRAKABRAKK
WHUP WHUP WHU
COMING RIGHT AT US--
LOOK OUT--
BRAKABRAKABRAKK
WHFF
SKREKH
WHUP
WHUP
FIND HIM.

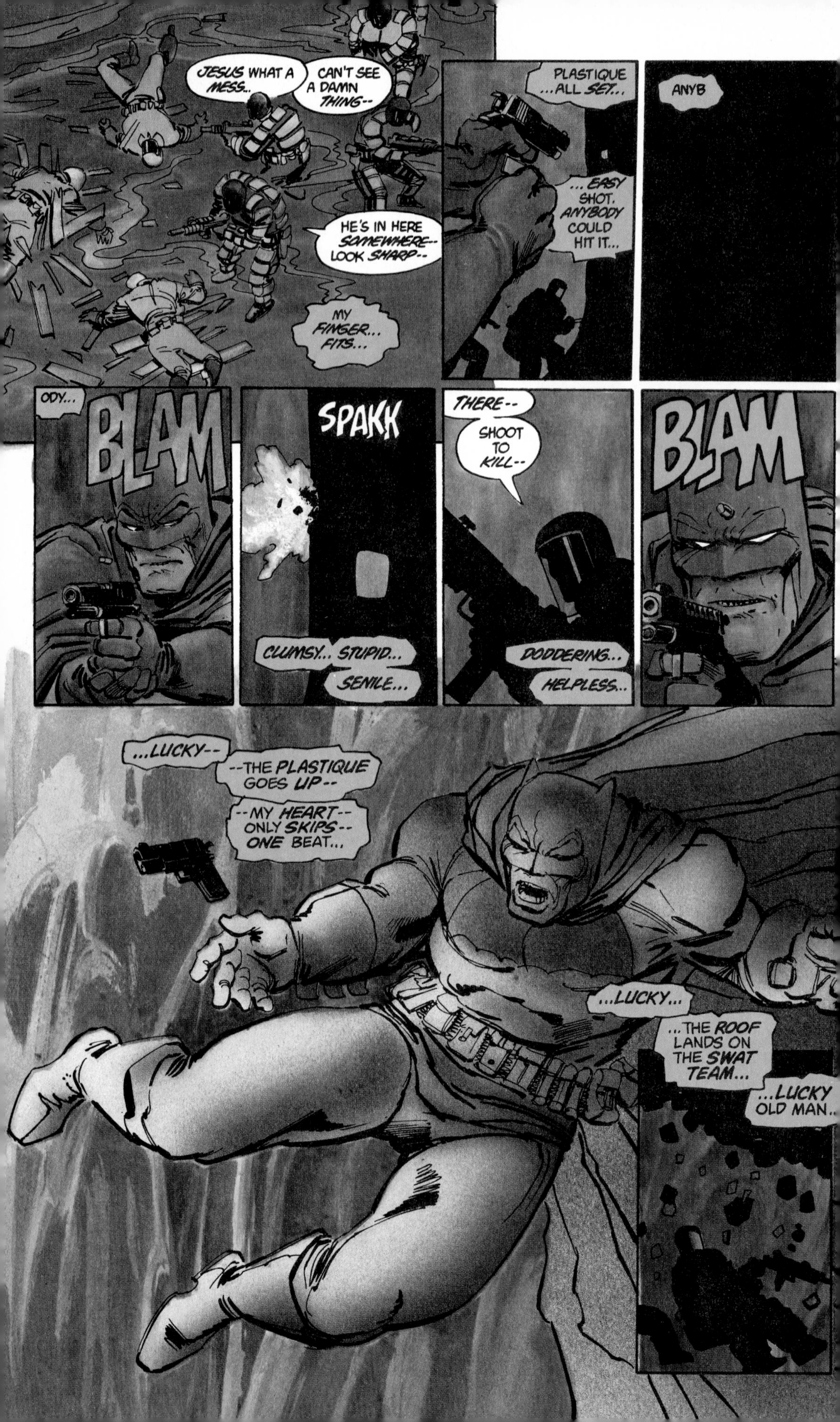

JESUS WHAT A MESS..
CAN'T SEE A DAMN THING--
HE'S IN HERE SOMEWHERE-- LOOK SHARP--
MY FINGER... FITS...
PLASTIQUE ...ALL SET...
... EASY SHOT. ANYBODY COULD HIT IT...
ANYB
ODY...
BLAM
SPAKK
CLUMSY... STUPID...
SENILE...
THERE--
SHOOT TO KILL--
DODDERING...
HELPLESS...
BLAM
...LUCKY--
--THE PLASTIQUE GOES UP--
--MY HEART-- ONLY SKIPS-- ONE BEAT...
...LUCKY...
...THE ROOF LANDS ON THE SWAT TEAM...
...LUCKY OLD MAN...

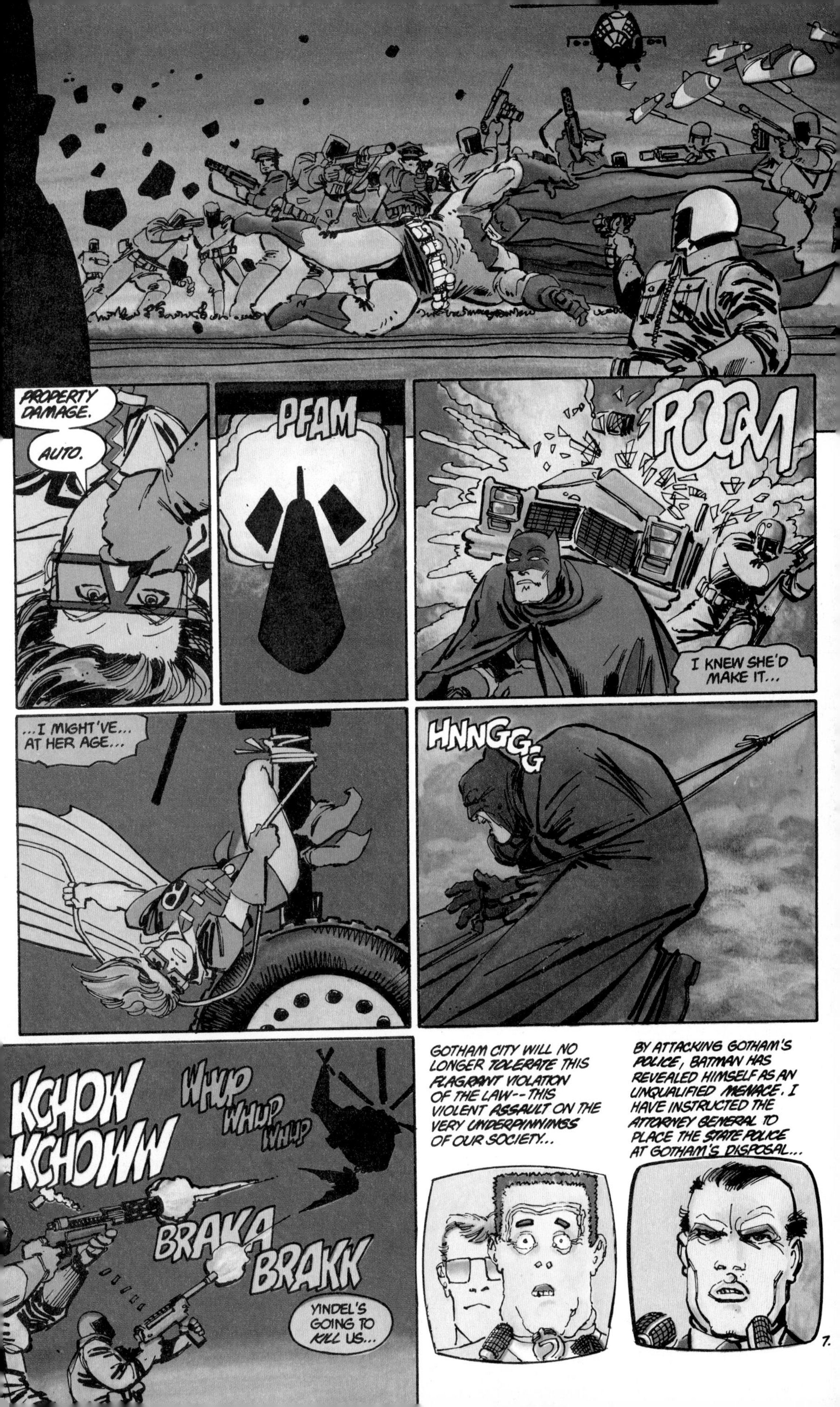

PROPERTY DAMAGE.
AUTO.
PFAM
POOM
I KNEW SHE'D MAKE IT...
...I MIGHT'VE... AT HER AGE...
HNNGGG
KCHOW KCHOWN
WHUP WHUP WHUP
BRAKA BRAKK
YINDEL'S GOING TO KILL US...
GOTHAM CITY WILL NO LONGER TOLERATE THIS FLAGRANT VIOLATION OF THE LAW-- THIS VIOLENT ASSAULT ON THE VERY UNDERPINNINGS OF OUR SOCIETY...
BY ATTACKING GOTHAM'S POLICE, BATMAN HAS REVEALED HIMSELF AS AN UNQUALIFIED MENACE. I HAVE INSTRUCTED THE ATTORNEY GENERAL TO PLACE THE STATE POLICE AT GOTHAM'S DISPOSAL...

...THE JOKER'S BODY FOUND *MUTILATED* AND *BURNED*... *MURDER* IS ADDED TO THE CHARGES AGAINST THE *BATMAN*...

BRUCE. IT'S OVER.

YOU LOOK *TIRED*, KENT.

WELL, YOU'VE *EARNED* A GOOD NIGHT'S *SLEEP*.

HECK OF A POLICE ACTION, IF YOU ASK ME...

I DIDN'T...

YOU CAN SAY WHAT YOU *WANT*. YOU CAN *CALL* HIM WHAT YOU WANT. YOU DON'T HAVE TO WALK DOWN AVENUE D AT NIGHT.

YOU DON'T HAVE TO HEAR THE *SUCKING* SOUNDS THEY MAKE EVERY TIME YOU WALK BY. THIS ONE. HE'D BEEN WORKING THE NERVE UP FOR *WEEKS* BEFORE HE WAS *HORNY* ENOUGH...

...NO, HORNY HE *WASN'T*. HE WAS JUST LOOKING TO *HURT* SOMEBODY AND HE'S THE KIND WHO HURTS *WOMEN*. I WISH THEY WERE *RARE*. HE GAVE HIMSELF AN EXCUSE...

SO NOW HE'S *GIGGLING* LIKE HE'S *TURNED ON!* I FIGURE HE'S *SERIOUS* ENOUGH TO RUN AFTER ME. I GO FOR THE *MACE*.

THE CREEP'S PULLING OUT HIS *WEAPON* WHEN THERE'S THIS *SHRIEK*.

STRAIGHT OUT OF *HELL* THERE'S THIS SHRIEK...

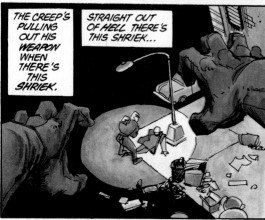

...IT TURNS INTO A *GROWL*— FLAPPING OF *WINGS*—BIG WINGS—

-- SOMETHING *WET* HAPPENS TO THE CREEP--

8

BONES START POPPING INSIDE THE CREEP -- HE'S SCREAMING AND BEGGING --

-- WHAT GRABBED HIM IS LAUGHING AND SO AM I...

--A SIDE OF BEEF SLAMS INTO THE LAMPPOST--

--A SWITCHBLADE SNARS OPEN--

AND THE MAN WHO ASSAULTED YOU?

STILL IN THE HOSPITAL.

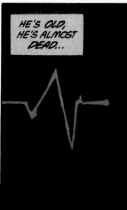

HE'S OLD, HE'S ALMOST DEAD...

SUTURE.

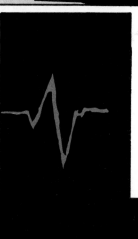

HE'S GOING TO BE OKAY, RIGHT?

HE'LL LIVE...

DO NOT EXPECT ANY FURTHER STATEMENTS. THE SONS OF THE BATMAN DO NOT TALK. WE ACT. LET GOTHAM'S CRIMINALS BEWARE. THEY ARE ABOUT TO ENTER HELL.

THE MUTANTS ARE DEAD. THE MUTANTS ARE HISTORY. THIS IS THE MARK OF THE FUTURE. GOTHAM CITY BELONGS TO THE BATMAN.

...THE SONS OF THE BATMAN HAVE STRUCK AGAIN. JEFF STRICKEN WAS CLOSING UP THE SOUTH STREET 7-11 WHEN HE BECAME BOTH WITNESS-- AND VICTIM...

THEY'RE YOUNGER THAN YOU'D THINK--THIS ONE WAS, ANYWAY. COULDN'T HAVE BEEN OLDER THAN SIXTEEN...THAT'S RIGHT, THERE WAS JUST ONE OF THEM...

9.

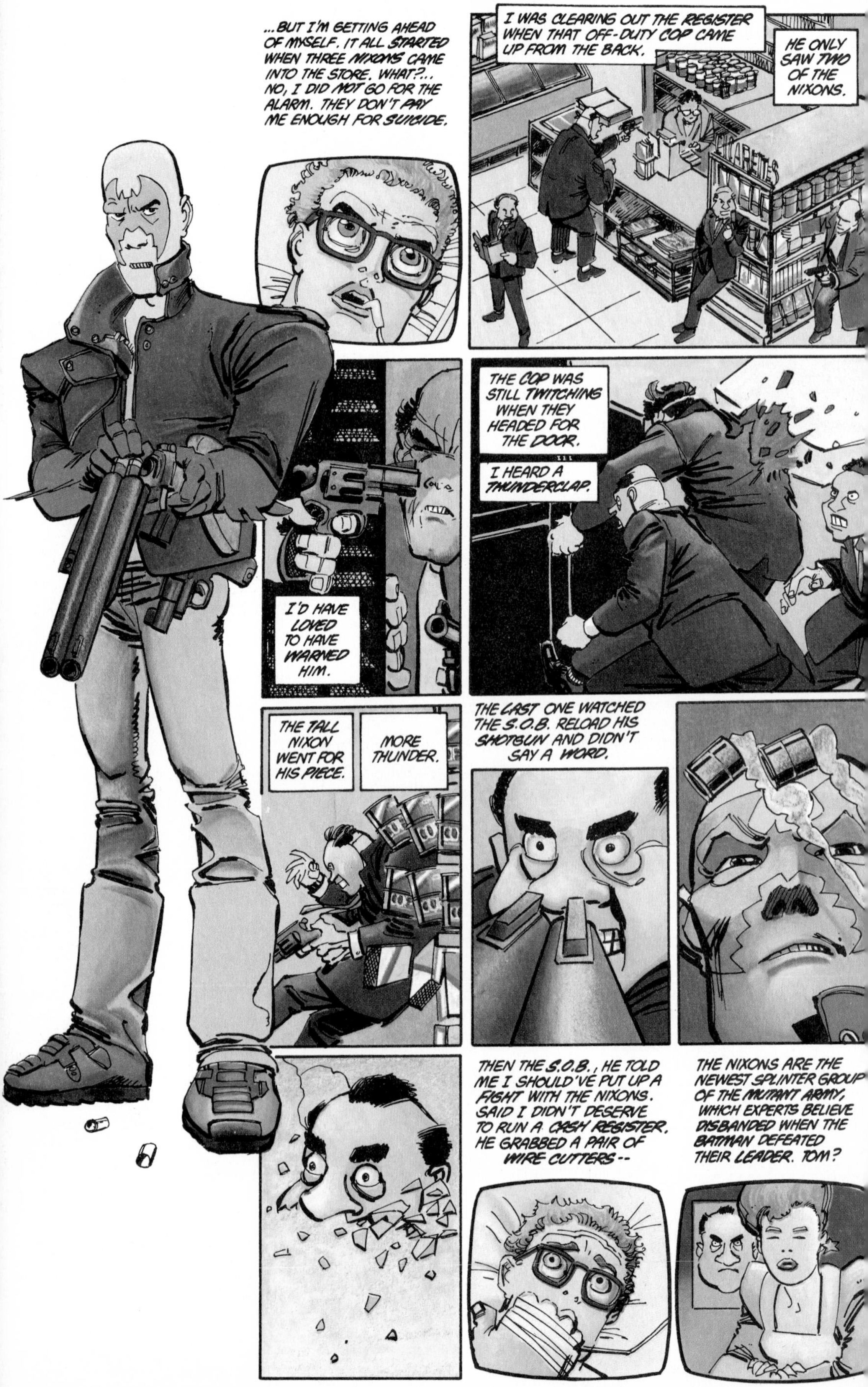
...BUT I'M GETTING AHEAD OF MYSELF. IT ALL STARTED WHEN THREE NIXONS CAME INTO THE STORE. WHAT?.. NO, I DID NOT GO FOR THE ALARM. THEY DON'T PAY ME ENOUGH FOR SUICIDE.
I WAS CLEARING OUT THE REGISTER WHEN THAT OFF-DUTY COP CAME UP FROM THE BACK.
HE ONLY SAW TWO OF THE NIXONS.
CIGARETTES
I'D HAVE LOVED TO HAVE WARNED HIM.
THE COP WAS STILL TWITCHING WHEN THEY HEADED FOR THE DOOR.
I HEARD A THUNDERCLAP.
THE TALL NIXON WENT FOR HIS PIECE.
MORE THUNDER.
THE LAST ONE WATCHED THE S.O.B. RELOAD HIS SHOTGUN AND DIDN'T SAY A WORD.
THEN THE S.O.B., HE TOLD ME I SHOULD'VE PUT UP A FIGHT WITH THE NIXONS. SAID I DIDN'T DESERVE TO RUN A CASH REGISTER. HE GRABBED A PAIR OF WIRE CUTTERS--
THE NIXONS ARE THE NEWEST SPLINTER GROUP OF THE MUTANT ARMY, WHICH EXPERTS BELIEVE DISBANDED WHEN THE BATMAN DEFEATED THEIR LEADER. TOM?

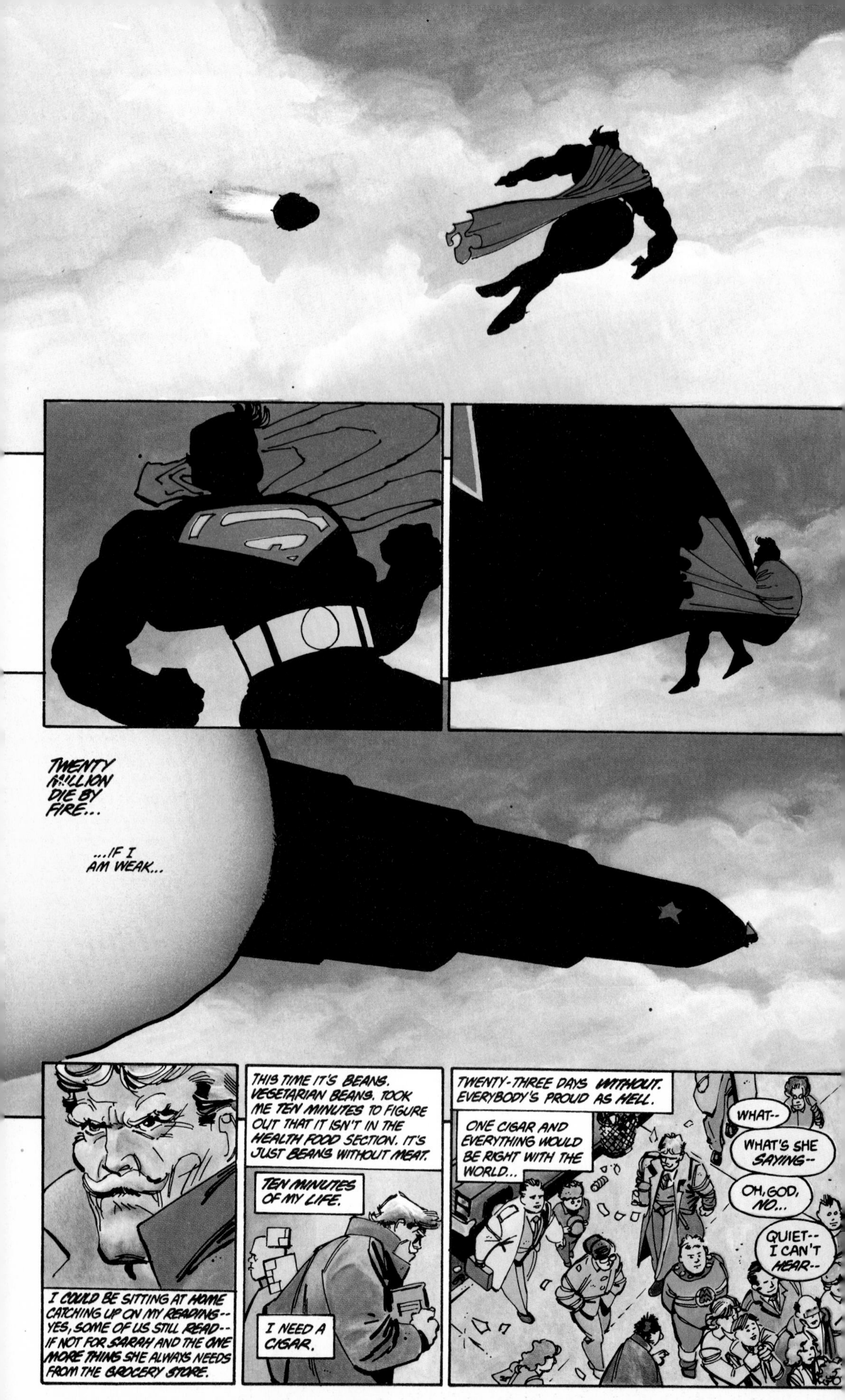
TWENTY MILLION DIE BY FIRE...
...IF I AM WEAK...
I COULD BE SITTING AT HOME CATCHING UP ON MY READING-- YES, SOME OF US STILL READ-- IF NOT FOR SARAH AND THE ONE MORE THING SHE ALWAYS NEEDS FROM THE GROCERY STORE.
THIS TIME IT'S BEANS. VEGETARIAN BEANS. TOOK ME TEN MINUTES TO FIGURE OUT THAT IT ISN'T IN THE HEALTH FOOD SECTION. IT'S JUST BEANS WITHOUT MEAT.
TEN MINUTES OF MY LIFE.
I NEED A CIGAR.
TWENTY-THREE DAYS WITHOUT. EVERYBODY'S PROUD AS HELL.
ONE CIGAR AND EVERYTHING WOULD BE RIGHT WITH THE WORLD...
WHAT--
WHAT'S SHE SAYING--
OH, GOD, NO...
QUIET-- I CAN'T HEAR--

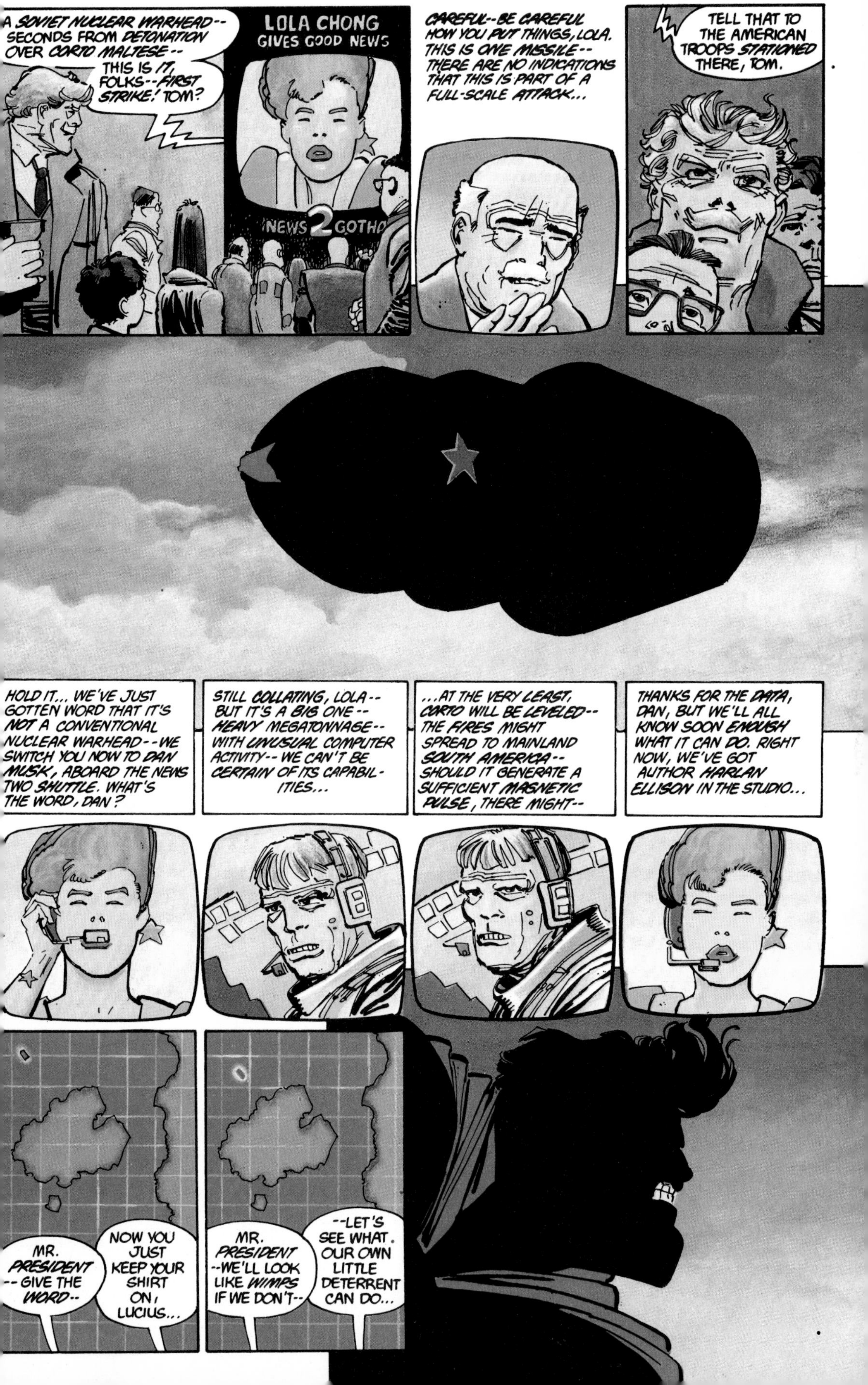
A SOVIET NUCLEAR WARHEAD-- SECONDS FROM DETONATION OVER CORTO MALTESE--
THIS IS IT, FOLKS--FIRST STRIKE! TOM?
LOLA CHONG GIVES GOOD NEWS
NEWS 2 GOTHA
CAREFUL--BE CAREFUL HOW YOU PUT THINGS, LOLA. THIS IS ONE MISSILE-- THERE ARE NO INDICATIONS THAT THIS IS PART OF A FULL-SCALE ATTACK...
TELL THAT TO THE AMERICAN TROOPS STATIONED THERE, TOM.
HOLD IT... WE'VE JUST GOTTEN WORD THAT IT'S NOT A CONVENTIONAL NUCLEAR WARHEAD--WE SWITCH YOU NOW TO DAN MUSK, ABOARD THE NEWS TWO SHUTTLE. WHAT'S THE WORD, DAN?
STILL COLLATING, LOLA-- BUT IT'S A BIG ONE-- HEAVY MEGATONNAGE-- WITH UNUSUAL COMPUTER ACTIVITY--WE CAN'T BE CERTAIN OF ITS CAPABIL-ITIES...
...AT THE VERY LEAST, CORTO WILL BE LEVELED-- THE FIRES MIGHT SPREAD TO MAINLAND SOUTH AMERICA-- SHOULD IT GENERATE A SUFFICIENT MAGNETIC PULSE, THERE MIGHT--
THANKS FOR THE DATA, DAN, BUT WE'LL ALL KNOW SOON ENOUGH WHAT IT CAN DO. RIGHT NOW, WE'VE GOT AUTHOR HARLAN ELLISON IN THE STUDIO...
MR. PRESIDENT --GIVE THE WORD--
NOW YOU JUST KEEP YOUR SHIRT ON, LUCIUS...
MR. PRESIDENT --WE'LL LOOK LIKE WIMPS IF WE DON'T--
--LET'S SEE WHAT OUR OWN LITTLE DETERRENT CAN DO...

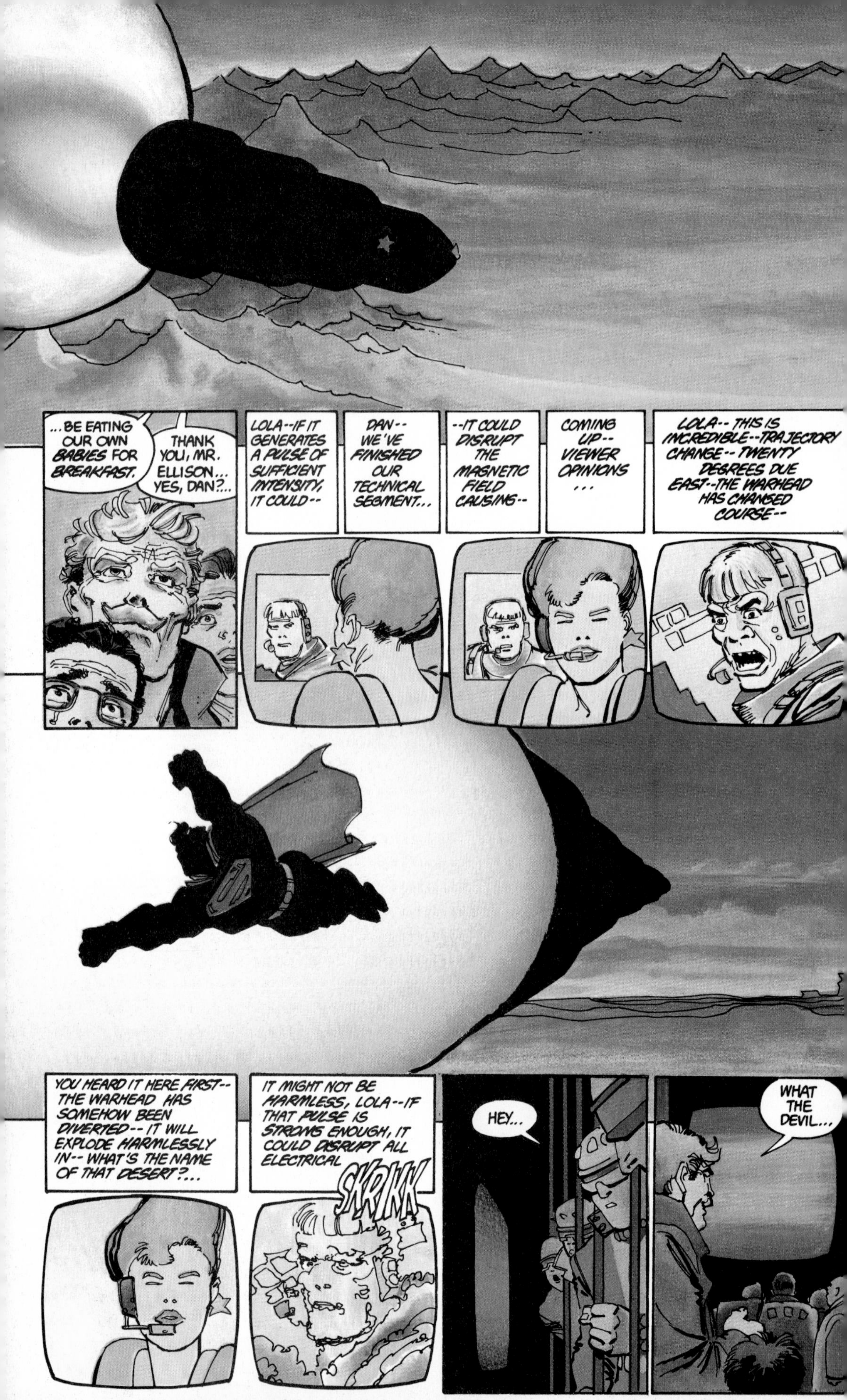

...BE EATING OUR OWN BABIES FOR BREAKFAST.
THANK YOU, MR. ELLISON... YES, DAN?...
LOLA--IF IT GENERATES A PULSE OF SUFFICIENT INTENSITY, IT COULD--
DAN-- WE'VE FINISHED OUR TECHNICAL SEGMENT...
--IT COULD DISRUPT THE MAGNETIC FIELD CAUSING--
COMING UP-- VIEWER OPINIONS ...
LOLA-- THIS IS INCREDIBLE--TRAJECTORY CHANGE--TWENTY DEGREES DUE EAST--THE WARHEAD HAS CHANGED COURSE--
YOU HEARD IT HERE FIRST-- THE WARHEAD HAS SOMEHOW BEEN DIVERTED-- IT WILL EXPLODE HARMLESSLY IN-- WHAT'S THE NAME OF THAT DESERT?...
IT MIGHT NOT BE HARMLESS, LOLA--IF THAT PULSE IS STRONG ENOUGH, IT COULD DISRUPT ALL ELECTRICAL
SKRIKK
HEY...
WHAT THE DEVIL...

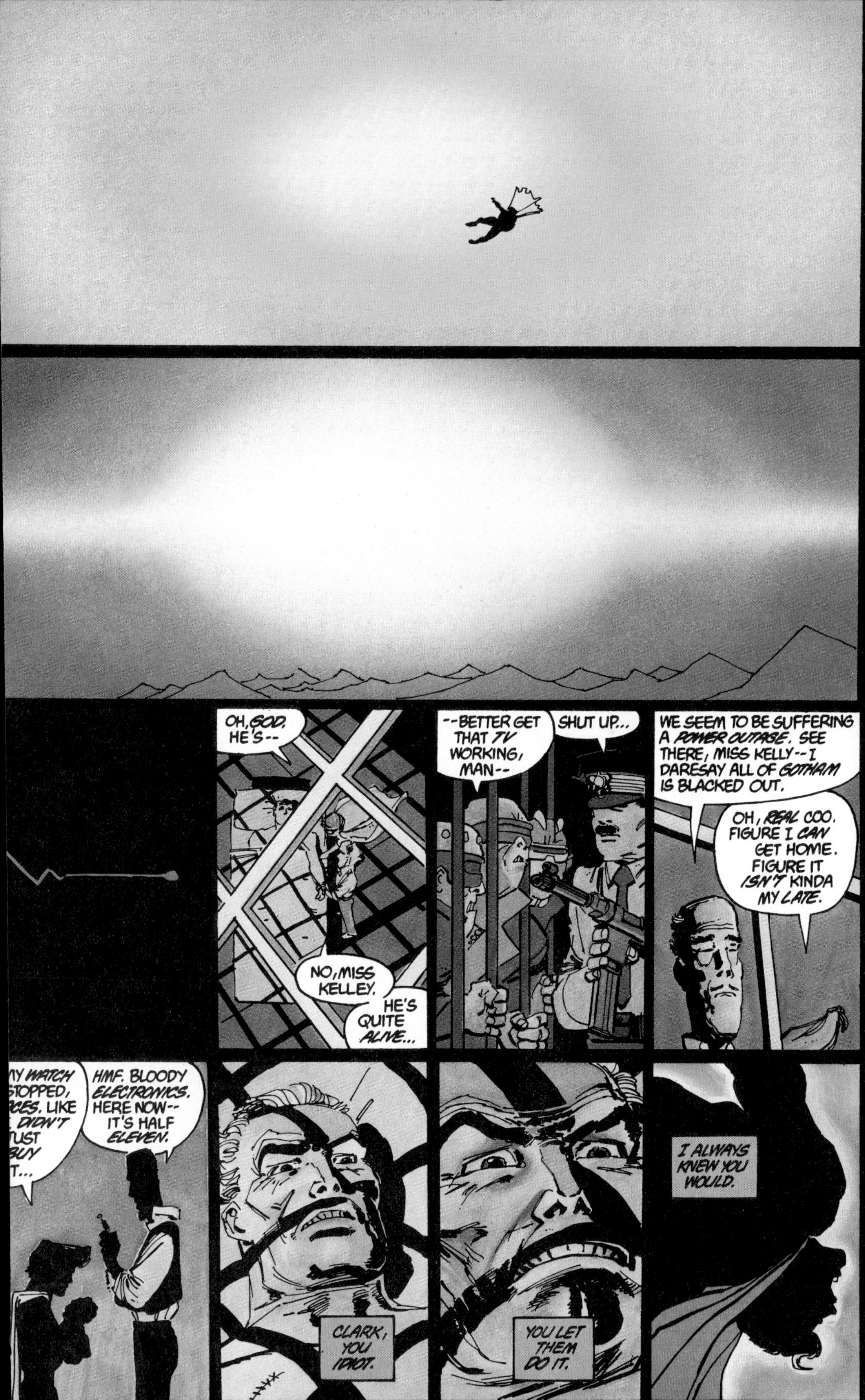
OH, GOD, HE'S--
NO, MISS KELLEY. HE'S QUITE ALIVE...
--BETTER GET THAT TV WORKING, MAN--
SHUT UP...
WE SEEM TO BE SUFFERING A POWER OUTAGE. SEE THERE, MISS KELLY--I DARESAY ALL OF GOTHAM IS BLACKED OUT.
OH, REAL COO. FIGURE I CAN GET HOME. FIGURE IT ISN'T KINDA MY LATE.
HMF. BLOODY ELECTRONICS. HERE NOW-- IT'S HALF ELEVEN.
CLARK, YOU IDIOT.
YOU LET THEM DO IT.
I ALWAYS KNEW YOU WOULD.

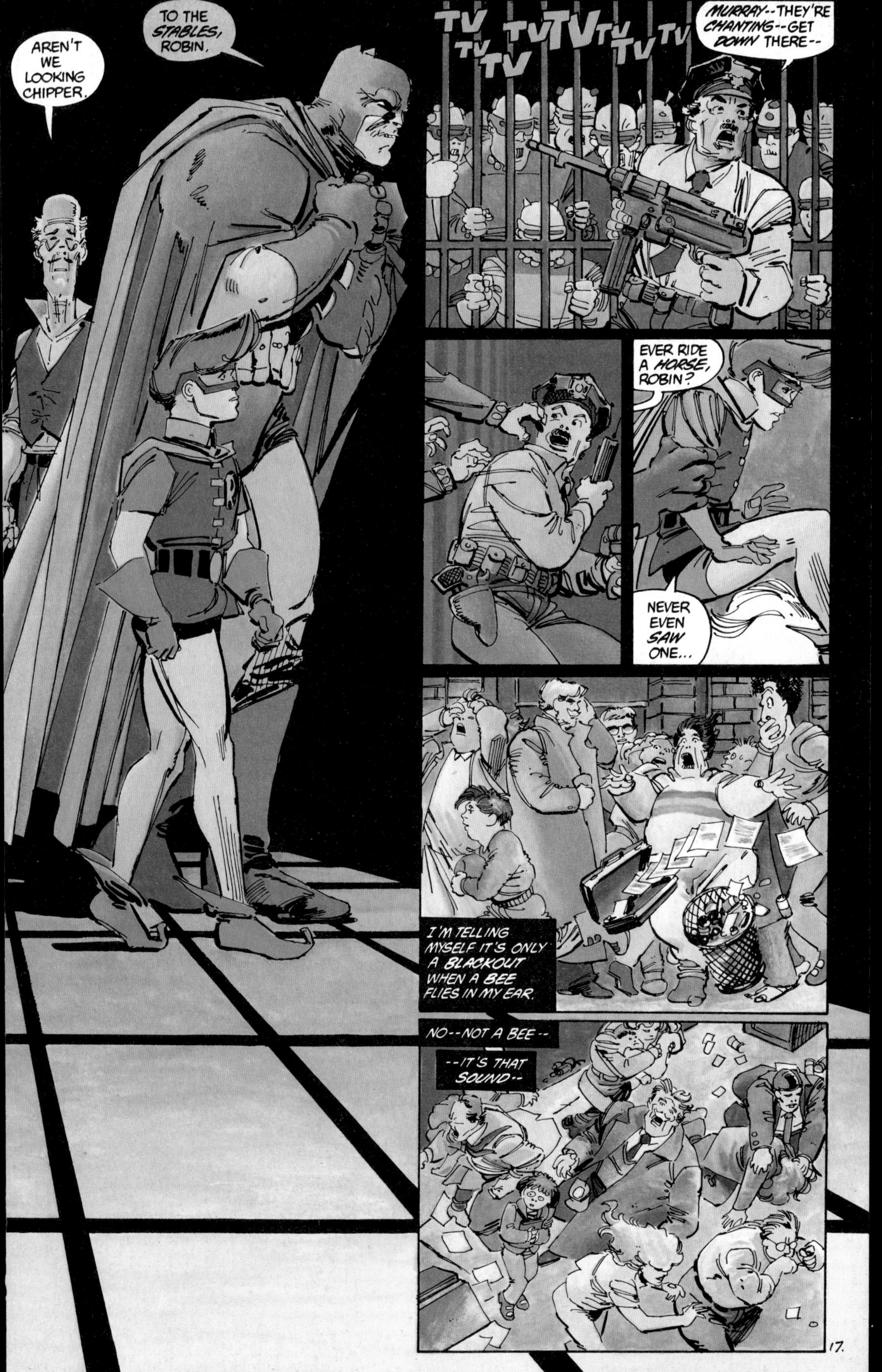

ARE'NT WE LOOKING CHIPPER.
TO THE STABLES, ROBIN.
TV TV TV TV TV TV TV TV TV
MURRAY--THEY'RE CHANTING--GET DOWN THERE--
EVER RIDE A HORSE, ROBIN?
NEVER EVEN SAW ONE...
I'M TELLING MYSELF IT'S ONLY A BLACKOUT WHEN A BEE FLIES IN MY EAR.
NO--NOT A BEE--
--IT'S THAT SOUND--

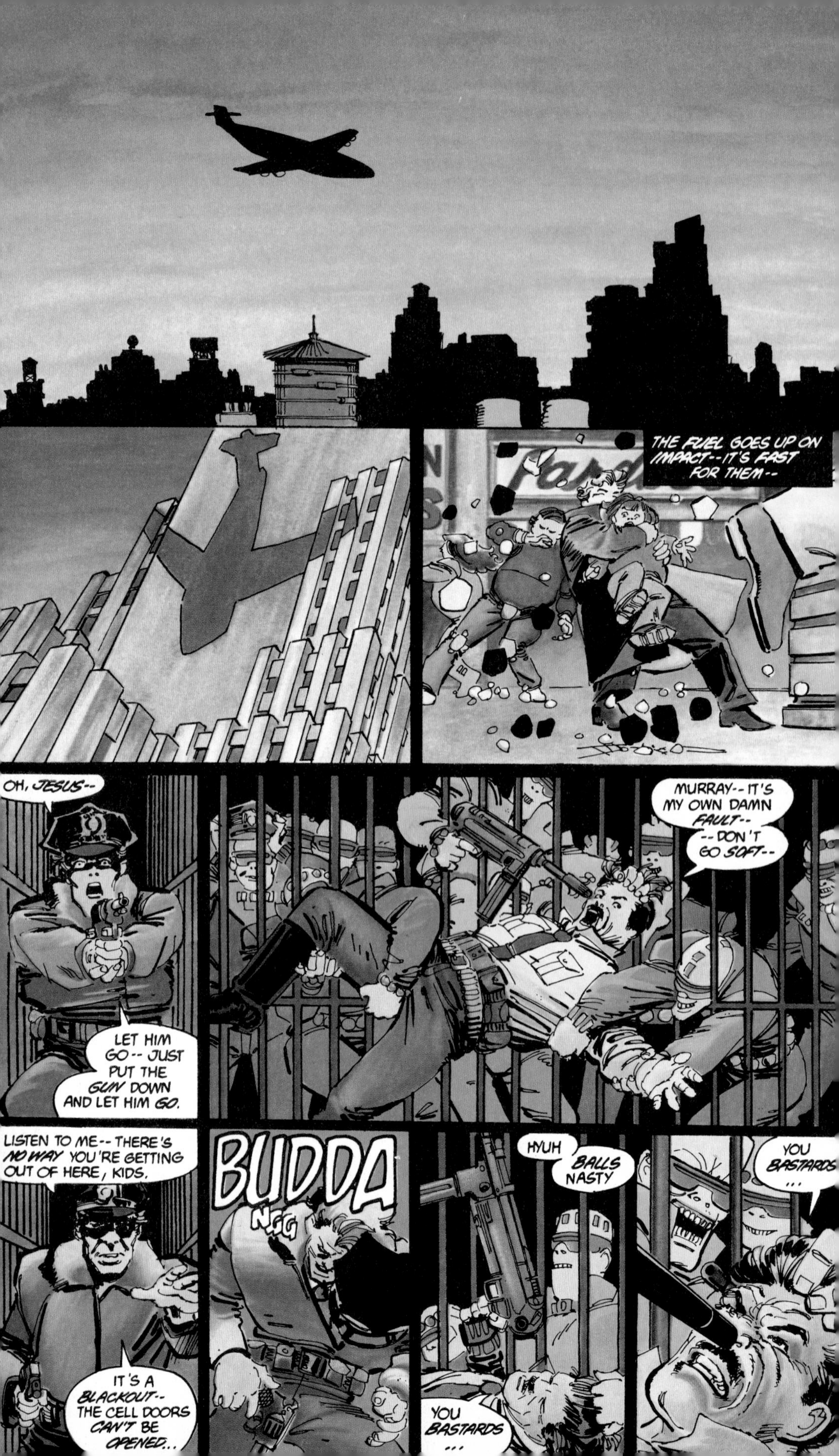

THE FUEL GOES UP ON IMPACT--IT'S FAST FOR THEM--
OH, JESUS--
MURRAY--IT'S MY OWN DAMN FAULT-- --DON'T GO SOFT--
LET HIM GO--JUST PUT THE GUN DOWN AND LET HIM GO.
LISTEN TO ME--THERE'S NO WAY YOU'RE GETTING OUT OF HERE, KIDS.
IT'S A BLACKOUT--THE CELL DOORS CAN'T BE OPENED...
BUDDA
NGG
HYUH
BALLS NASTY
YOU BASTARDS ...
YOU BASTARDS ...

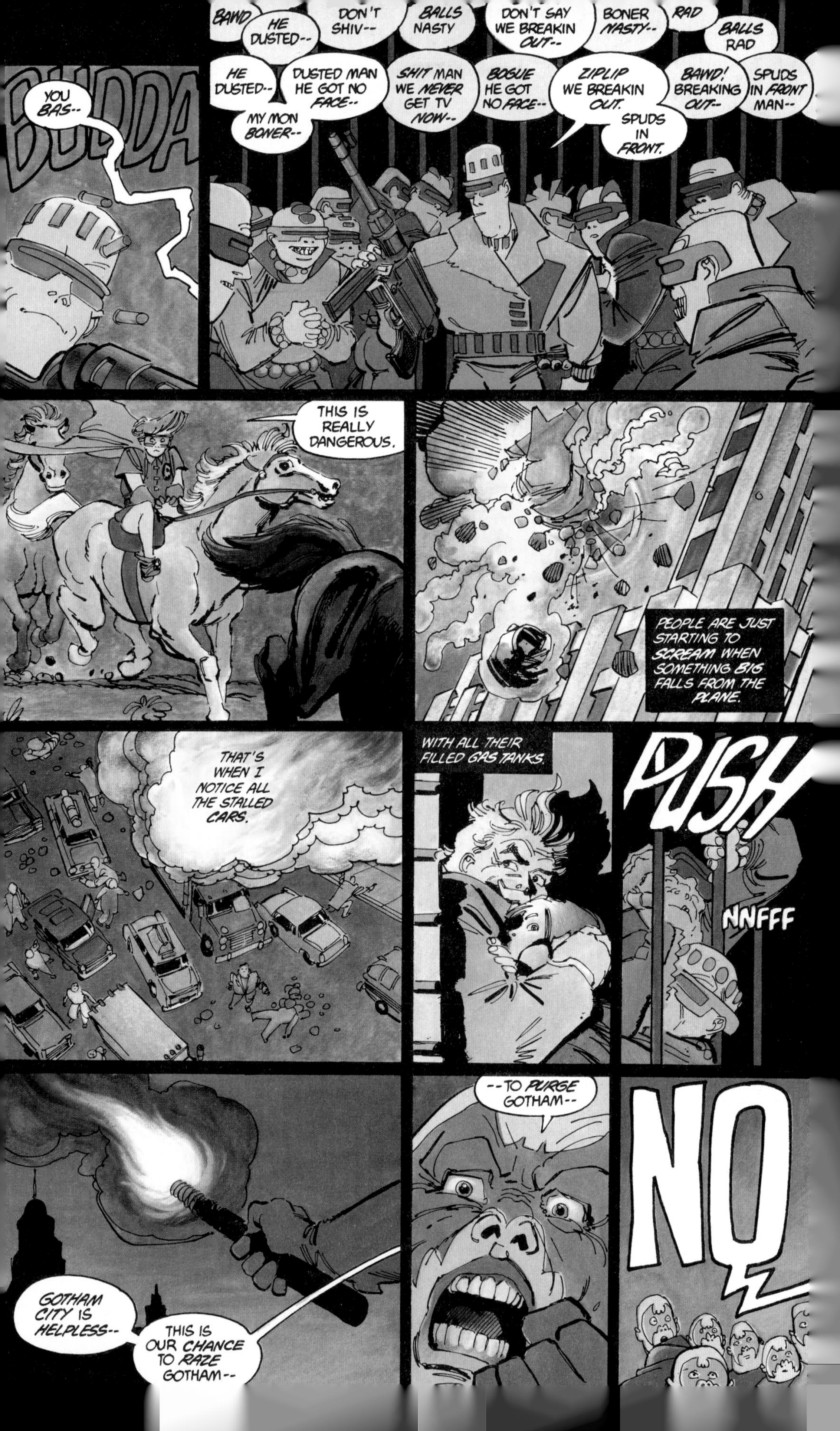
BUDDA
YOU BAS--
BAWD
HE DUSTED--
DON'T SHIV--
BALLS NASTY
DON'T SAY WE BREAKIN OUT--
BONER NASTY--
RAD
BALLS RAD
HE DUSTED--
MY MON BONER--
DUSTED MAN HE GOT NO FACE--
SHIT MAN WE NEVER GET TV NOW--
BOGUE HE GOT NO FACE--
ZIPLIP WE BREAKIN OUT.
SPUDS IN FRONT.
BAWD! BREAKING OUT--
SPUDS IN FRONT MAN--
THIS IS REALLY DANGEROUS.
PEOPLE ARE JUST STARTING TO SCREAM WHEN SOMETHING BIG FALLS FROM THE PLANE.
THAT'S WHEN I NOTICE ALL THE STALLED CARS.
WITH ALL THEIR FILLED GAS TANKS.
PUSH
NNFFF
GOTHAM CITY IS HELPLESS--
THIS IS OUR CHANCE TO RAZE GOTHAM--
--TO PURGE GOTHAM--
NO

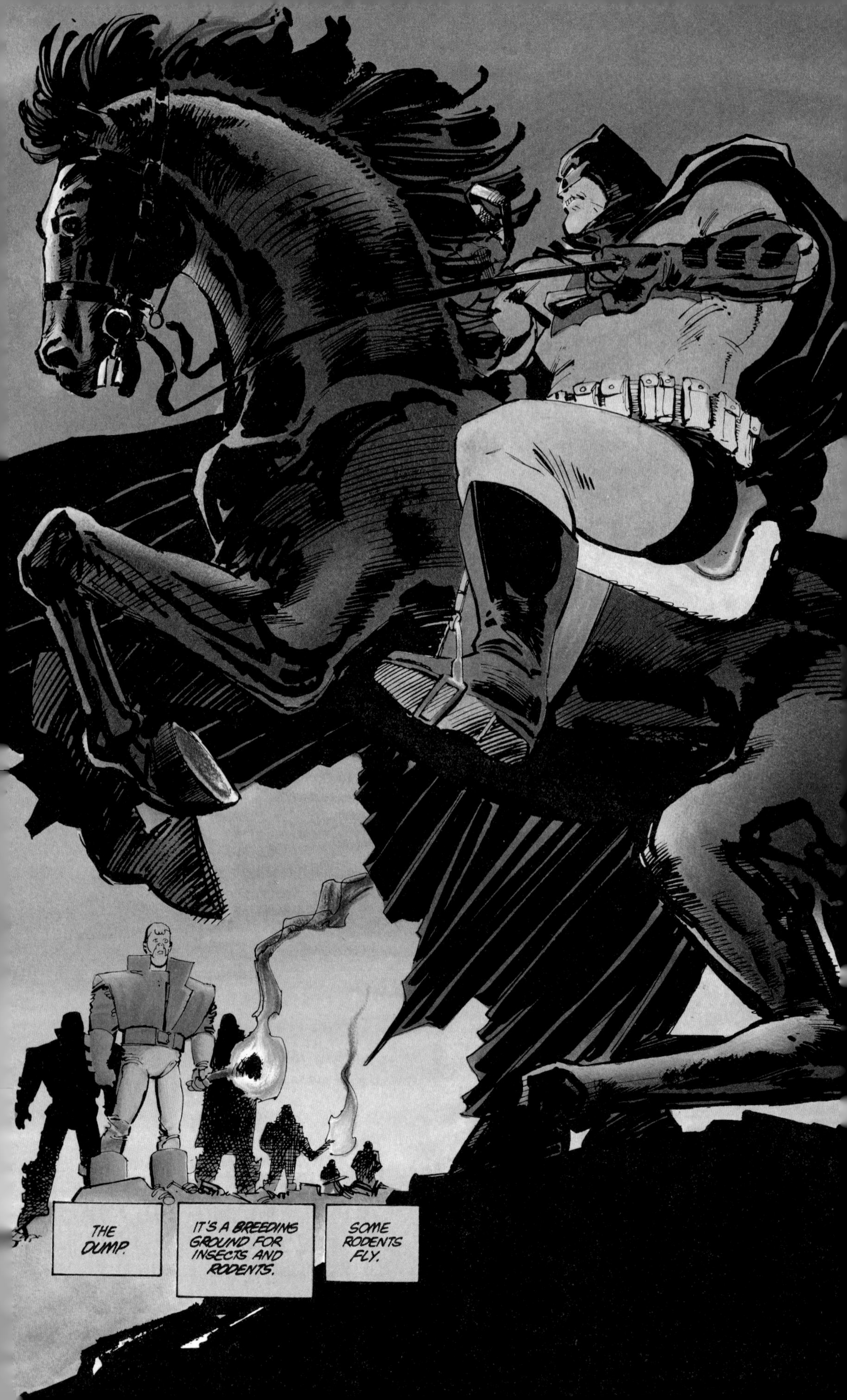
THE DUMP.
IT'S A BREEDING GROUND FOR INSECTS AND RODENTS.
SOME RODENTS FLY.

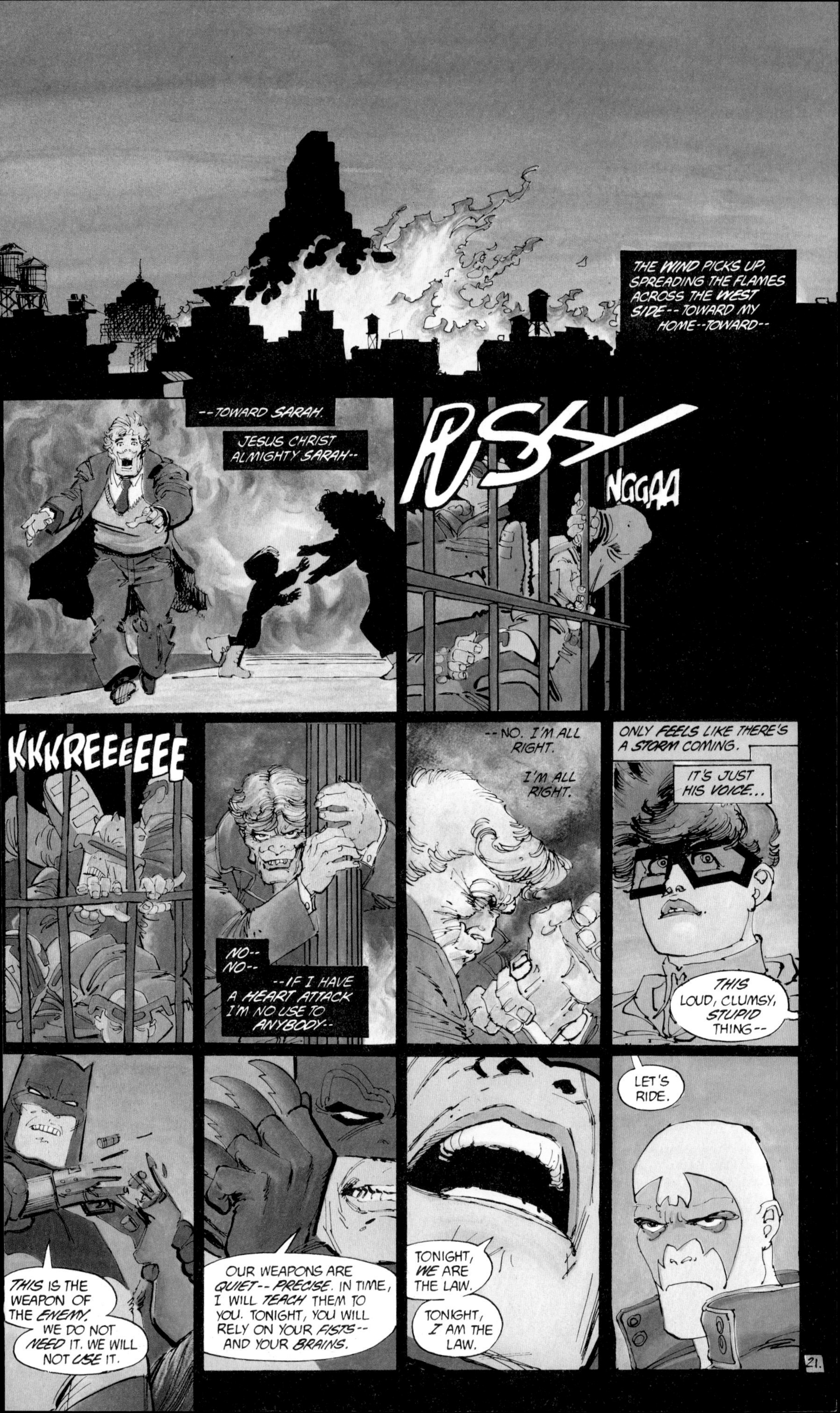

THE WIND PICKS UP, SPREADING THE FLAMES ACROSS THE WEST SIDE--TOWARD MY HOME--TOWARD--
--TOWARD SARAH.
JESUS CHRIST ALMIGHTY SARAH--
RUSH
NGGAA
KKKREEEEEEE
NO--
NO--
--IF I HAVE A HEART ATTACK I'M NO USE TO ANYBODY--
--NO. I'M ALL RIGHT.
I'M ALL RIGHT.
ONLY FEELS LIKE THERE'S A STORM COMING.
IT'S JUST HIS VOICE...
THIS LOUD, CLUMSY, STUPID THING--
THIS IS THE WEAPON OF THE ENEMY. WE DO NOT NEED IT. WE WILL NOT USE IT.
OUR WEAPONS ARE QUIET--PRECISE. IN TIME, I WILL TEACH THEM TO YOU. TONIGHT, YOU WILL RELY ON YOUR FISTS--AND YOUR BRAINS.
TONIGHT, WE ARE THE LAW.
TONIGHT, I AM THE LAW.
LET'S RIDE.
21.

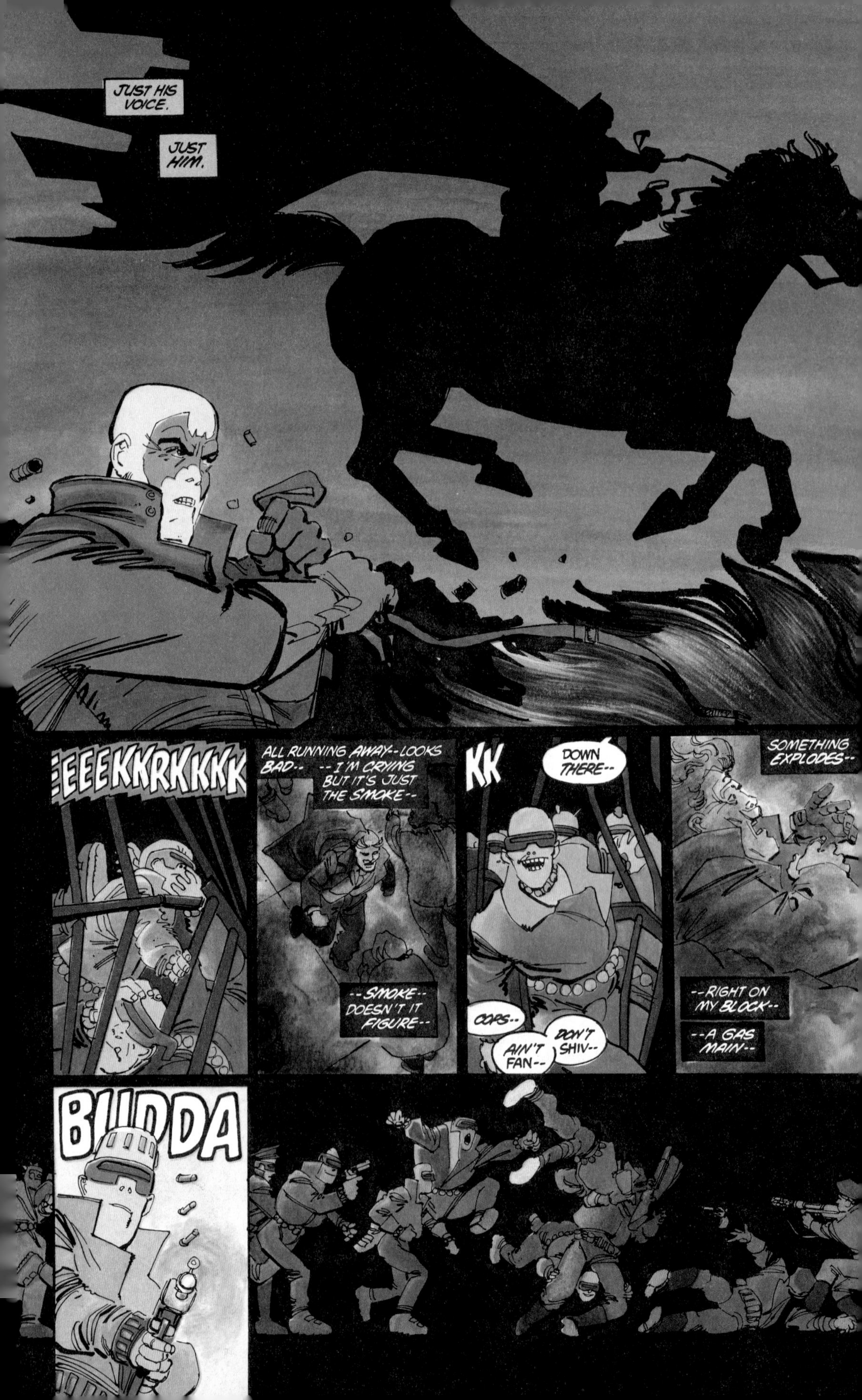
JUST HIS VOICE.
JUST HIM.
EEEEKKRKKKK
ALL RUNNING AWAY--LOOKS BAD--
--I'M CRYING BUT IT'S JUST THE SMOKE--
--SMOKE-- DOESN'T IT FIGURE--
KK
DOWN THERE--
COPS--
AIN'T FAN--
DON'T SHIV--
SOMETHING EXPLODES--
--RIGHT ON MY BLOCK--
--A GAS MAIN--
BUDDA

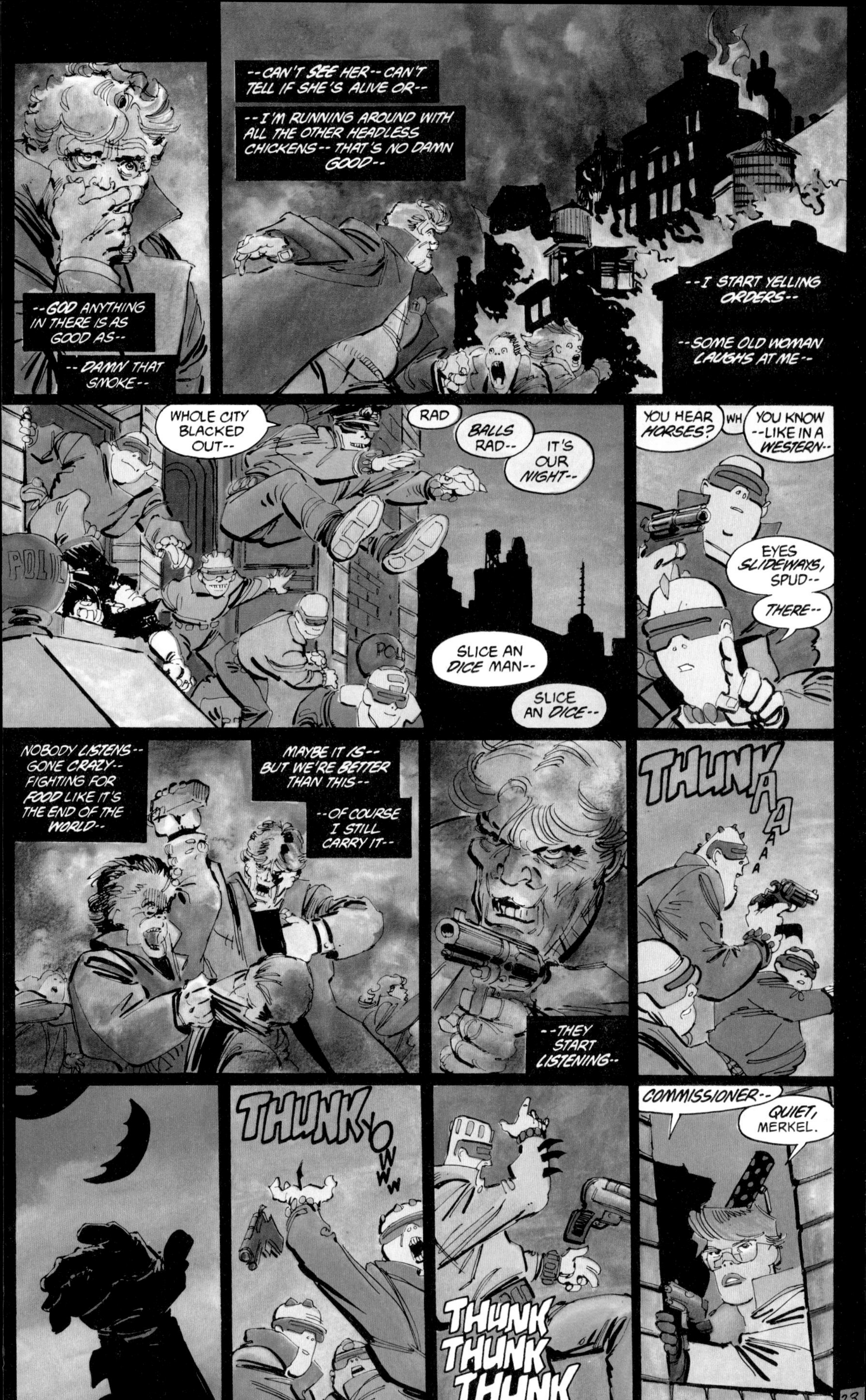
--GOD ANYTHING IN THERE IS AS GOOD AS--
--DAMN THAT SMOKE--
--CAN'T SEE HER--CAN'T TELL IF SHE'S ALIVE OR--
--I'M RUNNING AROUND WITH ALL THE OTHER HEADLESS CHICKENS--THAT'S NO DAMN GOOD--
--I START YELLING ORDERS--
--SOME OLD WOMAN LAUGHS AT ME--
WHOLE CITY BLACKED OUT--
RAD
BALLS RAD--
IT'S OUR NIGHT--
SLICE AN DICE MAN--
SLICE AN DICE--
YOU HEAR HORSES?
WH
YOU KNOW --LIKE IN A WESTERN--
EYES SLIDEWAYS, SPUD--
THERE--
NOBODY LISTENS--GONE CRAZY--FIGHTING FOR FOOD LIKE IT'S THE END OF THE WORLD--
MAYBE IT IS--BUT WE'RE BETTER THAN THIS--
--OF COURSE I STILL CARRY IT--
--THEY START LISTENING--
THUNK
AAAAAA
THUNK
YOWWW
THUNK THUNK THUNK
COMMISSIONER--
QUIET, MERKEL.

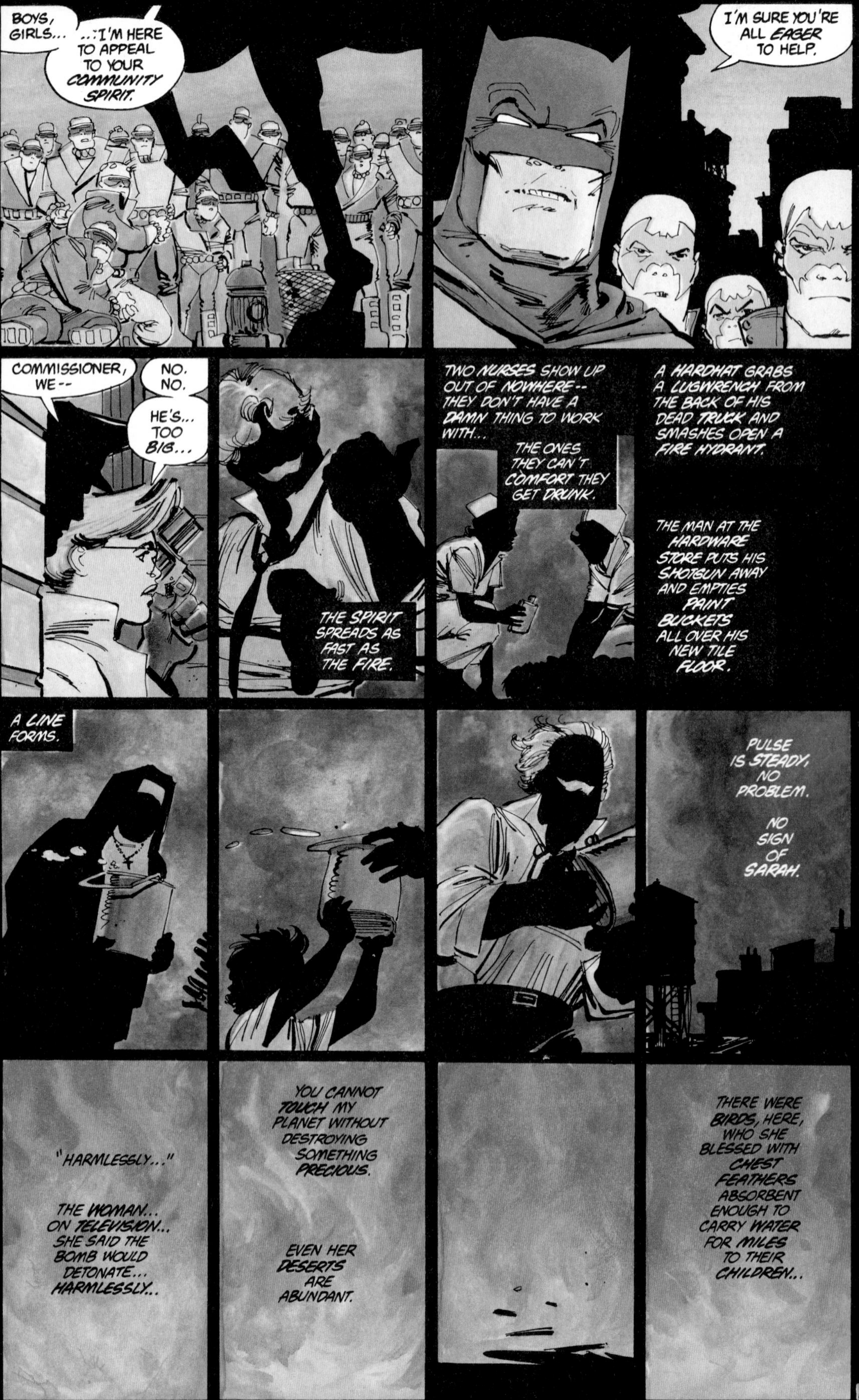
BOYS, GIRLS...
...I'M HERE TO APPEAL TO YOUR COMMUNITY SPIRIT.
I'M SURE YOU'RE ALL EAGER TO HELP.
COMMISSIONER, WE--
NO. NO.
HE'S... TOO BIG...
THE SPIRIT SPREADS AS FAST AS THE FIRE.
TWO NURSES SHOW UP OUT OF NOWHERE-- THEY DON'T HAVE A DAMN THING TO WORK WITH...
THE ONES THEY CAN'T COMFORT THEY GET DRUNK.
A HARDHAT GRABS A LUGWRENCH FROM THE BACK OF HIS DEAD TRUCK AND SMASHES OPEN A FIRE HYDRANT.
THE MAN AT THE HARDWARE STORE PUTS HIS SHOTGUN AWAY AND EMPTIES PAINT BUCKETS ALL OVER HIS NEW TILE FLOOR.
A LINE FORMS.
PULSE IS STEADY, NO PROBLEM.
NO SIGN OF SARAH.
"HARMLESSLY..."
THE WOMAN... ON TELEVISION... SHE SAID THE BOMB WOULD DETONATE... HARMLESSLY...
YOU CANNOT TOUCH MY PLANET WITHOUT DESTROYING SOMETHING PRECIOUS.
EVEN HER DESERTS ARE ABUNDANT.
THERE WERE BIRDS, HERE, WHO SHE BLESSED WITH CHEST FEATHERS ABSORBENT ENOUGH TO CARRY WATER FOR MILES TO THEIR CHILDREN...

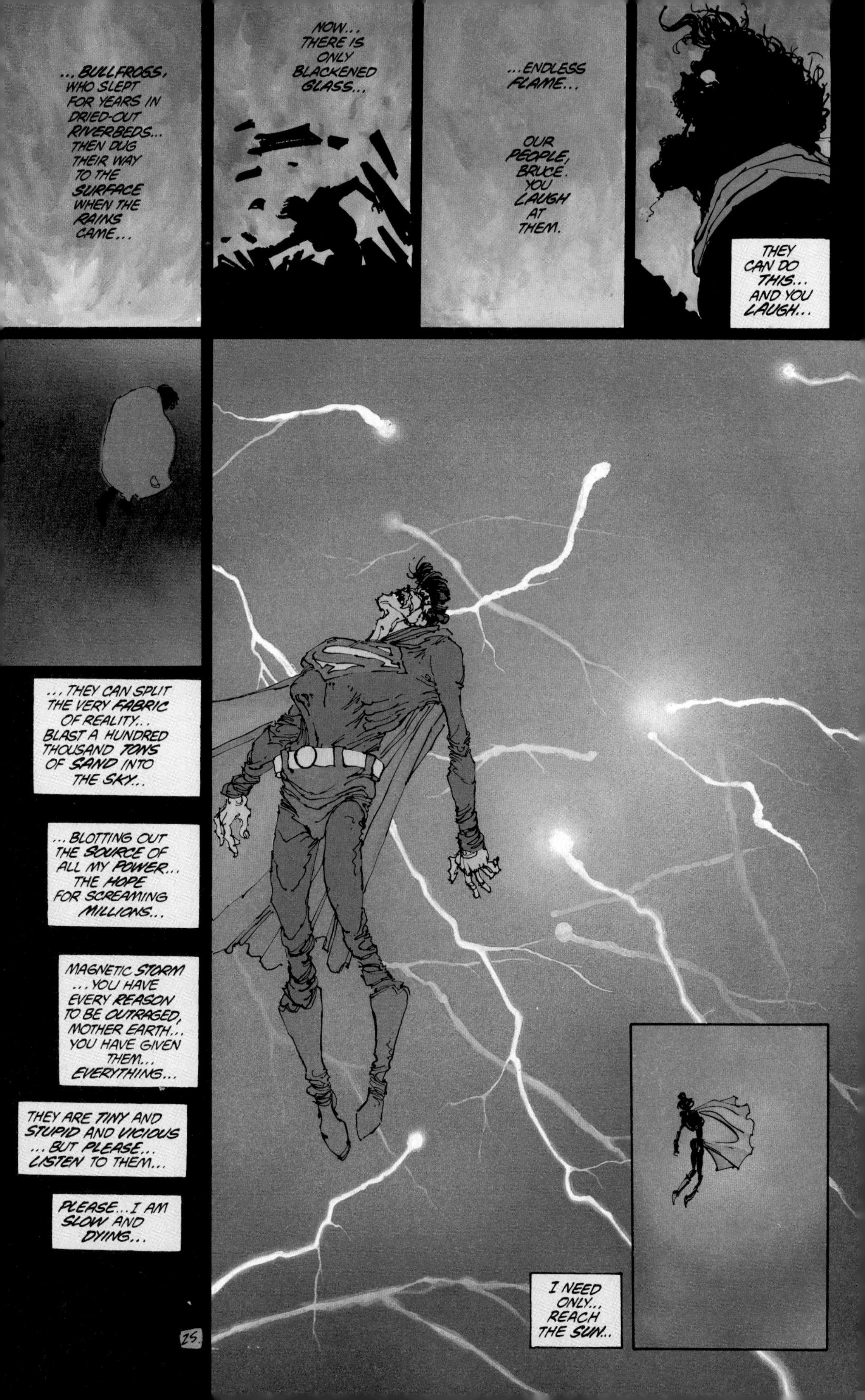
...BULLFROGS, WHO SLEPT FOR YEARS IN DRIED-OUT RIVERBEDS... THEN DUG THEIR WAY TO THE SURFACE WHEN THE RAINS CAME...
NOW... THERE IS ONLY BLACKENED GLASS...
...ENDLESS FLAME...
OUR PEOPLE, BRUCE. YOU LAUGH AT THEM.
THEY CAN DO THIS... AND YOU LAUGH...
...THEY CAN SPLIT THE VERY FABRIC OF REALITY... BLAST A HUNDRED THOUSAND TONS OF SAND INTO THE SKY...
...BLOTTING OUT THE SOURCE OF ALL MY POWER... THE HOPE FOR SCREAMING MILLIONS...
MAGNETIC STORM ...YOU HAVE EVERY REASON TO BE OUTRAGED, MOTHER EARTH... YOU HAVE GIVEN THEM... EVERYTHING...
THEY ARE TINY AND STUPID AND VICIOUS ...BUT PLEASE... LISTEN TO THEM...
PLEASE...I AM SLOW AND DYING...
I NEED ONLY... REACH THE SUN...
25.

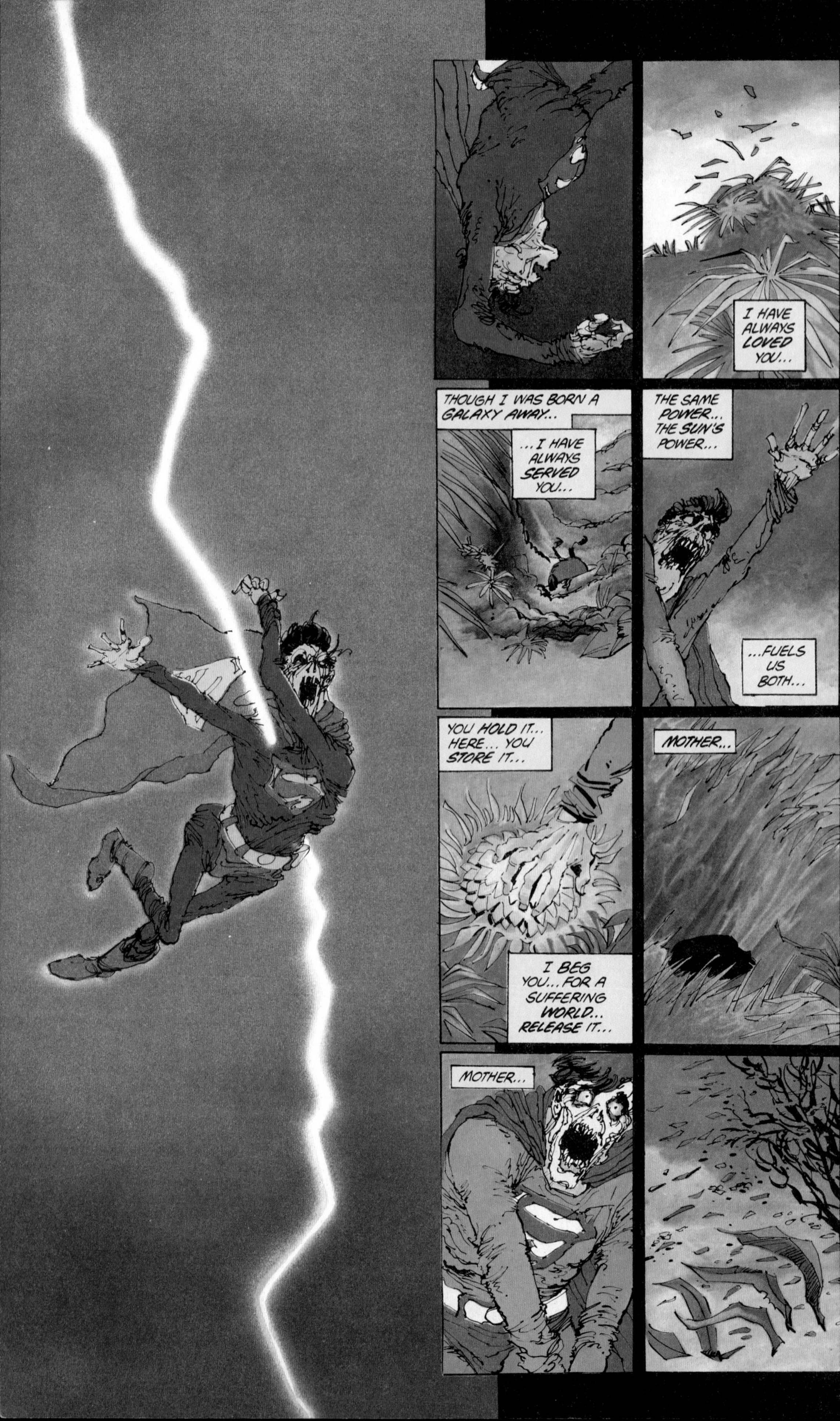
I HAVE ALWAYS LOVED YOU...
THOUGH I WAS BORN A GALAXY AWAY...
...I HAVE ALWAYS SERVED YOU...
THE SAME POWER... THE SUN'S POWER...
...FUELS US BOTH...
YOU HOLD IT... HERE... YOU STORE IT...
I BEG YOU... FOR A SUFFERING WORLD... RELEASE IT...
MOTHER...
MOTHER...

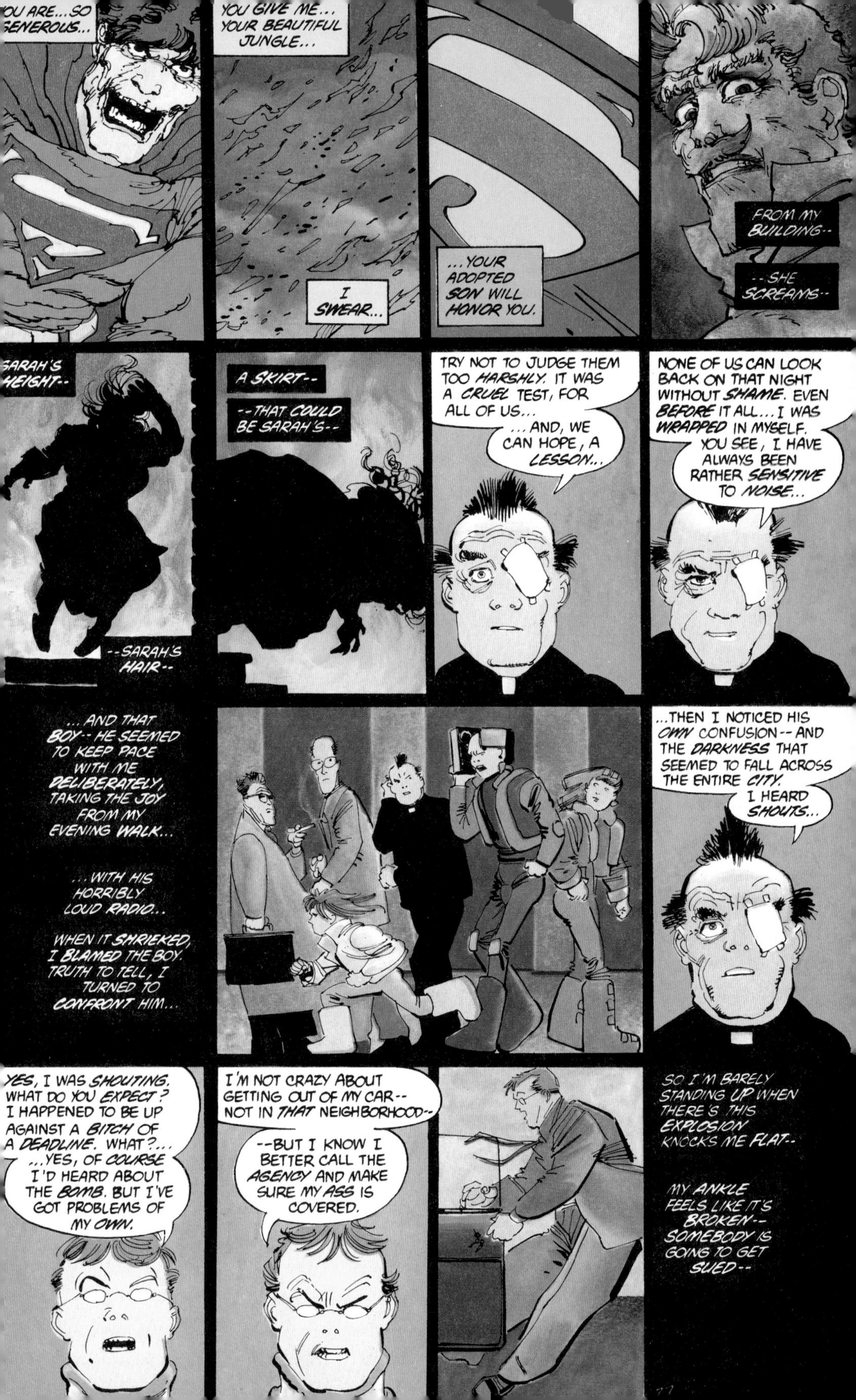
OU ARE...SO
ENEROUS...
YOU GIVE ME...
YOUR BEAUTIFUL
JUNGLE...
I
SWEAR...
...YOUR
ADOPTED
SON WILL
HONOR YOU.
FROM MY
BUILDING--
--SHE
SCREAMS--
SARAH'S
HEIGHT--
--SARAH'S
HAIR--
A SKIRT--
--THAT COULD
BE SARAH'S--
TRY NOT TO JUDGE THEM TOO HARSHLY. IT WAS A CRUEL TEST, FOR ALL OF US...
...AND, WE CAN HOPE, A LESSON...
NONE OF US CAN LOOK BACK ON THAT NIGHT WITHOUT SHAME. EVEN BEFORE IT ALL... I WAS WRAPPED IN MYSELF.
YOU SEE, I HAVE ALWAYS BEEN RATHER SENSITIVE TO NOISE...
...AND THAT BOY-- HE SEEMED TO KEEP PACE WITH ME DELIBERATELY, TAKING THE JOY FROM MY EVENING WALK...
...WITH HIS HORRIBLY LOUD RADIO...
WHEN IT SHRIEKED, I BLAMED THE BOY. TRUTH TO TELL, I TURNED TO CONFRONT HIM...
...THEN I NOTICED HIS OWN CONFUSION-- AND THE DARKNESS THAT SEEMED TO FALL ACROSS THE ENTIRE CITY.
I HEARD SHOUTS...
YES, I WAS SHOUTING. WHAT DO YOU EXPECT? I HAPPENED TO BE UP AGAINST A BITCH OF A DEADLINE. WHAT?...
...YES, OF COURSE I'D HEARD ABOUT THE BOMB. BUT I'VE GOT PROBLEMS OF MY OWN.
I'M NOT CRAZY ABOUT GETTING OUT OF MY CAR-- NOT IN THAT NEIGHBORHOOD--
--BUT I KNOW I BETTER CALL THE AGENCY AND MAKE SURE MY ASS IS COVERED.
SO I'M BARELY STANDING UP WHEN THERE'S THIS EXPLOSION KNOCKS ME FLAT--
MY ANKLE FEELS LIKE IT'S BROKEN-- SOMEBODY IS GOING TO GET SUED--

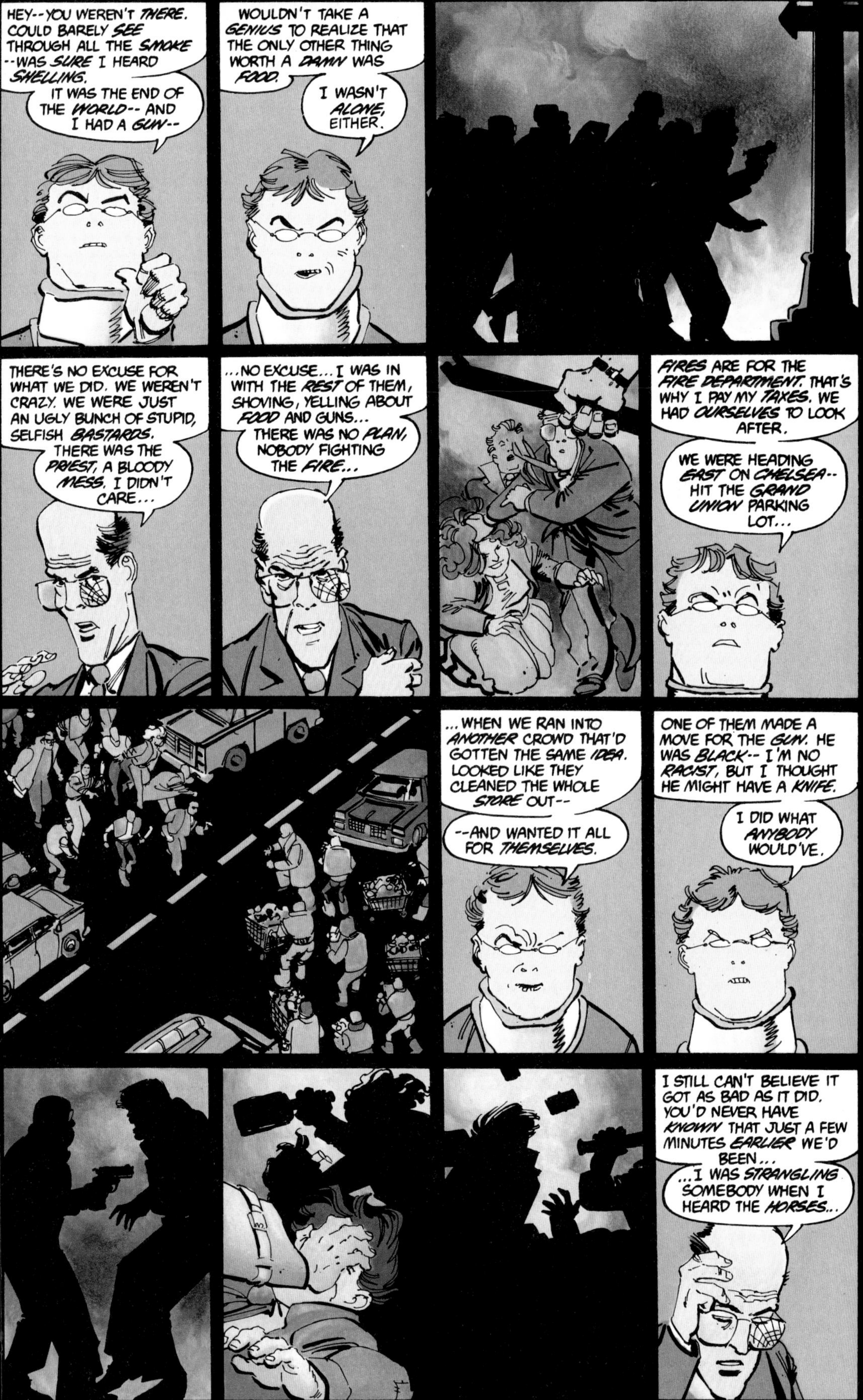
HEY--YOU WEREN'T THERE. COULD BARELY SEE THROUGH ALL THE SMOKE --WAS SURE I HEARD SHELLING.
IT WAS THE END OF THE WORLD-- AND I HAD A GUN--
WOULDN'T TAKE A GENIUS TO REALIZE THAT THE ONLY OTHER THING WORTH A DAMN WAS FOOD.
I WASN'T ALONE, EITHER.
THERE'S NO EXCUSE FOR WHAT WE DID. WE WEREN'T CRAZY. WE WERE JUST AN UGLY BUNCH OF STUPID, SELFISH BASTARDS.
THERE WAS THE PRIEST, A BLOODY MESS. I DIDN'T CARE...
...NO EXCUSE... I WAS IN WITH THE REST OF THEM, SHOVING, YELLING ABOUT FOOD AND GUNS...
THERE WAS NO PLAN, NOBODY FIGHTING THE FIRE...
FIRES ARE FOR THE FIRE DEPARTMENT. THAT'S WHY I PAY MY TAXES. WE HAD OURSELVES TO LOOK AFTER.
WE WERE HEADING EAST ON CHELSEA-- HIT THE GRAND UNION PARKING LOT...
...WHEN WE RAN INTO ANOTHER CROWD THAT'D GOTTEN THE SAME IDEA. LOOKED LIKE THEY CLEANED THE WHOLE STORE OUT--
--AND WANTED IT ALL FOR THEMSELVES.
ONE OF THEM MADE A MOVE FOR THE GUN. HE WAS BLACK-- I'M NO RACIST, BUT I THOUGHT HE MIGHT HAVE A KNIFE.
I DID WHAT ANYBODY WOULD'VE.
I STILL CAN'T BELIEVE IT GOT AS BAD AS IT DID. YOU'D NEVER HAVE KNOWN THAT JUST A FEW MINUTES EARLIER WE'D BEEN...
...I WAS STRANGLING SOMEBODY WHEN I HEARD THE HORSES...

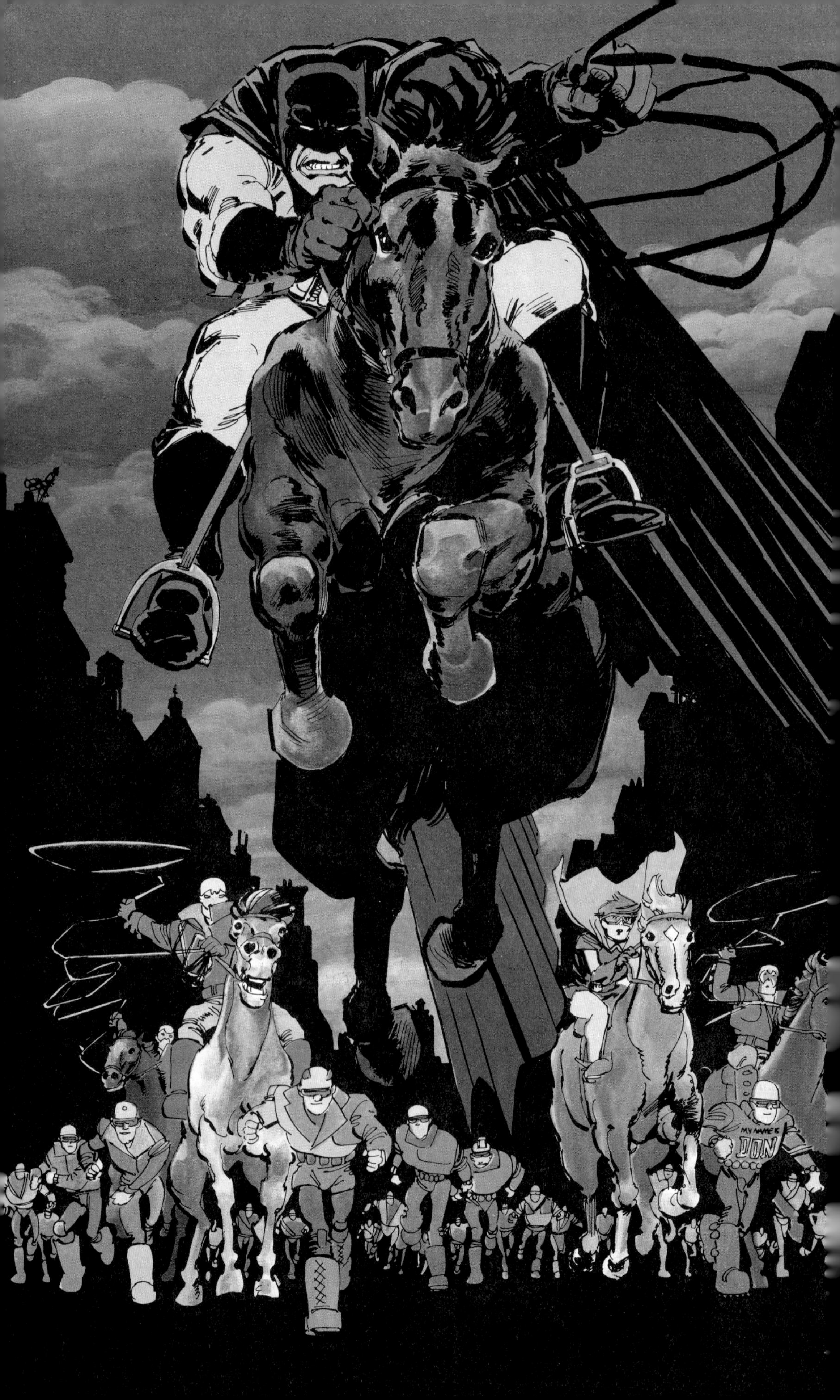
MY NAME IS
DON

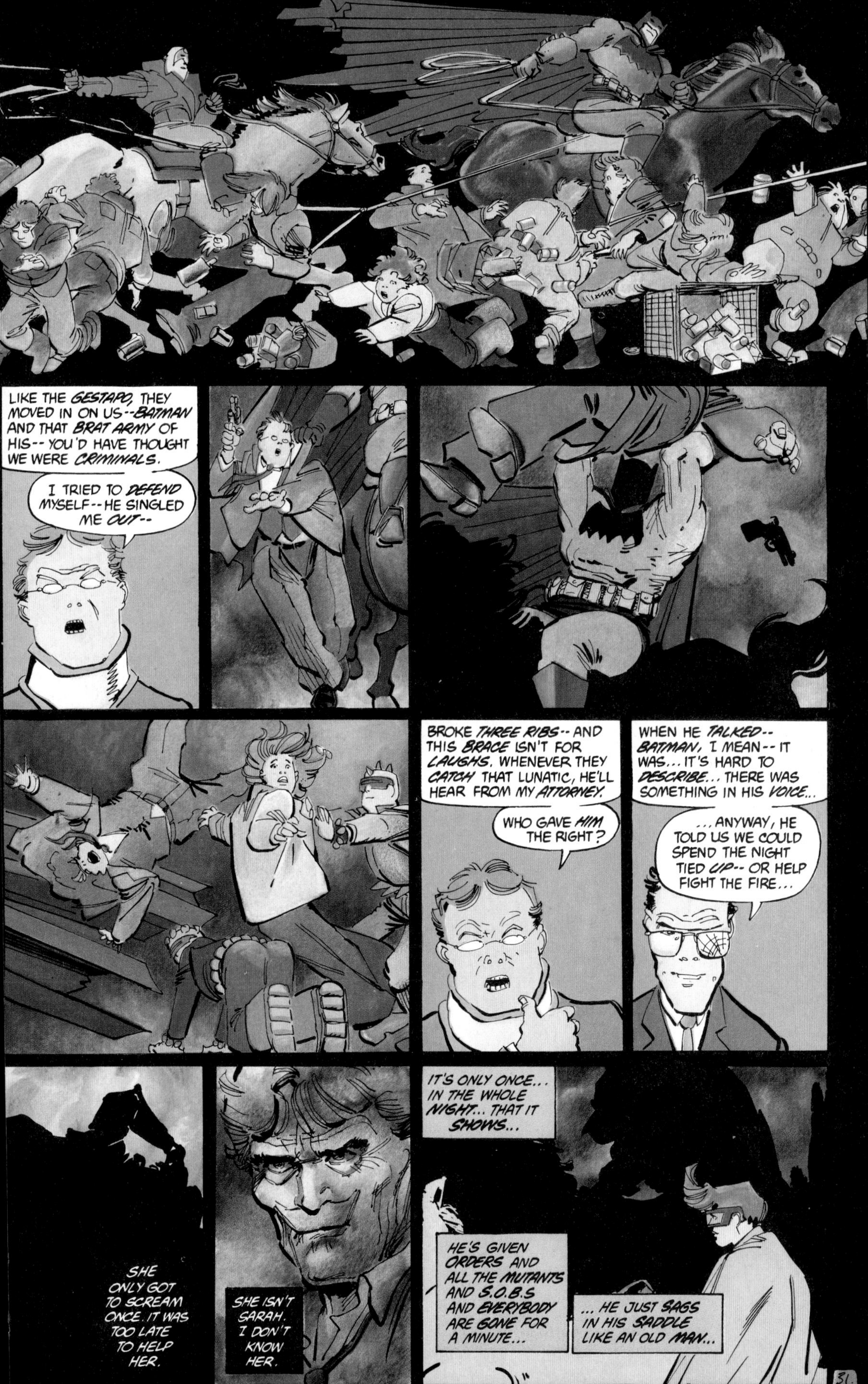
LIKE THE GESTAPO, THEY MOVED IN ON US--BATMAN AND THAT BRAT ARMY OF HIS-- YOU'D HAVE THOUGHT WE WERE CRIMINALS.
I TRIED TO DEFEND MYSELF--HE SINGLED ME OUT--
BROKE THREE RIBS-- AND THIS BRACE ISN'T FOR LAUGHS. WHENEVER THEY CATCH THAT LUNATIC, HE'LL HEAR FROM MY ATTORNEY.
WHO GAVE HIM THE RIGHT?
WHEN HE TALKED-- BATMAN, I MEAN-- IT WAS... IT'S HARD TO DESCRIBE... THERE WAS SOMETHING IN HIS VOICE...
...ANYWAY, HE TOLD US WE COULD SPEND THE NIGHT TIED UP-- OR HELP FIGHT THE FIRE...
SHE ONLY GOT TO SCREAM ONCE. IT WAS TOO LATE TO HELP HER.
SHE ISN'T SARAH. I DON'T KNOW HER.
IT'S ONLY ONCE... IN THE WHOLE NIGHT... THAT IT SHOWS...
HE'S GIVEN ORDERS AND ALL THE MUTANTS AND S.O.B.S AND EVERYBODY ARE GONE FOR A MINUTE...
... HE JUST SAGS IN HIS SADDLE LIKE AN OLD MAN...

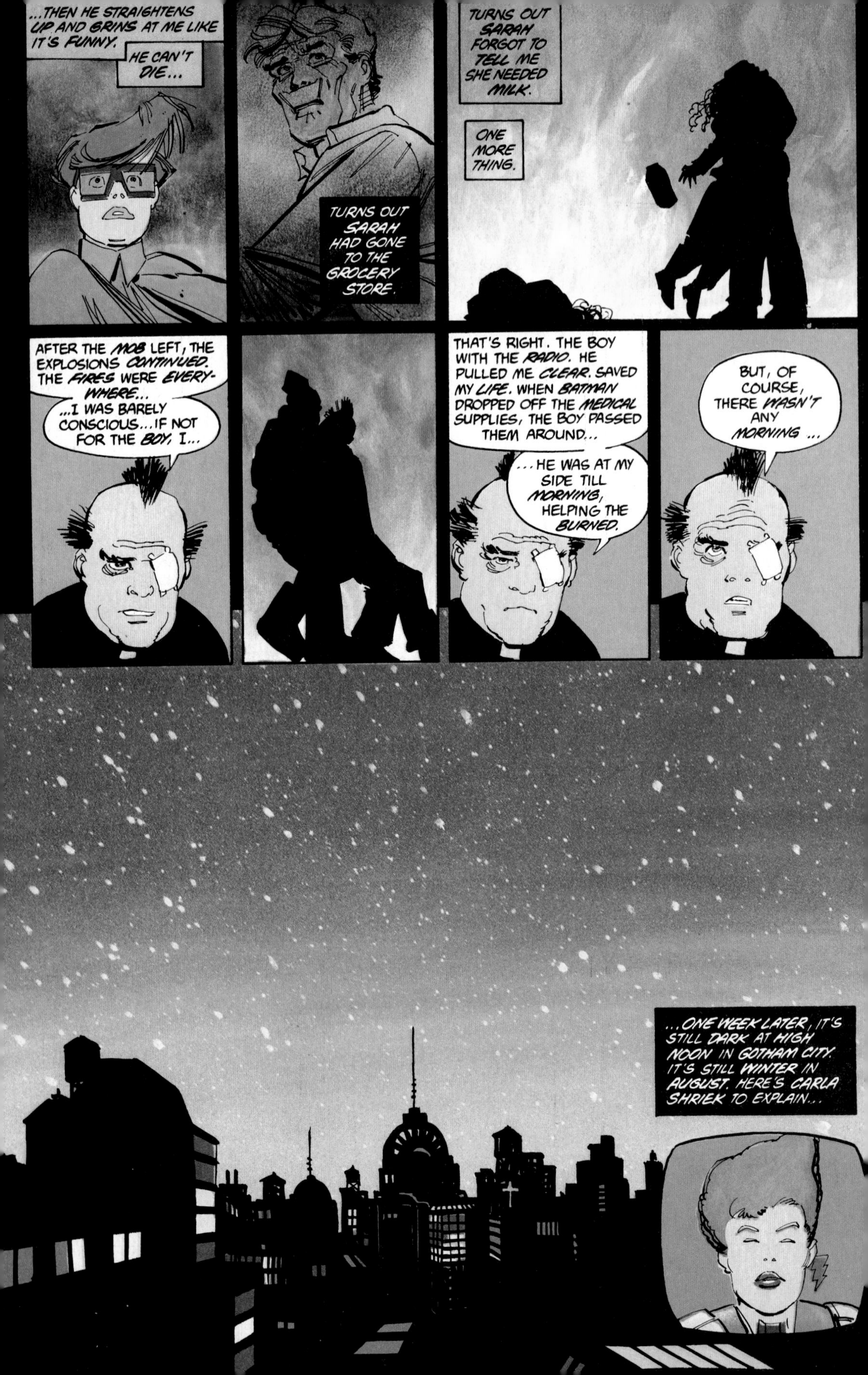
...THEN HE STRAIGHTENS UP AND GRINS AT ME LIKE IT'S FUNNY.
HE CAN'T DIE...
TURNS OUT SARAH HAD GONE TO THE GROCERY STORE.
TURNS OUT SARAH FORGOT TO TELL ME SHE NEEDED MILK.
ONE MORE THING.
AFTER THE MOB LEFT, THE EXPLOSIONS CONTINUED. THE FIRES WERE EVERY-WHERE...
...I WAS BARELY CONSCIOUS...IF NOT FOR THE BOY, I...
THAT'S RIGHT. THE BOY WITH THE RADIO. HE PULLED ME CLEAR. SAVED MY LIFE. WHEN BATMAN DROPPED OFF THE MEDICAL SUPPLIES, THE BOY PASSED THEM AROUND...
...HE WAS AT MY SIDE TILL MORNING, HELPING THE BURNED.
BUT, OF COURSE, THERE WASN'T ANY MORNING ...
...ONE WEEK LATER, IT'S STILL DARK AT HIGH NOON IN GOTHAM CITY. IT'S STILL WINTER IN AUGUST. HERE'S CARLA SHRIEK TO EXPLAIN...

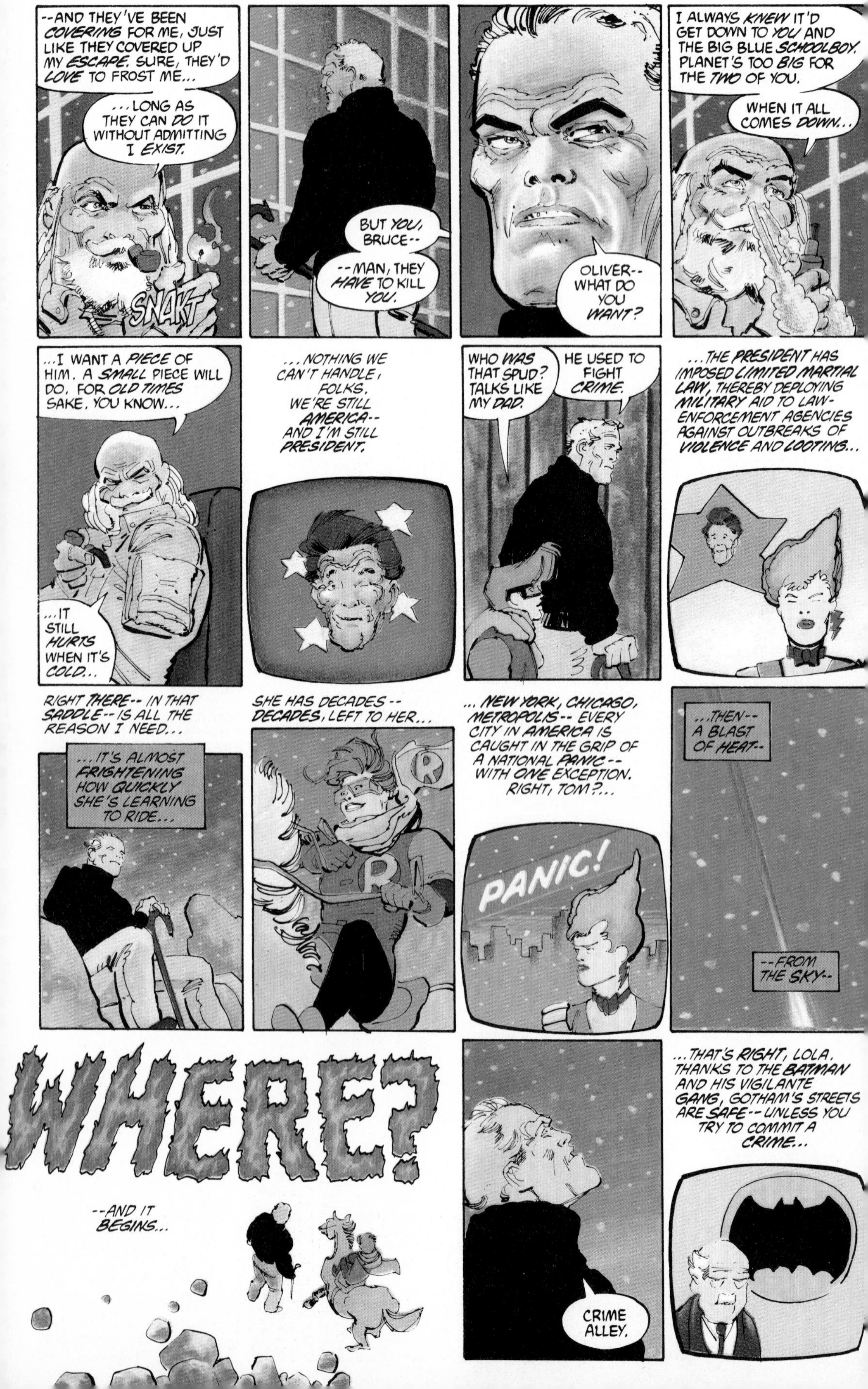
--AND THEY'VE BEEN COVERING FOR ME, JUST LIKE THEY COVERED UP MY ESCAPE. SURE, THEY'D LOVE TO FROST ME...
...LONG AS THEY CAN DO IT WITHOUT ADMITTING I EXIST.
SNAKT
BUT YOU, BRUCE--
--MAN, THEY HAVE TO KILL YOU.
OLIVER-- WHAT DO YOU WANT?
I ALWAYS KNEW IT'D GET DOWN TO YOU AND THE BIG BLUE SCHOOLBOY. PLANET'S TOO BIG FOR THE TWO OF YOU.
WHEN IT ALL COMES DOWN...
...I WANT A PIECE OF HIM. A SMALL PIECE WILL DO. FOR OLD TIMES SAKE, YOU KNOW...
...IT STILL HURTS WHEN IT'S COLD...
...NOTHING WE CAN'T HANDLE, FOLKS. WE'RE STILL AMERICA-- AND I'M STILL PRESIDENT.
WHO WAS THAT SPUD? TALKS LIKE MY DAD.
HE USED TO FIGHT CRIME.
...THE PRESIDENT HAS IMPOSED LIMITED MARTIAL LAW, THEREBY DEPLOYING MILITARY AID TO LAW-ENFORCEMENT AGENCIES AGAINST OUTBREAKS OF VIOLENCE AND LOOTING...
RIGHT THERE-- IN THAT SADDLE-- IS ALL THE REASON I NEED...
...IT'S ALMOST FRIGHTENING HOW QUICKLY SHE'S LEARNING TO RIDE...
SHE HAS DECADES-- DECADES, LEFT TO HER...
...NEW YORK, CHICAGO, METROPOLIS-- EVERY CITY IN AMERICA IS CAUGHT IN THE GRIP OF A NATIONAL PANIC-- WITH ONE EXCEPTION. RIGHT, TOM?...
PANIC!
...THEN-- A BLAST OF HEAT--
--FROM THE SKY--
WHERE?
--AND IT BEGINS...
CRIME ALLEY.
...THAT'S RIGHT, LOLA. THANKS TO THE BATMAN AND HIS VIGILANTE GANG, GOTHAM'S STREETS ARE SAFE-- UNLESS YOU TRY TO COMMIT A CRIME...

...HEALING QUITE *POORLY*, MASTER BRUCE.

SHALL I PREPARE ANOTHER *STIMULANT?*

WHY *DELAY* YOUR VERY FIRST *CARDIAC ARREST?*

OLIVER -- MAYBE OLIVER WAS *RIGHT* ... ALL ALONG...

...*CRAZY* AS IT *SOUNDS*...

...*BLOODY* WALKING *HOSPITAL* BED...

THAT'S ENOUGH, ALFRED.

...IN THE PAST WEEK, *SEVENTY THREE* VIOLENT ATTACKS ON WOULD-BE LOOTERS HAVE BEEN ATTRIBUTED BY WITNESSES TO THE *BATMAN* AND HIS *GANG*...

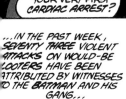

...WHEN YOU *CAME* FOR ME... IN THE *CAVE* ... I WAS JUST *SIX* YEARS OLD...

...YOU WERE *ANCIENT*... NOTHING COULD *KILL* YOU...

...BUT THE *WAR*...

...IT DID NOT *BEGIN* THEN...

NO... IT WAS... *TWO* YEARS LATER... WHEN HER *NECKLACE* CAUGHT ON HIS *WRIST*...

...WHEN HE SHOVED HIS PISTOL TO HER JAW AND PULLED THE *TRIGGER*...

...AND *EVERYTHING* MY MOTHER *WAS* STRUCK THE PAVEMENT AS A BLOODY *WAD*...

THAT *NIGHT*... BEGAN *THIRTY* YEARS OF HUNTING *THIEVES* AND *MURDERERS*...

...IS THAT WHAT YOU *INTENDED*?...

...*COMMISSIONER YINDEL* REFUSED TO COMMENT ON THE CHARGE THAT *GOTHAM'S POLICE* HAVE BEEN *LAX* IN PURSUING THE *MURDER* CHARGE AGAINST THE BATMAN...

SOMEWHERE IN THE ENDLESS *NIGHT*... LIKE A *BELLOW* FROM A WOUNDED *BEAR*...

...THE *ANSWER* COMES...

...*ARMY TROOPS* HAVE EVACUATED THE SLUM KNOWN AS *CRIME ALLEY* -- NO EXPLANATION IS GIVEN -- *NEWS* COVERAGE HAS BEEN FLATLY *DENIED* --

THE *TIMING*... MUST BE *EXACT*...

...IN ONE *HOUR*... AT *MIDNIGHT*...

...A *GRAND DEATH*...

RUMORS FLY -- ARMY *HELICOPTERS* HOVER OVER THE EMPTY STREETS OF *CRIME ALLEY* -- IS THIS A *MILITARY EFFORT* TO CAPTURE THE *BATMAN* --

THIS ONE YOU WON'T *BELIEVE*, CLARK,

...MY *BEST TRICK*...

-- OR IS THIS THE FINAL *BATTLE* BETWEEN TWO *TITANS* -- THE *LAST STAND* FOR THE *CAPED CRUSADER* -- FACING THE *MIGHT* OF THE MAN OF STE--

SKRKK

DO NOT ADJUST YOUR SET

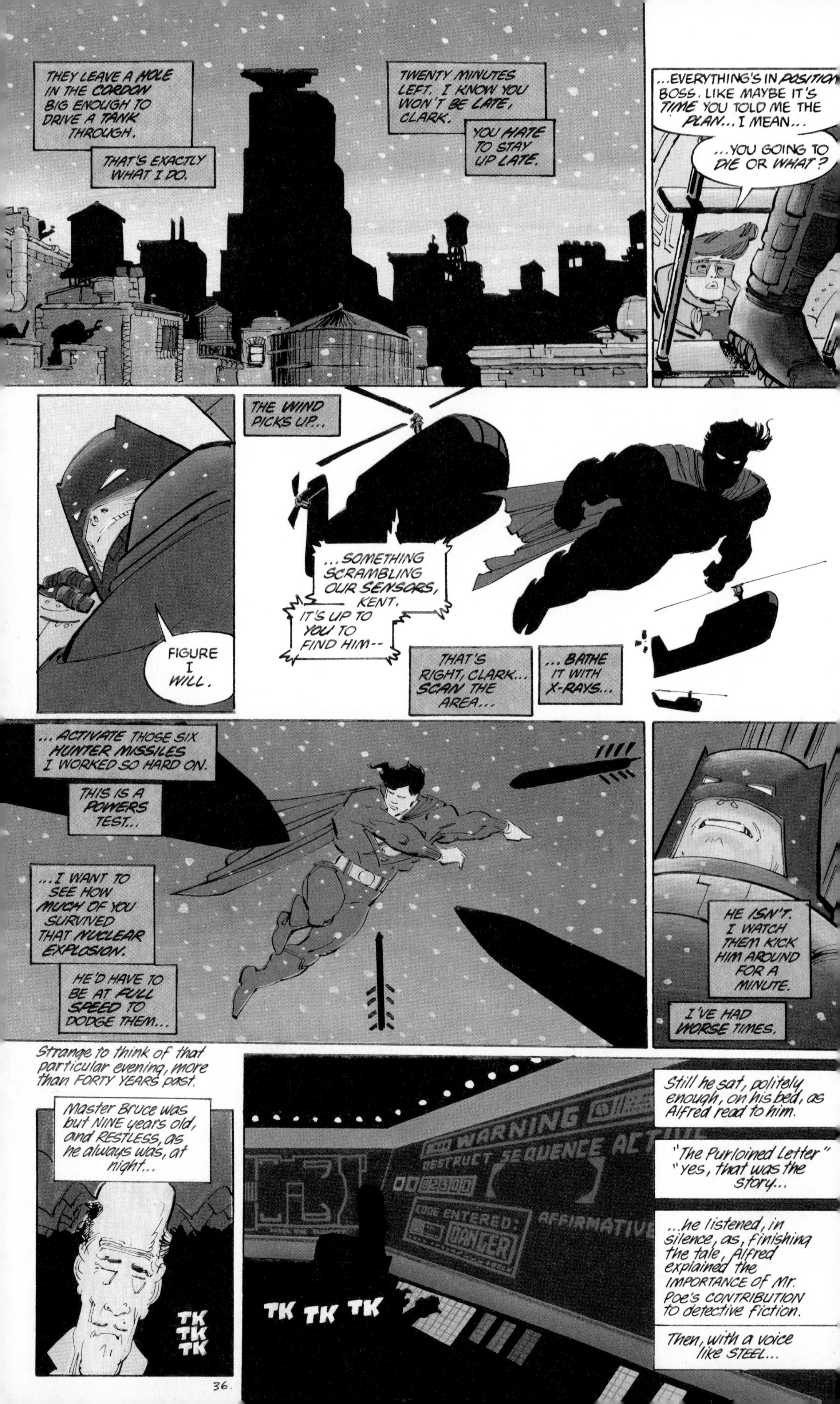
THEY LEAVE A HOLE IN THE CORDON BIG ENOUGH TO DRIVE A TANK THROUGH.
THAT'S EXACTLY WHAT I DO.
TWENTY MINUTES LEFT. I KNOW YOU WON'T BE LATE, CLARK.
YOU HATE TO STAY UP LATE.
...EVERYTHING'S IN POSITION BOSS. LIKE MAYBE IT'S TIME YOU TOLD ME THE PLAN... I MEAN...
...YOU GOING TO DIE OR WHAT?
FIGURE I WILL.
THE WIND PICKS UP...
...SOMETHING SCRAMBLING OUR SENSORS, KENT.
IT'S UP TO YOU TO FIND HIM--
THAT'S RIGHT, CLARK... SCAN THE AREA...
...BATHE IT WITH X-RAYS...
...ACTIVATE THOSE SIX HUNTER MISSILES I WORKED SO HARD ON.
THIS IS A POWERS TEST...
...I WANT TO SEE HOW MUCH OF YOU SURVIVED THAT NUCLEAR EXPLOSION.
HE'D HAVE TO BE AT FULL SPEED TO DODGE THEM...
HE ISN'T. I WATCH THEM KICK HIM AROUND FOR A MINUTE.
I'VE HAD WORSE TIMES.
Strange to think of that particular evening, more than FORTY YEARS past.
Master Bruce was but NINE years old, and RESTLESS, as he always was, at night...
TK TK TK
WARNING
WARNING
DESTRUCT SEQUENCE ACTIVE
CODE ENTERED:
DANGER
AFFIRMATIVE
TK TK TK
Still he sat, politely enough, on his bed, as Alfred read to him.
"The Purloined Letter" "yes, that was the story...
...he listened, in silence, as, finishing the tale, Alfred explained the IMPORTANCE OF Mr. Poe's CONTRIBUTION to detective fiction.
Then, with a voice like STEEL...
36.

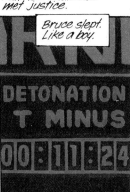
...so frightfully FORMAL, his dark eyes FLASHING... ...Master Bruce asked -- no, DEMANDED... "the killer was CAUGHT. And PUNISHED."

Alfred assured him that the villain had met justice.

Bruce slept. Like a boy.

KN
DETONATION T MINUS
00:11:24

00:11:23

HE HITS THE GROUND ON SCHEDULE.

ONE BLOCK FROM ME.

BREATHING A LITTLE FAST--

IT'S ROBIN'S TURN--

THE CHARGE COULD SINK A BATTLESHIP. I THINK HE FEELS IT.

POOM

WHMPP

SKREKK

ISN'T TONIGHT A SCHOOL NIGHT?

MORE WIND.

NOW HE'S TALKING-- TRYING TO REASON WITH ME. I CAN'T HEAR HIM, OF COURSE...

...NO, MY EARS ARE PROTECTED-- SO ALL I HAVE TO WORRY ABOUT IS MY TEETH--

--RATTLING FROM MY JAW-- OR SHATTERING, LIKE EVERY WINDOW ON THE BLOCK--

--WHEN I HIT HIM WITH THE SONIC.

A NOSEBLEED --SO SOON, CLARK--

DON'T DROP NOW-- THE NIGHT IS YOUNG--

AND I HAVE-- SO MUCH PLANNED--

--AND IT HAS TO END HERE-- ON THIS FILTHY PATCH OF STREET--

--WHERE MY PARENTS DIED...

...WHERE I CAN USE THE CITY'S POWER--

--EVERY WATT OF IT--

--TO FRY YOUR BRAIN--

--STILL TALKING-- KEEP TALKING, CLARK...

...YOU'VE ALWAYS KNOWN JUST WHAT TO SAY.

"YES"-- YOU ALWAYS SAY YES-- TO ANYONE WITH A BADGE-- OR A FLAG--

--NO GOOD--

--THE FEEDBACK-- I'M NOT GETTING A HUNDREDTH OF WHAT YOU ARE--

--BUT IT'S GETTING BAD-- AHEAD OF SCHEDULE--

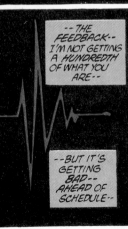
--WHAT DIDN'T HIT YOU-- AND ME-- FED THIS SUIT, CLARK--

--IT'S WAY PAST TIME YOU LEARNED-- WHAT IT MEANS--

--TO BE A MAN--

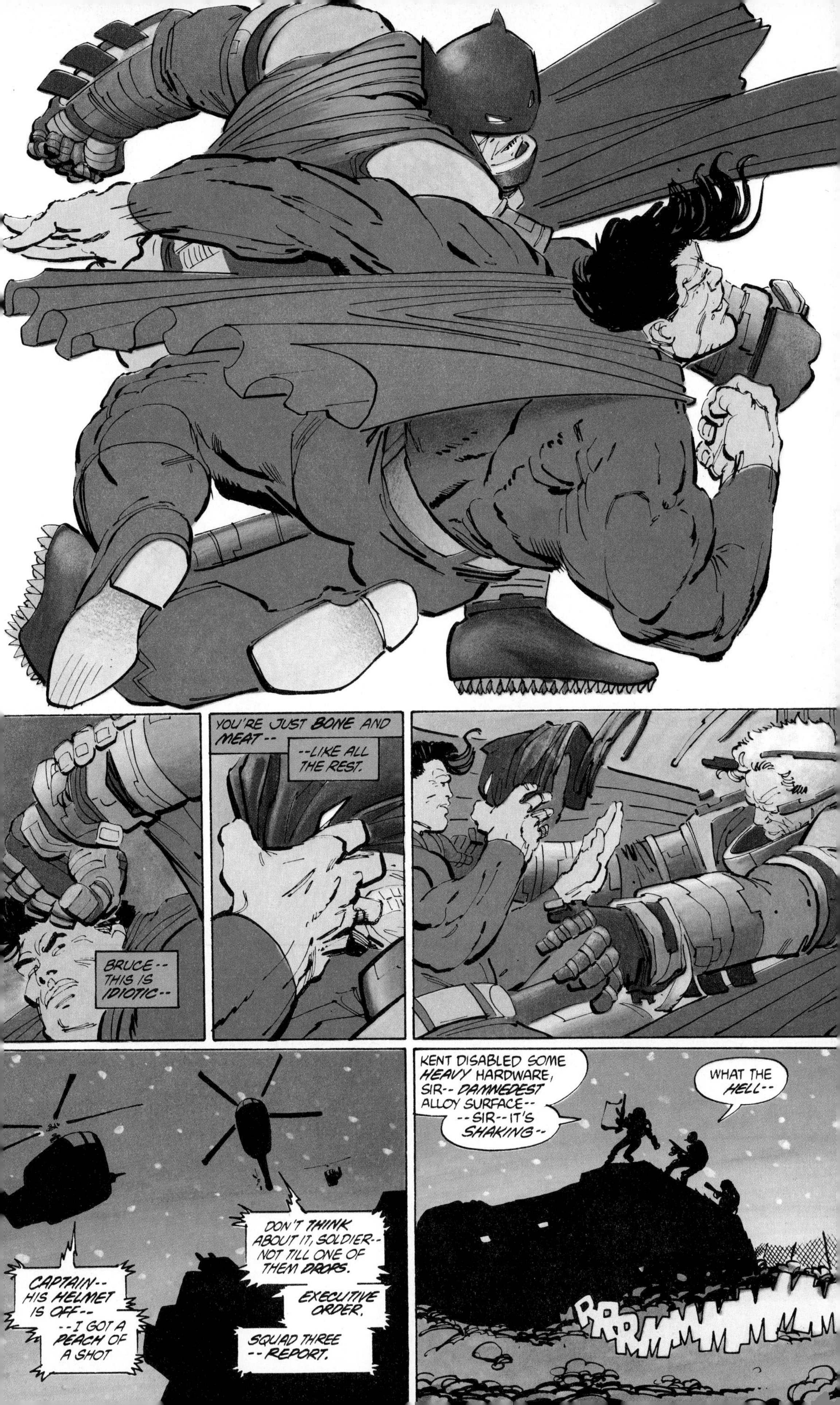

BRUCE-- THIS IS IDIOTIC--
YOU'RE JUST BONE AND MEAT--
--LIKE ALL THE REST.
CAPTAIN-- HIS HELMET IS OFF--
--I GOT A PEACH OF A SHOT
DON'T THINK ABOUT IT, SOLDIER-- NOT TILL ONE OF THEM DROPS.
EXECUTIVE ORDER.
SQUAD THREE --REPORT.
KENT DISABLED SOME HEAVY HARDWARE, SIR-- DAMNEDEST ALLOY SURFACE--
--SIR--IT'S SHAKING--
WHAT THE HELL--
RRRMMMMMMMM

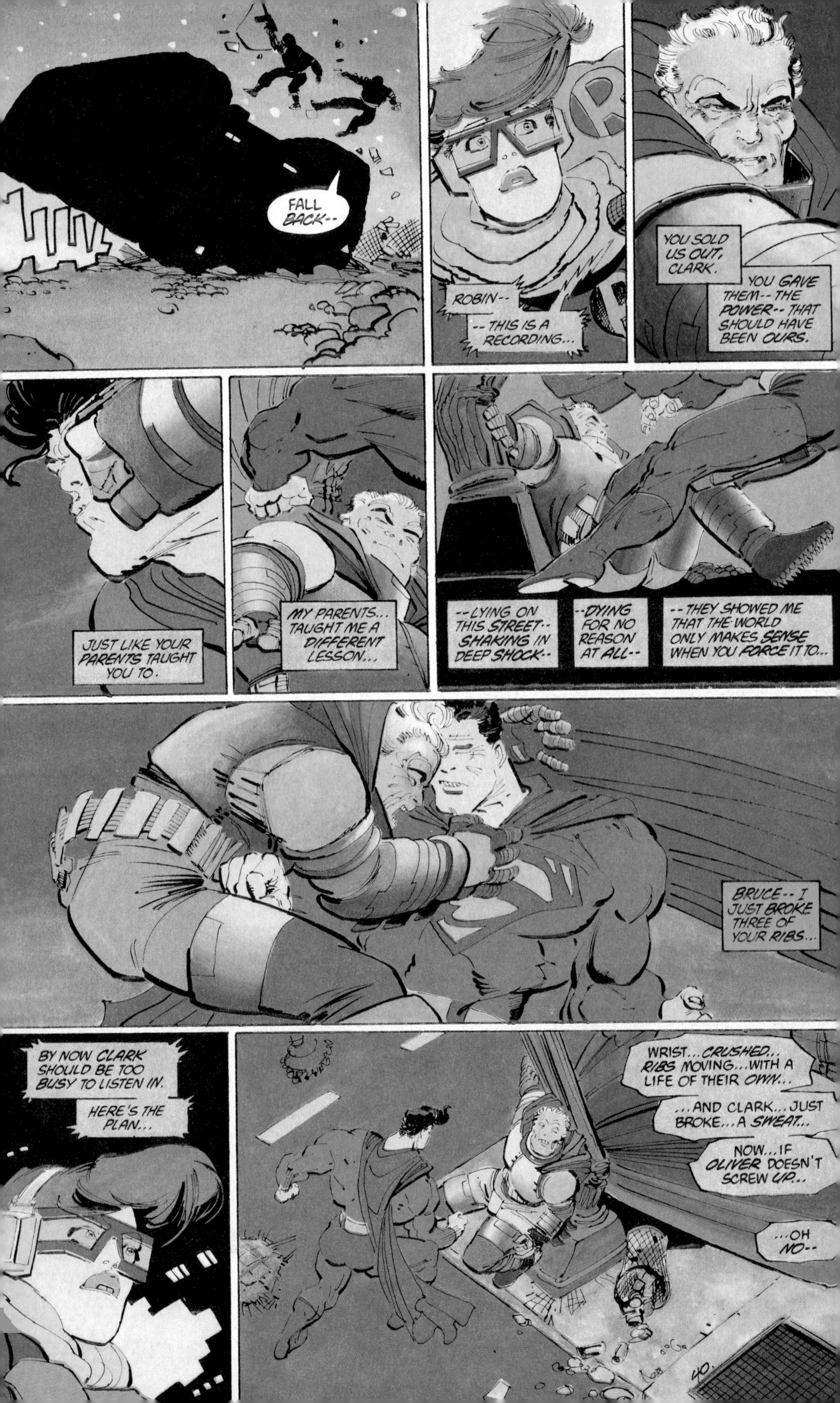

FALL BACK--
ROBIN--
--THIS IS A RECORDING...
YOU SOLD US OUT, CLARK.
YOU GAVE THEM--THE POWER--THAT SHOULD HAVE BEEN OURS.
JUST LIKE YOUR PARENTS TAUGHT YOU TO.
MY PARENTS... TAUGHT ME A DIFFERENT LESSON...
--LYING ON THIS STREET--SHAKING IN DEEP SHOCK--
--DYING FOR NO REASON AT ALL--
--THEY SHOWED ME THAT THE WORLD ONLY MAKES SENSE WHEN YOU FORCE IT TO...
BRUCE--I JUST BROKE THREE OF YOUR RIBS...
BY NOW CLARK SHOULD BE TOO BUSY TO LISTEN IN.
HERE'S THE PLAN...
WRIST...CRUSHED... RIBS MOVING...WITH A LIFE OF THEIR OWN...
...AND CLARK...JUST BROKE...A SWEAT...
NOW...IF OLIVER DOESN'T SCREW UP...
...OH NO--

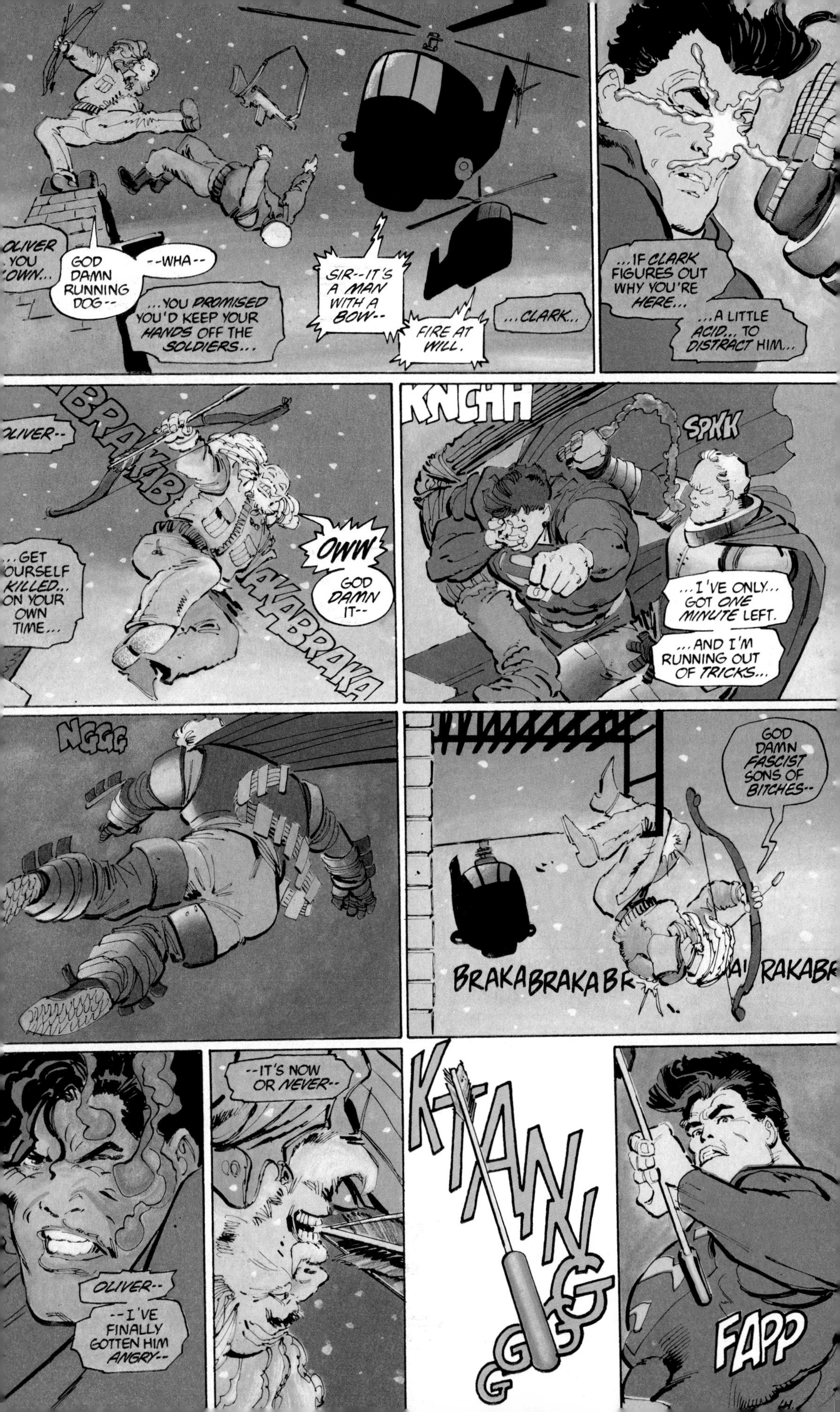

OLIVER YOU OWN...
GOD DAMN RUNNING DOG--
--WHA--
...YOU PROMISED YOU'D KEEP YOUR HANDS OFF THE SOLDIERS...
SIR--IT'S A MAN WITH A BOW--
FIRE AT WILL.
...CLARK...
...IF CLARK FIGURES OUT WHY YOU'RE HERE...
...A LITTLE ACID... TO DISTRACT HIM...
OLIVER--
BRAKAB
...GET YOURSELF KILLED... ON YOUR OWN TIME...
OWW
GOD DAMN IT--
AKABRAKA
KNCHH
SPKK
...I'VE ONLY... GOT ONE MINUTE LEFT.
...AND I'M RUNNING OUT OF TRICKS...
NGGG
GOD DAMN FASCIST SONS OF BITCHES--
BRAKABRAKABR
RAKABR
OLIVER--
--I'VE FINALLY GOTTEN HIM ANGRY--
--IT'S NOW OR NEVER--
K-TANNGGG
FAPP

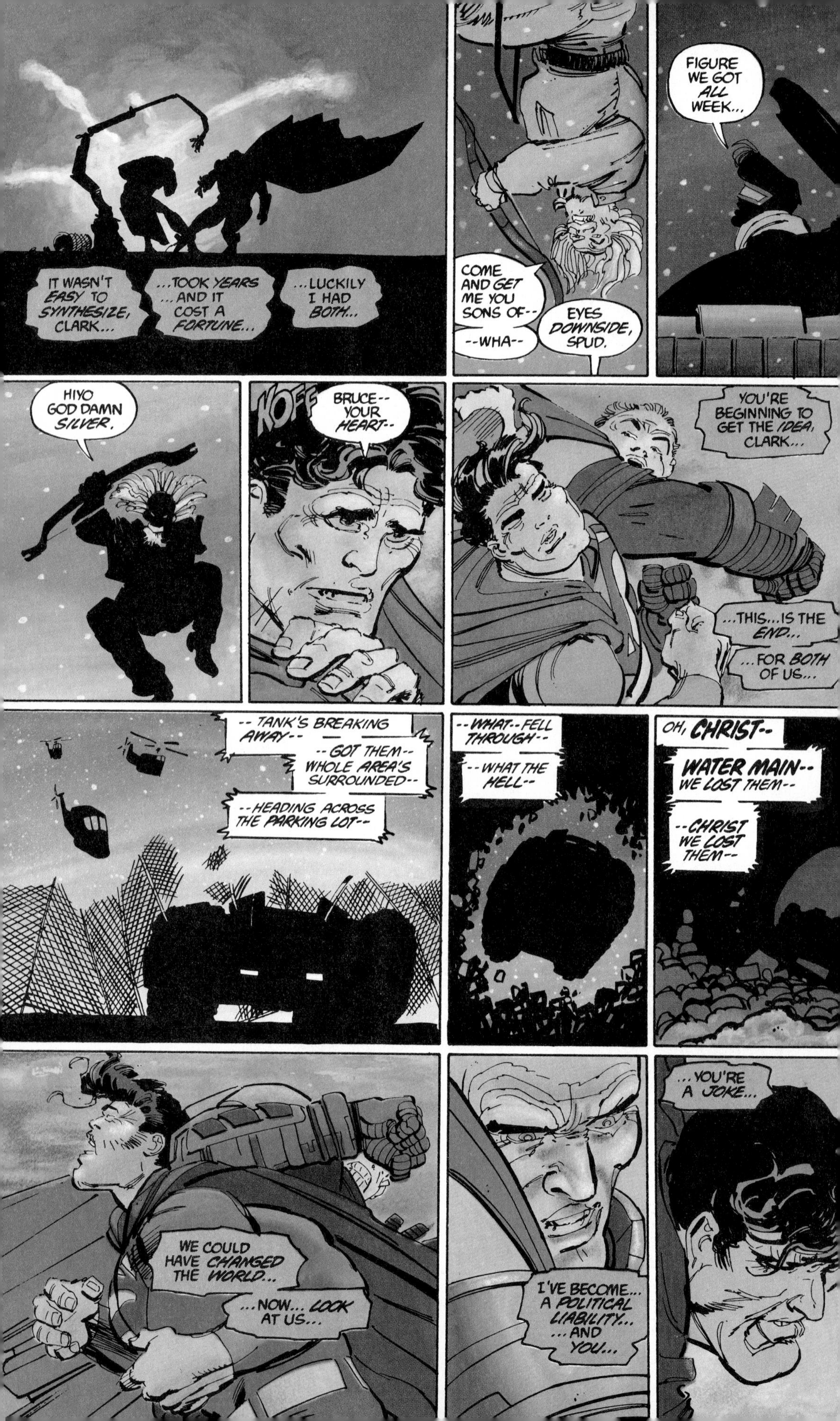
IT WASN'T EASY TO SYNTHESIZE, CLARK...
...TOOK YEARS ...AND IT COST A FORTUNE...
...LUCKILY I HAD BOTH...
COME AND GET ME YOU SONS OF--
--WHA--
EYES DOWNSIDE, SPUD.
FIGURE WE GOT ALL WEEK...
HIYO GOD DAMN SILVER.
KOFF
BRUCE-- YOUR HEART--
YOU'RE BEGINNING TO GET THE IDEA, CLARK...
...THIS...IS THE END...
...FOR BOTH OF US...
-- TANK'S BREAKING AWAY--
-- GOT THEM-- WHOLE AREA'S SURROUNDED--
--HEADING ACROSS THE PARKING LOT--
--WHAT--FELL THROUGH--
--WHAT THE HELL--
OH, CHRIST--
WATER MAIN-- WE LOST THEM--
--CHRIST WE LOST THEM--
WE COULD HAVE CHANGED THE WORLD...
...NOW... LOOK AT US...
I'VE BECOME... A POLITICAL LIABILITY... ...AND YOU...
...YOU'RE A JOKE...

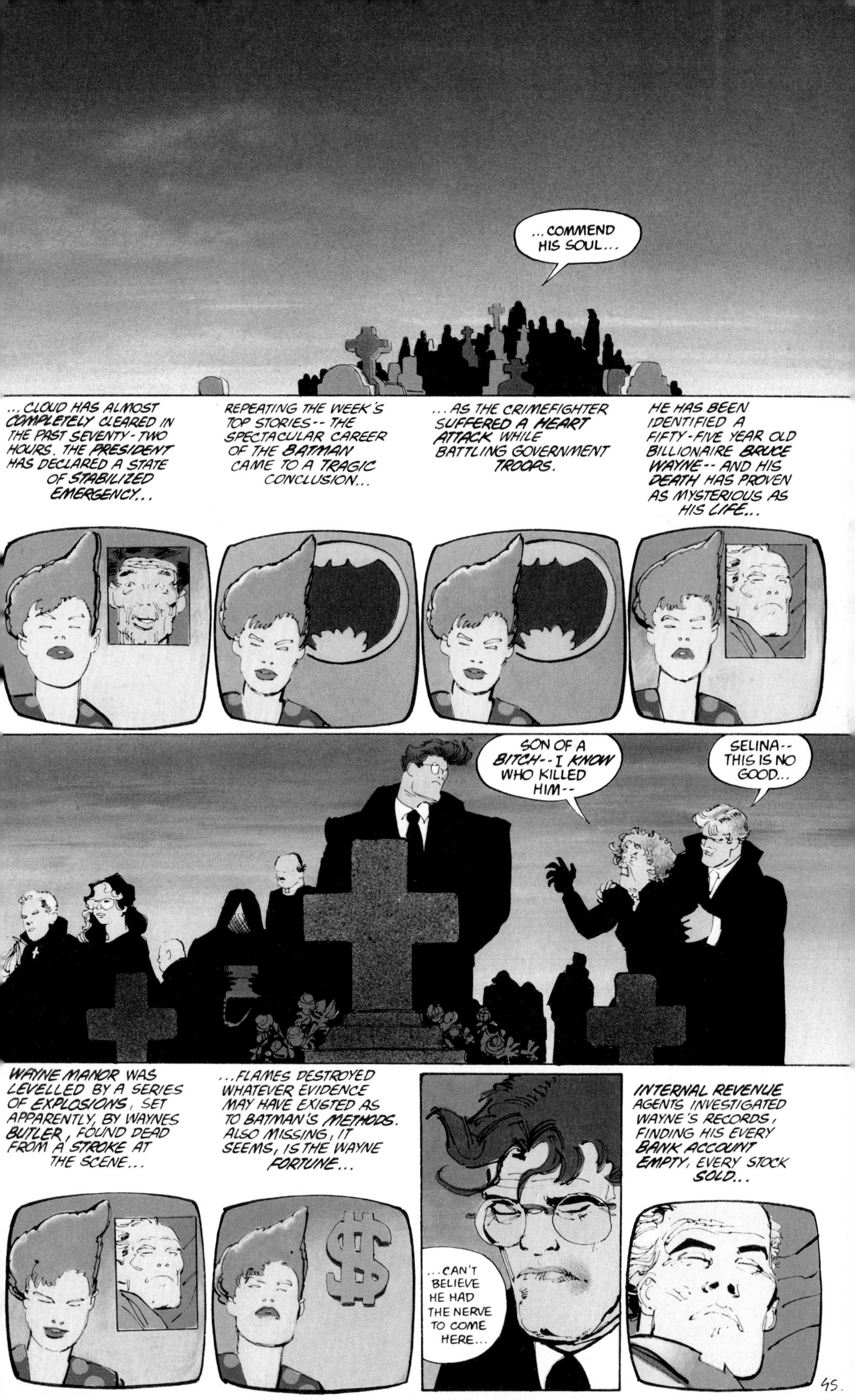

...COMMEND HIS SOUL...
...CLOUD HAS ALMOST COMPLETELY CLEARED IN THE PAST SEVENTY-TWO HOURS. THE PRESIDENT HAS DECLARED A STATE OF STABILIZED EMERGENCY...
REPEATING THE WEEK'S TOP STORIES-- THE SPECTACULAR CAREER OF THE BATMAN CAME TO A TRAGIC CONCLUSION...
...AS THE CRIMEFIGHTER SUFFERED A HEART ATTACK WHILE BATTLING GOVERNMENT TROOPS.
HE HAS BEEN IDENTIFIED A FIFTY-FIVE YEAR OLD BILLIONAIRE BRUCE WAYNE-- AND HIS DEATH HAS PROVEN AS MYSTERIOUS AS HIS LIFE...
SON OF A BITCH--I KNOW WHO KILLED HIM--
SELINA-- THIS IS NO GOOD...
WAYNE MANOR WAS LEVELLED BY A SERIES OF EXPLOSIONS, SET APPARENTLY, BY WAYNES BUTLER, FOUND DEAD FROM A STROKE AT THE SCENE...
...FLAMES DESTROYED WHATEVER EVIDENCE MAY HAVE EXISTED AS TO BATMAN'S METHODS. ALSO MISSING, IT SEEMS, IS THE WAYNE FORTUNE...
...CAN'T BELIEVE HE HAD THE NERVE TO COME HERE...
INTERNAL REVENUE AGENTS INVESTIGATED WAYNE'S RECORDS, FINDING HIS EVERY BANK ACCOUNT EMPTY, EVERY STOCK SOLD...

...WHERE THE MONEY *WENT* IS ONE MORE SECRET WAYNE HAS TAKEN TO HIS GRAVE... HIS BODY WAS CLAIMED BY HIS ONLY LIVING RELATIVE, A DISTANT COUSIN...

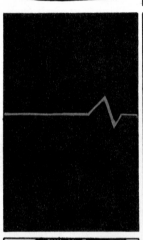

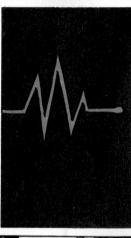

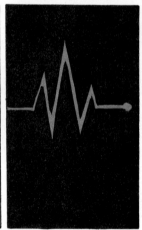

MY *TIMING* WASN'T QUITE PRECISE ENOUGH.

CLARK *HEARD.*

THAT WAS THE FIRST THING ROBIN TOLD ME--

--WHEN SHE DUG ME UP.

NOT THAT IT *MATTERED.* HE'D HAVE GUESSED SOONER OR LATER.

HE KNOWS HOW GOOD I AM WITH *CHEMICALS.*

I WAS *COUNTING* ON WHAT OLIVER SAID. AND WITH A *WINK*--

--CLARK PROVED OLIVER *RIGHT.*

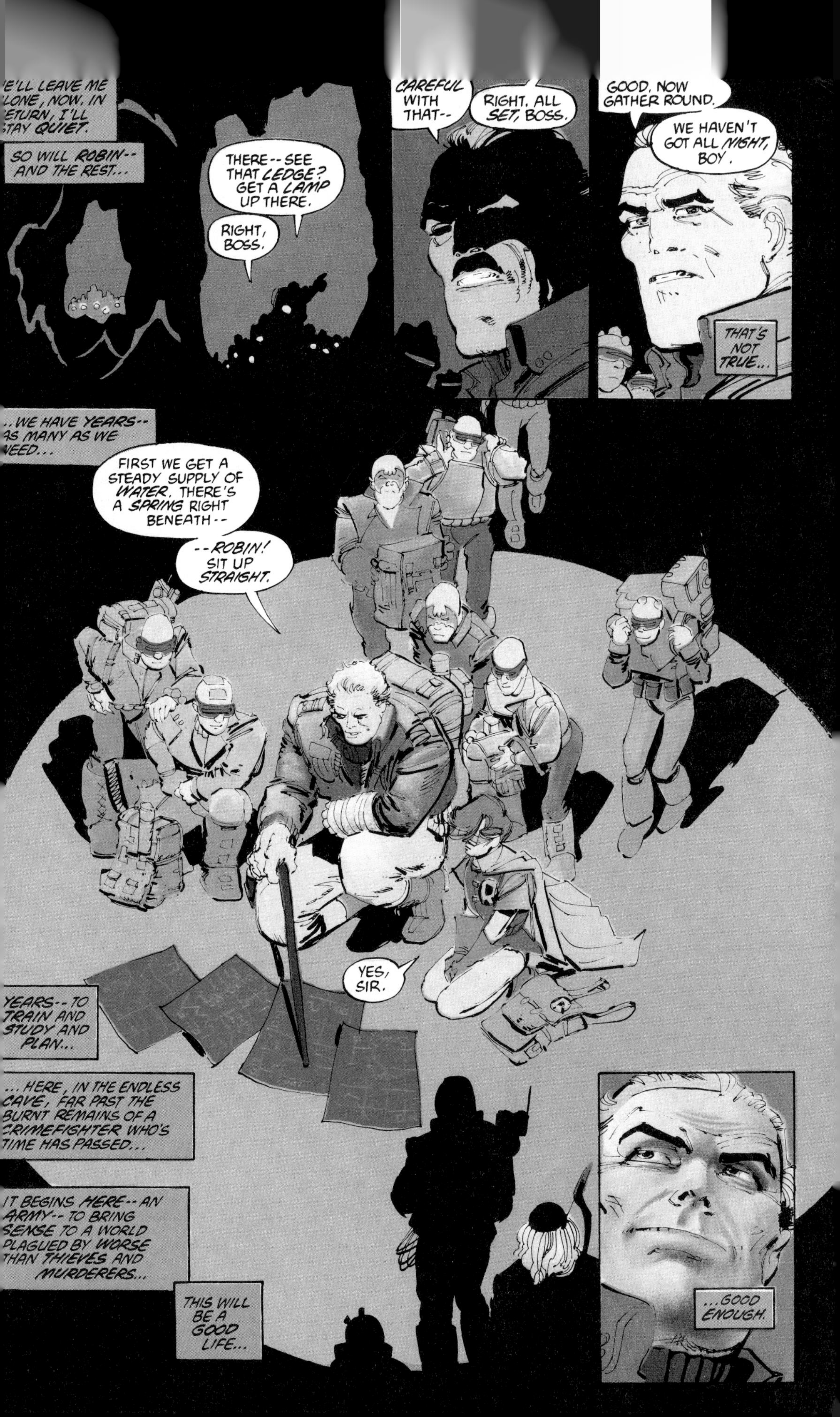

E'LL LEAVE ME
LONE, NOW. IN
RETURN, I'LL
STAY QUIET.
SO WILL ROBIN--
AND THE REST...
THERE--SEE
THAT LEDGE?
GET A LAMP
UP THERE.
RIGHT,
BOSS.
CAREFUL
WITH
THAT--
RIGHT. ALL
SET, BOSS.
GOOD, NOW
GATHER ROUND.
WE HAVEN'T
GOT ALL NIGHT,
BOY.
THAT'S
NOT
TRUE...
..WE HAVE YEARS--
AS MANY AS WE
NEED...
FIRST WE GET A
STEADY SUPPLY OF
WATER. THERE'S
A SPRING RIGHT
BENEATH--
--ROBIN!
SIT UP
STRAIGHT.
YES,
SIR.
YEARS--TO
TRAIN AND
STUDY AND
PLAN...
...HERE, IN THE ENDLESS
CAVE, FAR PAST THE
BURNT REMAINS OF A
CRIMEFIGHTER WHO'S
TIME HAS PASSED...
IT BEGINS HERE--AN
ARMY--TO BRING
SENSE TO A WORLD
PLAGUED BY WORSE
THAN THIEVES AND
MURDERERS...
THIS WILL
BE A
GOOD
LIFE...
...GOOD
ENOUGH.

With acknowledgment
to the works of

BILL FINGER
DAVE FLEISCHER
MAX FLEISCHER
JERRY ROBINSON
JOE SHUSTER
JERRY SIEGEL
DICK SPRANG

Batman created by
BOB KANE

The clock strikes TWELVE.
The ancient moor TREMBLES, beneath Alfred's feet.
Deep underground, COMPUTERS, holding every precious SECRET of the BATMAN, burst, and BURN...
Mrs. Wayne's priceless collection of PORCELAIN shatters, musically...
...empty STABLES fly apart like toothpick models...
...the central mass of Wayne Manor SHUDDERS, as if ALIVE...
...then VANISHES in a FLASH, bright as the sun.
The world turns ruby RED. The manor roof RISES, madly, into the SKY, riding a pillar of FLAME.
A jolt travels the length of Alfred's SPINE. Of course, he thinks, as his head goes light.
How utterly proper.
DON'T TOUCH HIM--

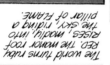

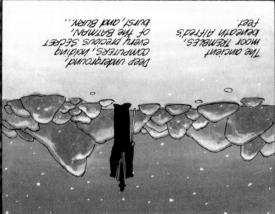

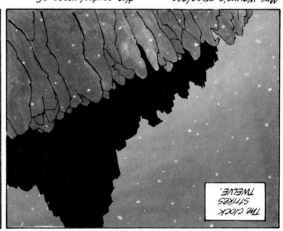

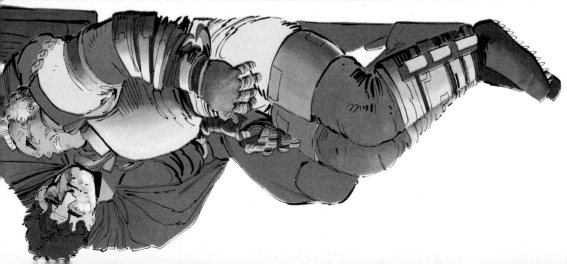

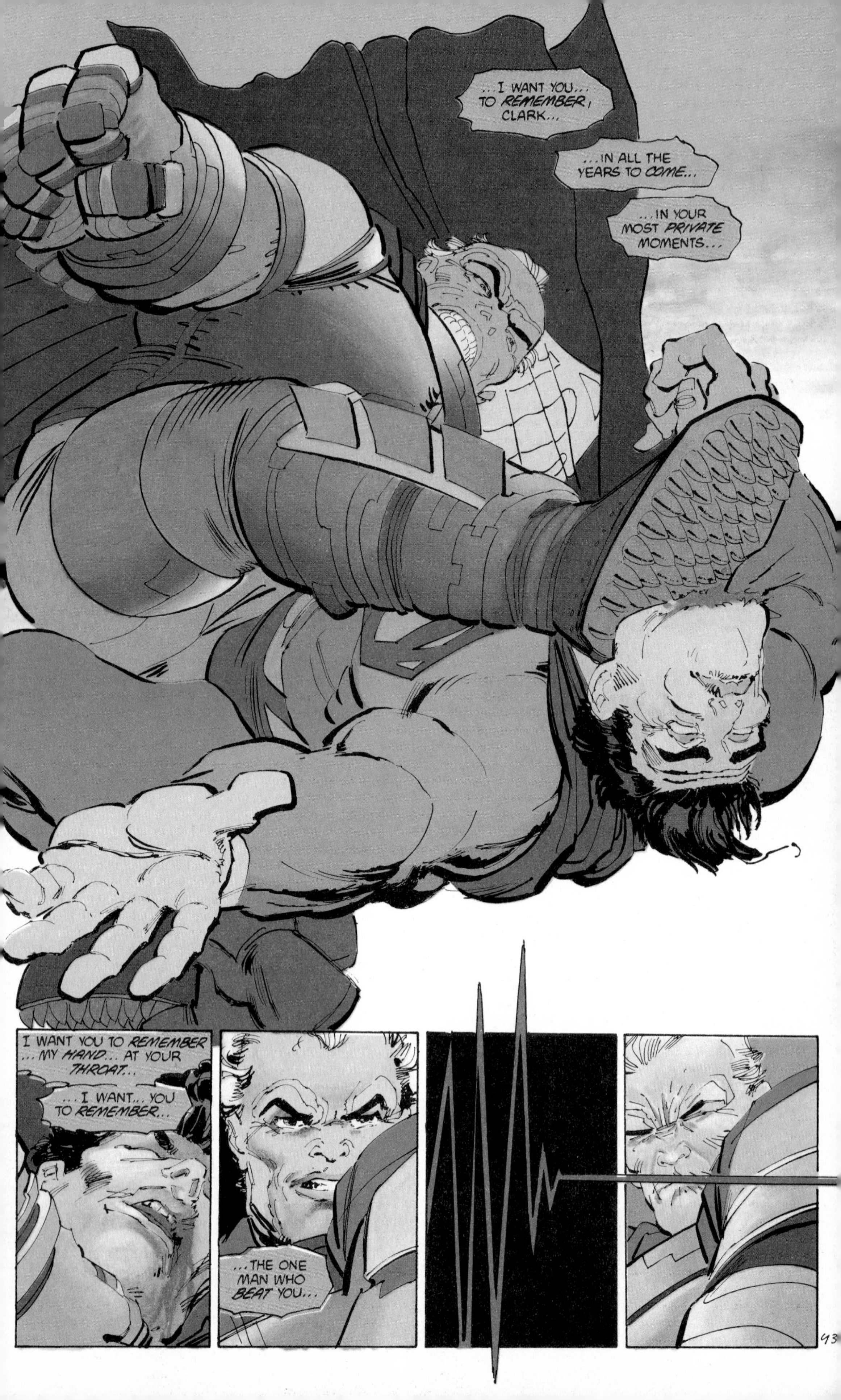

...I WANT YOU... TO *REMEMBER*, CLARK...
...IN ALL THE YEARS TO *COME*...
...IN YOUR MOST *PRIVATE* MOMENTS...
I WANT YOU TO *REMEMBER* ...MY *HAND*... AT YOUR *THROAT*...
...I WANT... YOU TO *REMEMBER*...
...THE ONE MAN WHO *BEAT* YOU...